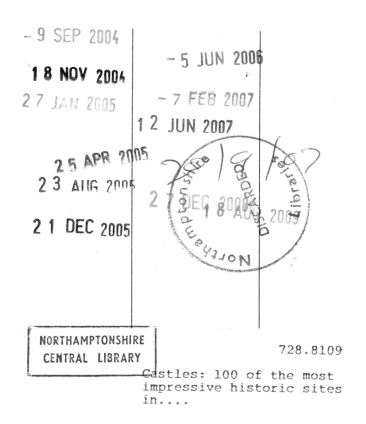
Please return or renew this item by the last date shown.
You may renew items (unless they have been requested
by another customer) by telephoning, writing to or calling
in at any library. 100% recycled paper *BKS 1 (5/95)*

AA

BEST OF BRITAIN'S

Castles

100 OF THE MOST IMPRESSIVE HISTORIC SITES IN BRITAIN

Produced by AA Publishing
© Automobile Association Developments Limited 2004
Map © Automobile Association Developments Limited 2004.
Crown copyright. All rights reserved. Licence number 399221.

Published by AA Publishing (a trading name of Automobile
Association Developments Limited, whose registered office is
Millstream, Maidenhead, Windsor SL4 5GD; registered office
1878835)

A01911A

ISBN: 0 7495 4046 X

A CIP catalogue record for this book is available from the
British Library.

The contents of this book are believed correct at the time of
printing. Nevertheless, the publishers cannot be held
responsible for any errors, omissions or for changes in the
details given in this book or for the consequences of any
reliance on the information provided by the same. This does not
affect your statutory rights. We have tried to ensure accuracy in
this book but things do change and we would be grateful if
readers would advise us of any inaccuracies they may
encounter.

We have taken all reasonable steps to ensure that the outdoor
activities are safe and achievable by persons with a realistic level
of fitness. However all outdoor activities involve a degree of risk
and the publishers cannot accept any responsibility for any
injuries caused to readers whilst following these activities.

Produced for AA Publishing by *The Bridgewater Book Company*

Printed and bound by Leo Paper. China

RUINS OF ARDVRECK CASTLE

ACKNOWLEDGMENTS

All images and illustrations belong to the Automobile
Association's own library (AA WORLD TRAVEL LIBRARY) with
the exception of p138l/139b courtesy of Warwick Castle
t (top), b (bottom), c (centre), l (left), r (right), bg (background)

M Adelman 2l; P Aithie 6/7, 28, 38, 56l, 56r; 78; M Alexander 27, 130b; M Alward-Coppin 117; S Anderson 136l; A
Baker 111; P Baker 121; S Bates 109; J Beazley 50t, 110l, 110r; 116l, 116r, 124, 137; A Besley 9l, 9r, 19r; M Birkitt 58b,
100r; J Blandford 64t, 64b; E Bowness 34; I Burgum 5, 29, 30l, 36l, 36br, 37, 81l, 103, 113, 140l; J Carnie 41r; C Coe
54tc, 100l; D Corrance 72b, 102; S Day 21l, 40, 45, 90l, 106l, 126l, 129; R Eames 120l, 120b; R Edwards 39; E Ellington
15, 55r, 77, 87; R Elliott 60, 123; D Forss 10l, 11, 16, 32cl, 33b, 52, 58t, 79, 97, 98l, 99, 114t, 114b, 115; J Gravell 31, 108;
A Grierley 68; J Henderson; 41l, 54tl, 61r; 62l, 62r, 63, 73l, 74, 75, 76, 92t, 92b, 93, 105l, 133; N Jenkins 30r; 47; C Jones
54tr, 55b, 107; M Jourdan 48; C Lees 2r, 12l, 14cl, 14cr; 14b, 19l, 65, 101, 104cc, 105tr; S&O Mathews 85; G Matthews
20; S McBride 32r, 32b, 33t, 135; E Meacher 21r, 104cr; J Miller 17, 24, 141b; C Molyneux 35; R Moss 96, 112, 118,
132; R Newton 43l, 43r, 46; H Palmer 139t; K Paterson 25, 53, 70t, 72t, 86l, 86r, 106r; 125, 130t; P Sharpe 26; J Smith
70cb, 70rb, 71r; F Stephenson 88, 89, 128l; R Strange 122; R Surman 44; T Teegan 67; R Tenison 119; T Timms 57, 82,
83l, 83r; M Trelawny 84l, 84r 104cl; A Tryner 18; W Voysey 51, 59, 142l, 143; W Voysey/the Dean and Canons of
Windsor 141t; R Weir 22, 23, 49, 50b, 69, 73r; 80, 94; S Whitehorne 55tr, 91, 127; H Williams 42, 66bl, 81r; 140r; T
Woodcock 13, 144 (Alnwick Castle).

Cover Kilchurn Castle - Steve Day
Cover br Caernarfon Castle - Pat Aithie
Spine Edinburgh Castle - Ken Paterson
Back Cover bl Castle Coch - Ian Burgum; bc Warwick Castle - Van Greaves;
br St George's Chapel, Windsor Castle - Wyn Voysey/the Dean and Canons of Windsor

Contents

Feature Spreads

LINDISFARNE CASTLE

Location Map
Best of Britain's Castles

Introduction

A castle is defined as a 'properly fortified military residence'. In medieval times, the castle was home not only to the owner and his family, but also to his retinue; it was designed as the centre of his military operations and to protect him from his enemies. This was a product of feudalism, whereby the lord of the castle agreed to protect his vassals and provide land, while his vassals worked the land and could be called on for military duty.

British castles tend to be one of two types – the fortified enclosure and the fortified tower – or a combination. Castles like Framlingham comprised strong walls (with towers), forming an enclosure. This was filled with buildings, and, in times of danger, people living outside the castle could take refuge there. An example of a fortified tower (or keep) is Hedingham.

As castles grew, owners built extra towers and walls to accommodate all their worldly goods, livestock and vassals. This was the origin of great castle complexes like the Tower of London. In the 12th century, powerful gatehouses were built into the walls to provide an additional layer of protection. In some cases, the gatehouse was even further fortified with walls and ditches, forming what is known as a 'barbican'.

THE FIRST CASTLES IN BRITAIN

Historians do not agree about whether there were castles in Britain before the Norman Conquest. After William the Conqueror invaded England in 1066, he had simple castles built known as mottes and bailies. The mottes were mounds of earth with flattened tops upon which wooden castles were built, sometimes surrounded by wooden pallisades or fences to form an enclosure (a bailey). Great ditches and banks called earthworks were constructed to provide additional protection, and these can still be seen at Castle Rising and Castle Acre. Later, the wooden pallisades were converted to stone, at many places forming small enclosure castles called shell keeps, of which Clifford's Tower in York is among the best examples.

Once the Normans had established a hold in Britain, more permanent structures were necessary and building in stone was started in castles like Chepstow, Rochester, Peveril, Colchester and, of course, the great Tower of London. Most of these early castles were simple towers, although Colchester and the Tower

THE 13TH-CENTURY CAERPHILLY CASTLE AND MOAT.

were – and are still – impressive for their sheer size and for the high quality of the craftsmanship.

Although Norman keeps were designed for defence and intended to dominate a defeated people, they were not all alike. The castle builders skilfully turned the unique character of each site to their advantage, and keeps were variously rectangular, circular, square, multi-sided and D-shaped. At Portchester, the splendid Norman keep was built inside the walls of an existing Roman fort.

LATER CASTLES

As methods of attacking castles became more refined, so the castles' protective measures and systems were further developed in attempts to keep the fortifications more or less impregnable. In the 12th century, castle owners became aware that a simple keep, however strong and well-built, would not be able to withstand a prolonged attack. They began to build layers of defences (including curtain walls) around the keep in a concentric arrangement, following the example of castle builders in the Near East. The great walls of Constantinople had repelled the Crusaders, and it seems likely that the Crusaders in turn borrowed this idea from their enemies. Dover was probably the first concentric castle in Britain, followed in the late 13th century by castles such as Beaumaris and Caerphilly.

Once the Normans were firmly established in power, castle building proceeded at a more leisurely pace. At later points in history, however, it was necessary for a king to embark on a fast and furious spate of castle raising, as during the reign of Henry VIII in the 16th century. Another such occasion followed the campaigns of Edward I in Wales between 1277 and 1284. The Welsh had not been idle during the previous century, and the sturdy fortress at Dolbadarn is an example of a Welsh-built castle. But Edward's Welsh masterpieces – magnificent, dominating structures such as Caernarfon, Conwy, Harlech and

Beaumaris – were the ultimate in defensive design of any castles in Britain, and perhaps in the world. Meanwhile, in Scotland clan leaders like the Douglases were also building mighty castles, like Tantallon, while Alexander II raised the impressive Kildrummy.

The fortified manor house began to emerge in the late 13th century as a new kind of castle. They were often surrounded by a moat, as at Bodiam, and although defence was still important, so was the comfort of the owners. Castles were expensive to build, and only the very rich could afford to do so. Some owners wanted a castle to display their wealth and power. The magnificent brick tower at Tattershall built by the Treasurer of England in the 15th century is a fine example of this.

THE CASTLE IN SCOTLAND

Scottish castles developed several distinctive features. The Border country was subject to raids by both Scots and English for many centuries after the Scottish wars of independence were won by Robert the Bruce. In the 14th century small fortified towers, or peles, were built to protect local areas against these raids in northern England, while in Scotland, the distinctive tower-house began to emerge. During the next 300 years, some 700 of these tower-houses were raised in Scotland, culminating in castles like Craigievar and Crathes.

Scottish tower-houses had thick walls, battlemented parapets and strong turrets on the corners. Many had the additional protection of extra walls, called barmkins, and ditches and banks. The small doorways were often protected by iron gates called yetts. After c1500, tower-houses were provided with specially designed holes so that guns could be fired from them.

DOLBADARN CASTLE ONCE OFFERED LLYWELYN THE LAST SANCTUARY FROM EDWARD I.

Aberystwyth Castle
Ceredigion
18 miles (29km) north of Aberaeron

OPEN ACCESS AT ANY
REASONABLE TIME.

ABERYSTWYTH CASTLE
WAS IRREPARABLY
DAMAGED DURING
THE CIVIL WAR.

Overlooking the harbour is the once mighty castle built in 1277 for Edward I as part of his impregnable 'iron ring', following his first successful campaign in Wales. Edward I became King of England in 1272 and was crowned two years later in Westminster Abbey. He was a natural military leader and tactician and set his sights on ruling the whole of England by conquering Scotland and Wales.

Following his successful campaigns in Wales, Edward reorganised Welsh law and government, creating counties in the north of Wales very similar to those in England. He also established boroughs for the English settlers, which the native Welsh were forbidden to enter, though with time and mixed marriages they soon were. This was also Edward's great castle-building period, when Harlech, Caernarfon and Conwy were built. Aberystwyth, Builth, Flint and Rhuddlan followed.

There has been a castle in Aberystwyth since 1110 when Gilbert of Clare built a castle near the mouth of the River Ystwyth, the hills and ditches of which are still visible. The present castle was located on the coast overlooking the town and was built during 1277. The castle took 12 years to complete but it appears that the building standards were poor, and the castle had to be extensively rebuilt at a cost of several thousand pounds.

The town and castle fell to the Welsh under Owain Glyndwr in 1404 and for a short time Wales had its Parliament there. With the demise of this last Welsh Prince of Wales, however, the castle again became tangled up in English politics and fell victim to the Civil War. This led to it being blown up and left to disintegrate into the ruins you see today.

Acton Burnell Castle

Shropshire

7 miles (11km) southeast of Shrewsbury

OPEN ACCESS AT ANY
REASONABLE TIME.

TEL: 0870 333 1181

A short walk from the car park along a wooded path reaches the elegant fortified manor house of Acton Burnell. It is a charming ruin, standing among the trees, a quiet, peaceful place disturbed by little more than the singing of birds. Roofless, with only the walls still standing, it has large windows on the ground floor – unusual for a fortified house because the windows would have been difficult to defend if the house had ever come under attack. In times of peace, however, they had the advantage of allowing plenty of light into what would otherwise have been a rather gloomy set of ground floor rooms.

Robert Burnell, after whom the house was named, originally built Acton Burnell as a comfortable manor house. Burnell was an important man in the 13th century, serving both as Edward I's Chancellor of England and as Bishop of Bath and Wells. Because medieval kings were usually worried about how much power their barons were amassing, no one was allowed to build a castle without the king's permission. In some cases, the king might give one of his subjects a 'licence to crenellate', which meant that an existing house might be given some defensive features, such as a new tower or battlements. In the 1280s, Robert Burnell was granted such a licence, and changed Acton Burnell from a simple dwelling place to a fortified house with battlemented parapets.

THE RUINS OF A FINE
FORTIFIED MANOR,
ACTON BURNELL WAS
ABANDONED IN 1420.

Allington Castle

Kent

2 miles (3km) northwest of Maidstone

The medieval castle at Allington, on the banks of the Medway just outside Maidstone, has had an eventful history that converted it from a 13th-century fortress to a grand Tudor mansion, a farmhouse, a stately home and finally a retreat for Carmelite friars.

The first castle on this site was raised in the 11th century, and was probably only a simple mound with a wooden structure on the top. Stephen of Penchester built a stone castle, under a licence granted by Edward I in 1281. (The king's concern about the power of the barons meant no one could build without royal permission.)

The oldest part of the early stone castle to survive is a section of wall that displays a distinctive herringbone pattern, made by laying the stones in zig-zags. The castle was converted into a mansion in the 15th century, but there was a serious fire in about 1600, leaving only enough of the mansion to make a farmhouse. Substantial restoration work was carried out before the castle was taken over by the Carmelite order in 1951.

PRIVATELY OWNED, THE CASTLE IS NOT OPEN TO THE PUBLIC EXCEPT FOR OCCASIONAL SPECIAL EVENTS. CONTACT THE TOURIST OFFICE, MAIDSTONE, FOR INFORMATION.

TEL: 01622 602169

ALLINGTON CASTLE, BYPASSED BY BATTLES AND SIEGES, HAS BEEN SHAPED BY MORE PEACEFUL EVENTS.

Alnwick Castle

Northumberland

Alnwick, 20 miles (32km) north of Morpeth

The clustered towers of this magnificent residential fortress have seen a good deal of action since the castle was founded in the 11th century. Its position near the border with Scotland made it vulnerable to attack from the Scots, and it played an important role in the Wars of the Roses during the 15th century.

In 1172 and 1174 William the Lion, King of Scotland, laid siege to Alnwick, but on the second occasion he was surprised by reinforcements from the south and was himself taken prisoner. Since the early 14th century, Alnwick has been the seat of the influential Percy family, Dukes of Northumberland.

OPEN DAILY FROM MARCH TO OCTOBER.

TEL: 01665 510777

A STONE PLAQUE ON FALCONER'S TOWER COMMEMORATES HENRY HUGH MANNERS PERCY RECEIVING THE GEORGE CROSS DURING THE CRIMEAN WAR.

THE CASTLE SHOWS A PASTORAL FACE ON THE SIDE FURTHEST FROM THE BUSY TOWN.

THE LAVISH ITALIANATE INTERIOR OF ALNWICK CASTLE HOUSES AN EXTENSIVE ART COLLECTION.

Although Alnwick was well fortified by the 12th century, the Percys, who rebuilt the keep and enclosed the castle inside walls with seven semi-circular towers, strengthened it further in the 14th century. Sturdy gatehouses were added to both the inner and the outer walls. After the Wars of the Roses in the 15th century, Alnwick began to decline. Restoration work started in the 18th century. In the 19th century it was further restored and embellished – its exterior an imposing re-creation of its medieval appearance, its interior an Italian Renaissance-style treasure house of works of art.

THE COLLECTION AT ALNWICK INCLUDES THIS ECCENTRIC CLUSTER OF OLD WALKING STICKS.

Ardvreck Castle

Highland

26 miles (41.5km) northeast of Ullapool

When the Civil War broke out in England in 1642, Scotland was inevitably drawn into the conflict. Two of the main protagonists in the north were Archibald Campbell, Marquess of Argyll, and James Graham, Marquess of Montrose. Montrose remained loyal to the King, while Argyll declared for Parliament. After the execution of Charles I in 1649, Montrose fled the country, but returned a year later. The Laird of Assynt captured him and held him in Ardvreck Castle until he could be safely handed over to Cromwell's forces. Montrose was hastily executed in the same year, while his rival, Argyll, was executed after the Restoration of the Monarchy in 1661.

The small 16th-century tower house is now a ruin, perched on a rocky peninsula that juts out into Loch Assynt. It was a simple structure – rectangular, with a staircase turret on the southeast corner. The basement had three chambers with vaulted roofs. One of the chambers is little more than a passage, but the gun loops pierced in its outer wall suggest that it could have been used to defend the castle. When observing Ardvreck Castle, visitors may notice other ruins nearby. These are the remains of Edderchalder House, a fine 17th-century mansion.

The castle can be seen from the A837, and is best admired from a distance, as it is in a dangerous condition.

Arundel Castle

West Sussex

Arundel, 12 miles (19km) east of Chichester

STILL A FAMILY HOME, ARUNDEL CASTLE REFLECTS THE CHANGES OF NEARLY A THOUSAND YEARS.

OPEN FROM APRIL TO OCTOBER, DAILY EXCEPT SATURDAY.

TEL: 01903 883136

The charming palace-castle, which sprawls among the trees in this attractive West Sussex town, has so many battlemented towers and chimneys that it has an almost fairy-tale appearance. There has been a castle at Arundel for some 900 years, ever since a castle mound was raised in about 1088. Around 100 years later, a circular shell keep was built on the mound and at the same time, or perhaps a little later, Henry II added walls, a chapel and a garden. It is possible that this was the first royal garden in England.

Most of the castle, however, is more recent, and owes much to the work of the 11th Duke of Norfolk who, in 1787, began to renovate and reconstruct Arundel so that it could become his main home outside London. Subsequent Dukes have continued this work, and today there are many splendid rooms packed with treasures on view to the public. The collection of paintings is especially fine, containing works by such artists as Van Dyck, Lely, Reynolds, Lawrence, Mytens and Gainsborough.

In the chapel, marble columns soar upwards to Gothic arches and an intriguing striped ceiling. Many of the staterooms contain exquisite furnishings dating from the 16th century.

Ashby de la Zouch

Leicestershire

Ashby-de-la-Zouch, 9 miles (14.5km) southeast of Burton upon Trent

A hall was founded at Ashby in the 12th century, but its principal feature, the keep, was not built until the 15th century. The owner, William, Lord Hastings, was granted a licence to convert the hall into a castle in 1474, at the same time as he started building his picturesque fortified house at Kirby Muxloe. Hastings' keep was about 90 feet (27m) tall and had four floors. There was also an extension on the northeast side of the tower, which had seven floors. Although there were already two wells in the castle, the keep had another of its own – a sensible precaution, for it meant that no one could tamper with the water supply.

Lord Hastings' own story shows how fortunes and the favour of kings could rise and fall in the Middle Ages. He rose to power dramatically under the Yorkist King Edward IV, becoming Lord Chamberlain as a reward for his loyalty throughout the Wars of the Roses. After Edward's death in 1483, Hastings, on the advice of Edward's mistress Jane Shore, refused to support his successor, Richard III. Richard had Hastings beheaded – a scene in history that was immortalised in Shakespeare's *Richard III*.

THE IMPRESSIVE RUINS OF ASHBY DE LA ZOUCH INCLUDE THE SPLENDID 15TH-CENTURY WARWICK TOWER.

OPEN DAILY FROM APRIL TO OCTOBER; WEDNESDAY TO SUNDAY FROM NOVEMBER TO MARCH; CLOSED CHRISTMAS AND NEW YEAR.
TEL: 01530 413343

Bamburgh Castle
Northumberland
Bamburgh, 16 miles (25.5km) north of Alnwick

OPEN DAILY FROM MARCH TO OCTOBER.

TEL: 01668 214208/214515

BAMBURGH IS ONE OF THE MOST DRAMATICALLY SET CASTLES IN ENGLAND.

Bamburgh's location, standing proud on a rocky promontory on the rugged Northumbrian coast, makes it one of the most spectacular of all the English castles. It is built high on a cliff, 150 feet (46m) above the North Sea. Its landward sides are protected by a forbidding display of strong walls. Bamburgh can be seen for miles, presenting a formidable obstacle to any would-be attackers.

There have been fortifications on the site for thousands of years. There was an Iron Age fort here, and the Romans, Anglo-Saxons and Vikings all left their marks. It is known that the Normans had established some kind of castle by 1095, for historical records mention that William II attacked it. Warwick, 'The Kingmaker', also attacked it during the Wars of the Roses in the 15th century, and much damage was done to its walls. Thereafter, it fell into disrepair, but was substantially restored during the 18th and 19th centuries.

Looking at the current structure of Bamburgh, it is not easy to distinguish its different periods of construction. The great tower, although altered over the years, is perhaps the most dominant feature, and there are traces of the original defensive walls, although these, too, have been much restored. The interior contains many fine paintings, tapestries, furniture and armour.

Beaumaris Castle

Isle of Anglesey

5 miles (8km) northeast of the Menai Bridge

OPEN ALL YEAR DAILY,
EXCEPT CHRISTMAS AND
NEW YEAR.

TEL: 01248 810361

THE CONSTRUCTION OF
BEAUMARIS INVOLVED
A HUGE WORKFORCE
INCLUDING 400 MASONS.

Sitting majestically on the shores of the Menai Straits, looking from the Isle of Anglesey across to mainland Wales, this powerful castle took more than 35 years to build, and even so was never completely finished. It was the last of the great castles built by Edward I following his conquest of Wales, and was designed by Edward's most famous castle-builder, Master James of St George.

The building of Beaumaris Castle was started in 1295, and with its wide moat, high walls and strong towers, it was thought to be impregnable. However, this was never put to the test. Less than 20 years after building work stopped on the still-unfinished castle, there were reports that it was already falling into decay.

Not merely a powerful fortress, the inner buildings had luxurious chambers, with an extensive array of kitchens, stables and a chapel. The castle itself is in two rings, one inside the other. The inner ring has two massive twin-towered gate-houses, while the outer ring is a wall 27 feet (8m) high, bristling with defensive towers and its own protected dock.

Berkeley Castle

Gloucestershire

Berkeley, 10 miles (16km) southwest of Stroud

OPEN APRIL TO SEPTEMBER, WEDNESDAY TO SATURDAY, AND SUNDAY AFTERNOONS IN OCTOBER.

TEL: 01453 810332

THIS RAMBLING AND ROMANTIC CASTLE HAS BEEN THE HOME OF THE BERKELEYS FOR ALMOST 850 YEARS.

Secluded Berkeley Castle, near the banks of the River Severn, was the site of one of the most infamous of all medieval murders. By 1327, Queen Isabella and her lover, the powerful baron Roger Mortimer, had wrested the Crown from Edward II and were running the country. Edward was taken secretly to Berkeley Castle in April 1327, where attempts were made to starve him to death. Dead animals were also thrown into a pit in his room, to make him sicken and die. But Edward was a strong man and Isabella saw that more drastic measures were necessary. In September, according to tradition, the unfortunate king was murdered by having a red-hot poker thrust into his bowels.

Although the chamber in which Edward is said to have been imprisoned remains, most of the castle dates from the mid-14th century. It is a great palace-fortress built around a courtyard. One room contains furniture said to have belonged to Sir Francis Drake, while the magnificent Great Hall has a superb timber roof dating from the 14th century.

Blair Castle
Perth & Kinross
Blair Atholl, 8 miles (13km) from Pitlochry

OPEN DAILY FROM APRIL TO OCTOBER.

TEL: 01796 481207

BLAIR, A STORY-BOOK CASTLE, IS SET AMONG FORESTED HILLS ABOVE THE RIVER GARRY.

In 1269 affairs of state forced David, Earl of Atholl, to spend a considerable amount of time in England. While he was away, his neighbour, John Comyn, began to build a castle on Atholl's land, causing Atholl to complain to the King, Alexander III. This early tower is now incorporated into a much bigger castle, but is still called Cummings (or Comyn's) Tower.

The Earls and Dukes of Atholl were prominent men in Scottish history. The simple tower-house was extended and rebuilt over the centuries according to the needs of its different owners. In the English Civil War, Blair, then a fortress with good defences, was captured by Cromwell's forces. In 1745 the Jacobites, in what was probably the last siege to take place in Britain, besieged it.

Most of the castle as it is seen today dates from the 18th century. It has become a splendid palace rather than a fortress, its gleaming white walls contrasting starkly with the rich woodland in which it stands. Many richly furnished rooms are open to the public, and some contain objects of great historical significance, including two cannons from an Armada galleon and an original copy of the National Covenant of 1638.

Bodiam Castle

East Sussex

12 miles (19km) north of Hastings

OPEN DAILY FROM MARCH TO OCTOBER, WEEKENDS ONLY NOVEMBER TO FEBRUARY; CLOSED CHRISTMAS.

TEL: 01580 830436

With its battlemented walls and towers reflected in a moat dotted with water lilies, Bodiam is one of the most picturesque castles in Britain. But beauty was hardly the prime objective of Bodiam's builder when he constructed his castle and dug his moat – this was a fortress designed to repel invaders and to provide a haven for those lucky enough to be secure within its walls.

Sir Edward Dalyngrygge built Bodiam between 1385 and 1388. Richard II had granted him a licence to fortify his manor house after the French had attacked the nearby port of Rye.

Interpreting the licence somewhat more liberally than had been intended, Dalyngrygge promptly abandoned his old manor house and set about building Bodiam Castle.

The castle is rectangular, with a round tower at each corner and a square tower midway along each wall. Bodiam is completely surrounded by the wide moat. These elaborate defences against attack were never seriously tested – Bodiam was involved in a skirmish in 1484, but during the Civil War it was surrendered without a shot being fired. To this day, the exterior is almost as it was when it was first built.

BODIAM CASTLE REMAINS RELATIVELY INTACT TODAY, PROOF OF ITS PEACEFUL PAST.

Brodick Castle

North Ayrshire

Arran, 2 miles (3km) from
Brodick pier head

After Robert the Bruce's defeat at Methven in 1306, he fled to Brodick Castle on the Isle of Arran. It was here that he is supposed to have waited for the beacon to be lit on the mainland, telling him the time was ripe to begin afresh his war with the English king, Edward I. Within a year, Edward was dead and Bruce was establishing himself as King of Scotland.

Nowadays, little remains of the 14th-century castle which, according to contemporary accounts, was 'levelled to the ground' in 1455 by the Earl of Ross. It was rebuilt, but in 1544 the Earl of Lennox destroyed it, acting on the orders of Henry VIII. The castle was repaired again in the 1630s so that it could be garrisoned for Charles I, but these buildings were largely swept away for the baronial mansion that was designed by James Gillespie Graham in the 19th century.

The mansion is an elegant red sandstone building, displaying clusters of chimneys, gables and towers, and nestling comfortably in its attractive gardens. A number of rooms are open, displaying a diverse collection of sporting trophies and some excellent paintings. Famous rhododendron gardens and extensive woodlands also form part of the estate.

OPEN DAILY FROM APRIL TO OCTOBER.

TEL: 01770 302202

FOR GENERATIONS, BRODICK CASTLE WAS THE HEART OF THE ISLE OF ARRAN ESTATE.

Brougham Castle
Cumbria
1 mile (1.5km) southeast of Penrith

OPEN DAILY FROM APRIL TO SEPTEMBER.

TEL: 01768 862488

The restoration of Brougham, and of the nearby castles at Appleby and Brough, is chiefly the work of the immensely rich and powerful Anne Clifford, Countess of Dorset, Pembroke and Montgomery. She wanted all three of her castles to be habitable, and spent large sums of money on making them so. She died in Brougham Castle in 1678 when she was almost 90 years old.

Brougham's origins date back to the time of Henry II when – probably around 1170 – the great tower was built. It was made of sandstone rubble, with more expensive, decorative cut stone at the corners and on windows and doors. The tower had buttresses on three walls, and a forebuilding on the fourth wall. It seems that the tower was originally intended to have only three storeys, but a fourth floor was added later. This later work is of a much better quality than the original, a difference that can be clearly distinguished today. Other buildings were added to the keep, most notably in the 17th century by Anne Clifford. However, the splendid great tower remains Brougham's most impressive feature, still standing almost to its original height.

Caerlaverock Castle
Dumfries & Galloway
12 miles (19km) southeast of Dumfries

OPEN ALL YEAR DAILY, EXCEPT CHRISTMAS AND NEW YEAR.

TEL: 01387 770244

THE RENAISSANCE WALLS AND CARVED STONE PANELS STILL REMAIN AT CAERLAVEROCK.

The imposing gatehouse at Caerlaverock Castle is so similar to those designed by Edward I's master castle-builder, James of St George, that it is often suggested that this was an English, rather than a Scottish, fortress. The high walls, their massive round towers, two moats and high ramparts, are very similar to the concentric castles built by Edward in Wales, such as Beaumaris and Harlech; but, unlike any other castle in Britain, Caerlaverock is triangular. It has three walls — two are protected by an arm of the sea that swings out round the back of the castle, and the third is protected by moats, earthworks and the great gatehouse.

Caerlaverock was built in the late 13th century, and exchanged hands several times when Edward invaded Scotland. Edward laid siege to it in 1300, after which it was besieged another four times during its eventful history. Often, if the Scots took a castle but were unable to hold it, they would destroy it so that the English could not use it. This happened to Caerlaverock in 1312, and it was almost completely rebuilt during the 15th century. Rebuilding followed the previous plan, although gun ports were added, and the great gatehouse was strengthened.

Caernarfon Castle

Gwynedd

Caernarfon, 7 miles (11km) southeast of Bangor

VIEWED FROM ANY ANGLE, DAY OR NIGHT, CAERNARFON IS AN IMPRESSIVE SIGHT.

OPEN ALL YEAR DAILY, EXCEPT CHRISTMAS AND NEW YEAR.

TEL: 01286 677617

In 1282, Llywelyn the Last, the last native Prince of Wales, was killed in an ambush, and Welsh resistance to English occupation began to crumble. The victorious Edward I offered the Welsh a prince who was born in Wales, could speak no word of English, and whose life and reputation no one would be able to stain. He had in mind his infant son, later Edward II, who became the first English Prince of Wales. Edward was invested in Wales in 1301, and the tradition has endured. In 1969, Prince Charles was invested as the current Prince of Wales.

The great creamy-grey walls of the castle dominate the little market town of Caernarfon. Building started in 1283, but a decade later the unfinished fortress came under attack during a Welsh rebellion, and much damage was done. Believing he could not trust the native Welsh, Edward press-ganged English craftsmen and labourers to rebuild the castle, creating the most impressive of all Welsh castles. Edward intended his castle to be not only a fortress, but also the seat of his government in Wales and his own official residence there. The massive building was also a clear statement of English victory over a defeated nation.

Caernarfon Castle is shaped like an hourglass. Great walls with stones in banded colours (inspired by the walls of Constantinople, which Edward admired while on a crusade) run between the great towers, topped by battlemented wall-walks. The castle's defences were formidable. In order to gain access to the courtyard, visitors were obliged to cross two drawbridges, pass through five heavy doors and walk under six portcullises. The entire way was protected by arrow slits and murder-holes, through which an unpleasant array of deadly missiles could be hurled onto unwelcome guests.

Caerphilly Castle

Caerphilly

Caerphilly, 8 miles (13km) north of Cardiff

THE EXPANSIVE SITE CAERPHILLY CASTLE OCCUPIES MAKES IT THE SECOND LARGEST BRITISH CASTLE AFTER DOVER.

OPEN ALL YEAR DAILY, EXCEPT CHRISTMAS AND NEW YEAR.

TEL: 029 2088 3143

When the huge water systems that make up some of the defences of Caerphilly Castle are taken into account, this is one of the biggest, and certainly one of the most spectacular military complexes in Britain. The sheer size of the defences at Caerphilly can only truly be appreciated from a distance, taking in the vast outer walls, the lakes and the inner concentric castle itself.

After 1066, the Normans established themselves in southern Wales, although they left the unfarmable north to the Welsh. In the mid-13th century, the last of the Welsh-born princes, Llywelyn the Last, decided he should unite Wales under his rule. He began to threaten the lands held by the Normans, causing Henry III to build castles to protect them. One such castle was Caerphilly, started in 1268, funded by the wealthy baron Gilbert de Clare, Earl of Gloucester and Hertford.

The castle itself comprises a rectangular enclosure with outer and inner walls. The inner walls contain the two great gatehouses and the remains of the hall. Here the living quarters were situated, along with domestic buildings such as kitchens, storerooms, a chapel, butteries and pantries. The outer walls, well fortified with towers and their own gatehouses, gave additional protection to the inner ward and were surrounded by a moat. Beyond the moat, to the east, lay a further complex of defences in the form of great walls studded with towers. The artificial lake lent protection to the north and south sides, while a walled island defended the west.

Cardiff Castle

Cardiff

Cardiff, 21 miles (34km) southeast of Merthyr Tydfil

CARDIFF CASTLE IS A ROMANTIC VICTORIAN RE-CREATION OF THE MIDDLE AGES.

OPEN ALL YEAR DAILY, EXCEPT CHRISTMAS AND NEW YEAR.

TEL: 029 2087 8100

The Romans, who built a fortress here, knew the site of Cardiff Castle. When the Normans arrived in the 11th century, they built a motte about 40 feet (12m) high, and topped it with a wooden building. Later, a 12-sided keep was erected, and a gatehouse and stairs were added in the 15th century. Robert, the eldest son of William the Conqueror, was held prisoner here for many years by his youngest brother, Henry I, and died in Cardiff Castle in 1134. A short distance away from the keep is a magnificent Victorian reconstruction, which owes its existence to the rich 3rd Marquess of Bute, who employed William Burges, an architect who shared his love of the past, to construct a great palace in the style of a medieval castle. Burges designed rooms with intricately painted ceilings, elaborately marbled bathrooms, spiral staircases and an impressive clock tower. The Banqueting Hall has a fine wooden roof, decorated with brightly coloured shields. The high walls have murals showing scenes from the Civil War, as well as a small painting of the Conqueror's son, Robert, gazing wistfully from behind his barred prison window.

Carew Castle

Pembrokeshire

Carew, 5 miles (8km) east of Pembroke

Although today Carew appears to be more of a palace than a castle, it still possesses some of its original defensive features. Of these, perhaps the most impressive are the two great cylindrical towers with their jutting bases. Parts of the medieval castle were altered in the 15th and 16th centuries, when its many different owners built new wings and exchanged the small narrow windows for larger stately ones.

One of Carew's first owners is said to have been the Norman Gerald of Windsor, who was married to a Welsh princess named Nest. Before her marriage, Nest had been a hostage of Henry I, and legend has it that she bore his illegitimate son. Nest's grandson was Gerald of Wales, whose detailed description of life in the 12th century is an important source of information for medieval historians.

Another legend attached to Carew is that of Sir Roland Rhys, who lived in the castle during the reign of James I. When his son eloped with the daughter of a Flemish merchant, Rhys attacked the merchant with his pet ape. Later, the ape attacked Rhys himself, and during the struggle which followed the castle caught fire. However, the most serious damage to be inflicted on Carew Castle's elegant buildings was to occur during the Civil War.

THE STATELY RUINS OF CAREW CASTLE, SCENE IN 1507 OF THE LAST MEDIEVAL TOURNAMENT TO BE HELD IN WALES.

OPEN DAILY EASTER TO NOVEMBER.

TEL: 01646 651782

Carisbrooke Castle

Isle of Wight

Carisbrooke, just southwest of Newport

Combine an invigorating downland walk with a visit to a magnificent castle and discover more about Charles I, Carisbrooke's famous prisoner.

Carisbrooke's Medieval Castle Set on the site of a Roman fort, Carisbrooke Castle was originally a fortified camp built by the Saxons as defence against the Vikings, and later strengthened by the Normans, who built the impenetrable stone walls, gatehouse and keep, it overlooks the Bowcombe Valley and the approaches to the central downs and the heart of the island. But the castle only experienced military action twice, in 1136 and in 1377. In the late 16th century the outer bastions were built to guard against the threat of Spanish invasion. The most important episode in the castle's history was the imprisonment of Charles I in 1647. You can walk the battlements in his footsteps, view the bowling green created for his amusement, and see the window from which he tried to escape.

The Rise and Fall of Charles I There had been an uneasy relationship between Crown and Parliament during the reign of James I, and after the accession to the throne of his son, Charles I, in

THE CASTLE HOLDS REGULAR HISTORICAL RE-ENACTMENTS.

VIEWS OF THE GATEWAY TO THE RUINS OF CARISBROOKE CASTLE.

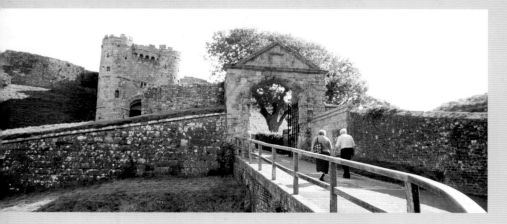

1625 matters deteriorated. Charles's High Church views and demands for war funds provoked a series of crises and disputes, and in 1630 he dispensed with Parliament and embarked on a period of personal rule.

There was nearly a decade of relative political calm and stability before Charles's lack of empathy, stubbornness and high-minded approach to statecraft led to the collapse of royal authority in the late 1630s and the descent into rebellion and civil war by 1642. Bitter battles between the Royalist and Parliamentarian armies raged across the country for four years, until major strategic errors by Charles led to crushing defeats at Naseby, Langport, Bristol and, finally, at Oxford in May 1646. A virtual prisoner of his rebellious Scottish army, Charles still considered it his divine right to rule the country as an autocrat, and he refused to negotiate a political settlement with the Parliamentarians.

SET ON A SWEEPING RIDGE OF CHALK DOWNLAND, THE MEDIEVAL RUINS OF CARISBROOKE CASTLE.

THE LIGHT AND AIRY PRIVATE CHAPEL AT CARISBROOKE CASTLE HOUSES AN ETHEREALLY BEAUTIFUL ALTARPIECE.

Rumours spread of a plot to murder him, and Charles escaped from Hampton Court Palace in 1647 and sought refuge at Carisbrooke Castle. Governor Robert Hammond was torn between his loyalty to the King and his duty to Parliament, but promised to do what he could for Charles. The King was treated with respect, had the best rooms in the castle and was allowed freedom to move around the island. However, on hearing that Charles had signed a secret treaty with the Scots in December 1647, by which they undertook to invade England and restore him to the throne, Hammond imprisoned Charles in the castle. During his ten-month incarceration Charles made two unsuccessful attempts to escape before being taken to London for trial and execution in 1648.

Exploring Carisbrooke Castle's Downland Vista

❶ Facing Carisbrooke Priory, turn left along the road and take the footpath, opposite Quarr Business Park, to Carisbrooke Castle – built on a Roman site Carisbrooke once marked the capital of the island. At the castle walls, follow the grassy rampart right around the walls, continuing past the castle entrance. Take the footpath, signed Millers Lane, to the right of the car park entrance and descend to a lane. Turn left, cross a ford, then at a T-junction, turn right to Froglands Farm. Pass the farm, then bear right at gates to follow a bridleway through Bowcombe Valley.

❷ After a sharp right bend, gently descend and cross the stile on your left. Keep straight on, following the grassy path to a track. Turn left and keep right at a fork. At the field boundary on the left, follow the field edge to a gate. Ascend through a copse to a gate, then keep to the left-hand field edge, steadily uphill to a gate. Maintain direction to a further gate. Keep to the wide track beside a coniferous plantation and take the footpath left, signed Gatcombe. Go through a gate and keep ahead, passing a dew pond, to a further gate. On reaching a stile on the left, bear right downhill to a T-junction of paths and turn left, signed Garstons.

❸ Descend off the down. Go through a gate and shortly bear right beside Newbarn Farm. Turn right along the metalled access lane into the hamlet. Keep right on merging with Snowdrop Lane and turn left along the Shepherds Trail, signed Carisbrooke.

❹ Ascend a concrete drive and pass a house. At the top, keep to the main path (Shepherds Trail) across fields via gates. Disregard the path merging from the left and shortly follow the sunken path gently downhill to Whitcombe Road. Keep ahead back to the car park.

Distance: 5.25 miles (9km)

Total ascent: 600ft (183m)

Paths: generally firm but can be muddy in wet weather

Terrain: farmland and open downland

Gradients: undulating; one steep ascent and one long steady climb

Refreshments: Coach House tea room at Carisbrooke Castle

Castle: Open all year daily, except at Christmas and New Year. Tel: 01983 522107

OS Map: OS Outdoor Leisure 29 Isle of Wight

Carlisle Castle

Cumbria

Carlisle, 20 miles (32km) north of Penrith

OPEN ALL YEAR DAILY, EXCEPT CHRISTMAS AND NEW YEAR.

TEL: 01228 591922

A STONE WALKWAY ACROSS THE DRY INNER DITCH, WHICH ONCE PROTECTED THE CASTLE FROM ATTACKERS.

Carlisle's location so close to the Scottish border ensured that it played an important role in British history. It was held by David I and Malcolm IV, Kings of Scotland, from 1136 until 1157, and was taken back into English hands by Henry II. Another Scottish king, William the Lion, besieged the castle between 1173 and 1174.

The first castle overlooking the River Eden was nothing more than a triangular area of land encircled by a wooden fence. William Rufus, the son of William the Conqueror, erected it in 1092. When William Rufus was killed in a hunting accident in the New Forest, his brother Henry became king. Henry ordered that

walls and a castle should protect the town of Carlisle and a castle was built in 1093. His precautions seemed well advised, as 14 years later David I attacked. Despite the new fortifications the castle fell to the Scots.

Although Carlisle has been greatly altered and restored through the years, there is still much of the original to see. There is a fine 14th-century gatehouse in the inner enclosure, and visitors can still admire the buttressing on some of the walls. Queen Mary's Tower, named after Mary, Queen of Scots who was imprisoned here, now houses the Museum of the Border Regiment & King's Own Royal Border Regiment.

Carreg Cennen Castle
Carmarthenshire
Near Llandeilo, 16 miles (25.5km)
east of Carmarthen

Perched on a limestone crag, the dramatic ruins of Carreg Cennen overlook miles of rolling Welsh countryside. Steep cliffs and slopes protect the castle on three sides, while the one vulnerable approach is well defended with walls, watchtowers, pits and gates.

Roman coins have been found at Carreg Cennen, suggesting that the site was a fortress long before the present buildings were erected. The original Welsh castle was demolished in the 13th century to make way for the complex, heavily fortified buildings that remain today. It suffered extensive damage, first at the hands of Owain Glyndwr in the 15th century and then by the Yorkists during the Wars of the Roses.

Under the castle, burrowed into the rock itself, is a huge natural cavern, reached from the castle by a narrow vaulted passageway along the edge of the cliff. Although water drips almost constantly into the cave at one end, it would have been insufficient to supply a whole garrison, and the passage was probably built to ensure that invaders could not use the cave as a point from which to attack the castle. It would appear that at one time the passage was used as a dovecote, presumably to supply the castle kitchens.

OPEN ALL YEAR DAILY, EXCEPT CHRISTMAS AND NEW YEAR.

TEL: 01558 822291

CARREG CENNEN'S WALLS COMMAND WONDERFUL VIEWS ACROSS TO THE BLACK MOUNTAINS.

Castell Coch

Cardiff

Tongwynlais, 6 miles (9.5km) northwest of Cardiff

OPEN ALL YEAR DAILY, EXCEPT CHRISTMAS AND NEW YEAR.

TEL: 029 2081 0101

Rising out of wooded parklands, and clearly visible from the main road from Cardiff to Pontypridd, stands Castell Coch, a vast, elegant building with conical towers and a working drawbridge. Castell Coch, meaning 'red castle' in Welsh (it is built of red sandstone), is just like a castle from a fairy tale. It was built during the 19th century, at a time when Victorians were expressing a great interest in the past, especially in the seemingly idyllic, industry-free Middle Ages.

The architect William Burges designed Castell Coch for the 3rd Marquess of Bute, and it was not the first time these two men had worked together. They were also responsible for work on Cardiff Castle, with Bute providing the fortune and Burges the plans. Castell Coch was never intended to be a permanent residence, but was, in Burges' words, 'for occasional occupation in the summer'. It even has a dungeon, but the only prisoners have been actors, since Castell Coch has proved to be a popular ready-made film set.

If the exterior of the castle is impressive, the interior is a breath-taking jumble of rich colours and minute detail. There are fabulously decorated ceilings in many rooms, while others boast intricately painted wall-panels. The total effect is the kind of exuberant gaudiness that is indisputably Victorian.

ONE OF CASTELL COCH'S MANY HIGHLY ORNATE CEILINGS.

CASTELL COCH'S COAT-OF-ARMS.

SECURE ON ITS WOODED HILLSIDE, CASTELL COCH IS MORE LIKE A FRENCH CHATEAU THAN A TRADITIONAL BRITISH CASTLE.

Castell-y-Bere

Gwynedd

Near Abergynolwyn, 9 miles (14.5km) south of Dolgellau

OPEN ACCESS AT ANY REASONABLE TIME.
TEL: 029 2050 0200

The mountains that tower above dwarf the site of this once-powerful Welsh-built castle. Cader Idris is one of the great peaks looming steeply over the site of Castell-y-Bere. The castle is reached by a path that leads around the rocky spur on which it is perched, and approaching from this angle gives an accurate impression of the natural strength of the site. Castell-y-Bere once controlled one of the primary routes through central Wales, but today the major road runs further south and the castle is abandoned and lonely.

ABANDONED IN THIS REMOTE AREA, CASTELL-Y-BERE HAS BEEN LEFT TO DETERIORATE SINCE THE 13TH CENTURY.

Little remains and foundations alone represent most of the buildings. Llywelyn the Great built the castle in the 1220s, probably more to secure his position as Prince of Wales against his warring compatriots than to stand against the invading Normans. The castle was roughly triangular, following the shape of the rock, with towers at each angle. The entrance was defended by an impressive array of ditches, as well as a drawbridge and a portcullis.

During Edward I's wars against the Welsh princes, Castell-y-Bere was besieged and damaged. Although Edward paid more than £260 to have the castle repaired, it was not occupied for long, and was abandoned by around 1295.

Castle Rising

Norfolk

Castle Rising, 5½ miles (9km) northeast of King's Lynn

THE CASTLE IS FAMOUS FOR ITS CONNECTION WITH EDWARD II's QUEEN, ISABELLA.

OPEN ALL YEAR DAILY, EXCEPT MONDAY AND TUESDAY IN WINTER, AND CHRISTMAS AND NEW YEAR.

TEL: 01553 631330

In 1327 Edward II was horribly murdered in Berkeley Castle on the orders of his wife, Queen Isabella, and her lover, Roger Mortimer. At this time, Edward's heir, Edward III, was only 15 years old, and Mortimer and Isabella were able to rule England together by manipulating the young king. This state of affairs continued for three years, until Edward III began to take matters back into his own hands.

Learning of the roles of his mother and Mortimer in the death of his father, Edward had Mortimer tried for treason and hanged in 1330. Isabella was spared trial and execution but was banished from the court. She spent the last 30 years or so of her life at Castle Rising, joining an order of nuns called the Poor Clares in her old age.

There are many fascinating points about Castle Rising. As late as the 18th century, paintings of the castle show ships in the background, for when the castle was built in the 12th century it was near the sea, or at least accessible from the sea.

Visitors to Castle Rising cannot fail to notice the massive Norman earthworks that surround the castle. Great ditches and mounds were thrown up, with walls added later, and still today – even without the threat of archers sending out hails of arrows – the grassy earthworks are difficult to scale.

The mighty square keep was built between 1138 and 1140, although alterations to entrances and fireplaces were carried out later, and several rooms remain in excellent condition. They include a handsome wall passage and a chapel on one of the upper floors. The castle had a good water supply within the grounds – there is a well in the basement of the main tower and another in the castle grounds.

Castle Stalker

Argyll & Bute

18 miles (29km) north of Oban

THE CASTLE IS OPEN TO THE PUBLIC SOMETIMES BY APPOINTMENT. IT IS CLEARLY VISIBLE FROM THE MAIN ROAD.

TEL: 01631 730354

CUT OFF FROM THE LAND, CASTLE STALKER'S DEFENCES WERE EFFECTIVE THROUGHOUT ITS HISTORY.

Standing on a tiny island in Loch Laich, this small tower-house can be seen from the road that runs from Ballachulish towards Oban. It bears some resemblance to the castle of Eilean Donan, since both are set in lonely sites, surrounded by water, and are simple tower structures.

Historically, it would appear that access to Castle Stalker has always been by boat, and no causeway has ever been built to make it more easily accessible. However, at low tide it is possible to wade across the shallow waters of the loch. The castle itself is a rectangular tower, about 45 feet (14m) by 36 feet (11m) at its base, and was built in the 16th century. The fact that its walls were nine feet (3m) thick, coupled with the inaccessibility of its site, meant that it was fairly well protected against would-be invaders. The entrance was at first floor level, and access originally would have been up wooden steps, or a ladder that could have been drawn up into the tower in times of danger. The stone stairway that can be seen today was a later addition.

Castle Stalker was abandoned and became derelict after the second Jacobite uprising in the 18th century. It was not rebuilt and restored until the 1960s.

Cawdor Castle

Highland

Cawdor, 6 miles (9.5km) southwest of Nairn

OPEN DAILY FROM MAY
TO MID-OCTOBER.

TEL: 01667 404615

Cawdor Castle has had a violent history. It was home to the Thanes of Cawdor, who played an active role in local Scottish politics throughout the centuries, but the 9th Thane was branded on the hip with a hot key as a child, and both the 4th and the 11th Thanes were murdered.

Cawdor is also associated with Macbeth's murder of King Duncan, but as Macbeth lived during the 11th century, and Cawdor was not built until the 14th century, the link between the bloody murder and the castle may well be poetic licence.

Nevertheless, the appearance of the austere tower and battlements makes it easy to imagine why Shakespeare chose it as the location for his grim tale of madness and regicide. The keep dates from the 15th century and is a forbidding grey tower. The later buildings sprout an attractive array of steep-sided roofs, crow-stepped gables and small turrets dating from the 17th and 19th centuries. Inside, visitors can explore parts of the keep and rooms in the later buildings. There is a fine 17th-century kitchen displaying an array of antique household utensils.

THE CASTLE IS THE ANCIENT SEAT OF THE THANES OF CAWDOR.

CAWDOR CASTLE WAS BUILT AROUND A THORN TREE, STILL ON VIEW IN THE THORN ROOM.

Chepstow Castle

Monmouthshire

Chepstow, 15 miles (24km) east of Newport

OPEN ALL YEAR DAILY, EXCEPT CHRISTMAS AND NEW YEAR.

TEL: 01291 624065

CHEPSTOW CASTLE STANDS IN A STRATEGIC POSITION ABOVE THE RIVER WYE.

Chepstow was one of the first stone castles ever to be built in Britain. It was started in 1068, a mere two years after the invasion of England by William the Conqueror. William knew that in order to continue to hold what he had acquired at the Battle of Hastings, it was necessary to dominate the newly conquered people with a show of Norman power. This was achieved by castle building – at first simple mounds topped with wooden structures, and later, more permanent stone towers.

Chepstow was of great strategic importance, and William entrusted one of his best generals, William FitzOsbern, to build the castle and control the Marches. FitzOsbern chose a site that was naturally protected on one side by cliffs plummeting down into the brown waters of the Wye, and on another by a valley. He protected the remaining sides with stone walls.

Around 1190, Chepstow passed to the Marshall family, who set about improving defences by adding strong curtain walls with towers set into them. They extended the castle too, and were also responsible for the imposing gatehouse – this has a prison in one of its round towers, a dismal chamber with only an airshaft to break the monotony of the dank walls.

After 1270 a second hall, a D-shaped tower and another gatehouse were built on by one of Edward I's most powerful barons, Roger Bigod. Bigod's buildings contain comfortable living quarters, well equipped with kitchens, larders and storerooms. A double-seated latrine was also provided for visitors to the hall.

Chepstow, though never besieged in medieval times, played an important role in the Civil War. Afterwards its importance declined, and it began to fall into the romantic ruin it is today.

Clifford's Tower
York

York, 22 miles (35km) east of Harrogate

The site of Clifford's Tower was the scene of one of the bloodiest incidents in York's history. In 1190 the city's Jewish population was rounded up and put into the castle, which was then burned to the ground. This unpleasant episode was merely one event in a whole series of anti-Jewish riots that culminated in their expulsion from the country in 1290.

A second castle was quickly built, which involved raising the mound – originally built in about 1070 from layers of clay and marl, gravel and stones, and timber – to its present height of about 60 feet (18m). The new tower did not last long, but was blown down in a gale in 1228. Henry III ordered that a third tower should be built, and during the following 25 years the quatrefoil shell keep was erected on top of the mound. This unusual structure, very similar to the great tower at Etampes, near Paris, was known as the King's Tower until the 16th century. Walls and towers were also built at the bottom of the mound.

CLIFFORD'S TOWER IS A MEMORABLE LANDMARK ATOP THIS GRASS-COVERED MOUND.

OPEN ALL YEAR DAILY, EXCEPT CHRISTMAS AND NEW YEAR.

TEL: 01904 646940

Colchester Castle

Essex

Colchester, 17 miles (27km) south of Ipswich

OPEN ALL YEAR DAILY, EXCEPT CHRISTMAS AND NEW YEAR.

TEL: 01206 282939

Colchester is the largest Norman keep ever to have been built in Britain – larger even than the enormous Tower of London. Its dimensions are staggering – 150 feet (46m) from north to south, 110 feet (34m) from east to west and as much as 110 feet (34m) high at its corner turrets. At their splayed bases, the walls are 17 feet (5m) thick, but taper slightly as they rise. Because it bears some similarities to the White Tower, the central keep of the Tower of London, some scholars believe that Gandulf, Bishop of Rochester, designed both.

Unfortunately, the keep lost its upper storeys in the 17th century. There were originally four floors, but in 1683 the castle was sold to one John Wheeley, who wanted to pull it down and sell the stones. The great keep proved stronger than Wheeley had anticipated, and he gave up his demolition after the top two floors had proved something of a struggle. The idea of plundering ancient buildings arouses feelings of horror in these days of heritage conservation, but the castle itself was built from stones taken from nearby Roman ruins, and stands on the foundations of the Roman Temple of Claudius.

In the 18th century, MP Charles Gray patched up the castle to its present state. It now houses a museum, including archaeological finds from Colchester – the first capital of Roman Britain.

THE SAXONS KNEW COLCHESTER CASTLE AS KING COEL'S PALACE, AFTER THE OLD KING COLE OF THE NURSERY RHYME.

Conisbrough Castle

Doncaster

Conisbrough, 6 miles (9.5km) southwest of Doncaster

OPEN ALL YEAR DAILY,
EXCEPT CHRISTMAS AND
NEW YEAR.

TEL: 01709 863329

CONISBROUGH CASTLE
FEATURES IN SIR WALTER
SCOTT'S NOVEL *IVANHOE*.

In the early 12th century, Geoffrey, the young Count of Anjou, plucked a sprig of gorse – *Planta genista* – and wore it as a badge in his helmet. What began as a joke ended as a habit, earning the name 'Plantagenet' not only for himself but also for the ruling dynasty, which he founded. He married Matilda, the arrogant, embittered daughter of Henry I, and had a number of children, one of whom would later become Henry II – the first Plantagenet king of England.

Geoffrey was several years younger than his wife, and their marriage was far from happy. Like many medieval barons, he had children from other liaisons, and it was one such illegitimate child, Hamelin Plantagenet, who built the unusually shaped tower at Conisbrough. Hamelin began his building around 1174, and some 15 years later the keep, surrounded by walls with towers, was completed. The walls are 35 feet (11m) tall and 7 feet (2m) thick. The tower is basically round, but with six projecting buttresses, one of which houses a six-sided chapel and some comfortable accommodation. The immensely thick walls of the 95-foot (29m) high tower contain staircases, latrines, fireplaces and hand basins. Despite this economical use of the thick walls, visitors will notice that there are very few windows or arrow loops in the tower.

Conwy Castle
Conwy
Conwy, 4 miles (6.5km) south of Llandudno

OPEN ALL YEAR DAILY,
EXCEPT CHRISTMAS AND
NEW YEAR.

TEL: 01492 592358

CONWY OFFERS
A SUPERB 13TH-
CENTURY FORTRESS
BUILT BY EDWARD I.

Eight massive round towers and two barbicans linked by thick walls form the castle at Conwy, which, although perhaps overshadowed by Caernarfon, is one of the most spectacular in Wales.

Building at Conwy began in 1283 and was completed around 1287. During this very short time the town's defences were also built, taking in some ¾ mile (1km) of walls with 22 towers and three gateways. Conwy was Edward I's most expensive Welsh castle and was designed by his talented castle architect Master James of St George. Although Conwy's circular towers are its most dominant feature, there are the remains of other buildings in the two wards. One is the huge Great Hall, which would have been the heart of the medieval castle, where meals were eaten and audiences held, and where some people would have slept.

Shortly after Conwy was built there was a Welsh rebellion, led by Prince Madog, and a number of Edward I's castles were badly damaged.

Edward marched to Wales to suppress the rebellion, setting up his headquarters at Conwy. However, as soon as he was inside the castle, the river flooded, trapping Edward and his men inside. They were stranded for several days, and supplies of food and fresh water became dangerously low before the waters receded and they were able to escape.

THE IMPRESSIVE CONWY
SUSPENSION BRIDGE
WAS DESIGNED BY
THOMAS TELFORD.

Corfe Castle

Dorset

Corfe, 6 miles (9.5km) southeast of Wareham

OPEN ALL YEAR DAILY,
EXCEPT CHRISTMAS.

TEL: 01929 481294

BUILDING FIRST BEGAN ON CORFE IN THE 1080s, ON A NATURAL HILL WITH FINE VIEWS OVER THE COUNTRYSIDE.

Once regarded as one of the finest castles in England, Corfe was reduced during the Civil War to the collection of ragged walls and shattered towers that today loom over the small town like broken teeth.

During the first siege of Corfe in 1643, 500 Parliamentians were soundly repelled by Royalist troops under the command of the formidable Lady Bankes. The second siege occurred in 1646, conveniently timed when Lady Bankes was away. A small group of soldiers purporting to be Royalists was welcomed into the castle as much-needed additional manpower, but the soldiers were, in fact, Cromwell's men and they opened the gates and allowed the besiegers in. As soon as Cromwell's forces had taken the last prisoner, orders were given to destroy the castle so that it would never again withstand a siege.

Several kings contributed to Corfe Castle's stone construction. Most notably, King John paid £1400 for walls, a deep ditch-and-bank defence and his 'gloriette'. Corfe was John's favourite castle and the gloriette was an unfortified residential block containing lavish accommodation for the king, a chapel and offices. Henry III and Edward I added more towers and walls, making Corfe one of the strongest castles in the country.

Corfe Castle was particularly important to King John – he imprisoned his wife here and, four years later, he used it as a hiding place for his treasure and crown. Other notable prisoners kept at Corfe included Robert of Normandy, William the Conqueror's eldest son, who was kept captive for most of his life by his youngest brother, Henry I. Edward II was also imprisoned here before his fateful journey to Berkeley.

Craigievar Castle

Aberdeenshire

7 miles (11km) south of Alford

OPEN DAILY FROM APRIL TO SEPTEMBER, EXCEPT WEDNESDAY AND THURSDAY.

TEL: 01339 883635

Standing amid attractive woodland, and built of delicate rose-pink granite, Craigievar is one of the most romantic of the 17th-century Scottish tower houses. Although it is perhaps one of the most lavish and ornate, it was also one of the last of its kind to be built. Within two decades of its completion the Civil War broke out in England, and many castles and fortified houses came under devastating bombardment from cannon. Since it was no longer possible to build a house that could withstand such firepower indefinitely, fortresses became obsolete, and in their places came the elegant Classical-style mansions and tower houses of the 18th century.

The wealthy merchant, Sir William Forbes, who built Craigievar in the 1620s, spared no expense. It was he who ordered the decorative turrets that adorn each corner and the elegant carvings high up on the walls. Inside the castle are more reminders of Forbes' wealth. Many rooms have retained their impressive Renaissance plaster ceilings, and the elegant hall has arcaded panelling with a royal coat of arms over the granite fireplace.

The National Trust for Scotland now owns this magical L-plan castle, and nearly all the rooms are open to visitors.

Crathes Castle

Aberdeenshire

Crathes, 3 miles (5km) east of Banchory

OPEN DAILY FROM APRIL
TO OCTOBER.

TEL: 01330 844525

THE CASTLE'S BEAUTIFUL GARDENS COVER SOME 3 ACRES (1.2HA).

Crathes Castle is said to have a ghost that haunts one of its rooms. One version of the story is that the illegitimate child of a lady was murdered and buried under the hearth in the Green Room. It is said that moans and wails are sometimes heard echoing through Crathes' lonely halls, and that a mysterious green light has been seen by some visitors to the castle. Whether or not the story is true, a great deal more is on offer here.

Crathes, one of the most beautiful and best-preserved 16th-century castles in Scotland, was built in the 1550s for the wealthy Burnett family, and when the splendid multi-storey building proved too small for Thomas Burnett and his 21 children, some time in the early 18th century, he set about enlarging and restoring the castle. The outcome was the beginnings of the stately gardens that still surround the house, and an elegant building known as the Queen Anne Wing. Unfortunately, this was gutted in a serious fire in 1966, although the original L-plan tower escaped serious harm.

The National Trust for Scotland has restored the building. Crathes is in the same mould as Glamis and Craigievar, harled with delicately shaded rose granite, and capped with attractive clusters of turrets and chimneys.

PEPPER-POT TOWERS CLING TO THE 16TH-CENTURY CRATHES CASTLE.

Criccieth Castle

Gwynedd

Criccieth, 5 miles (8km) west of Porthmadog

OPEN ALL YEAR DAILY, EXCEPT CHRISTMAS AND NEW YEAR.

TEL: 01766 522227

CRICCIETH CASTLE SITS NEATLY ABOVE THE LITTLE TOWN.

In 1404 Criccieth Castle was taken from the English by Owain Glyndwr, the last of the Welsh leaders to rebel against the English crown. Shortly afterwards, the castle was so badly damaged by fire that it was never used again. In the 1930s, an archaeological investigation found proof of the fire that brought the castle's role in history to such an abrupt end, when charred timbers were discovered dating to the 15th century.

Criccieth, like many castles, was built in several different stages. The first stage, which included the solid twin-towered gatehouse, was built by Llywelyn the Great, while his grandson, Llywelyn the Last, added more walls and a rectangular tower. Edward I took the castle after Llywelyn the Last's defeat, and ordered the building of more walls and a tower strong enough to mount a siege engine on the roof.

Today, Criccieth is in ruins, although its commanding position on a promontory overlooking the picturesque Tremadog Bay gives an idea of the status this castle must once have enjoyed. Llywelyn the Great's massive gatehouse still presents a forbidding face to the world, and the thickness of its crumbling walls imbues it with an aura of strength and permanence.

Deal Castle
Kent
Deal, 9 miles (14.5km)
northeast of Dover

In 1533 Henry VIII, disappointed at not having produced a healthy son, divorced his Catholic wife, Catherine of Aragon. This move resulted not only in Henry being excommunicated, but also brought him into direct conflict with Catholic France and Spain. In order to protect England's southern coasts, Henry built a series of forts, which were financed largely from the proceeds of the dissolved monasteries.

Deal and nearby Walmer are two of these forts, both plain, functional buildings, where the sole purpose was defence. At Deal, six semi-circular bastions are joined to form a tower, which is further protected by an outer wall of the same shape. All were liberally supplied with gun loops and cannon ports, so that, in all, an attacker faced five tiers of guns.

Walmer has a simpler plan, involving a circular tower and a quatrefoil outer wall, but the defensive principle is the same, and from every angle an invader would face a bristling armoury of handguns and cannon.

As it happened, Henry's precautions were not necessary and Deal was not attacked until 1648, during the Civil War. It suffered extensive damage, but was not attacked again until a bomb fell on it during World War II.

OPEN ALL YEAR, EXCEPT MONDAY AND TUESDAY FROM NOVEMBER TO MARCH.

TEL: 01304 372762

DEAL CASTLE HOUSES A DISPLAY OF IRON AGE WEAPONS AND RELICS OF THE TOWN'S HISTORY.

Dirleton Castle

East Lothian

Dirleton, 11 miles (17.5km) northeast of Edinburgh

OPEN ALL YEAR DAILY, EXCEPT CHRISTMAS AND NEW YEAR.

TEL: 01620 850330

DIRLETON IS BUILT ON A ROCK OUTCROP, SURROUNDED BY THE REMAINS OF A MOAT.

This sturdy castle was raised in the 13th century, probably on the remains of an earlier fortress. The principal building was the impressive three-storey round keep or 'drum' tower, supported by a complex arrangement of other towers and walls. In the 14th and 15th centuries the castle was considerably enlarged, to include a chapel with a prison beneath, and a pit-prison hewn from the rock below that. Although a ruin, Dirleton still presents an imposing face to the world and, crossing the modern wooden footbridge to the great gatehouse, it is easy to appreciate the difficulties faced by any would-be attacker.

Dorothea, wife of the rebellious Earl of Gowrie, was probably one of the saddest residents of Dirleton Castle. Her husband was executed in 1585 after a plot to seize Stirling Castle was discovered, and King James VI took all his lands and castles, leaving Dorothea and her 15 children poverty-stricken. The king granted Dirleton Castle to Gowrie's great rival, the Earl of Arran, who kept it until the castle and its lands were restored to Dorothea almost two years later. Then, in 1600, two of her sons were involved in the mysterious 'Gowrie Conspiracy', when it was alleged that they tried to kill the king.

FAR LEFT: KILDRUMMY
CASTLE
LEFT: LINCOLN CASTLE
RIGHT: CARDIFF CASTLE

Siege and Strife

The Castle Under Attack It was not easy to overpower great medieval fortresses designed to repel invaders. Most attackers therefore opted for a siege – a waiting game where the defences of the castle were pitted against the equipment and cunning of the attacking army. Treachery was not unknown, as was the case when a Scottish blacksmith sabotaged Kildrummy Castle, allowing the English to take it.

Defence Tactics Defenders might make use of the 'sally port', or back door, to harry the camp of the attackers. They could use war machines (called mangonels and trebuchets) to hurl missiles at them and, as long as supplies lasted, keep up a constant shower of arrows. Meanwhile, the attackers could hurl missiles back, use battering rams on the gates, or advance using the protection of 'belfries' or siege towers. If they could get close enough, attackers could undermine the walls by tunnelling underneath to weaken the foundations. A tunnel at St Andrew's was aiming to do just that when it was met with a 'countermine' dug by the castle defenders. Unable to dig further the attackers were forced to abandon their plan. King John successfully undermined one corner of Rochester's keep, with the aid of 40 dead pigs that he set alight in the tunnel. When the heat caused the tunnel to collapse, part of the keep also fell, allowing John's troops in.

Harlech Castle Harlech was built in 1283-81 by Edward I, with a sheer drop to sea on one side. today the sea has slipped away and the castle stands among the dunes. Castle sieges often resulted in the occupants starving or surrendering themselves to horrible consequences. Harlech was the scene of a last, desperate siege in the

Wars of the Roses. In 1461 Edward IV had all but obliterated the opposition, but Harlech held out against a siege that would drag on for seven years. When his rival Jasper Tudor arrived to join forces with the 'Men of Harlech', Edward took drastic action. and sent his troops on a rampage through the local communities. Harlech finally surrendered and two of its garrison were executed.

Cardiff Castle Despite its present of Victorian mock-Gothic extravagance, Cardiff Castle has a long and bloody history. Its site was originally occupied by a Roman fort. In the post-Roman era the locals suffered terribly as fights raged between the Welsh and the Saxons, and marauding Vikings raided the coast. The defences were strengthened in the 10th and 11th centuries, and in 1112 the castle was captured by Ifor Bach, chief of Glamorgan, who held the occupants captive until he was paid off.

Conwy Castle One of the bloodiest events occurred during the siege of Conwy Castle. The castle was built by Edward I to subjugate the Welsh but the tables were briefly turned in 1401, during Owain Glyndwr's uprising. On 1 April, only two warders were on duty in the castle when a Welsh carpenter turned up for work. As they let him in, 40 of Glyndwr's soldiers burst through the gates, killed the guards and prepared to sit out a long siege. After three months, supplies were running low, and the impasse was broken by desperate means. In one version, nine heroic warriors surrendered their lives to the English in return for their companions' release. Another claims that they were ambushed by their comrades during the night, and offered up to the enemy. All versions agree that the nine victims were butchered by Edward's army, who had them hanged, drawn, disembowelled, beheaded and quartered.

ABOVE: Eilean Donan Castle in Scotland was pounded by the guns of an English man-of-war in 1719.

LEFT: Conwy Castle's serene location gives no hint of the fortress's long and bloody history.

55

Dolbadarn Castle

Gwynedd

7½ miles (12km) east of Caernarfon

Huge steep-sided mountains loom on both sides of the Llanberis Pass as the road winds down towards Caernarfon and the coast. Here can be found Dolbadarn Castle, still standing sentinel to the route it once guarded. Although Dolbadarn was never large, it was of great importance to the Welsh princes. When Llywelyn the Last retreated to his mountain stronghold to escape from Edward I, the Llanberis Pass was the main route to the farmlands of Anglesey, whence most of Llywelyn's supplies came.

The castle's most striking feature is the single round tower that still survives to a height of 40 feet (12m). The entry was on the first floor, with wooden steps that could be pulled up inside the castle in the event of an attack. It was probably built by Llywelyn the Great in the early 13th century, and is much stronger and better built than the rest of the castle, of which little remains but the foundations. The contrasting views of Dolbadarn are one of its most remarkable features. On one side lie the gently undulating hills with the lake twinkling in the distance, while on the other stand the stark mountains of the Snowdonia National Park, some ripped open by slate quarries.

DOLBADARN CASTLE OVERLOOKS THE WATERS OF LLYN PERIS.

OPEN ACCESS AT ANY REASONABLE TIME.

Dolwyddelan Castle
Conwy
Dolwyddelan, 6 miles (9.5km) southwest of Betws-y-Coed

OPEN ALL YEAR DAILY, EXCEPT CHRISTMAS AND NEW YEAR.

TEL: 01690 750366

This sturdy three-storey tower appears almost insignificant among the sweeping hills of the Welsh countryside, especially next to the rugged green-brown slopes of Moal-Siabod that lie to one side. The precise origins of the castle are obscured by time, but it was built by the Princes of Wales to guard the ancient pathway that ran from Merionnydd to the Vale of Conwy. It may have been built by Iorwerth Trwyndwn ('the flat-nosed'), and it is said that one of Wales' most famous princes, Llywelyn the Great, was born here around 1173. Edward I's forces attacked it in 1283 during his Welsh campaign, and seeing its great strategic value, the king had it refortified and manned by English soldiers: thus the Welsh-built castle became a stronghold for the English. The castle itself was originally a rectangular tower of two storeys; it was later given an extra floor and a battlemented roof line. Later still, thick walls were added to form an enclosure with another rectangular tower, all protected by ditches cut into the rock. Although it was built by the Welsh, the architect of Dolwyddelan borrowed heavily from the Norman style of castle building, and there was a door on the first floor, protected by a drawbridge.

DOLWYDDELAN CASTLE WAS REPUTEDLY THE BIRTHPLACE OF LLYWELYN THE GREAT.

Dover Castle

Kent

Dover, 7 miles (11km) east of Folkestone

OPEN ALL YEAR DAILY,
EXCEPT CHRISTMAS AND
NEW YEAR.
TEL: 01304 211067

Dover Castle is so enormous, and contains so many fascinating features, that it is difficult to know where to start in its description. It was a state-of-the-art castle in medieval times, displaying some of the most advanced defensive architecture available. Its strategically vital position at the point where England is nearest to the coast of France has given it a unique place in British history. And it is without doubt a most powerful, massive, imposing and splendid building.

RICH IN HISTORY,
DOVER CASTLE
WAS USED DURING
WORLD WAR II TO
PLAN THE EVACUATION
OF DUNKIRK.

The castle stands on a spur of rock overlooking the English Channel. Walls bristling with towers and bulwarks protect the entire site. These include the formidable Constable's Gate, erected in the 1220s, a pair of D-shaped towers that not only served as a serious obstacle for would-be invaders, but provided comfortable lodgings for the castle constables (or, nowadays, their deputies). Outside the walls are earthworks and natural slopes that provide additional defence.

William the Conqueror began the castle, but Henry II built the great keep in the 1180s. It is surrounded by yet another wall, studded with square towers and two barbicans. The keep itself is 95 feet (29m) tall, and around 95 feet (29m) across at its base. There are square turrets at each corner, and even at the top of the tower, where the walls are thinnest; they are still 17 feet (5m) thick. The well is carved into the thickness of the wall, and plunges 240 feet (73m) to reach a steady water supply.

Dover has had a rich and eventful history, and one especially important episode occurred during the last year of the reign of King John (1216). John's barons had been growing increasingly frustrated with him, and had invited Prince Louis, heir to the French throne, to invade England and take over. Louis landed at Dover and laid siege to Dover Castle, which was held by Hubert de Burgh, a baron loyal to John. Ever since the castle was founded, kings had laid down vast sums of money for its repair and development (notably Henry II and Richard I), and it looked as though this investment had paid off. Louis, it seemed, would be unable to breach Dover's powerful walls. Then the unthinkable happened – the French managed to take the outer barbican and undermine the gate. Despite de Burgh's efforts, Louis was poised to enter the inner enclosure. With fortunate timing, John died, the barons proclaimed allegiance to his successor, Henry III, and Louis went home. Lessons were learned, however, and Henry spent a good deal of money in improving Dover's defences.

Duart Castle
Argyll & Bute
Criagnure, east coast of Isle of Mull

OPEN DAILY FROM MAY TO MID-OCTOBER.

TEL: 01680 812309

DUART CASTLE, ON
THE ISLE OF MULL,
OVERLOOKS THE WATERS
OF LOCH LINNHE.

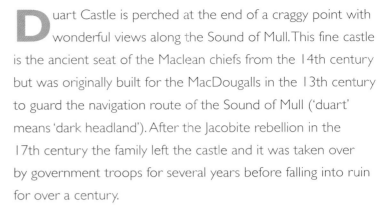uart Castle is perched at the end of a craggy point with wonderful views along the Sound of Mull. This fine castle is the ancient seat of the Maclean chiefs from the 14th century but was originally built for the MacDougalls in the 13th century to guard the navigation route of the Sound of Mull ('duart' means 'dark headland'). After the Jacobite rebellion in the 17th century the family left the castle and it was taken over by government troops for several years before falling into ruin for over a century.

This impressive castle, like similar castles such as Eilean Donan, is the result of careful and expensive restoration work. It was purchased and restored in 1911 by Sir Fitzroy Maclean to be the home of the Clan Chief and house much of the Maclean memorabilia, but the site still retains many fragments from the 13th century. You can visit the dungeons and view the state-rooms in the keep, then climb to the top for spectacular views.

Dunnottar Castle
Aberdeenshire
1 mile (1.5km) southeast of Stonehaven

OPEN ALL YEAR DAILY,
EXCEPT TUESDAY TO
THURSDAY IN WINTER.
TEL: 01569 762173

THE DRAWING-ROOM
FIREPLACE AT
DUNNOTTAR WAS A
FOCAL POINT FOR THE
ENTIRE HOUSEHOLD.

DUNNOTTAR CASTLE
SQUATS ON TOP OF A
VAST FLAT-TOPPED ROCK,
160 FEET (50M) ABOVE
THE SEA.

On the rugged coastline south of Aberdeen a great stack of rock projects into the stormy North Sea, topped by a jumbled collection of buildings spanning several centuries. Joined to the land by a narrow crumbling neck of rock, great cliffs protect this natural fortress on all sides, while a thick wall and a gatehouse protect the castle entrance.

The first castle here was built in the 12th century, but virtually nothing remains of this early building. In the 14th century an L-plan tower-house was built by William Keith, the Marischal of Scotland. This building dominates the rest of the castle, its 50-foot (15m) walls still in good repair, although it is roofless.

More buildings were raised in the 16th century, forming a handsome quadrangular courtyard. Although the emphasis was on comfort rather than on defence, the castle was equipped with gun ports as a safeguard against possible attack. These were used twice in the Civil War when the castle came under siege, first by the Royalists and then by Cromwell.

In a dark episode in its history, Dunnottar Castle was used as a prison for 167 Scottish Presbyterians. These people were crammed into a long, narrow chamber known as the Whigs Vault, and the conditions there were so appalling that many of the prisoners died.

Dunskey Castle
Dumfries & Galloway
6 miles (9.5km) southwest of Stranraer

Little is known of this ruined tower-house standing on a rocky peninsula that juts out into the sea. A castle is mentioned in records dating to 1330, but was burned down early in the 15th century. William Adair of Kinhilt raised a new tower, but this was deserted in the middle of the 17th century, and was little more than a ruin by 1684.

Dunskey is a simple L-plan tower-house, with cellars, a ground floor and a first floor. Walls were built around the small peninsula, so that the castle would have been surrounded by two lines of defence: firstly, the sea and ditches hewn from the rock and, secondly, the walls. Virtually nothing remains of these walls, although there are traces of other buildings in what would have been the courtyard.

It is likely that Dunskey Castle would once have been a fine, proud house. The windows and doors were at one time all decorated with dressed stones, but these, being expensive and much in demand for building work, have been stripped away over the centuries by local looters. It is the absence of these stones that gives the roofless walls of Dunskey Castle their forlorn, rugged appearance.

DUNSKEY, LYING JUST SOUTH OF PORTPATRICK, OCCUPIES A SPECTACULAR COASTAL LOCATION.

OPEN ACCESS AT ANY REASONABLE TIME.

Dunstanburgh Castle
Northumberland
12 miles (19km) north of Alnwick

OPEN DAILY, EXCEPT
MONDAY AND TUESDAY
IN WINTER, AND
CHRISTMAS AND
NEW YEAR.

TEL: 01665 576231

ON A LONELY CLIFF-TOP, THE RUINED TOWERS OF DUNSTANBURGH FORM A DRAMATIC SILHOUETTE AGAINST THE SKY.

Lonely and ruined, Dunstanburgh is one of the most dramatic and atmospheric castles in Britain. Its low walls hug the rocky coastline, and only the cries of gulls and the roar of the waves disturb its peace. In order to see the castle you must walk from the nearby village, a distance of over a mile (1.2km), but the effort is well worth it, and the absence of traffic does much to enhance the feeling of timelessness of this splendid fortress.

Dunstanburgh was built by Thomas of Lancaster, the most powerful baron in the reign of Edward II. The earl and his king were constantly at loggerheads, especially over the favouritism shown by Edward to certain of his Court – and in particular, to Piers Gaveston. Lancaster ordered Gaveston's brutal murder, and in the turmoil that followed the Scots seized the opportunity to begin a series of raids in northern England. Dunstanburgh was

therefore built both as a stronghold against a possible Scottish invasion and as a retreat for Lancaster from the King's wrath.

The site occupied by Dunstanburgh is large, and there would have been plenty of space for local people and their livestock to take refuge from Scottish raids within the great thick walls that swept around the site. The sea and steep cliffs provided further protection from attack on two sides.

Lancaster's impressive gatehouse was built between 1313 and 1325, and even in its ruinous state it exudes a sense of power and impregnability. It had three floors, and all the building materials were of the finest quality. Dunstanburgh is unusual in that it acquired a second gatehouse about 60 years later. By this time, the castle had come into the hands of another Duke of Lancaster, the powerful John of Gaunt, third son of Edward III.

Dunster Castle

Somerset
3 miles (5km) southeast of Minehead

OPEN ALL YEAR.

TEL: 01643 702624

Set on the eastern edge of Dartmoor, Dunster Castle dominates one of the most picturesque medieval villages. There has been a castle on this site since Norman times and during the early medieval period the sea provided the occupants with a natural defence. In the late 14th century the castle came into the possession of the Luttrell family, where it remained for the next six hundred years. When the sea receded in the 15th century they created a deer park, but during the Civil War Dunster shared the fate of many other Royalist strongholds under siege and all the medieval fortifications were destroyed, except for the gatehouse and two ruined towers.

Now in the care of the National Trust, Dunster Castle was substantially altered between 1868 and 1872 but its medieval character was preserved to a large extent. The architect, Anthony Salvin, attuned the castle for comfortable living, but retained the 17th-century plasterwork, panels and oak staircase, which date from about 1683. Sub-tropical plants flourish in the 28-acre (11.2ha) park and the terraced gardens are noted for exotica such as a giant lemon tree, yuccas, mimosa and palms. St George's Church, once both a Benedictine priory and parish church, is the largest in Exmoor and dates mainly from the 15th century.

DUNSTER CASTLE HAS AN EXCEPTIONALLY PICTURESQUE SETTING ON AN ELEVATED SITE.

THE CASTLE BOASTS A SUPERB 17TH-CENTURY OAK STAIRCASE.

THE EXTENSIVE GARDENS AT DUNSTER ARE FAMOUS FOR THEIR THRIVING COLLECTION OF EXOTIC PLANTS.

Duntulm Castle

Highland

Duntulm, Isle of Skye, 24 miles (38.5km) north of Portree

OPEN ACCESS AT ANY
REASONABLE TIME.

REMAINS OF THE 15TH
TO 17TH-CENTURY
DUNTULM CASTLE.

This stronghold of the island clan of MacDonald stands in a commanding position overlooking a natural harbour at the extreme northern end of Skye. The rectangular tower dates from the 15th century, but a smaller tower was added in the 17th century, when the little fortress was at the height of its glory. Contemporary accounts tell of the lavish hospitality that could be enjoyed at the fine MacDonald house at Duntulm, and soil was imported from seven different countries to make the castle gardens fertile.

Several legends are attached to the atmospheric ruins of Duntulm Castle. One such legend tells of the baby son of the clan chief, who was dangled from a window by his nurse to see a passing ship, when she inadvertently dropped him. The chief was reported to have quit Duntulm immediately before any further misfortunes should befall him.

A different tale involves another chief and his heir, Hugh. The story goes that Hugh was keen to inherit sooner, rather than later, and so arranged for his kinsman's murder. In an act of appalling incompetence, Hugh misaddressed his letters, sending to the chief not an invitation to dine, but instructions to the hired killer outlining how the foul deed was to be done. Hugh was arrested and incarcerated in Duntulm's vaults with salt beef and nothing to drink. It is said that many years later a skeleton was unearthed, still clutching an empty water pitcher.

Dunvegan Castle
Highland
Dunvegan, Isle of Skye,
23 miles (37km) west of Portree

Open all year daily, except Christmas and New Year.

Tel: 01470 521206

Dunvegan Castle has been the home of the MacLeod family for nearly 800 years.

The story of Dunvegan Castle, one of Scotland's oldest inhabited castles, and its owners, the MacLeods, stretches back to the 13th century. In 1237 Leod, a son of the King of the Isle of Man and the North Isles, inherited the island of Lewis and Harris, and part of Skye. When Viking claims to the Scottish islands were finally crushed, Leod controlled a good portion of the Hebrides. He chose the rocky peninsula jutting out into the sea at Dunvegan on which to establish his fortress and headquarters. Dunvegan has remained the home of the MacLeods (meaning 'son of Leod') ever since.

Leod died in 1280, but before his death a thick wall had been built around the site, leaving only a small sea gate, through which supplies could be brought to the castle in times of siege. Between 1340 and 1360, a keep was added, which contained kitchens and a dungeon. The 'Fairy Tower' was built around 1500, while further improvements were made in the 17th century.

The entire castle was reconstructed in the 19th century, complete with noble battlements and little corner turrets, and is an impressive sight, whether approached from land or sea.

Edinburgh Castle
City of Edinburgh
Edinburgh

There was no capital city of Scotland, as such, until the end of the Middle Ages. Before that, Scotland's capital was wherever the king and his court happened to be. But the magnificent fortress squatting firmly on its plug of rock was a great favourite with Scottish kings, and has played a vital role in history on many occasions. It changed hands several times when the Scots were fighting for independence from England under Robert the Bruce, and became a royal residence under the Stuart kings.

Today it is a museum – it houses the Scottish National War Memorial and the Scottish crown jewels – and is the venue for the spectacular annual Edinburgh Military Tattoo. It still dominates the ancient city from its rocky pinnacle, and even though it has been battered and bruised through the centuries, remains one of the most impressive and best-known castles in the world.

The origins of Edinburgh Castle are shrouded in mystery. Although the great rock on which the castle stands would probably have attracted earlier strongholds, there is no archaeological evidence to prove the site was used earlier than the 11th century. Malcolm III, before his death in 1093, raised a wooden fortress here and his son, David I, built a church to the memory of his mother in the 1120s. This tiny chapel is the oldest

THE VAST SPRAWL OF THE CASTLE CONTAINS BUILDINGS FROM MANY CENTURIES, SUCH AS THE PALACE BUILT FOR KING JAMES IV.

THE MILITARY TATTOO HAS BEEN A FEATURE OF THE EDINBURGH FESTIVAL FOR ABOUT 50 YEARS AND TAKES PLACE ON THE ESPLANADE.

surviving building in the castle. Thereafter, Edinburgh became an important gamepiece in the struggles between Edward I and Robert the Bruce in the late 13th century. Edward seized it in 1296, bombarding it with huge boulders from his great war machines. The garrison surrendered after only eight days, and Edward installed 350 of his own soldiers to hold it securely.

In 1313 the Earl of Moray, acting for Bruce, scaled the cliffs with only 30 men and routed the English. Bruce ordered the castle be destroyed, so that Edward's forces could never again use it. He underestimated Edward's tenacity, for a few years later Edward retook the site, and set about repairing the damage, even planting gardens in anticipation of a lengthy stay. But the Scots were undeterred, and in 1341 a small party of Scottish soldiers disguised themselves as merchants and ambushed the garrison.

A FINE STATUE OF ROBERT THE BRUCE CONVEYS THE HERO'S NOBLE BEARING AND POWERFUL AUTHORITY.

EDINBURGH CASTLE, AT THE HEART OF THIS GREAT CITY, IS ONE OF THE MOST FAMOUS IN THE WORLD.

OPEN ALL YEAR DAILY, EXCEPT CHRISTMAS.

TEL: 0131 225 9846

Edzell Castle

Angus
Edzell, 8 miles (13km) north of Brechin

The most remarkable feature of this sturdy little fortified tower-house is its unusual gardens, complete with bath-house and summer-house. In 1604 a walled enclosure was added onto the already existing tower-house and courtyard. It was designed to surround one of the most elegant and notable gardens of any castle in western Europe.

OPEN ALL YEAR DAILY, EXCEPT FRIDAY IN WINTER AND CHRISTMAS.

TEL: 01356 648631

EDZELL CASTLE HAS A REMARKABLE WALLED GARDEN, BUILT IN 1604 BY SIR DAVID LINDSAY.

The garden walls are a triumph in themselves: they have been divided into sections, and they are richly adorned with carvings and sculpted panels. Exquisite in their detail, the carvings embrace several themes: the first set depicts a number of planetary deities, including Mars, Jupiter, Venus and Saturn; the second represents 'the liberal arts'. In medieval learning, the three basic subjects were grammar, rhetoric and logic, while arithmetic, music, geometry and astronomy were the more advanced topics, and each of these is illustrated by seated figures busily practising their art.

The tower-house was built in the 15th century as a home for the Lindsay family. Other buildings arranged around a courtyard were added in the 16th century.

Edzell has seen little military action since it was built, although it was occupied by Cromwell's troops in 1651, and was badly damaged in the second Jacobite uprising in 1747.

Today, the tower remains the most complete section, along with the quaint summer-house in the southeast corner of the garden. The two-storey summer-house has its own stair tower and gun loops.

THE CASTLE GROUNDS INCLUDE ATTRACTIVE ORNAMENTAL AND BORDER GARDENS.

FLOWER-FILLED RECESSES IN THE GARDEN WALLS ARE ALTERNATED WITH HERALDIC AND SYMBOLIC SCULPTURES OF A SORT NOT SEEN ELSEWHERE IN SCOTLAND.

Eilean Donan Castle
Highland
Dornie, 8 miles (13km) east of Kyle of Lochalsh

OPEN DAILY FROM
EASTER TO OCTOBER.

TEL: 01599 555202

THE BEAUTIFUL EILEAN DONAN CASTLE STANDS GUARD ON A PROMONTORY WHERE THREE LOCHS MEET.

Dwarfed by the brooding hills surrounding Loch Duich, the castle of Eilean Donan stands picturesquely on its rocky island. A fortress was built here in 1220 by Alexander II to protect himself against raids by Vikings. During the Jacobite Rebellion the Macraes, owners of the castle, opted to support the Old Pretender and garrisoned a small force of Spanish soldiers here. In 1719 the guns of an English man-of-war pounded the castle to pieces.

It remained in ruins until 1912, when Colonel John Macrae decided to restore his ancestral home. Paying great attention to detail, the lakeside castle was lovingly rebuilt, along with an arched bridge that affords easier access to the castle than the ancient Macraes would have known.

Some rooms in the castle are open to visitors, all furnished in the style of the home of a country laird. There are fine collections of pistols and powder horns, and, although it is mostly a 20th-century restoration, it allows the imagination to return to the time when the wild Macraes owned it. A fearsome clan, they relished the displaying of the heads of their enemies from the battlements, and local legends tell how, on one occasion, they defended the castle successfully when outnumbered by their attackers 400-to-one.

Flint Castle

Flintshire

Flint, 10 miles (16km) northwest of Chester

OPEN ACCESS AT ANY
REASONABLE TIME.

TEL: 01352 733078

ONCE AN IMPORTANT
FORTRESS, FLINT CASTLE
RECEIVES VERY FEW
VISITORS TODAY.

In August 1399 Richard II, fleeing from the forces of his cousin Henry of Bolingbrooke, arrived at Flint Castle. Within days, Bolingbrooke had captured Richard and had him taken to London, where he abdicated in Bolingbrooke's favour. Bolingbrooke became King Henry IV, while Richard was eventually taken to Pontefract Castle in Yorkshire, where he was probably murdered.

Flint was the first of the castles built by Edward I during his Welsh campaigns. Building started in 1277 with an enormous workforce of 2300 labourers, who were paid handsomely, since building a castle in a hostile land was not popular work. The castle consisted of a rectangular enclosure with four round towers at the corners. Additional walls, a moat and some deep ditches further protected this. One of the round corner towers was larger than the others, and was protected by a moat. It also had its own kitchens, living quarters and chapel, and was probably the residence of the constable and his family.

Nowadays, this once vitally important castle is hidden behind the modern town, bypassed by tourists heading west and standing lonely and forgotten on the marshy shores of the River Dee.

Framlingham Castle
Suffolk
Framlingham, 18 miles (29km) northeast of Ipswich

OPEN ALL YEAR DAILY, CLOSED CHRISTMAS AND NEW YEAR.

TEL: 01728 724189

THE MAGNIFICENT CURTAIN WALLS OF FRAMLINGHAM CASTLE.

The battlemented towers and walls of Framlingham Castle have had some notable owners. The powerful Earl of Norfolk, Roger Bigod, probably built the castle that survives today between about 1189 and 1200 on the site of an earlier castle. The Bigods traditionally had tempestuous relationships with their kings – Hugh Bigod supported Henry II's eldest son when he rebelled against his father in 1173, Roger Bigod II held Framlingham against King John in 1216 and Roger Bigod IV refused to go to Flanders to fight for Edward I in 1297.

The Mowbray family also owned Framlingham, one of whom was engaged to marry one of the unfortunate princes who disappeared in the Tower of London. It was at Framlingham that Mary Tudor learned that she had become Queen of England in 1553. Later, Elizabeth I used the castle as a prison for priests who defied the new Church of England.

Framlingham has 13 towers, all connected by walls, and a wall-walk that is still open to visitors runs right round the castle. When Framlingham was no longer used as a ducal residence, it took on several different roles through the centuries, including that of poorhouse (the buildings for which survive in the courtyard), parish meeting place, dance hall, courtroom, drill hall and fire station.

Glamis Castle

Angus

Glamis, 12 miles (19km) north of Dundee

OPEN DAILY FROM
MARCH TO OCTOBER.
TEL: 01307 840393

Legends and myths about Glamis Castle are plentiful. Malcolm II is said to have been murdered here in the 11th century; James V burnt Lady Janet Douglas, the widow of the Earl of Glamis, at the stake as a witch in 1540; and there is said to be a secret room where one lord of Glamis played cards with the devil. It is difficult to associate such dark tales with the splendid dark red castle, with its ornate turrets and chimneys.

There was probably a castle at Glamis in the early 14th century, but it was not until after 1376 that John Lyon built the L-plan tower-house on land presented to him by Robert II. The Lyon family, now Earls of Strathmore and Kinghorne, have owned the castle ever since.

If Glamis today looks more like a French château than a medieval fortress, then that is because it was extensively restored and developed in the 17th and 18th centuries. The original tower-house, although strengthened, heightened, and re-roofed, remains the central part of this rambling palace. Tours of the house range from the medieval hall to the 17th-century chapel, and include the small suite of rooms used by George VI and his queen.

A MAGNIFICENT AND MYSTERIOUS CASTLE, GLAMIS WAS THE FAMILY HOME OF THE QUEEN MOTHER AND THE BIRTHPLACE OF PRINCESS MARGARET.

Goodrich Castle

Herefordshire

Goodrich, 6 miles (9.5km) northeast of Monmouth

OPEN ALL YEAR DAILY, EXCEPT MONDAY AND TUESDAY FROM NOVEMBER TO MARCH, AND CHRISTMAS AND NEW YEAR.

TEL: 01600 890538

A RED SANDSTONE RUIN, GOODRICH CASTLE HAS WONDERFUL VIEWS IN ALL DIRECTIONS.

Goodrich does not possess the elegance or the picturesque quality of some castles – it was built for strength and defence. However, time has given these ruins a beauty their builders never intended and Goodrich today is one of the castles which are most evocative of Norman dominance.

In the middle of the 12th century the first stone building at Goodrich was raised – a sturdy, pale-red keep. It stands 60 feet (18m) high today, although it was originally taller and would probably have had battlements. In the late 13th century the de Valence family, who owned the castle, decided to turn the simple keep into a formidable fortress. Round the keep, they built four massive walls. At three of the corners were cylindrical towers with great square bases that seem to grow out of the rock on which they are anchored. Undermining these towers would have been extremely difficult, especially as the whole castle was surrounded by a deep moat. The fourth corner had a huge gatehouse tower that led out into the barbican.

Harlech Castle

Gwynedd

Harlech, 16 miles (25.5km) south of Porthmadog

The last great uprising of the Welsh against the occupying English occurred in the early 15th century under the leadership of the great hero Owain Glyndwr. In the spring of 1404, Glyndwr gathered his forces against the mighty fortress of Harlech, but the castle was too strong to be taken in a battle and so Glyndwr began a siege. For many months the castle garrison held out, despite Glyndwr's efficient blockade of all the castle's supply routes. Food began to run low, and then disease broke out, doubtless aggravated by the shortage of clean water for drinking, cooking and washing. After some of the soldiers had made an unsuccessful attempt to escape, Glyndwr stood at the castle's gate and demanded surrender.

Harlech was Glyndwr's home and headquarters for the next four years, and it is possible he even held a Welsh parliament there. It is also said that he crowned himself Prince of Wales in Harlech. Finally, in 1409, Henry IV sent a powerful force to recapture the castle and stamp out the rebellion. After a short siege, the castle fell. Glyndwr's wife and children were taken prisoner, and although Glyndwr himself escaped, the fall of Harlech marked the beginning of the end for him. Within four years he had disappeared.

The great castle that allowed its garrison to withstand intense and prolonged sieges was one of Edward I's 'iron ring' of castles built during his second castle-building campaign. Unlike Beaumaris, on which building continued for 35 years, Harlech was completed within seven years (1283–90). Master James of St George personally supervised the building, and it does not take much imagination to envisage what a remarkable feat of engineering was required to erect such a vast fortress in such a short space of time.

Harlech is concentric, with outer walls giving further protection to the inner walls, which contained the main living quarters. The inner walls also contain the great gatehouse, with its comfortable residential apartments. The gatehouse is perhaps Harlech's finest feature, a vast structure that presents a forbidding display of thick grey walls and impregnability.

Harlech's mighty walls were not its only defence. Two sides of the castle were protected by deep dry moats hacked out of the rock on which the castle stands, while cliffs plunging down to the sea made any assault on the back of the castle virtually impossible.

HARLECH CASTLE
WAS BUILT TO
WITHSTAND FIERCE
ATTACK AND INTENSE
PROLONGED SIEGES.

RISING 200 FEET (60M)
ON A ROCKY
PROMONTORY, THE
STRIKING CASTLE IS
LARGELY INTACT.

OPEN ALL YEAR
DAILY. TELEPHONE
FOR CHRISTMAS
OPENING TIMES.

TEL: 01766 780552

Hedingham Castle

Essex

Castle Hedingham, 7 miles (11km) southwest of Sudbury

Open from Easter to October daily, except Saturday.
Tel: 01787 460261

When the barons forced King John to sign the Magna Carta in 1215, they doubtless thought that it would bring an end to John's unpopular policies, but John was not bowed for long. Robert de Vere was the owner of Hedingham Castle, and was one of the barons who sided against the king, and had his castle attacked twice in what became known as the Magna Carta Wars. John died soon afterwards, and Hedingham and other properties were restored to de Vere, whose family continued to own the castle until 1703.

Today, only the keep remains of the great 12th-century fortress, but it is one of the finest in England. It was probably built between 1120 and 1140. It has four storeys, although the second floor is double the height of the others. This floor forms a magnificent hall, with elegant arched windows on two levels to provide plenty of light. A vast Norman arch spans the whole room, and a gallery runs around the upper half of the chamber.

THE GREAT KEEP OF HEDINGHAM CASTLE IS ONE OF THE BEST PRESERVED IN EUROPE.

AT HEDINGHAM, THE LORD CHAMBERLAIN'S CARVED CHAIR STILL HAS PRIDE OF PLACE.

Herstmonceux Castle

East Sussex

8 miles (13km) north of Eastbourne

GROUNDS OPEN DAILY
EXCEPT SATURDAY, APRIL
TO OCTOBER. CASTLE
OPEN FOR GUIDED
TOURS ONLY.

TEL: 01323 834457

HERSTMONCEUX IS ONE
OF THE MOST STRIKING
15TH-CENTURY CASTLES
IN BRITAIN.

Many people will associate the fine brick palace at Herstmonceux with the Royal Observatory, which moved here from Greenwich in 1948. In 1989 the Royal Observatory moved yet again, leaving Herstmonceux to adjust to its new existence as a conference centre.

Herstmonceux was one of the first castles in England to be built of brick, and the effect is stunning. Its clusters of elegant chimneys and the many towers, all in a pleasing shade of rich red, are reflected in the wide moat that surrounds it, rendering it one of the most attractive castles built in the Middle Ages.

Sir Roger Fiennes was granted a licence to build Herstmonceux in 1441. The fact that the castle was built in a lake afforded some protection, and the impressive gatehouse presented a formidable array of murder holes and arrow slits with which to greet hostile visitors.

Once the castle had passed from the Fiennes family, it had a sad history of careless owners. In the 17th century, one owner shamelessly ripped out the interior of the castle in order to provide himself with the raw materials to build another house, and a great deal of work has been necessary to restore it to its former grandeur.

Huntingtower

Perth & Kinross

2 miles (3km) west of Perth

Huntingtower is one of the most interesting castles in Scotland. It is essentially two towers joined together as one, but intended to be fully independent of each other. The first tower dates from the 15th century and is three storeys tall. In the late 15th or early 16th century, a second rectangular tower was built, a floor higher than the earlier building. In the 17th century, the space between these two towers was walled in and roofed. This remarkable building still displays some original painted ceilings.

One of the most famous events in Scottish history was the 'Raid of Ruthven', which took place at Huntingtower in August 1582. At that time, the castle was called the House of Ruthven and was owned by the powerful Scottish noble, the Earl of Gowrie. The young king, James VI, was heavily under the influence of two of Gowrie's rivals, the Duke of Lennox and the Earl of Arran. Gowrie and his ally, the Earl of Mar, persuaded the young king to visit the House of Ruthven and then proclaimed him a prisoner. When Arran tried to free the king, he too was imprisoned. Later, Gowrie was executed, and the king ordered that the name of the castle be changed from Ruthven to Huntingtower.

HUNTINGTOWER WAS THE SCENE OF A FAMOUS ROYAL KIDNAPPING.

OPEN ALL YEAR DAILY, EXCEPT FRIDAY IN WINTER AND CHRISTMAS.

TEL: 01738 627231

Huntly Castle

Aberdeenshire

Huntly, 12 miles (19km) southeast of Keith

The once magnificent, palatial castle that is now decayed and crumbling has been described as one of the noblest baronial ruins in Scotland. Approaching the castle along the avenue of trees, you are faced with the vast five-storey façade, with its inscriptions, fine oriel windows and handsome carvings. A former Catholic stronghold, Huntly Castle remains an elegant and imposing ruin.

There have been three castles at Huntly. In the 12th century a mound and wooden structure were raised by the Normans, and Robert the Bruce stayed here in 1307, but this building was burned down. In the early 15th century, the Gordons built a second castle, of which only the foundations remain. However, in the 1450s the 4th Earl of Huntly began what he called his 'new werk' and this was basis of the palatial castle that can be seen today. Although it was intended to be an elegant residence, defence was not totally abandoned for comfort. The walls are thick, and there are gun ports and iron gates for added protection.

In 1594 the 5th Earl revolted against James VI, who then attacked Huntly with gunpowder. Royal favour was lost and won quickly, however; three years later the castle was restored to the Earl, and building resumed. In 1640 the Covenanters occupied Huntly.

OPEN ALL YEAR DAILY,
EXCEPT FRIDAY AND
SUNDAY IN WINTER,
AND CHRISTMAS.

TEL: 01466 793191

HUNTLY CASTLE,
LAST REBUILT IN
1620, IS NOW AN
IMPRESSIVE RUIN.

Kenilworth Castle
Warwickshire
Kenilworth, 5 miles (8km) southwest of Coventry

OPEN ALL YEAR DAILY, EXCEPT CHRISTMAS AND NEW YEAR.
TEL: 01926 852078

ENOUGH REMAINS OF KENILWORTH CASTLE TODAY TO SHOW WHAT A MAGNIFICENT FORTRESS IT ONCE WAS.

The deep red stone of one of Britain's mightiest keeps was the scene of one of the most important sieges in English history. In 1238 a young French noble, who had claimed a tenuous hold on the earldom of Leicester, secretly married Henry III's recently widowed sister. The young noble was Simon de Montfort, and during the next 27 years he would become one of Henry's greatest friends and most bitter enemies. Henry gave Kenilworth to his brother-in-law in 1244, but later de Montfort voiced his opposition to the absolute power of the monarchy and openly declared war on the king, making Kenilworth his rebel headquarters. At first, many nobles were struck by the sense of de Montfort's proposals, and they flocked to his cause. Even Henry's son Edward, heir to the throne of

England, took de Montfort's side against his father at first. When he eventually changed sides, de Montfort imprisoned him at Kenilworth Castle. Edward escaped and played a vital role in the defeat and death of de Montfort at the Battle of Lewes in 1265.

De Montfort's supporters fled to Kenilworth, where the rebellion continued under his son. The siege that was to follow lasted six months, and was perhaps one of the most violent ever to take place on English soil. Because the castle was protected on three sides by water, the attackers could not undermine the walls and had to concentrate instead on trying to breach the great defences of the gatehouse and walls. Contemporary accounts tell how besiegers and besieged hurled missiles at each other from great war machines. So intense was this fire that the stones exploded as they crashed into each other in mid-air. The castle was finally overcome by starvation, not because the castle could no longer be defended.

The first castle at Kenilworth was a simple mound with wooden buildings, and the magnificent keep was not raised until the 12th century. It was a massive building, with an entrance on the first floor that was protected by a substantial forebuilding. Robert Dudley, Earl of Leicester, was responsible for changing the narrow windows into large ones that would flood the upper chambers with light. Dudley was the favourite of Elizabeth I, and he lived in constant expectation of a visit from her. He built a fine gatehouse and a graceful residential suite, intended specifically for the queen.

Much has survived of this important castle. The great red keep looms powerfully over the elegant 16th-century residences, all still protected by strong walls, earthworks and the great mere.

Kilchurn Castle
Argyll & Bute
18 miles (29km) east of Oban

In an area of reeds and marshes at the northern end of Loch Awe stands Kilchurn Castle, its granite walls and chimneys rising like jagged teeth above the trees. Its position on a peninsula reaching out into the loch gave it some protection from attack on three sides. The beauty of Kilchurn's setting on this loch has attracted many an artist, but on closer inspection, time has not dealt kindly with the little lakeside fortress and only a shell remains.

Kilchurn Castle began as a simple square tower with five floors. Colin Campbell, 1st Earl of Breadalbane, raised it in the 15th century. In the 16th and 17th centuries, the castle was extended. The square tower was incorporated into a small courtyard, with three corner towers, forming an irregular quadrangle. Oddly, the only way into the castle seems to have been through the main door of the keep and across its ground floor. Gun loops placed at intervals all around the walls suggest Kilchurn's builders were more concerned with repelling sudden attacks by Highlanders than in resisting lengthy sieges.

KILCHURN'S WALLS, CLOSE TO TOPPLING OVER, HAVE RECENTLY BEEN STRENGTHENED.

OPEN ACCESS AT ANY REASONABLE TIME.

TEL: 0131 688 8800

Kildrummy Castle

Aberdeenshire

Kildrummy, 15 miles (24km) south of Huntly

THIS STONE GARGOYLE CARVING SURVIVED THE DESTRUCTION OF KILDRUMMY CASTLE.

Robert the Bruce was married twice. His first wife was a daughter of the powerful Earl of Mar and his second was from the English de Burgh family. Through his first marriage, Robert came into possession of Kildrummy Castle, and it figured prominently in the Scottish wars of independence against Edward I of England.

Like Stirling and Bothwell castles, Kildrummy changed hands several times, most notably after the siege of 1306. Robert's brother, Nigel, had been left in charge of Kildrummy while other supporters of the defeated Bruce hurried north, away from Edward's advancing troops. When Edward laid siege to Kildrummy, Nigel withstood every assault, and his constant counter-attacks made life in the siege camp unbearable. The castle finally fell because of Osbourne, a treacherous blacksmith who was offered gold in return for setting Kildrummy on fire. The garrison surrendered, and Nigel was later executed at Berwick.

Kildrummy Castle today is a seven-sided enclosure with two round towers, two D-shaped towers and a sturdy gatehouse, very much like the one at Harlech. Today, most of this once mighty fortress exists only as foundations in the grass, although some of the towers have survived to first-floor level.

KILDRUMMY CASTLE, RUINED SINCE 1717, PLAYED AN IMPORTANT PART IN SCOTTISH MEDIEVAL HISTORY.

OPEN DAILY FROM APRIL TO SEPTEMBER.

TEL: 01975 571331

FIREPLACE

Kisimul Castle
Island of Barra, Western Isles
On a rock, just off the south coast

Kisimul translates as 'the rock in the bay' and the origin is obvious from the castle's location. The early history of Kisimul Castle is obscure. It is possible that the rock in the bay was fortified as early as the 1000s. However, the earliest significant structures still standing today probably date back to the early 1400s, construction beginning after the granting of Barra to Gilleonan MacNeil in 1427 by Alexander MacDonald, Lord of the Isles.

The original design had a massive three-storey tower-house with a curtain wall shaped to fit the rock on which the castle stands. Inside the wall a number of other structures were built, including the hall you see today and the building referred to as the chapel. Additions were made over the next 200 years.

During the 15th and 16th centuries the castle successfully withstood several attempts to take it by the MacNeils' enemies, but by the 1700s the MacNeils abandoned it as their main residence. It was later gutted by fire, and much of its stonework was stolen. In 1838 the chief of the MacNeil clan became bankrupt and was forced to sell Barra, but in 1937 American architect Robert MacNeil, recognised as the 45th clan chief, managed to buy most of the Barra estate back, including Kisimul Castle. The following year he began to restore the castle as the family home. In 2000 the 1000-year lease on Kisimul Castle was made over to Historic Scotland.

OPEN DAILY FROM APRIL TO SEPTEMBER. ACCESS SUBJECT TO WEATHER CONDITIONS.
TEL: 01871 810313

KISIMUL CASTLE CAN ONLY BE REACHED BY FERRY FROM CASTLEBAY VILLAGE ON BARRA.

Laugharne Castle
Carmarthenshire
Laugharne, 14 miles (22km) southwest of Carmarthen

OPEN DAILY FROM APRIL TO SEPTEMBER.
TEL: 01994 427906

ONCE A PLACE FOR BATTLES AND SIEGES, LAUGHARNE CASTLE IS NOW JUST A ROMANTIC SHELL.

The Laugharne Castle that can be seen today bears very little resemblance to the building that was erected in the 12th century. The Welsh princes Rhys ap Gruffydd, Llywelyn the Great and Llywelyn the Last seized the original castle from the English three times before the end of the 13th century.

Parts of the ivy-clad building that can be visited today date from the early 14th century, and the gatehouse is thought to have been constructed in the 15th century. The grand entrance arch in the gateway was added later still, probably during the 16th century.

In Tudor times, Laugharne was leased to Sir John Perrott, said to be the illegitimate son of Henry VIII, who did not find the medieval castle to his courtly taste and set about converting it into a fine Tudor mansion. The foundations of his hall can be seen in the courtyard near the well.

Laugharne Castle came under siege during the Civil War, and some of the cannonballs fired at it by the Parliamentarians have been found deeply embedded in its sturdy stone battlements. The small town of Laugharne is perhaps best known for its associations with the poet Dylan Thomas.

Launceston Castle

Cornwall

Launceston, 23 miles (37km) northwest of Plymouth

OPEN DAILY APRIL TO OCTOBER; FRIDAY TO SUNDAY ONLY FROM NOVEMBER TO MARCH.
TEL: **01566 772365**

LAUNCESTON CASTLE WAS AN IMPORTANT MILITARY FORTRESS IN ITS TIME.

Henry III had a younger brother named Richard. It was, perhaps, an unfortunate twist of fate that made Henry the older of the two boys, for Richard was a skilful politician, a cunning diplomat and was wiser by far than his brother the king. Richard used his considerable talents to make himself one of the richest barons in the country – amassing far more wealth than Henry had ever possessed – and with his wealth came a different sort of power. He was elected King of the Romans, and even tried to secure himself the position of Holy Roman Emperor. In 1227, Richard was made Earl of Cornwall, and it was he who built the fine castle at Launceston.

Launceston is a good example of what is known as a shell keep, which consists of a circular wall with buildings inside. Within this outer wall Richard built another tower, roofed over the space between the two walls and added a fighting platform around the outside of the outer wall.

After Richard's death in 1272, Launceston declined in importance as a military fortress, and by 1353 it was reported that pigs were endangering its foundations by trampling the moat. Launceston Castle was also used as a prison, and it is believed that George Fox, the founder of the Quakers, was held here for eight months in 1656.

Leeds Castle

Kent

5 miles (8km) east of Maidstone

Open all year daily, except concert days and Christmas.

Tel: 01622 765400

The castle, set in 500 acres (200ha) of landscaped parkland, has been beautifully restored.

Leeds Castle is not, as many would-be visitors might suppose, in the city of Leeds in West Yorkshire, but in the depths of the beautiful Kent countryside. It takes its name from its first owner, a man named Leed, or Ledian, who built himself a wooden castle in 857. Leed was the Chief Minister of the King of Kent, and in a time where a fall from grace or an attack by rival parties was a way of life, Leed was very wise in building a stronghold for his family on the two small islands in the lake formed by the River Len.

It is difficult to imagine what the original Leeds Castle must have looked like, especially when confronted by the grandeur of the building that stands on the two islands today. Edward I rebuilt the earlier Norman castle, providing it with a set of outer walls, a barbican and the curious 'gloriette', a D-shaped tower on the smaller of the two islands, which was altered extensively in the Tudor period. Much of Leeds Castle was restored and rebuilt in the 19th century, and many of the rooms are open to the public, all lavishly decorated, with superb collections of art and furniture.

97

THE FORBIDDING
PORTCULLIS GATE AT
LEEDS CASTLE IS NOW
RAISED IN WELCOME.

THE ELEGANT CASTLE
WAS ONCE THE ROYAL
PALACE OF HENRY VIII.

Lincoln Castle

Lincolnshire

Lincoln, 16 miles (26km) northeast of Newark-on-Trent

OPEN ALL YEAR DAILY, EXCEPT CHRISTMAS AND NEW YEAR.

TEL: 01522 511068

In 1068 William the Conqueror ordered that a castle should be built in Lincoln on a site that had been occupied since Roman times, and 166 houses were cleared away in order to make room for it. It seems inconceivable today that so many people could be uprooted from their homes at a moment's notice, but such cavalier actions on the part of landowners were not uncommon in medieval times, and the historical records of many castles tell of such clearances.

LINCOLN CASTLE DATES BACK TO NORMAN TIMES, AND SUBSTANTIAL PARTS OF IT REMAIN.

Lincoln is one of the very few castles in Britain that has two 'mottes' or castle mounds (Lewes Castle in East Sussex is another example). The larger of these two mottes has a 15-sided keep called the Lucy Tower, named after Lucy, Countess of Chester, the mother of a 12th-century owner. The smaller motte has a square tower with a 19th-century observatory, and huge 12th-century walls join the two mottes and enclose an area of about 5 acres (2ha).

The castle has been a centre of justice for the last 900 years and it still houses Lincoln Assizes Court. Between 1787 and 1878 the castle acted as the city's prison, and one of its most interesting features is the Victorian prison chapel, designed as a series of small, coffin-like pews to remind prisoners of their fate, and to ensure they could not see each other. Many prisoners were deported to Australia and others were executed on the castle ramparts.

Lindisfarne Castle

Northumberland

13 miles (21km) southeast of Berwick-upon-Tweed

OPEN FROM APRIL TO OCTOBER DAILY, EXCEPT FRIDAY, BUT OPEN GOOD FRIDAY.

TEL: 01289 389244

LINDISFARNE CASTLE IS A 16TH-CENTURY FORT, TURNED INTO A PRIVATE HOME BY SIR EDWIN LUTYENS IN 1903.

Twice a day, the tide covers the ancient causeway that connects Holy Island, or Lindisfarne, to the mainland. Anyone who misjudges the tide must wait until the causeway opens up again in several hours, and it is not unknown for people and vehicles to be trapped by the rising tide while halfway across.

Perhaps it was this daily encroachment by the sea that attracted the early Christians to the island, for Lindisfarne has a rich history that dates back to the saints of the 7th century. In the 11th century, the Benedictines founded a monastery here, the remains of which can still be visited.

The castle, however, is comparatively modern. It was built in the 16th century, when raids by the Scots were a serious problem, and used stones taken from the recently dissolved Benedictine monastery. However, when James I of England and VI of Scotland united the two countries, the need for border defences declined and Lindisfarne was allowed to fall into disrepair. It saw action briefly in the second Jacobite uprising, when two Jacobite supporters seized control of the little fortress and its garrison of seven men, and held it for one night.

In 1903 the leading country house architect Sir Edwin Lutyens lovingly restored Lindisfarne for Edward Hudson (the founder of *Country Life* magazine). Lutyens changed very little of the structure, but used his considerable skills to convert the austere stone-vaulted ammunition rooms into comfortable living quarters. The castle is a labyrinth of small tunnels and bizarrely shaped rooms, all decorated in the style of a 17th-century Dutch mansion, with an abundance of sturdy oak furniture, brass candlesticks and attractive blue and white pottery.

Linlithgow Palace

Falkirk

7 miles (11km) south of Grangemouth

OPEN ALL YEAR DAILY, EXCEPT CHRISTMAS AND NEW YEAR.

TEL: 01506 842896

ONE OF SCOTLAND'S FOUR ROYAL PALACES, LINLITHGOW WAS BUILT FOR JAMES I OF SCOTLAND.

Rising dramatically from the shores of Linlithgow Loch is a great square palace-fortress, which dates from the 15th century. Although there was a fortified residence here as early as the mid 12th-century, and Edward I built a manor here in 1302, it was not until 1425 that work began on the castle that may be seen today.

The Scottish King, James I, gave orders that a royal residence should be constructed on the site of the earlier buildings, and although Linlithgow was primarily a palace, the architect incorporated a number of defensive features. There was a drawbridge and a barbican, and the walls of the four corner towers were immensely thick. Iron bars, the holes for which can still be seen in the stone, protected the windows in the lower floors. Around the early 1500s, machicolations were added.

Linlithgow has played its part in Scotland's history. Mary, Queen of Scots was born here in 1542, Charles I slept here in 1633 and Cromwell stayed in the Palace in the winter of 1650–51. When the Duke of Cumberland's army bivouacked in Linlithgow in 1746 en route to its encounter with the army of Prince Charles Edward Stuart (the last of the Stuart claimants to the Crown) at Culloden Moor, fires were left burning which gutted this handsome building.

Llansteffan Castle

Carmarthenshire

Llansteffan, 8 miles (13km) southwest of Carmarthen

OPEN ACCESS ALL YEAR.
TEL: 01267 241756

LLANSTEFFAN'S RUINS STAND MAJESTICALLY ON THE WEST BANK OF THE TOWY ESTUARY.

Running like a finger across the gently undulating farmland of the Dyfed coast is a ridge that ends in a rocky bluff. The advantages of this site for defence were recognised long before the Normans arrived, and charcoal from an Iron Age hill fort has been dated to the 6th century BC.

When the Normans established themselves in Wales, they were quick to make use of this ready-made site, protected on three sides by natural slopes, and a ditch was dug to strengthen the fourth side. The castle has two baileys, or enclosed areas. The smaller area is the older of the two, and battlemented walls defended the small square tower, which can still be seen.

When the Welsh took Llansteffan Castle in 1257 (which was apparently achieved with great ease), the English de Camville family decided that they would make improvements to the castle's defences. They built thick walls around the lower bailey, as well as several towers and a fine gatehouse. In Tudor times the gatehouse was converted from a functional military building into a comfortable residence.

Before Llansteffan came into the hands of Cadw: Welsh Historic Monuments (the official guardian of the built heritage of Wales) to be carefully restored as an historic monument, it was used as farm buildings for some 400 years.

LEFT: THE NORMAN GREAT HALL IN THE 12TH-CENTURY FORT, HEDINGHAM CASTLE. RIGHT: THE TAPESTRY-HUNG FIREPLACE AT 14TH-CENTURY BERKELEY CASTLE.

Life in a Castle

Protection and Comfort Early castles were more like military garrisons than homes, but even so, their occupants had to live, and even the most desolate and inhospitable fortress was expected to have a modicum of comfort. In many rooms there were fireplaces, but many windows would not have had glass, the stone walls and gaps at the shutters must have made them cold and gloomy places, especially in the winter. Castles would also have been noisy, with The lord, his family, servants, soldiers, cooks, grooms and a host of others crammed inside, Privacy was an impossible luxury, even for the lord himself.

Decoration and Function Many of the chambers would have had paintings or perhaps tapestries, to decorate the walls. In most castles, there would have been rushes on the floors, although some wealthy owners might have been able to afford rugs. The heart of the castle was the hall. Meals were eaten there, and some would have used the hall as sleeping quarters after the lord had retired to bed. Later castles often had a 'solar' above the hall – an airy, pleasant room, perhaps the forerunner of the drawing room, where the lord could relax away from the bustle of the hall. During the daytime, the large windows would have allowed sufficient light for various household tasks to be performed, like sewing and mending. It is likely that the lord of Tolquhon used his solar to display his fine collection of books.

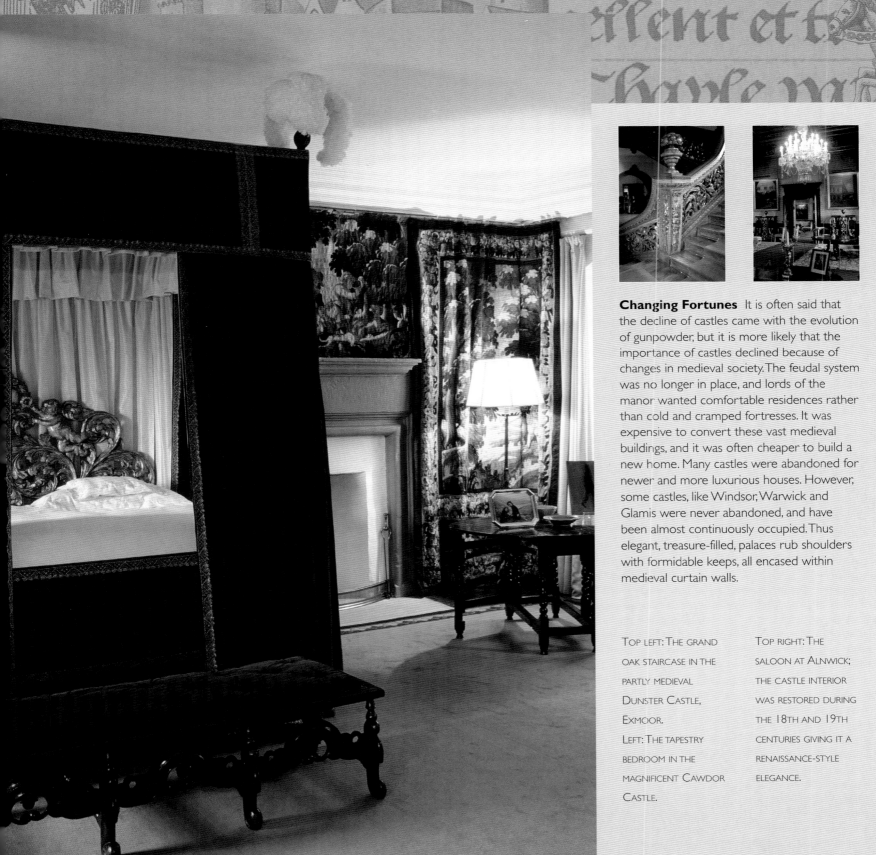

Changing Fortunes It is often said that the decline of castles came with the evolution of gunpowder, but it is more likely that the importance of castles declined because of changes in medieval society. The feudal system was no longer in place, and lords of the manor wanted comfortable residences rather than cold and cramped fortresses. It was expensive to convert these vast medieval buildings, and it was often cheaper to build a new home. Many castles were abandoned for newer and more luxurious houses. However, some castles, like Windsor, Warwick and Glamis were never abandoned, and have been almost continuously occupied. Thus elegant, treasure-filled, palaces rub shoulders with formidable keeps, all encased within medieval curtain walls.

TOP LEFT: THE GRAND OAK STAIRCASE IN THE PARTLY MEDIEVAL DUNSTER CASTLE, EXMOOR.
LEFT: THE TAPESTRY BEDROOM IN THE MAGNIFICENT CAWDOR CASTLE.

TOP RIGHT: THE SALOON AT ALNWICK; THE CASTLE INTERIOR WAS RESTORED DURING THE 18TH AND 19TH CENTURIES GIVING IT A RENAISSANCE-STYLE ELEGANCE.

Loch Leven Castle
Perth & Kinross
Kinross, 10 miles (16km) north of Dumfermline

LOCH LEVEN CASTLE IS FOREVER ASSOCIATED WITH THE IMPRISONMENT OF MARY, QUEEN OF SCOTS.

OPEN DAILY FROM APRIL TO SEPTEMBER.

TEL: 01786 450000

The only way to reach the ancient fortress of Loch Leven is by boat, even though the waters of the loch today are lower than they were in the 14th century when the castle was built. This is because the course of the River Leven was altered in the 19th century, and the level of the loch was lowered as a result. The castle itself is a simple square tower of five storeys, surrounded by a towered wall that was a later addition. The third floor of the tower was possibly where Mary, Queen of Scots was imprisoned between June 1567 and May 1568. There are also the remains of what may have been a private chapel, complete with an altar shelf containing a basin, and a small wall cupboard. In another window is a closet that may have been used as a strong-room in which to store valuables.

Queen Mary was unwell for much of the time she was imprisoned at Loch Leven, and she suffered a miscarriage. She escaped from the castle by befriending the boat keeper, but after the Battle of Langside, during which Mary and her supporters were soundly defeated, she fled the country.

Ludlow Castle
Shropshire
Ludlow, 12 miles (19km) north of Leominster

OPEN DAILY FROM FEBRUARY TO DECEMBER, WEEKENDS ONLY JANUARY.

TEL: 01584 873355

THE TOWN OF LUDLOW IS DOMINATED BY THIS MASSIVE RED SANDSTONE CASTLE, WHICH DATES FROM ABOUT 1086.

Throughout 1138, England was wracked by a civil war fought between supporters of King Stephen and his cousin Empress Matilda, both of whom thought they were rightful heirs to the English throne. Stephen laid siege to the castle at Ludlow, which was then held by one of Matilda's supporters. While he was walking outside the castle walls with Prince Henry of Scotland, a metal hook on a rope was lowered from the castle, catching on the Prince's cloak. As the Prince began to rise up the walls, quick-thinking Stephen cut the rope and managed to free him. He did not, however, take the castle, and was forced to abandon his siege and fight elsewhere.

The extensive ruins of Ludlow Castle contain much that is interesting or unusual. There is a circular chapel modelled on the Church of the Holy Sepulchre in Jerusalem, one of only six round churches in England.

There are curtain walls with flanking towers that are among the earliest such defensive features in England, and a gatehouse that was later blocked up to make a square tower and then, later still, reduced in size.

Many of the existing domestic buildings, such as the kitchens, halls and service rooms, were built in the 14th century, but were given Tudor facelifts.

Manorbier Castle

Pembrokeshire

Manorbier, 5½ miles (9km) southwest of Tenby

THE REMAINS OF THE MANORBIER CASTLE SET ON THE PEMBROKESHIRE COAST.

OPEN DAILY FROM EASTER TO SEPTEMBER.

TEL: 01834 871394

The strong limestone walls of Manorbier Castle have weathered the centuries well and still stand largely intact after 800 years. The first stone buildings were a three-storey square tower and a long hall. In the 13th century the curtain walls were raised, with flanking towers and a fine gatehouse. Two large barns were built in the castle in the 17th century. Manorbier's considerable defences, including the sturdy walls, battlements, portcullises and ditches, were never put to the test by a serious siege, and the Norman de Barri family lived their lives happily unassailed by attacks from the local Welsh people.

Manorbier Castle is perhaps most famous as the birthplace of Giraldus Cambrensis, or Gerald of Wales as he is also known. Gerald was a scholar who travelled extensively before he became an archdeacon, and his sensitive and incisive observations provide a valuable record of life in medieval Wales and Ireland. Beside his analyses of Welsh politics and history, he described the people and their way of life – how they slept on communal beds of rushes wearing all their clothes, and how their feuding and vengeful natures were balanced by their love of music and poetry.

Norham Castle
Northumberland
7 miles (11km) southwest of Berwick-upon-Tweed

Norham was so close to the Scottish border, and was besieged or captured by either the English or the Scots with such frequency, that repairs were being carried out almost constantly from the 12th to the 16th centuries. In fact, the first building, founded by Flambard, Bishop of Durham, in 1120, survived only 20 years before the Scots destroyed it.

James IV of Scotland and his army surrounded the castle in 1513 and bombarded it with heavy artillery, destroying parts of the newly renovated great tower. The castle garrison surrendered, just a few days before James was killed at the Battle of Flodden Field.

Although foundations and walls of what was once a strong fortress remain, the most imposing feature at Norham is the huge rectangular keep, its thick walls still towering up to 90 feet (27m) in places. It originally had three floors (including the vaulted basement), and the Prince-Bishop of Durham, who held the castle for many years, completed most of this after 1158. It passed to the Crown in 1173, and King John may have been responsible for the building of the Sheep Gate. In the 15th century, a further two floors were added.

NORHAM CASTLE HAS BEEN THE SCENE OF MANY BATTLES AND SIEGES SINCE THE 12TH CENTURY.

OPEN DAILY FROM APRIL TO SEPTEMBER.

TEL: 01289 382329

Nunney Castle
Somerset
Nunney, 3 miles (5km) southwest of Frome

Supposedly modelled on the Bastille, Nunney Castle has one of the deepest moats in England.

Open access at any reasonable time.

Tel: 0870 333 1181

In 1645 Cromwell's men set up a cannon on high ground near Nunney, preparing to lay siege to a castle which was at the time held for Charles I. Almost immediately, a hole was made in the north wall, and Cromwell's troops continued firing to widen the breach. Two days later the castle garrison surrendered and the soldiers swarmed into Nunney, removing everything of value. The damaged wall remained standing until 1910, when it collapsed into the moat, but this has since been cleared.

Sir John Delamere built Nunney in 1373. By this time, the church had already been built in the best position in the village, and so the castle is sited on a stretch of land that most castle-builders would have rejected as too low. But Delamere was perhaps not so much interested in building a strongly defensible fortress as a splendid palace that would reflect his own rising glory (he later became Sheriff of Somerset and a Knight of the Shire). It is a roughly oblong building, with round towers at each corner, more reminiscent of a French château than an English castle, and is an attractive feature of a delightful village.

Okehampton Castle

Devon

Okehampton, 24 miles (38.5km) east of Exeter

OPEN DAILY FROM APRIL TO OCTOBER.

TEL: 01837 52844

OKEHAMPTON CASTLE STANDS ON THE NORTHERN EDGE OF DARTMOOR NATIONAL PARK.

Set among richly wooded hills in the rolling Devon countryside, the size and strength of Okehampton Castle come as something of a surprise. Okehampton's history was relatively uneventful, and the only episode of national significance that occurred here was when Henry VIII executed one of its owners, Henry, Marquis of Exeter, for conspiracy in 1539, after which the castle was seized by the Crown and dismantled.

Okehampton Castle is, in fact, one of the largest and most extensive castle ruins in the West Country, and is sadly neglected by tourists. It started as a simple mound, probably before 1070, and a stone keep was erected in the late 11th century. In the early 14th century a second building was added to the keep, with thick walls and fine round-arched windows. At the same time, other buildings were added below the keep, producing an elongated enclosure protected by walls and steep slopes. These other buildings included kitchens, more accommodation, a solar and hall, guardrooms and a chapel. A gatehouse was also raised, connected to the rest of the castle by a long, narrow tunnel. Many of the buildings are in an excellent state of preservation, and this neglected castle is well worth a visit.

Pembroke Castle
Pembrokeshire

Pembroke, 10 miles (16km) southeast of Milford Haven

OPEN ALL YEAR DAILY,
EXCEPT CHRISTMAS
AND NEW YEAR.

TEL: 01646 681510

HENRY TUDOR WAS
BORN AT PEMBROKE
CASTLE IN THE 15TH
CENTURY IN THE TOWER
NOW NAMED AFTER HIM.

Pembroke Castle's most outstanding feature is its great tower – a vast circular keep that stands almost 80 feet (24m) high, with walls that are 16½ feet (5m) at the thickest part, all capped by an unusual stone dome. Although the keep once had four floors, these have long since disappeared, and today you can stand in the basement and gaze all the way up to the stone dome. The great tower was built between 1200 and 1210, probably by William Marshall, one of Richard I's most powerful barons.

There are two other unusual features to note about this castle. The first is the medieval graffiti scored into the plaster walls of the Monkton Tower, and the second is the 'Wogan', a great natural cavern under the Northern Hall of the castle, once occupied by Stone Age cave-dwellers. This cavern can be reached by a spiral stair.

Cromwell besieged the rest of the castle – great battlemented walls liberally studded with defensive towers and a mighty gatehouse – during the Civil War. Once the defending garrison had surrendered, Cromwell blew up the barbican and some of the towers to ensure that Pembroke Castle could not become a refuge for Royalist forces again. Much of the castle was restored during the last century.

Pevensey Castle
East Sussex
4 miles (6.5km) northeast of Eastbourne

At nine o'clock in the morning of Thursday, 28 September 1066, an invading army landed on the English coast. Their leader, William, Duke of Normandy, a veteran of many battles, immediately seized the Roman fort at Pevensey and dug ditches to provide his troops with added protection in the event of an attack. The attack did not come, and William quickly moved his army to a better site along the coast at Hastings, to prepare himself for the coming battle with King Harold, his rival for the English throne. The simple castle that William built at Hastings was the first of many built in England by the Normans.

Once the Battle of Hastings was over, and Duke William had become King William, the Normans consolidated their position by building castles and controlling the land around them. William gave Pevensey to his half-brother, Robert of Mortain, who built a castle inside the old Roman fort. Years later, perhaps about 1100, work started on raising a large keep.

The castle has had many owners, and has been besieged on several occasions, notably by William II in 1088, Stephen of Penchester in 1147, and Simon de Montfort in 1264–65. The last siege is perhaps the most famous. It happened after the Battle of Lewes, in which his barons defeated Henry III. The King's supporters took refuge in the town of Pevensey, but Simon de Montfort was unable to take the castle.

PEVENSEY CASTLE,
ALTHOUGH THREATENED
ON OCCASIONS, HAS
NEVER BEEN TAKEN
BY FORCE.

OPEN ALL YEAR DAILY
EXCEPT MONDAY
AND TUESDAY FROM
NOVEMBER TO MARCH.
TEL: 01323 762604

Portchester Castle

Hampshire

4 miles (6.5km) east of Fareham

LEFT TO FALL INTO DISREPAIR, ONLY PARTS OF PORTCHESTER CASTLE REMAIN TODAY.

OPEN ALL YEAR DAILY, EXCEPT CHRISTMAS AND NEW YEAR.

TEL: 01705 378291

The origins of Portchester Castle stretch much further back in time than its Norman buildings, for Portchester was a Roman coastal fortress built in the 3rd century AD, and the Roman walls still stand tall and strong today.

The Roman fort was a great square enclosure, protected by high walls studded with protective towers. In 1120 the Normans built a fine keep using cut stone imported from Caen in France. Originally the keep was two storeys high, but about 50 years later it was given an additional two floors, and 200 years after this, Richard II added battlements.

Because of its strategically important position on the coast, several medieval kings spent a good deal of money on maintaining and improving the castle. Richard II is believed to have raised the buildings between the keep and the gatehouse, called Richard's Palace. Edward I presented the castle first to his mother and then to his wife. Before the castle came into royal hands, Augustinian Canons built a priory in the south-eastern corner of the fort, and visitors to the castle can still see their splendid chapel, which is remarkably complete.

Prudhoe Castle
Northumberland
Prudhoe, 10 miles (16km) west
of Newcastle upon Tyne

When Prudhoe's attractive square keep was raised around 1175, it was one of the first great towers to be built in Northumberland. At the same time, or perhaps slightly later, a gatehouse was added, along with stone curtain walls. However, the castle's history pre-dates the Norman keep, for in 1173 and again in 1174, William the Lion, King of Scotland, laid siege to the early 12th-century earthworks. Although these sieges were ultimately unsuccessful, it was doubtless the threat of further Scottish attacks that prompted Henry II to grant permission for a stone castle to be built.

Prudhoe was provided with a moat and drawbridge, two barbicans and a stronger gatehouse in the 13th century. A vaulted basement was built under the gatehouse, and a chapel added on the first floor. The chapel had a beautiful oriel (bay) window, thought to be one of the earliest of its kind in any English castle. In 1381 Prudhoe passed into the hands of the Percy family.

FEW VISITORS STOP AT PRUDHOE TODAY, BUT IT IS A FINE CASTLE SET IN LOVELY GROUNDS.

OPEN DAILY FROM APRIL TO OCTOBER.
TEL: 01661 833459

Raglan Castle
Monmouthshire
Raglan, 7 miles (11km) southwest of Monmouth

OPEN ALL YEAR DAILY,
EXCEPT CHRISTMAS AND
NEW YEAR.

TEL: 01291 690228

THE HANDSOME RUINS
OF RAGLAN CASTLE
CAN BE SEEN FROM
SEVERAL MILES AWAY.

It is said that Charles I once played bowls on the grass on Raglan's terraces, under the shadow of the great Yellow Tower of Gwent, the most imposing part of this magnificent 15th-century castle. A short time later the country was at war, and the Earl of Worcester, who owned Raglan, immediately garrisoned the castle for the King. Cromwellian forces laid siege to the castle in June 1646, and the powerful walls underwent weeks of devastating bombardment. On 19 August Worcester was forced to surrender, and Cromwell's troops poured into the castle. Worcester was taken to London, where he died shortly after, and Raglan Castle was stripped of anything portable and left derelict. Further destruction took place after the Restoration,

when the newly created Duke of Beaufort ransacked Raglan for fittings for his new home at Badminton. By the 19th century, Raglan was a romantic ivy-clad ruin.

There had been a castle at Raglan since about 1070. In the 1400s this building fell into the hands of William ap Thomas, a Welsh knight who had fought at the Battle of Agincourt with Henry V. Thomas began to build a tower in an unusual hexagonal shape, a keep with thick, tapering walls. He surrounded the tower with more walls and a moat, and the pale gold stone from which it is built earned it its name: the Yellow Tower of Gwent. Thomas' son William, Earl of Pembroke, continued the building work his father had begun.

Restormel Castle

Cornwall

Near Lostwithiel, 1 mile (1.5km) north of Fowey

OPEN DAILY FROM APRIL TO OCTOBER.

TEL: 01208 872687

HIGH ON A MOATED MOUND, RESTORMEL OFFERS SPECTACULAR VIEWS ACROSS THE CORNISH COUNTRYSIDE.

Norman castle sites are often reduced to a few grassy humps amid towering nettles, but this is an exception, occupying a lofty mound defended by a deep moat, high above the Fowey Valley. The views from the top of the castle walls are magnificent, and the extensive dry-moated ruins are wonderfully atmospheric – the oldest and best-preserved example of Norman motte and bailey construction in Cornwall.

There is evidence of an earlier wooden castle, dating from about 1100, which took advantage of a high spur of land overlooking Fowey a mile north of the town, but the stone castle we see today was the result of a refurbishment in the 13th century by Edmund, Earl of Cornwall. This rebuilding programme was not carried out for defensive purposes: it is likely that Restormel was his main residence and, situated in the largest deer park in the country, that it was developed as a forceful symbol of Norman power and prosperity, and used largely for entertainment purposes.

The considerable 12th- and 13th-century remains include the gate, keep, kitchens and private rooms, with the walls standing almost at their original height. The castle was a symbol of power and wealth and was once home of Edward, The Black Prince (1330–76), heir to the English throne. It was abandoned long before the Civil War, but briefly held a Parliamentarian garrison before falling to the Royalists in 1644.

Rhuddlan Castle
Denbighshire
Rhuddlan, 3 miles (5km) south of Rhyl

This concentric castle was built by Edward I, but now stands uncomfortably next to a modern housing development. Its once-powerful round towers are crumbling around their bases, and time has eaten away at their roofless tops. Yet Rhuddlan was a vitally important part of Edward I's campaign in Wales and was designed by his master castle-builder, James of St George. Indeed, it was here that the Great Statute of Wales was issued in March 1284, proclaiming Edward's dominance over the defeated country.

Rhuddlan Castle guards the mouth of the River Clwyd and the coastal route into North Wales, and is a good example of how a castle developed over the centuries. It is diamond-shaped with towers at each corner, and has two sets of outer walls. It also has its own dock tower. The building of the castle in its present location necessitated a great feat of military engineering. The site was already historically important because it was on a ford over the River Clwyd. Edward wanted his new castle to have access to the sea, so that boats might supply it, but the Clywd was a shallow river that meandered lazily towards the sea. Edward cut a new channel, which was deeper and straighter than the one the river had made for itself, and 700 years later it still more or less follows this course.

RHUDDLAN CASTLE TOWERS MAJESTICALLY OVER THE RIVER CLWYD.

OPEN DAILY FROM MAY TO SEPTEMBER.

TEL: 01745 590777

Richmond Castle
North Yorkshire
Richmond, 4 miles (6.5km) southwest of Scotch Corner

Open all year daily, except Christmas and New Year.

Tel: 01748 822493

Never seriously threatened, Richmond has now surrendered itself gracefully to time.

Commanding a powerful position on the banks of the River Swale, this mighty fortress was never put to the test, for Richmond has never seen military action. Its location is superb, with steep cliffs protecting one side, and thick walls defending the other sides.

The Normans started constructing a castle here in the 1080s, and it is thought that Scolland's Hall, a fine two-storey hall with typical round-headed windows, is one of the earliest stone-built halls in England. The towers at Richmond have romantic names:

Robin Hood Tower, now in ruins, is said to have been the prison of William the Lion, King of Scotland; the Gold Hole Tower may have a poetic ring to its name, but it was actually the latrine tower, complete with pits at its base, spanned by an interesting 11th-century arch. By far the largest building of the entire complex is the keep. It started life as a gatehouse in the 11th century, but in the mid-12th century it was extended upwards to a height of 100 feet (30m). Straight flights of stairs ran between the floors, rather than the traditional spiral stairways.

Rochester Castle

Kent

Rochester, 10 miles (16km) north of Maidstone

OPEN ALL YEAR DAILY, EXCEPT CHRISTMAS AND NEW YEAR.

TEL: 01634 402276

THE MASSIVE NORMAN KEEP OF ROCHESTER CASTLE LIES BESIDE THE RIVER MEDWAY.

The magnificent Norman keep at Rochester has seen more than its share of battles and sieges, but perhaps the most famous one was in 1215. Shortly after the barons forced King John to sign the Magna Carta, he turned against them in a bitter war. Rochester Castle was held for the barons, and John laid siege to it with incredible ferocity. The siege lasted for about seven weeks, during which time those in the castle were reduced to a diet of horsemeat and water. Meanwhile, John kept up a constant barrage of missiles from crossbows and ballistas (stone-throwing machines), and began to dig a tunnel under the keep itself. Part of the keep collapsed, but the defenders bravely fought on. Those men who could no longer fight were sent out, whereupon it is said John had their hands and feet cut off. But Rochester finally fell, and the defenders were imprisoned.

Building on the keep started in about 1127, and it is one of the largest in England. Its walls soar to 113 feet (34m) and are up to 12 feet (3.5m) thick. Although mainly a defensive building, there are some beautifully carved archways and windows.

St Andrews Castle

Fife

St Andrews, 13 miles (21km) southeast of Dundee

OPEN ALL YEAR DAILY, EXCEPT CHRISTMAS AND NEW YEAR.

TEL: 01334 477196

THE JAGGED RUINS OF ST ANDREWS CASTLE CLING TO A LOW GRASSY CLIFF ON THE COAST.

In March 1546 the ambitious Archbishop of St Andrews, Cardinal David Beaton, burnt the Protestant preacher George Wishart in front of the walls of St Andrews Castle. Beaton was not a popular man, chiefly because he refused to agree to the marriage of Henry VIII's Protestant son to the Scottish king's Catholic daughter. Later that year, a group of Protestant Fife lairds gained access to the castle and murdered Beaton, hanging his body from the castle walls in a pair of sheets. Following this, a long siege began, as the forces of the Regent of Scotland tried to oust them from the castle.

It was during this turbulent time that the famous mine and counter-mine were dug. The attackers' mine was intended to go under the foundations, so that the wall would weaken, while the counter-mine attempted to stop it. You can still walk through these two tunnels, which give a unique insight into medieval warfare.

This ancient castle, built and used by the Bishops and Archbishops of St Andrews, comprises a five-sided enclosure, protected on two sides by the sea, with buildings dating from the 12th to the 16th centuries. One of its most famous features is a sinister bottle dungeon, a pit 24 feet (7m) deep, narrower at the top (like a bottle), hewn out of solid rock.

Skipton Castle
North Yorkshire
Skipton, 9 miles (14.5km) northwest of Keighley

OPEN ALL YEAR DAILY,
EXCEPT CHRISTMAS.

TEL: 01756 792442

SKIPTON'S HANDSOME
900-YEAR-OLD CASTLE
IS IN A WONDERFUL
STATE OF PRESERVATION.

Two cannon stand on either side of the stalwart doors of Skipton Castle's powerful medieval gatehouse. Although the castle dates from much earlier, it is strongly associated with the Civil War, when the busy market town and the castle came under heavy attack from cannon such as these. The castle was so badly damaged that by the time the troops had left, it was almost totally destroyed, and the gatehouse that stands proudly at the head of the main street today is the result of some painstaking restoration work.

Skipton Castle is the result of several building phases. The earliest stonework was raised during the 12th century on the site of an earlier castle. More towers and some sturdy walls were added in the 13th and 14th centuries. Some of these walls were 12 feet (3.5m) thick in places, and so it is not surprising that Skipton was able to hold out against the siege of the Civil War for so long. There was a moat here, too, although this has long since disappeared. Today, Skipton Castle is one of the most complete and well-preserved medieval castles in England.

Stirling Castle
Stirling
Stirling, 22 miles (35.5km) west of Dunfermline

OPEN ALL YEAR DAILY.
TEL: 01786 450000

STIRLING CASTLE'S
PALACE, VIEWED ACROSS
THE BEAUTIFULLY KEPT
BOWLING GREEN
GARDENS.

Perched high and proud on its towering cliffs, Stirling Castle is a complex arrangement of buildings, some plain and functional, others splendid and palatial, that reflect its long history as one of the most important castles in Scotland.

Most of the buildings that can be seen today date from the 15th century or later, and it is not known exactly what the castle was like before this, when it was being fought over by William Wallace, Robert the Bruce and Edward I. This eventful history

began in the late 11th century, when a wooden structure was raised. Edward I seized Stirling in 1296 and Wallace took it back in 1297. He lost it again in 1298, but the Scots reclaimed it once more in 1299. Edward retrieved the castle after a furious siege in 1304, and this time held it until the English defeat at Bannockburn in 1314.

There are many fine buildings to explore in this splendid fortress. Perhaps the most impressive is the Great Hall, which is one of the earliest Renaissance buildings in Scotland. The elegant Palace was built for James V in the 1540s, and there are some exquisite carvings, both inside (around the fireplaces) and on the exterior walls.

THE CASTLE HOUSES THE REGIMENTAL MUSEUM OF THE ARGYLL AND SUTHERLAND HIGHLANDERS.

SET ON A VOLCANIC HIGH ROCK, STIRLING CASTLE HAS PLAYED A MAJOR ROLE IN SCOTLAND'S HISTORY.

Sudeley Castle
Gloucestershire
Off the A46, south of Winchcombe

A compelling mixture of ruined fortress and Victorian gentleman's residence, built in local stone, the castle is set in wooded countryside below the Cotswold scarp. It was built in the 15th century and was subsequently owned by both Edward IV and Richard III, but it is best known as the home of Katherine Parr, last wife and widow of Henry VIII. She lived here after his death in 1547. Anne Boleyn, Lady Jane Grey and Elizabeth I all stayed at or visited Sudeley Castle too.

The castle was later owned by the Brydges family and was the headquarters of Prince Rupert in the Civil War. In 1644 Sudeley was attacked and badly knocked about by Parliamentarian troops.

Parts of the castle are still glamorously ruined, but the estate was bought in the 19th century by the wealthy Dent family, Worcester glovers who had the house partly restored by Sir George Gilbert Scott. He designed the beautiful tomb of Katherine Parr in the church. The restored apartments are royally appointed and the walls are hung with Old Masters. The castle also houses an interesting collections of curios, porcelain and tapestries.

OPEN DAILY FROM APRIL
TO OCTOBER.

TEL: 01242 602308

SUDELEY CASTLE IS SET
IN ATTRACTIVE GARDENS.

ENJOYING A GLORIOUS
COTSWOLDS SETTING,
THE CASTLE IS AN
IMPRESSIVE SIGHT.

Tantallon Castle

East Lothian

2½ miles (4km) east of North Berwick

The great red walls of Tantallon Castle form one of the strongest and most daunting castles in Scotland. Perched on a spur of rock, with sheer cliffs plummeting into frothing seas on three of its sides, the castle's fourth side is protected by a formidable array of ditches and walls. Rising from one of the three great gaping ditches, and sweeping clear across the neck of the promontory, is a vast curtain of red sandstone. This mighty wall is 12 feet (3.5m) thick, and a staggering 50 feet (15m) tall.

Tantallon is associated with one of Scotland's most famous families – the Red Douglases, Earls of Angus. It came into their hands at the end of the 14th century, and became their base as they plotted and fought against their enemies. But it was not until 1528 that the mighty fortress of Tantallon was seriously put to the test, when James V laid siege to it.

Sixteenth-century Scottish politics were complicated, but, essentially, Archibald Douglas, 6th Earl of Angus, had kept the young James V a virtual prisoner in Edinburgh during his minority. James finally managed to escape, and once he was old enough to act for himself, charged Douglas with treason. James brought a great battery of guns from Dunbar Castle, and for 20 days pounded the Tantallon's walls. Tantallon, however, stood firm – perhaps because the great ditches in front of the castle prevented the guns from being brought too close. The castle eventually fell to James, but as a result of negotiations rather than firepower. Douglas fled the country, and James began work to reinforce and repair Tantallon's medieval defences. After the King's death, Douglas returned from exile in 1543 and immediately began plotting against the Regent of Scotland, the Earl of Arran.

Tattershall Castle

Lincolnshire

8 miles (13km) southwest of Horncastle

Surrounded by a moat and earthworks, the great red-brick tower of Tattershall Castle stands proudly in the rolling Lincolnshire countryside. The tower is vast, its red-brown brick contrasting vividly with the bright white stone of its windows and 'machicolations' – projecting parapets with holes in them to permit objects to be thrown or fired at attackers.

Records show that nearly one million bricks were used to build the 100-foot (30m) high tower and associated buildings. It was constructed between 1430 and 1450 for Ralph, Lord Cromwell, who was Treasurer of England. Cromwell wanted Tattershall to be an aggressive statement of his power and authority, hence the formidable array of machicolations 80 feet (24m) above the ground, and the once extensive systems of water-filled moats and earthworks.

Like many barons of his day, Cromwell wanted his home comforts as well as security, and inside the tower are six floors of fine chambers, each with small rooms in the corner towers. Visitors may well have the curious feeling that the rooms are getting larger as they head upwards, and this is actually the case – it was not necessary to have such thick walls in the upper floors, which were less likely to be attacked than the lower ones.

Open from April to October daily, except Thursday and Friday and some weekends in winter.

Tel: 01526 342543

Lord Curzon, Viceroy of India, bought and restored Tattershall, presenting it to The National Trust in 1925.

Tintagel Castle
Cornwall
Tintagel, 2 miles (3km) north of Camelford

In the winter, ferocious storms whip up around the rugged Cornish coast, wearing away at the rocky peninsula that is home to the scanty remains of Tintagel Castle. Each year parts are swept away, and so what remains today is not what would have existed when Reginald, an illegitimate son of Henry I, first raised his castle here.

Tintagel is traditionally associated with the legend of King Arthur, who, it is said, was conceived here while Merlin waited in a cave under the castle. The cave that pierces the thin neck of rock, which joins the peninsula to the mainland, is still called Merlin's Cave, and it can be visited at low tide. This is a wild and desolate place, where it is easy to imagine the romantic image of the legendary hero, but there is no concrete evidence to support the connection.

About 100 years after Reginald had built his square hall, Richard, Earl of Cornwall, built two more enclosures and raised some walls. The Black Prince built another hall, and there is evidence that yet another was raised over the remains of the previous two. Archaeologically, Tintagel is difficult to understand, and there are foundations of buildings and several tunnels, the purpose of which remains unknown – all adding to the castle's air of mystery.

OPEN ALL YEAR DAILY, EXCEPT CHRISTMAS AND NEW YEAR.

TEL: 01840 770328

SUBJECT TO CONSTANT EROSION BY THE SEA, TINTAGEL CASTLE IS A DRAMATIC SIGHT.

Tolquhon Castle
Aberdeenshire
Pitmedden, 15 miles (24km) north of Aberdeen

OPEN DAILY FROM
APRIL TO SEPTEMBER,
WEEKENDS ONLY IN
WINTER.

TEL: 01651 851286

NOW A ROOFLESS RUIN,
TOLQUHON REMAINS AN
IMPRESSIVE AND
HANDSOME CASTLE.

*Al this warke excep the auld tour was begun
be William Forbes 15 Aprile 1584 and
endit be him 20 October 1589.*

These words are inscribed in a panel high up on the right-hand side of the imposing gatehouse at Tolquhon Castle (pronounced 'Tuh-hon'). They refer to the work of the 7th Lord of Tolquhon, the cultured William Forbes, who inherited the castle in the late 16th century. Before Tolquhon came into Forbes' possession, it was a single tower (the 'auld tour') with some adjoining walls. But in 1584, Forbes decided the tower was insufficient for his needs and set about extending it. The result was the fine palatial building that can be visited today, and, although Tolquhon is now a ruin, it takes little imagination to envisage how splendid this castle must have looked in its heyday.

The 'auld tour', or Preston's Tower, was raised in the early 15th century, probably by John Preston, its namesake. It was built of granite, with thick walls, and had small rooms. Little remains of it today. Forbes used it as one of the corners of his new castle, and extended the building to make a four-sided structure around a large courtyard. The castle was entered through a gatehouse, which, although it appears to be formidable with its gun loops and round towers, had thin walls and would not have withstood a serious attack. It was designed for show, rather than defence.

Impressive buildings line all four sides of the fine cobbled courtyard. To the east are the kitchens and a pit-prison, while the main house is to the south. This building contained the hall and the laird's personal chambers, which looked out over a formal garden. Although this has long since disappeared, the remains of a dovecote and recesses for bees have been found in the walls.

Tower of London
Central London
Tower Hill, EC3

OPEN ALL YEAR DAILY,
EXCEPT SUNDAYS
FROM NOVEMBER TO
FEBRUARY AND
CHRISTMAS.

TEL: **0870 756 6060**

Standing proud and strong in the very heart of England's capital city, the Tower of London has had a long and eventful history. It conjours up many images for visitors – Beefeaters and ravens, the Crown Jewels, Traitors' Gate – and a multitude of executions.

William the Conqueror began work on the keep, known as the White Tower, in about 1078, but it was probably completed by William II some 20 years later. Building in the Tower of London complex has continued throughout history, right up to the Waterloo Barracks, built in 1845, and the brand new high-security jewel house. The variety of the buildings reflects the Tower's use as a royal residence, a prison, the Mint, the Royal Zoo, a public records office, the Royal Observatory and the stronghold for the Crown Jewels.

The Tower is noted for its bloody history. The first execution here is thought to have been that of Sir Simon Burley, who was beheaded in 1388. Two different places of execution are connected with the tower: Tower Hill, a patch of land outside the castle walls which was for public executions, and the more discreet Tower Green, inside the castle in the shadow of the White Tower. In 1465 Edward IV erected a permanent scaffold on Tower Hill. Countless heads followed the unfortunate Simon Burley's, including those of Sir Thomas More (1535), Thomas Cromwell, the Earl of Essex (1540), and John Dudley, the Duke

THE TOWER OF LONDON IS ONE OF THE MOST OUTSTANDING EXAMPLES OF NORMAN ARCHITECTURE IN EUROPE.

ORIGINALLY KNOWN AS WATER GATE, TRAITORS' GATE GOT ITS NEW NAME WHEN IT WAS USED AS THE LANDING FOR PRISONERS WHO WERE THE CROWN'S ENEMIES.

 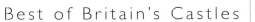

of Northumberland, and his son Guilford (1553). Tower Green witnessed the execution of two of Henry VIII's wives and the unlucky 16-year-old Lady Jane Grey, executed by Mary I in 1554.

Not everyone detained at the Tower was executed, and famous prisoners who languished within the gloomy walls included Princess Elizabeth (later Elizabeth I), Judge Jeffries and William Penn. But even when not under the threat of execution, prisoners were not necessarily safe. Henry VI was murdered in the Wakefield Tower in 1471, and the boy king, Edward V and his brother, the Duke of York, are believed to have been murdered in the Bloody Tower. A number of prisoners attempted an escape – some successfully, like the charismatic Ranulf Flambard, Bishop of Durham, who climbed down a rope smuggled in to him in a jug of wine. Others were less fortunate – Gruffudd, the son of Llywelyn the Great, attempted a similar escape, but the rope broke as he climbed down it and he fell to his death.

TRADITION HAS IT THAT IF THE RAVENS EVER LEAVE THE TOWER, THE MONARCHY WILL FALL. TODAY, PRECAUTIONS ARE TAKEN AGAINST SUCH AN EVENT, INCLUDING CLIPPING THE RAVENS' WINGS.

Urquhart Castle
Highland
Drumnadrochit, 16 miles (26km) southwest of Inverness

In 1545 the fearsome MacDonald clan swept into the quiet Glen of Urquhart, looting and pillaging as they went. They laid siege to the castle and plundered it mercilessly, taking chairs, tables, gates, armour, food and even the pillows from the beds. After the castle had been thoroughly sacked, the raiders turned their attention to the homesteads in the valley. This was just one incident in a long history of warfare and bloodshed that had raged since a castle was first built on the shores of Loch Ness in the early 13th century.

In view of its turbulent history, it is not surprising that Urquhart's defences are formidable. A walled causeway, with a drawbridge halfway along, led to the castle gatehouse. Great walls that followed the contours of the rock protected it from attack, strengthened by a ditch at the front and the loch at the back. Inside the walls were a variety of buildings, including living quarters, a chapel, kitchens and a dove-cote.

Although much is ruined, apart from the 16th-century tower house, which is still largely intact, this romantic ruin huddled on the loch shore is well worth a visit.

URQUHART CASTLE IS A FAMOUS LANDMARK ON THE SHORES OF LOCH NESS.

OPEN ALL YEAR DAILY, EXCEPT CHRISTMAS.

TEL: 01456 450551

Warkworth Castle
Northumberland
Warkworth, 10 miles (16km) southeast of Alnwick

THE KEEP AND THE GATEHOUSE DOMINATE THE CRUMBLING WALLS OF WARKWORTH CASTLE.

When William the Lion, King of Scotland, seized Warkworth in 1173, it was widely thought that this had been possible because the castle was 'feeble in wall and earthwork'. Subsequent owners apparently decided that this description should not be applied to Warkworth a second time, for the castle that can be seen today is one of the most powerful fortresses in northern England.

The Earl of Northumberland raised the unusually shaped keep in around 1390. It is square, but has towers projecting from each of its four sides. One of these towers contained an elegant chapel, and there were comfortable living quarters in some of the others. Rainwater was collected on the roof and channelled to tanks in the basement, permitting a supply of clean water to basins and latrines – a great luxury in a medieval castle.

The Earl and his famous son, Hotspur, are perhaps the most renowned residents of the castle, for it was they who fought so hard to put Henry IV on the throne in 1399, and to force the rightful king, Richard II, to abdicate. Four years later, these two men fought equally hard to wrest the Crown from Henry once more. The King promptly marched to Warkworth and blasted its walls with cannon-fire until the garrison surrendered.

The King then gave Warkworth to his brother, later the Duke of Bedford, although it was restored to Hotspur's son in 1416. The Percys' political favour continued to wax and wane during the 15th century, and in 1572 Sir Thomas Percy was executed for his part in a plot against Elizabeth I. With his death, this great fortress began to decline in importance and gradually fell into ruins.

Warwick Castle

Warwickshire

Warwick, 3 miles (5km) from Leamington Spa

When not at war, England's 14th-century knights were stars of the country's favourite spectator sport: The Tournament

An Impregnable Stronghold After the 17th century, Warwick Castle evolved into a stately home, whose lavish house parties often included the Monarch among the guests. Earlier, it had served more utilitarian purposes and, well before the Normans arrived, there had been a Saxon fort to defend against Viking raiders. Henry de Beaumont, one of William the Conqueror's vassals, built the first stone castle, but that was largely destroyed during the Barons Revolt in 1264. Today's castle dates mostly from 14th- and 15th-century rebuilding and was designed to be both imposing and impregnable. The only assault on its formidable defences was an unsuccessful attack by Royalist forces during the Civil War.

Entertainment Medieval Style

Despite the disturbances of the 14th century, there was some comfort within the castle's spartan exterior and, for the nobility at least, life had many pleasurable diversions. Knights were the superstars of the day and, when not seeking honour on the battlefield, spent their time practising combat or competing in tournaments. These were great spectacles, the champions and their horses clad in shining armour and colourful liveries which, besides adding glamour to the occasion, served a practical purpose on the battlefield by identifying the combatants. Jousting and single combat contests were popular, with prizes for the victor, the possible bonus of the loser's forfeited armour and horse, and favours from lady admirers. More unruly was the mêlée, a mock battle between opposing teams. Although the objective was victory through surrender, by unseating, knocking down or disarming opponents, things often got well out of hand.

Hunting parties led by the lord, were more civilised. These, too, gave an opportunity to demonstrate skills with horse, bow and sword, and to display favourite hunting birds and dogs. Many castles had menageries, with collections of hawks and dogs, but there were also more exotic animals, such as bears and lions. It is said that Richard the Lionheart had a crocodile, before it escaped into the Thames.

Little excuse was needed for a feast, and while the poor were lucky to have coarse bread, pottage and weak beer, the tables of the rich were a gastronomic delight. Beef, mutton, venison and boar were served, together with fish and game birds and delicacies such as peacock and heron. Rich and spicy sauces often flavoured the dishes, probably to disguise the taints of over-ripe food. Pastries, sweets and puddings were also popular, all washed down with imported wine. Jesters, jugglers and acrobats provided a floorshow to a musical background from the minstrel gallery and, once the tables were cleared, it was time to dance.

A VIEW OF WARWICK CASTLE ACROSS THE WILLOW-FRINGED RIVER AVON.

THE RICHLY ADORNED GREAT HALL IN WARWICK CASTLE.

THE AGE OF CHIVALRY IS REVIVED IN THE CASTLE GROUNDS.

A Wander around Warwick

❶ Walk through St Nicholas' Park to the river and turn left. Past a footbridge beyond the park, continue along a wooded riverside path. After a railway bridge and then the Grand Union Canal, carried high above on a three-arched aqueduct, turn left and climb steps to the canal's towpath. Instead of crossing the bridge, turn right and follow the canal around the town's northern edge, passing old warehouses and workshops that exploited the canal's cheap and relatively swift transport. After some 2 miles (3km), immediately before bridge number 51, leave the canal and climb on to the road above. Turn left over the bridge and then go right into Budbrooke Road. Walk through a small car park on the left and carry on, following a short length of canal, to the Saltisford Arms.

❷ Forced back to the road beyond its far end, pass beneath a railway bridge and immediately go right, crossing a redundant canal bridge. Over a gate/stile on the right, climb left up a tree-planted bank on to Warwick Racecourse and keep going between a driving range and golf course. Where the range ends, turn left past the clubhouse and continue off the course.

❸ Carry on ahead up Linen Street and then turn right, down to the main road. At the main road, go left through West Gate, past the Lord Leycester Hospital and along the High Street. At Castle Street, turn right and then fork right beside Oken House. Cross the road at the bottom and enter a gate to Warwick Castle. Its entrance is to the left.

❹ After visiting the castle, leave the courtyard by the opposite gate and turn right down a flight of steps. Go left at the bottom and walk out to the main road. The car park is down to the right.

Distance: 5.25 miles (8.5km)

Total ascent: minimal

Paths: riverside and canal paths may be muddy; otherwise well-surfaced paths and tracks

Terrain: river and canalside; pavements

Refreshments: plenty within Warwick and at the castle

Parking: car park off A41, by St Nicholas' Park and the River Avon

Castle: open all year daily, except Christmas. Tel: 0870 442 2000

OS Map: Explorer 221 Coventry & Warwick, Royal Leamington Spa

White Castle

Monmouthshire

7 miles (11km) northeast of Abergavenny

WHITE CASTLE WAS ONE OF A FORMIDABLE TRIO BUILT TO DEFEND THE WELSH MARCHES.

OPEN DAILY FROM MAY TO SEPTEMBER.
TEL: 01600 780380

White Castle gained its name from the white plaster that once covered it, but only traces of this can be seen today on the castle's crumbling walls. White's sister castles, Grosmont and Skenfrith, were built by Hubert de Burgh. While he owned the so-called Three Castles of Gwent between 1201 and 1204 and from 1219 to 1232, White itself had a rather different origin.

Like Skenfrith and Grosmont, White Castle began as earthworks with wooden buildings. In the 12th century, a stone curtain wall was added, and in the 13th century a gatehouse and additional towers were built. White Castle was near land claimed by Llywelyn the Last during his wars with Edward I, and the King ensured that its defences were strengthened. Even in its ruined state, the sophistication of the castle's defences can be appreciated, especially the height and strength of the great walls.

Windsor Castle

Berkshire

Windsor, 2 miles (3km) south of Slough

Windsor Castle is not only the official residence of HM The Queen, but also the largest inhabited castle in the world. The battlemented towers and turrets have been fortress, home and court to English monarchs since the 11th century.

William the Conqueror began work on the castle, raising a simple motte and bailey structure on a chalk cliff. Since then, Windsor has been almost continuously occupied, and many kings changed or added buildings during the next 900 years.

THE ELEGANT ST GEORGE'S CHAPEL IN THE CASTLE IS DISTINCTLY REGAL.

WINDSOR CASTLE HAS BEEN COMPLETELY RESTORED AFTER SIGNIFICANT FIRE DAMAGE IN 1993.

Thus Henry II remodelled the great Round Tower, Edward III began to convert the military buildings into a royal residence, Edward IV started (and Henry VIII completed) the elegant St George's Chapel, and Henry VIII added the fine gatehouse. In the 1820s George IV spent a million pounds on modernising and repairing this splendid medieval fortress. The castle remained virtually unchanged from that time until the devastating fire in 1993, which destroyed parts of the historic buildings.

Windsor was a favourite among kings. Henry I was married here, Henry II planted a herb garden and regarded the castle as home, and Henry III famously entertained the local poor to a great feast here one Good Friday. Edward III was born in the castle, and his Knights of the Order of the Garter were later to adopt St George's Chapel as their place of worship. The castle withstood two sieges by King John during the Magna Carta Wars.

WINDSOR CASTLE STANDS MAJESTICALLY ON A CLIFF ABOVE THE RIVER THAMES AND THE TOWN OF WINDSOR.

GUARDS MARCHING IN THE CASTLE PRECINCTS ARE A REMINDER OF ITS PAST AS A FORTRESS.

STATE APARTMENTS OPEN ALL YEAR EXCEPT CHRISTMAS AND GOOD FRIDAY. SUBJECT TO CLOSURE AT SHORT NOTICE.

TEL: 020 7766 7304

Index

B-Hannël

A COLOR ATLAS OF
HEART DISEASE

A COLOR ATLAS OF HEART DISEASE

PATHOLOGICAL, CLINICAL AND INVESTIGATORY ASPECTS

George C. Sutton
Hillingdon Hospital, Middlesex, UK

Kim M. Fox
National Heart Hospital, London, UK

Contributors

John Bayliss
St Albans City Hospital, Herts, UK

John Swales
University of Leicester School of Medicine,
Leicester, UK

Foreword by
Burton E. Sobel M.D.

Current Medical Literature Ltd, London

Acknowledgements

The authors are grateful to John Swales, Professor of Medicine, University of Leicester, for the chapter on Hypertension, and to John Bayliss, National Heart Hospital, and John Davies, Royal Gwent Hospital, for their help on the sections dealing with Heart Failure and Restrictive Cardiomyopathy, respectively. Many of the illustrations used in Chapter 3 on Hypertension were generously made available by Dr EH Mackay of Leicester General Hospital.

The authors gratefully acknowledge the contributions of Michael Davies, Simon Rees, Robert Anderson, Stuart Hunter, Ian Kerr, Graham Leech, Fergus McCartney, Michael Rigby and the authors, editors and contributors to the following publications:

The Slide Atlas of Cardiology and Supplement (Sutton, Anderson and Fox. Medi-Cine Ltd, 1978 and 1986)

Physiological and Clinical Aspects of Cardiac Auscultation (Harris, Sutton, Towers. Medi-Cine Ltd, 1976)

An Introduction to Echocardiography (Leech, Kisslo. Medi-Cine Productions, 1981)

An Introduction to Nuclear Cardiology (Walton, Ell. Current Medical Literature, 1985)

An Introduction to Cardiovascular Digital Subtraction Angiography (Hunter, Walton, Hunter. Current Medical Literature, 1987)

An Introduction to Magnetic Resonance of the Cardiovascular System (Underwood, Firman. Current Medical Literature, 1987)

In the preparation of this second edition, the authors wish to thank Dr John Cleland, Hammersmith Hospital, Dr David Hackett, Royal Postgraduate Medical School and Dr Richard Underwood, National Heart Hospital, for their meticulous review and constructive suggestions. In addition, they also wish to thank Dr Cleland for supplying figure 17 in Chapter 1, and Dr Underwood for supplying the illustrations used in the sections on Nuclear Techniques in Chapters 1 and 2.

Published by Current Medical Literature Ltd,
40–42 Osnaburgh Street, London,
NW1 3ND, UK.

ISBN 1 85009 058 0

Contents

Foreword

Because cardiology is both a cognitive and interventional specialty, its mastery requires assimilation of information and acquisition of technical expertise. Definitive illustration can contribute to both. Kim Fox and George Sutton have thoughtfully compiled meticulously prepared illustrations that will enhance the diagnostic and therapeutic skills of the fortunate readers of 'A Color Atlas of Heart Disease.' They will benefit from a logical and thorough presentation, superb graphics, and attractive photography and artwork, all of which elucidate concepts, algorithms, and techniques essential to the practice of modern cardiology. The comprehensive breadth and incisive analysis provided by the Atlas will well serve students, residents, fellows, faculty, and practitioners of cardiology while equipping them to better provide optimal care for the patients they serve.

Burton E. Sobel, M.D.
Lewin Distinguished Professor of Cardiovascular Diseases,
Washington University
Cardiologist-in-Chief,
Barnes Hospital

Chapter 1.
Ischemic Heart Disease

Abbreviations

AMVL	Anterior Mitral Valve Leaflet	IVS	Interventricular Septum	N	Negative Contrast Effect
		LA	Left Atrium	PVW	Posterior Ventricular Wall
Ao	Aorta	LAO	Left Anterior Oblique	RA	Right Atrium
AoV	Aortic Valve	LAT	Lateral	RV	Right Ventricle
AP	Antero-posterior	LV	Left Ventricle	TV	Tricuspid Valve
Eff	Effusion	MV	Mitral Valve	VSD	Ventricular Septal Defect
		MVL	Mitral Valve Leaflet		

Note

The small images which accompany the text at the beginning of each chapter appear later in the chapter in a larger format.

Pathology

Patients with ischemic heart disease almost always have atheroma of the coronary arteries [1] though episodes of myocardial ischemia can occasionally result from spasm of normal coronary arteries. Rarer pathologic lesions include coronary artery emboli or non-atheromatous disease of the coronary arteries or of the coronary ostia.

Although atheroma may occur to a variable extent in the coronary arterial tree, the histologic pattern is consistent. Severe areas of stenosis show eccentric intimal thickening or plaques [2] containing large amounts of lipid. Lipid is often present as large pools of free cholesterol crystals separated from the lumen only by a thin layer of fibrous tissue. Thrombotic material is frequently present. Many areas of severe stenosis (>75%) have two or more lumina suggesting that they are recanalized total occlusions. Thrombotic total occlusions are due to a mass of fibrin and platelets plugging the lumen [3]. Calcification deep in the intima is common in atherosclerosis.

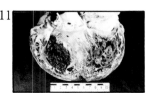

Although the initiating event causing myocardial infarction is unknown, plaque rupture leading to thrombosis of a coronary vessel may be important. This may lead to an area of muscle necrosis. The site of the infarct depends on the vessel involved. Thrombosis of the anterior descending coronary artery typically leads to an antero–septal infarct [4,5]. Disease in the right coronary artery results in a diaphragmatic infarct.

In transmural infarction, recent total occlusion due to thrombus in the supplying artery is invariably present [3]. Somewhat different pathologic changes may be found when the infarct is non-transmural. These consist of subendocardial and focal areas of necrosis scattered throughout the ventricle. Occlusive thrombi are less consistently found.

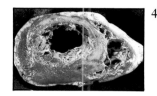

Complications of acute myocardial infarction include rupture of the left ventricle into the pericardium [6,7], ruptured interventricular septum [8], ruptured papillary muscle [9], ischemic papillary muscle resulting in severe mitral regurgitation [10], and formation of mural thrombus within the ventricles [11,12]. Later complications include the formation of a localized left ventricular aneurysm and dilatation of the left ventricle including areas of scarring [12].

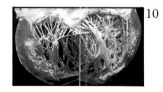

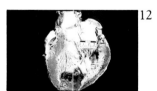

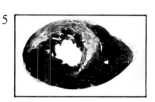

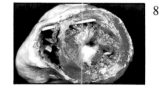

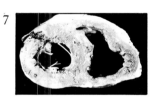

Presentation

Symptoms

Patients with ischemic heart disease may be asymptomatic in spite of widespread severe coronary atheroma. In contrast, other patients may die suddenly without extensive disease. The usual clinical presentation includes angina, acute myocardial infarction and heart failure. Some patients may present with arrhythmias (including sudden death) without any previous symptoms due to ischemic heart disease.

Chest pain due to myocardial ischemia typically occurs on physical exercise or during stress probably due to myocardial oxygen demand exceeding the coronary blood supply. Episodes of chest pain may also occur at rest. Such episodes may be due to a

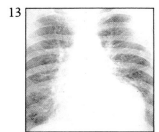

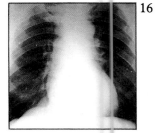

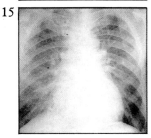

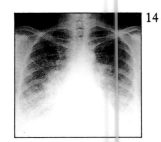

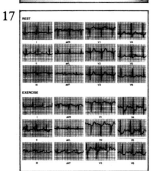

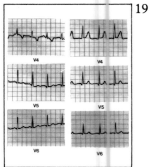

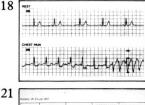

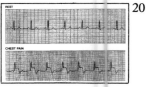

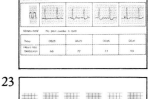

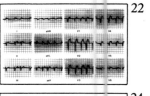

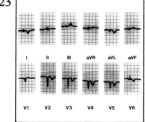

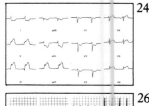

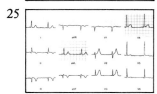

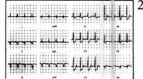

sudden reduction in oxygen delivery to the myocardium (e.g. coronary artery spasm).

Patients whose symptoms appear to be stable may develop more readily provoked pain and episodes of pain that are entirely unprovoked. Occasionally such symptoms in some patients precede the development of acute myocardial infarction, while in others the unprovoked episodes fade and the patient often returns to, or establishes, a stable pattern of chest pain.

Many patients develop myocardial infarction without premonitory symptoms. Prolonged severe chest pain is a characteristic feature. The acute development of breathlessness following infarction may be due to extensive myocardial necrosis with resulting pulmonary edema or rarely rupture of the ventricular septum or a papillary muscle. Arrhythmias are very common in acute infarction and may be asymptomatic or result in acute breathlessness or further chest pain or syncope.

Patients with chronic ischemic heart disease may develop heart failure without recent myocardial infarction. Such patients may have either a localized left ventricular aneurysm or left ventricular dilatation with widespread areas of scarring resulting in severely compromised left ventricular function.

Signs

Many patients with chronic ischemic heart disease do not have any abnormal physical signs. If there is left ventricular dysfunction, a double apical impulse will frequently be palpated and a fourth heart sound may be heard. In some patients with severe left ventricular disease, a loud pulmonary valve closure sound will be heard suggesting pulmonary hypertension. There may be a pansystolic murmur either due to chronic papillary muscle dysfunction with resultant mitral regurgitation or due to tricuspid regurgitation in patients with severe chronic heart failure with fluid retention. A third heart sound may be heard either in the patient with chronic severe ventricular dysfunction or in the acute phase of myocardial infarction with severe heart failure. The development of a pansystolic murmur shortly after acute myocardial infarction would suggest ischemic damage to a papillary muscle, rupture of the ventricular septum or rupture of the papillary muscle. In patients with severe heart failure sinus tachycardia is common with summation of third and fourth heart sounds giving rise to the gallop rhythm. Reduced cardiac output, either as an acute or chronic complication, results in reduced perfusion of vital organs with consequent oliguria and renal failure, confusion due to poor cerebral perfusion and peripheral vasoconstriction.

Investigations

Radiology

Most patients presenting with angina in the absence of left ventricular dysfunction have a normal plain chest radiograph. With long standing generalized left ventricular dysfunction or a localized left ventricular aneurysm there may be cardiomegaly and features of pulmonary venous hypertension. In about 50% of

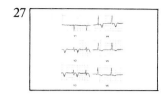

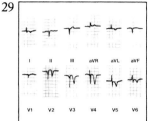

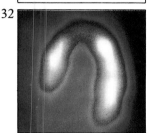

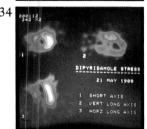

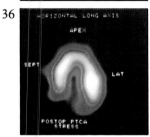

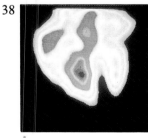

27

29

32

34

36

38

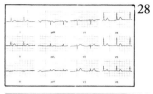

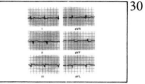

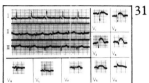

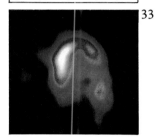

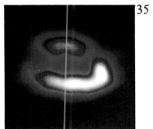

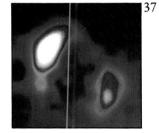

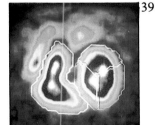

28

30

31

33

35

37

39

patients with a localized left ventricular aneurysm, the aneurysm may be visible on the radiograph as an abnormal bulge on the left heart border [13]. Pulmonary edema may develop in the patient with chronic ischemic heart disease or may follow acute myocardial infarction or one of its complications [14], such as ruptured interventricular septum or mitral regurgitation. In ruptured ventricular septum the pattern of pulmonary vessels sometimes suggests a left to right shunt [15,16].

Electrocardiography

The resting ECG may often be normal. However, it may show evidence of an old myocardial infarction, ST-T abnormalities, or left bundle branch block.

The electrocardiogram recorded during exercise is likely to show ST-segment abnormalities. The most specific change is down sloping ST-segment depression particularly in association with the development of chest pain [17]. Usually 1mm ST-segment depression is suggestive of myocardial ischemia. The ST-segment may be upsloping, horizontal or down-sloping. Occasionally arrhythmias are recorded in association with ST-segment changes during exercise [18]. The presence of an abnormal resting ECG, particularly left bundle branch block, makes interpretation of ST-segment changes difficult.

During episodes of chest pain due to myocardial ischemia, the 12 lead ECG is likely to show ST-T wave changes that resolve when the pain is relieved [19]. The rare patient with angina due to coronary artery spasm with or without coronary atheroma (Prinzmetal's angina) shows striking ST-segment elevation during an episode of chest pain [20].

Ambulatory monitoring of ST-segments in patients with ischemic heart disease will often show ST-T wave changes during episodes of chest pain; frequently, however, such ECG changes may be recorded in the absence of chest pain [21] and are also likely to be due to myocardial ischemia.

Patients who have acute myocardial infarction usually show pathologic Q waves and ST-T abnormalities which evolve with time. The location of the infarct can be roughly determined from the electrocardiogram; thus an acute anterior infarct shows Q waves and ST-elevation in the anterior precordial leads (V1 to V4) with similar changes in leads 1, AVL and V5 to V6 [22]. As time passes the ST-T changes evolve into T wave inversion [23]. More localized ECG changes are seen in septal (V2-V4) or lateral (I, AVL, V5, V6) infarction. An inferior infarct shows similar changes in the inferior leads (2,3 and AVF) [24,25]. A true posterior infarction shows dominant R waves in V1 reflecting the absence of posterior forces [26].

When the infarct is non-transmural (subendocardial) Q waves are not seen but there are usually striking ST-T changes which may resolve with time [27,28].

Patients with rupture of the ventricular septum following myocardial infarction usually show electrocardiographic features of a septal infarct [29] whereas those with papillary muscle infarction or ischemia resulting in mitral regurgitation often show evidence of infero-lateral infarction [30]. These electrocardiographic features may help in distinguishing these two complica-

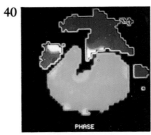

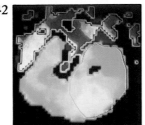

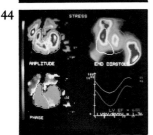

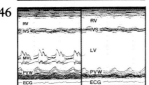

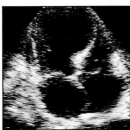

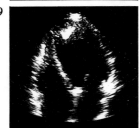

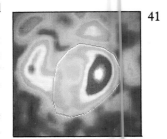

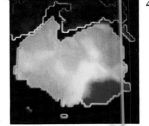

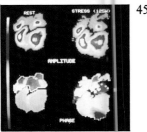

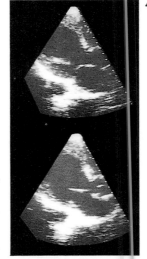

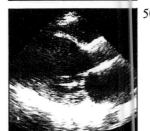

tions of myocardial infarction clinically. Patients with a localized left ventricular aneurysm may continue to show ST-segment elevation as well as Q waves in the electrocardiogram persisting after the acute phase of myocardial infarction [31]. However, this feature is not invariable and patients with a left ventricular aneurysm may show any kind of electrocardiographic abnormality associated with coronary artery disease.

Patients with heart failure due to ischemic heart disease almost always have ECG evidence of previous myocardial infarction, ST-T wave abnormalities or left bundle branch block at rest.

Nuclear Techniques

Nuclear techniques show functional information which complements the anatomic information provided by, for instance, coronary arteriography. Thallium-201 is an isotope that is actively taken up by myocardial cells in proportion to myocardial perfusion. Subsequent imaging therefore provides a map of myocardial perfusion with defects representing areas either with impaired perfusion or with cellular ischemia. The isotope is normally given at peak exercise with imaging immediately afterwards and again following a variable period of redistribution. Areas of infarction have reduced uptake in both images, but reversibly ischemic myocardium has impaired uptake initially and improved uptake at rest. It is therefore possible to define normally perfused [32], reversibly ischemic [33], and infarcted myocardium, and to assess the site and extent of abnormalities. The importance of such an assessment lies in the fact that the likelihood of future cardiac events is closely related to the extent of ischemia. It is therefore possible to select patients at high risk, independently of coronary anatomy, and to concentrate revascularization procedures in this subgroup [34-36]. Planar images have traditionally been used, but a significant advance has been the use of rotating gamma cameras to acquire images from many angles from which to reconstruct emission tomograms. The three dimensional view of myocardial perfusion provided by tomographic imaging greatly increases the accuracy of assessment and hence the clinical value of the technique. A further development that has increased the scope of the technique is the use of intravenous dipyridamole, a coronary arterial dilator, to induce abnormalities of thallium uptake in patients with coronary artery disease without the need for dynamic exercise [37].

The second important nuclear cardiologic procedure is radionuclide ventriculography using technetium-99m to label the intracardiac blood pools. Imaging is either performed during the first passage of the bolus through the central circulation or when it has reached equilibrium [38]. Left ventricular volumes, ejection fraction and parameters of diastolic function such as filling rates can be measured. Regional wall motion can also be assessed and helpful methods of displaying both the extent and the timing of contraction are the Fourier amplitude and phase images [39-42]. The phase image is particularly helpful in defining areas of dyskinesis suggesting left ventricular aneurysm [43]. Imaging during stress allows the response to exercise to be measured and a fall in LVEF and/or new regional wall motion abnormalities are suggestive of exercise induced ischemia [44,45]. The LVEF during peak

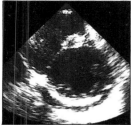

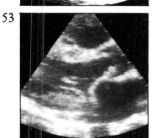

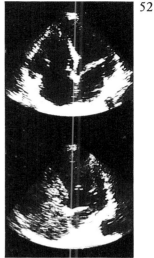

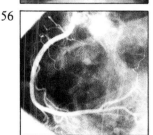

stress is, like the extent of ischemia shown by thallium imaging, a powerful prognostic indicator.

Echocardiography

In patients with ischemic heart disease and normal resting left ventricular function the echocardiogram is usually normal except in the rare circumstances where a recording is made during chest pain when regional wall motion abnormalities may be detected by 2-dimensional echocardiography. In those patients with chronic ischemic heart disease who have abnormal left ventricular function, this may be detected by various techniques using echocardiography. M-mode echocardiography may show an increase in left ventricular dimension and reduction of wall motion when left ventricular disease is severe and generalized [46]. Sometimes, an M-mode echocardiogram showing lack of motion of either the septum or posterior wall will indicate permanent damage or scarring in those regions. 2-Dimensional echocardiography may visualize regional abnormalities within the overall function of the ventricle. Cases of extreme systolic wall thinning and/or dyskinesia are readily apparent from inspection of the systolic and diastolic images [47]. A localized left ventricular aneurysm may be detected by 2-dimensional echocardiography [48]. Thrombus within an abnormal ventricle may sometimes be seen [49].

In acute myocardial infarction, M-mode echocardiography may show outward movement of the endocardium during systole of either septum or posterior wall due in part to a reduction in wall thickness of either of these affected regions. 2-Dimensional echocardiography is usually superior in locating and determining the extent of infarcted myocardium [50].

Complications of acute myocardial infarction such as the development of a pericardial effusion [51], rupture of the ventricular septum resulting in a ventricular septal defect [52] and rupture of a papillary muscle causing flail-like motion of mitral valve leaflets may be identified using 2-dimensional echocardiography [53].

Cardiac Catheterization and Angiography

Although left ventricular pressures are often normal the most likely hemodynamic abnormality in patients with chronic ischemic heart disease is an elevation of left ventricular end-diastolic pressure. This occurs most frequently if there is extensive chronic damage of the left ventricle or during an episode of myocardial ischemia. In acute myocardial infarction, left ventricular end-diastolic and pulmonary capillary wedge pressure may be elevated and cardiac output reduced.

If the myocardial infarct is complicated by ventricular septal rupture, a left-to-right shunt at ventricular level will be demonstrated often with significant pulmonary hypertension. If the infarct is complicated by significant mitral regurgitation, the left atrial or pulmonary capillary wedge pressure will show a high 'V' or systolic wave. Cardiac output is likely to be reduced with either of these complications. In order to demonstrate the exact pattern of coronary artery narrowing coronary arteriography is required [54-60]. This technique may be required either in the patient

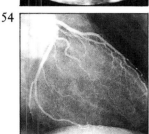

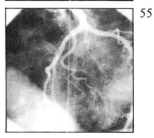

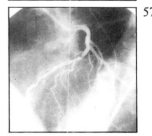

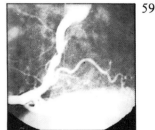

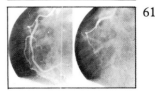

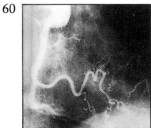

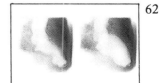

63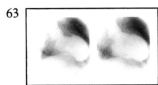

64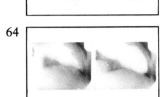

with chronic ischemic heart disease or in the acute phase of myocardial infarction. The absence of angiographically demonstrable coronary artery narrowing does not exclude the possibility of the patient having transient myocardial ischemia. Occasionally patients with normal or near normal coronary arteries may develop coronary spasm [61].

Left ventricular angiograms may demonstrate local [62] or generalized abnormalities of left ventricular contraction, localized left ventricular aneurysm [63], mitral regurgitation [64], and ruptured septum [65].

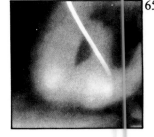 65

1 Longitudinal slice of coronary artery showing at least 80% narrowing of the lumen.

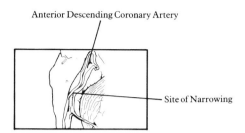

Anterior Descending Coronary Artery

Site of Narrowing

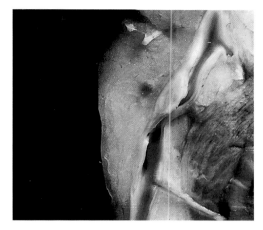

2 Narrowed coronary artery due to atherosclerosis - transverse section. The lumen is reduced to a small rather crescentic opening by a mass of intimal fibrous tissue containing lipid.

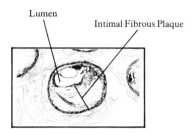

Lumen

Intimal Fibrous Plaque

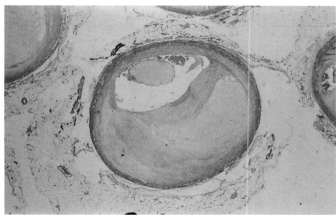

3 Thrombosed coronary artery in transverse section. The lumen is completely occluded by a mass of red thrombus. Above and to the left of the thrombus is a plaque of atheroma which contains lipid.

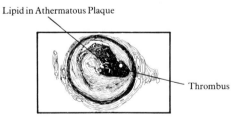

Lipid in Athermatous Plaque

Thrombus

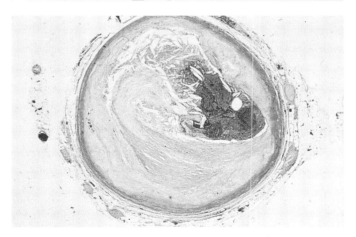

4 Transverse slice (fresh) of the ventricles. A recent (four day old) full-thickness myocardial infarction is present in the anterior wall of the left ventricle which extends into the interventricular septum.

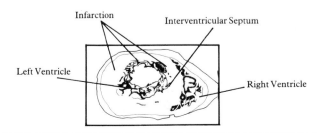

Infarction

Interventricular Septum

Left Ventricle

Right Ventricle

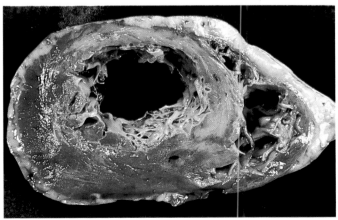

5 Slice of the ventricles stained to show succinic dehydrogenase enzyme activity (dark). An acute infarct is demonstrated as a white area due to the loss of enzyme activity.

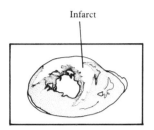

6 Pericardial sac filled with blood clot as a result of cardiac rupture due to myocardial infarction.

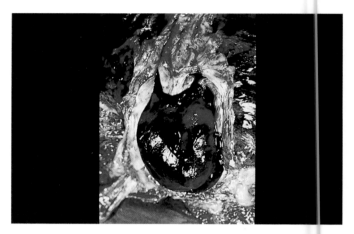

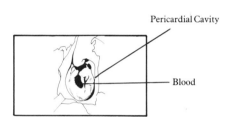

7 Rupture of the anterior wall of the left ventricle due to acute infarction.

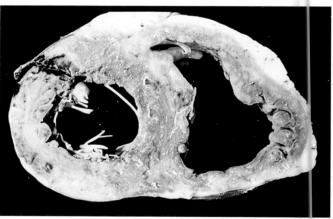

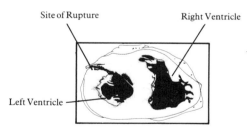

8 Acute myocardial infarction of the septum with rupture resulting in a ventricular septal defect (probe is shown passing through the defect).

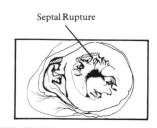

9 Acute myocardial infarction resulting in rupture of a papillary muscle.

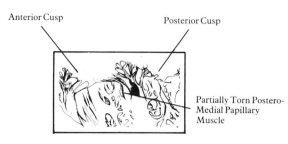

Anterior Cusp

Posterior Cusp

Partially Torn Postero-Medial Papillary Muscle

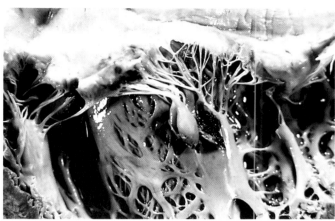

10 The left ventricle has been opened to show a papillary muscle infarct resulting in mitral regurgitation. The posterior papillary muscle is pale and shrunken due to infarction. The anterior papillary muscle (normal) is larger and darker. Subendocardial ischemic scarring is present in the left ventricle.

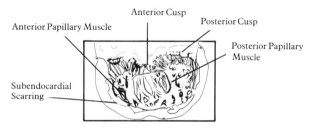

Anterior Cusp

Anterior Papillary Muscle

Posterior Cusp

Posterior Papillary Muscle

Subendocardial Scarring

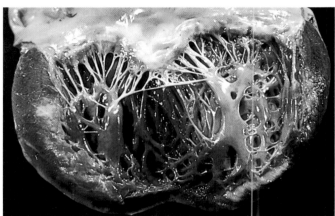

11 Widespread ischemic scarring of the myocardium producing a dilated thin-walled ventricle. A thrombus has formed in one area in relation to the aneurysmal bulge of the ventricular wall.

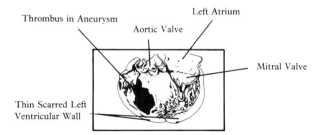

Thrombus in Aneurysm

Left Atrium

Aortic Valve

Mitral Valve

Thin Scarred Left Ventricular Wall

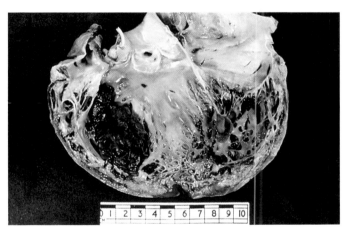

12 Localized left ventricular aneurysm due to ischemic damage. The aneurysm does not contain more than a fine deposit of thrombus and has a larger central cavity opening into the ventricle.

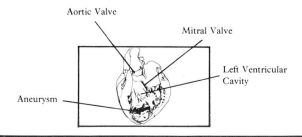

Aortic Valve

Mitral Valve

Left Ventricular Cavity

Aneurysm

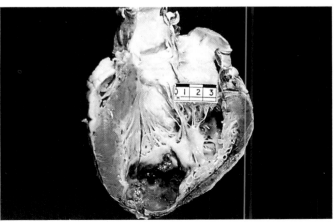

13 Chest radiograph showing an abnormal bulge on the left heart border due to a ventricular aneurysm. There is pulmonary edema.

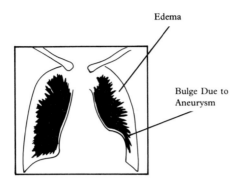

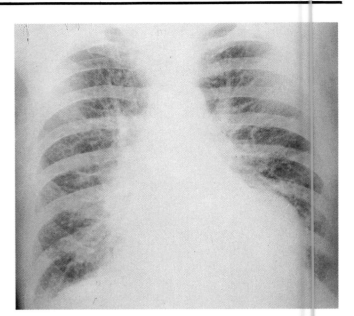

14 Chest radiograph showing pulmonary edema and bilateral pleural effusions following acute myocardial infarction.

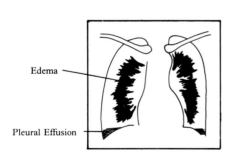

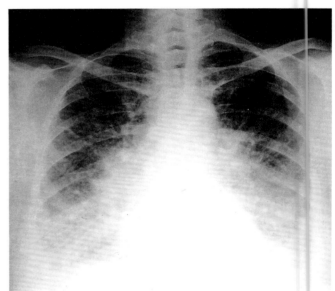

15 Chest radiograph showing cardiac enlargement with hilar edema and generalized increase in pulmonary vessel size due to left-to-right shunt through a ventricular septal defect complicating myocardial infarction.

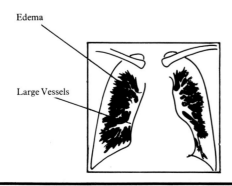

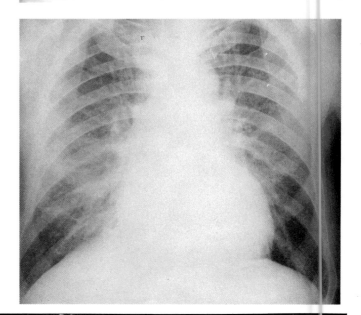

16 Chest radiograph of the same patient as [15] showing normal pulmonary vascularity following surgical closure of the defect.

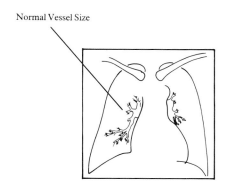

Normal Vessel Size

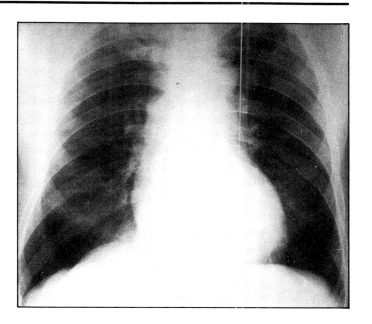

17

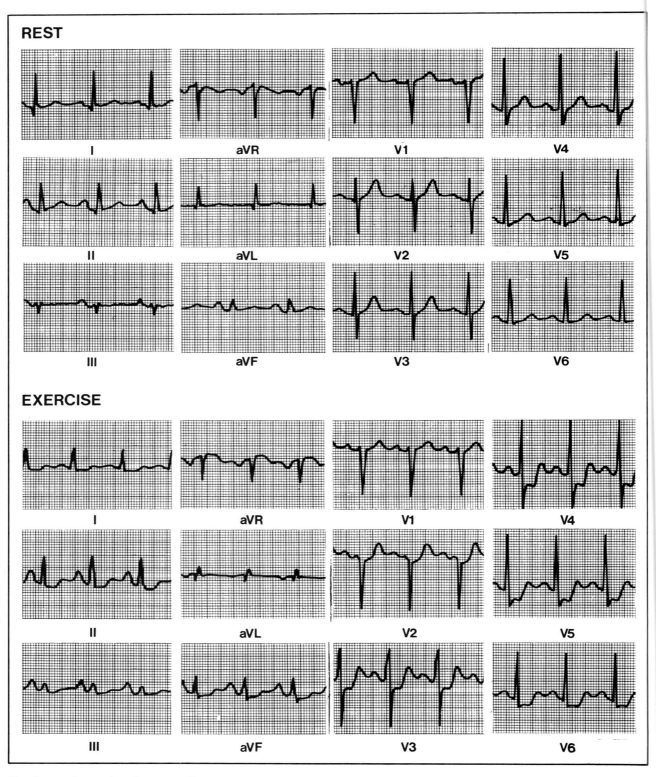

Resting and exercise electrocardiograms in a patient with angina. The resting electrocardiogram is normal. On exercise there is both horizontal and down sloping ST segment depression in the anterior chest leads associated with the development of chest pain.

18

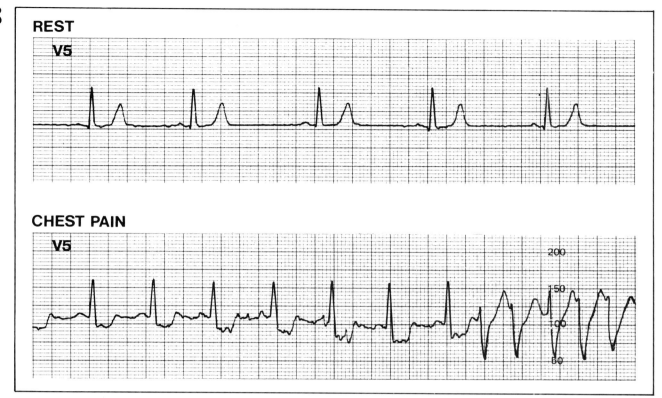

Electrocardiogram recorded during 24-hour ambulatory monitoring showing ST depression and the development of ventricular tachycardia during chest pain.

19

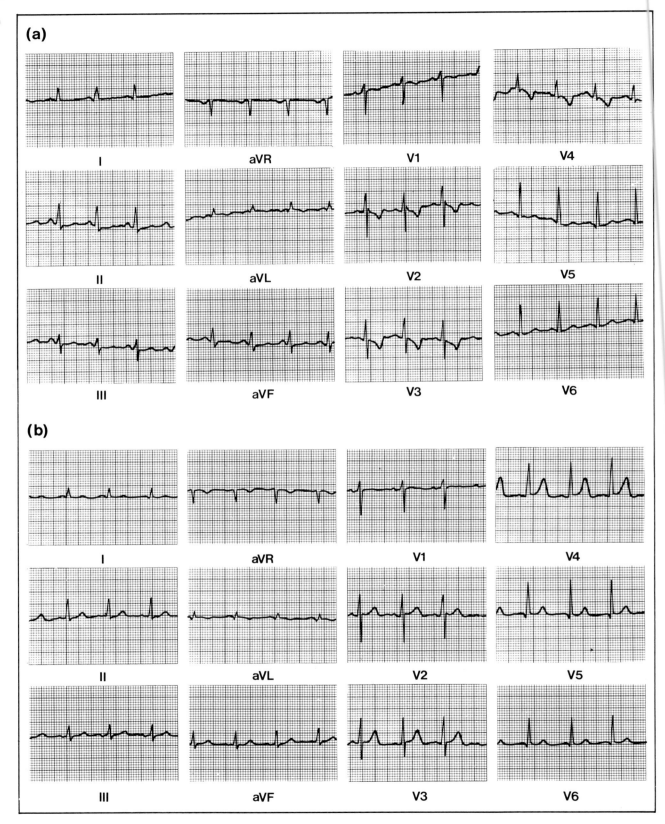

Resting electrocardiograms taken during chest pain in a patient with ischemic heart disease showing ST-T wave abnormalities in the anterior chest leads (a). After the pain has subsided the ST-segment changes return to normal (b).

20

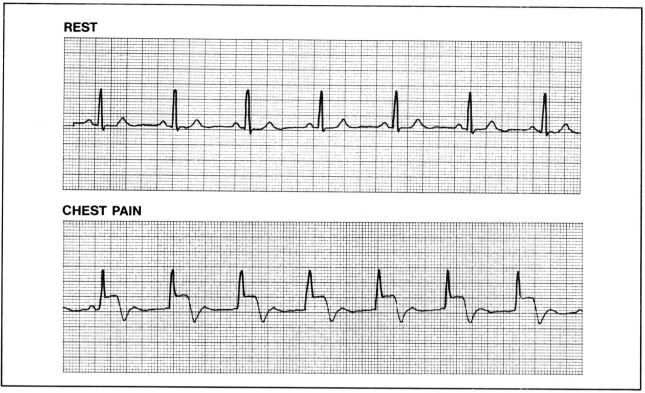

Electrocardiogram recorded during ambulatory monitoring showing ST-segment elevation during chest pain.

21

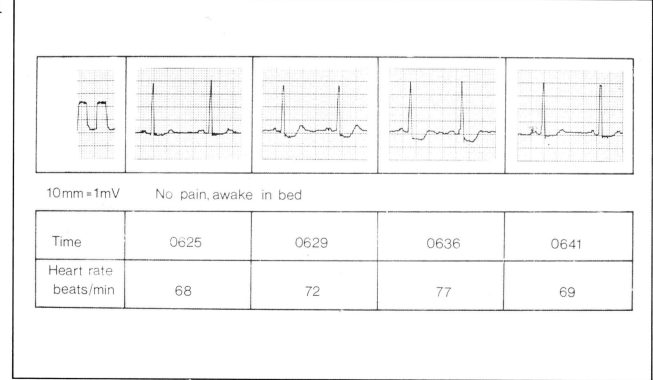

Electrocardiogram recorded during 24-hour monitoring. There are transient ST-segment changes whilst the patient was lying awake in bed. He did not complain of chest pain.

22

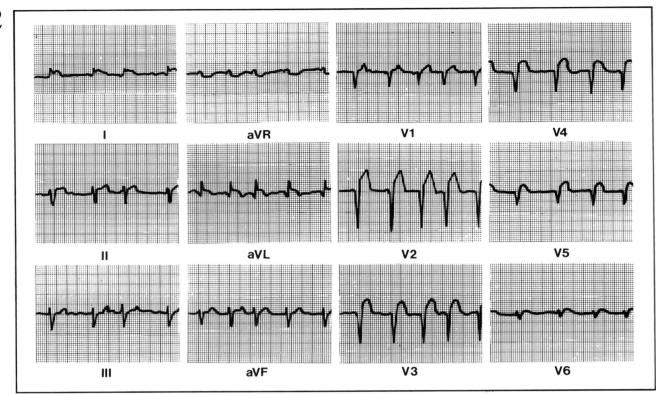

Electrocardiogram in a patient with acute anterolateral myocardial infarction showing Q waves and ST elevation in V2-V5, I and aVL.

23

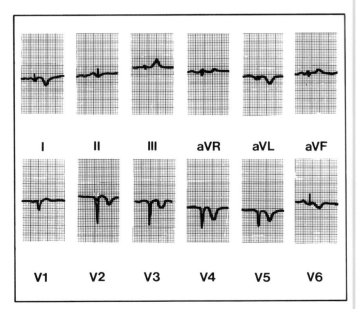

Electrocardiogram in the same patient as [22] taken several days later, showing T wave inversion in leads previously showing ST elevation with persisting Q waves.

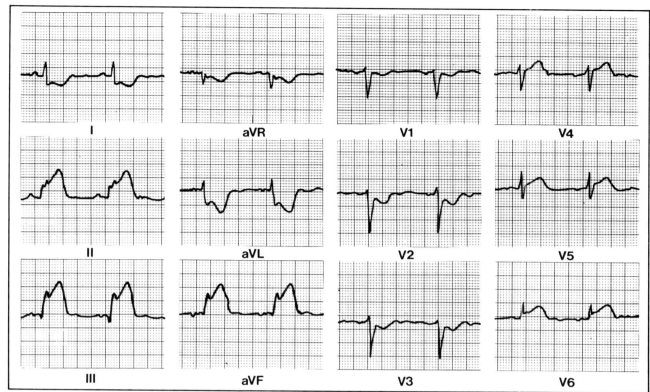

Electrocardiogram showing acute inferior myocardial infarction with ST elevation in II, III and aVF. There is also ST elevation in V5 and V6 and ST-segment depression in I, aVL, V2 and V3.

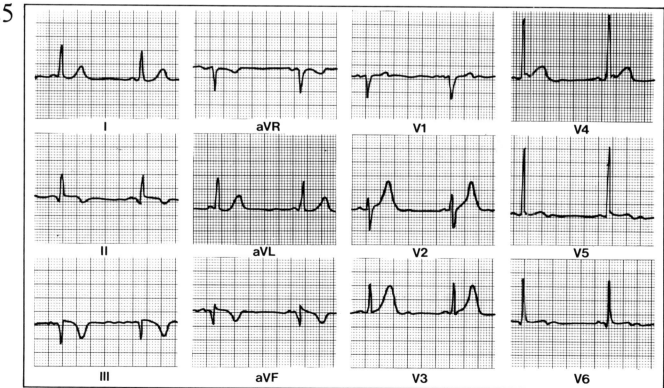

Electrocardiogram from the same patient as [24] showing Q waves and T wave inversion in leads II, III and aVF.

26

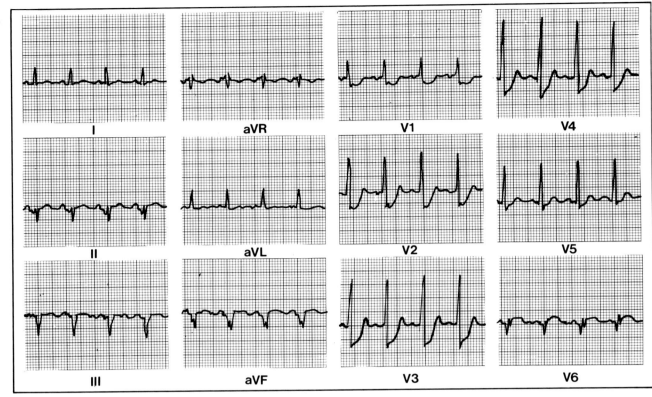

Electrocardiogram showing a true posterior myocardial infarction. There are Q waves in II, aVF and V6 with dominant R waves in V1-V4 together with ST-segment depression in the anterior chest leads.

27

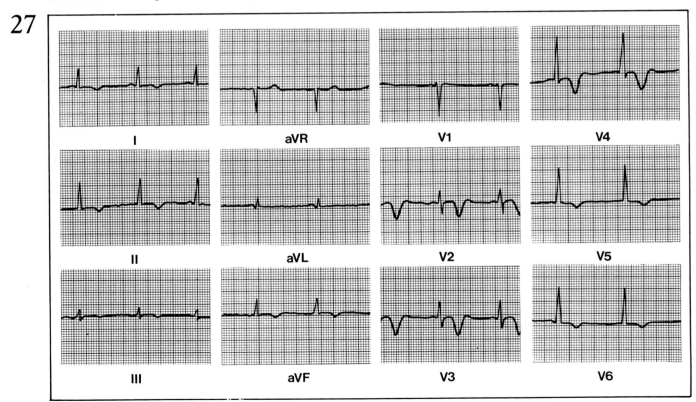

Electrocardiogram from a patient with a subendocardial infarction showing widespread T wave inversion.

28

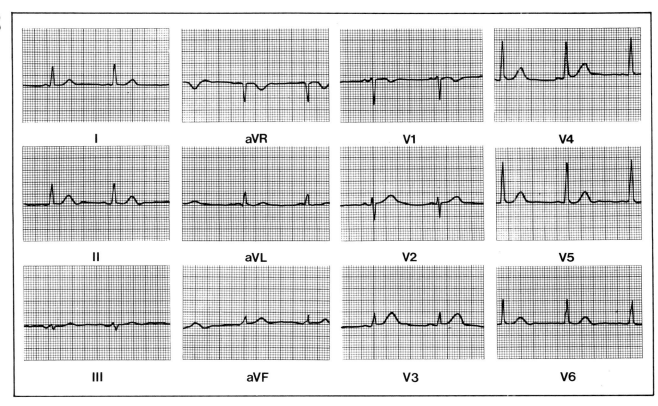

Electrocardiogram from the same patient as [27] several months later showing resolution of the T wave changes.

29

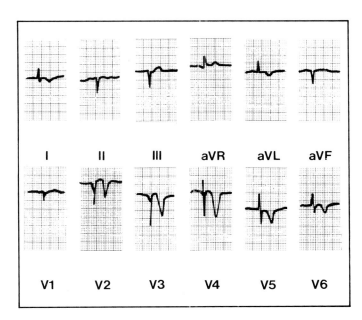

Electrocardiogram from a patient with a ruptured ventricular septum following myocardial infarction. There are Q waves in leads V1–V3 indicating septal infarction.

30

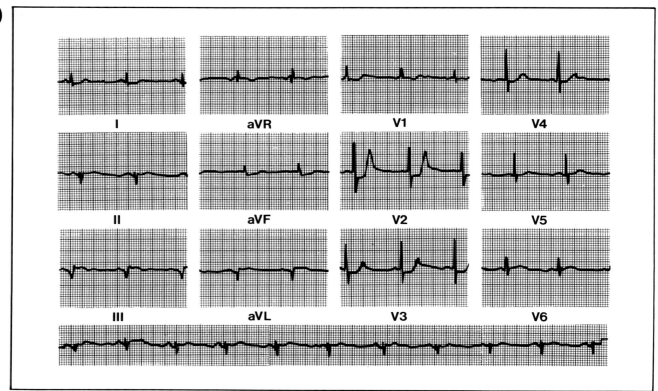

Electrocardiogram from a patient with mitral regurgitation secondary to inferior myocardial infarction. There are Q waves in the inferior leads, and incomplete right bundle branch block. The changes of true posterior infarction are also present.

31

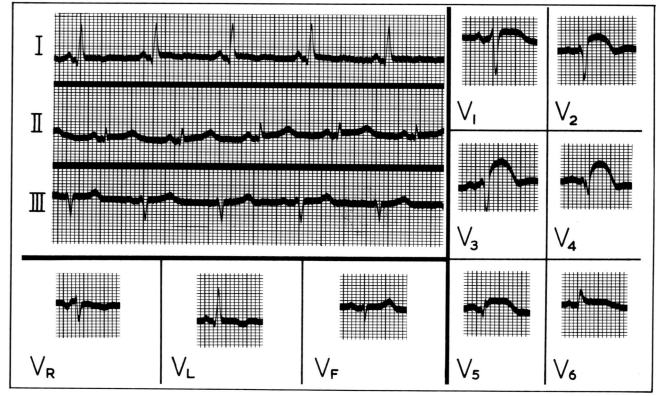

Electrocardiogram from a patient with a left ventricular aneurysm. There are Q waves and ST-segment elevation in the anterior leads some months following acute infarction.

32 Normal emission tomograms in vertical (top) and horizontal long axis (middle) and short axis planes (bottom). There is uniform uptake of thallium-201 throughout the myocardium.

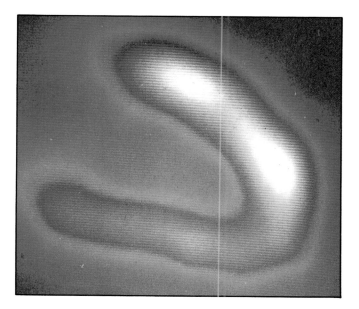

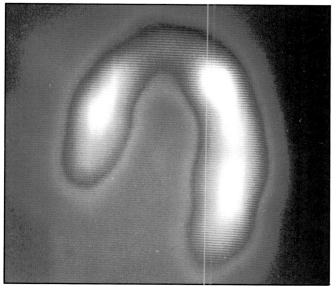

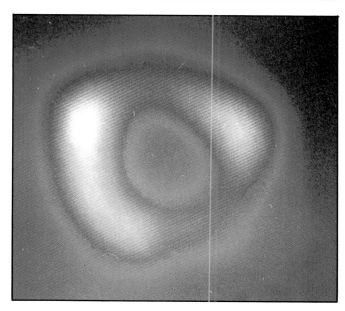

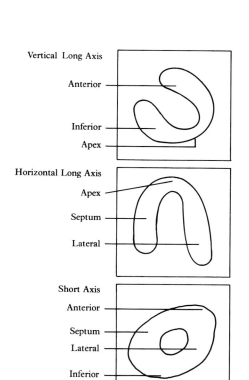

Vertical Long Axis

Anterior

Inferior

Apex

Horizontal Long Axis

Apex

Septum

Lateral

Short Axis

Anterior

Septum

Lateral

Inferior

33

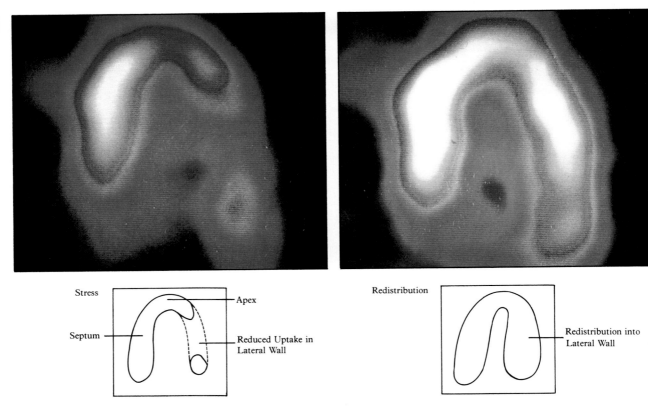

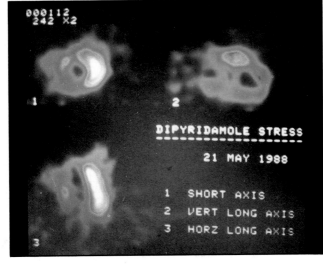

Stress (left) and redistribution (right) horizontal long axis tomograms showing reversible lateral wall ischemia in a patient with left circumflex coronary artery disease.

34

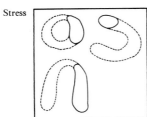

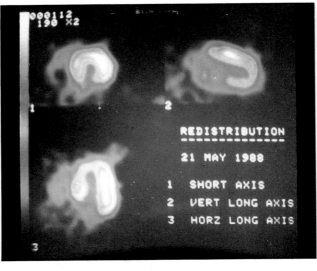

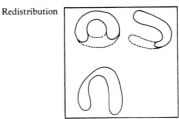

Stress (left) and redistribution (right) tomograms showing inferior infarction and reversible anteroseptal and apical ischemia. This is a high risk scan because of the extent of ischemia.

35

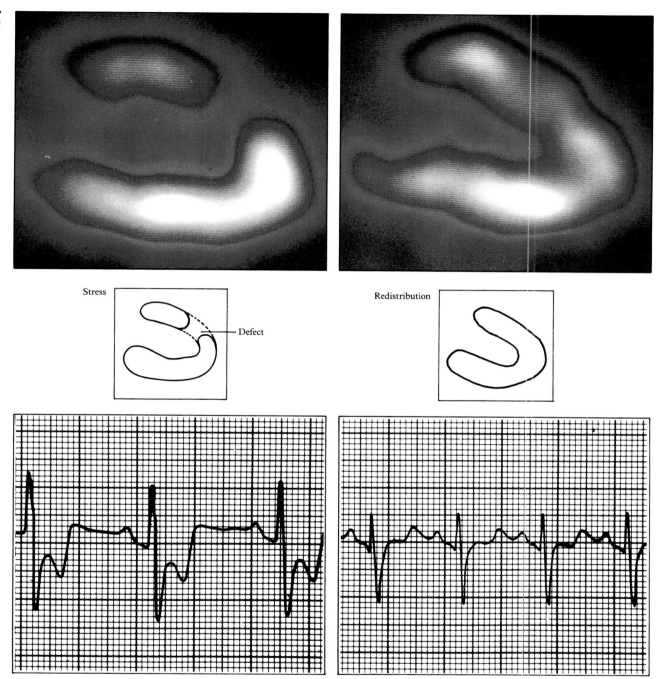

Stress (left) and rest (right) vertical long axis tomograms (top) and ECG (bottom) showing reversible anterior ischemia. Because of the limited area of ischemia, this is a low risk scan.

36

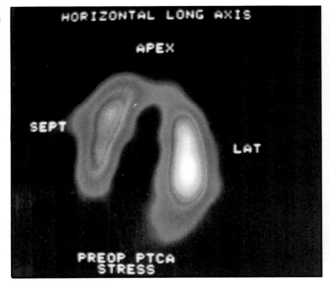

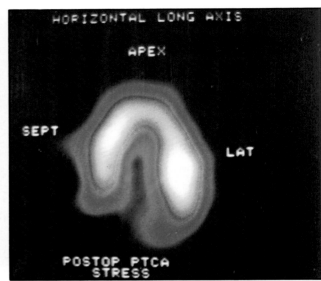

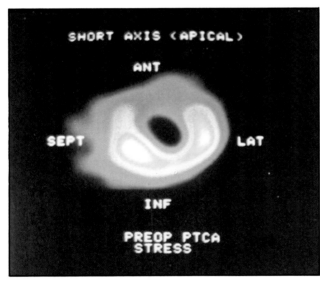

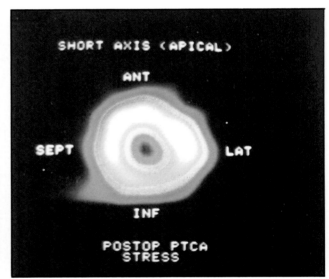

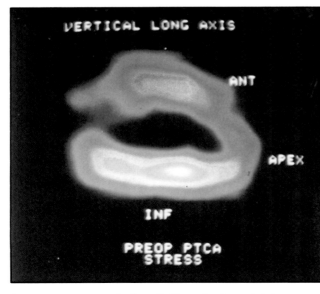

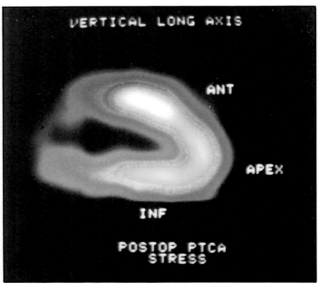

Stress tomograms before (left) and after (right) angioplasty to a left anterior descending lesion after the first septal branches. The small distal anterior area of ischemia is abolished.

37

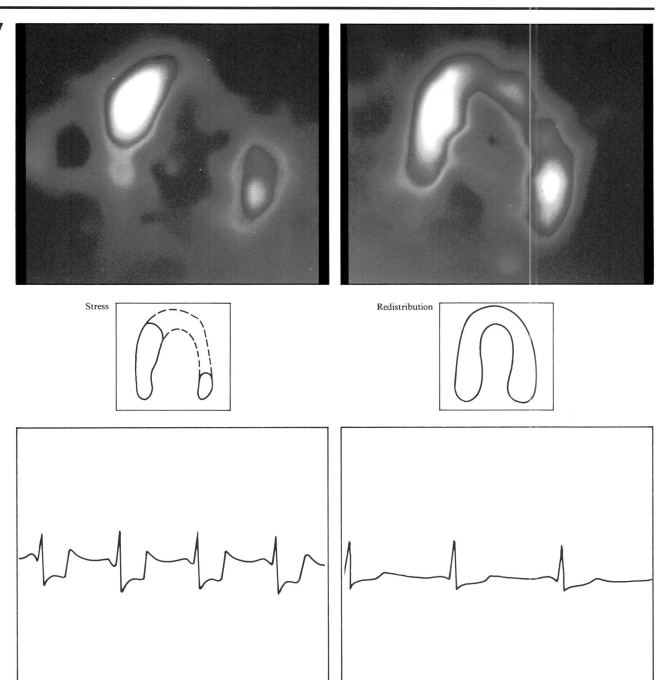

Stress (left) and redistribution (right) horizontal long axis tomograms (top) with ECG (bottom) showing reversible ischemia of the lateral wall and basal septum. In this case, the abnormality was produced by intravenous infusion of dipyridamole and no exercise was necessary.

38 Normal left anterior oblique end diastolic image from an equilibrium radionuclide ventriculogram.

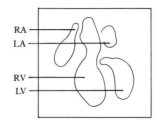

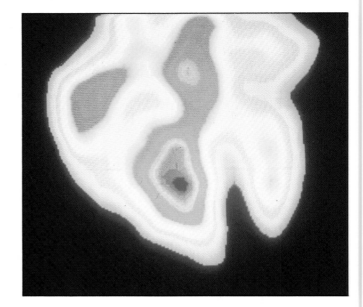

39 Normal amplitude image showing high amplitude of all parts of the left ventricle.

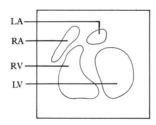

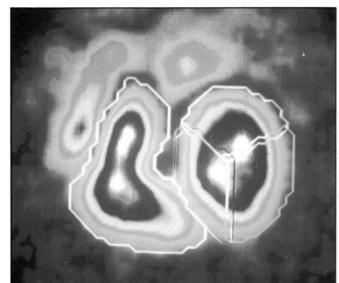

40 Normal phase image showing synchronous contraction of all parts of both ventricles in green. The atria and great vessels are 180° out of phase and are seen in red.

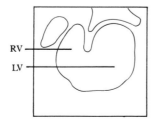

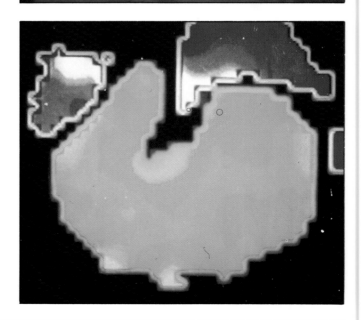

41

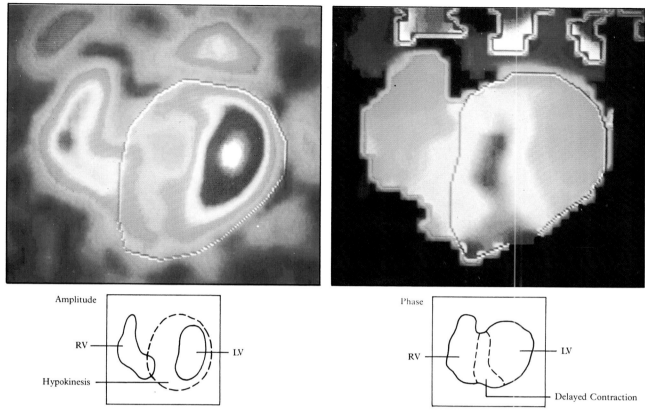

Amplitude (left) and phase (right) images in anteroseptal infarction. There are reduced values of amplitude and high phase in the region of the septum. This indicates hypokinesis and delayed contraction.

42

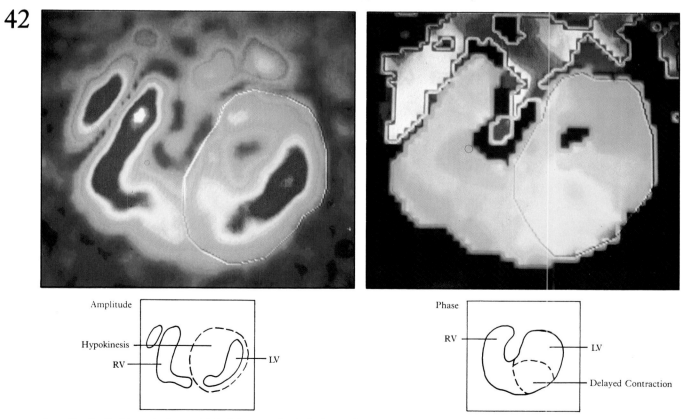

Amplitude (left) and phase (right) images in inferior infarction. The central amplitude defect and the delayed apical contraction are typical.

43 Phase image in left ventricular aneurysm showing apical dyskinesis (red).

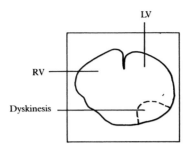

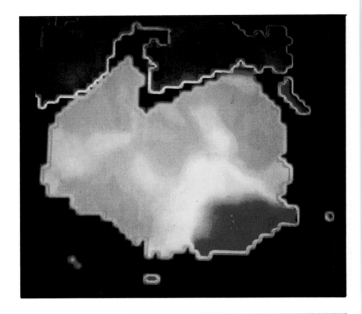

44

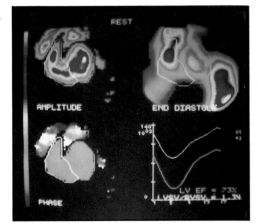

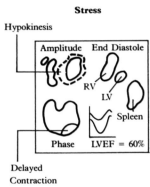

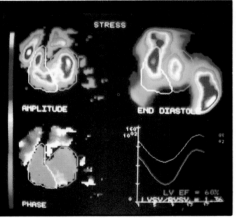

Rest (left) and stress (right) radionuclide ventriculograms with phase and amplitude images in a patient with coronary artery disease. The LVEF is normal at rest (73%) with normal regional wall motion shown on the amplitude and phase images. During stress, the LVEF falls (60%) and the amplitude and phase images show septal hypokinesis with delayed contraction.

45 Rest (left) and stress (right) amplitude and phase images. Regional wall motion is normal at rest, but delayed apical contraction develops during stress.

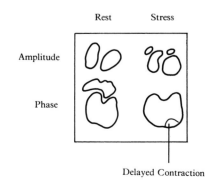

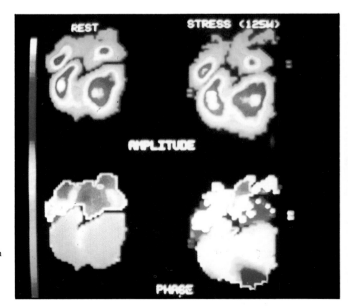

46

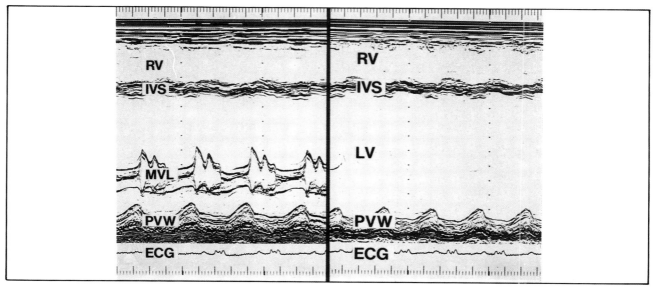

M-mode echocardiogram of the mitral valve (left) and left ventricle (right) in a patient with severe generalized left ventricular dysfunction due to coronary artery disease.

47

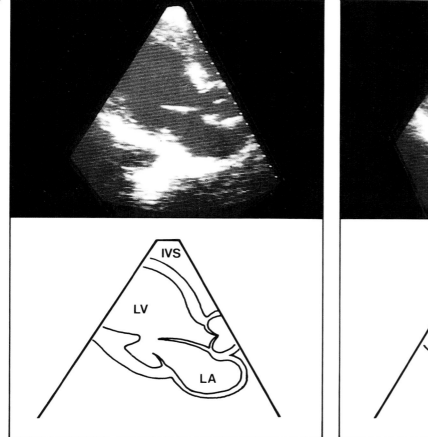
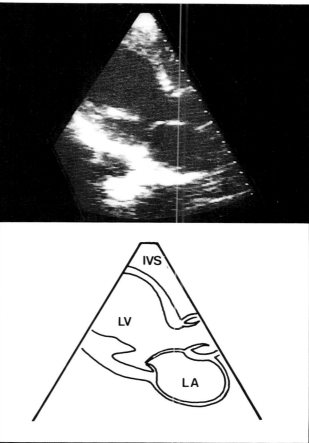

2-D echocardiographic parasternal long axis views in diastole (left) and systole (right) showing the thinning, anterior bulging and lack of movement of the septum following myocardial infarction.

48

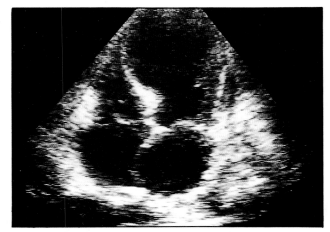
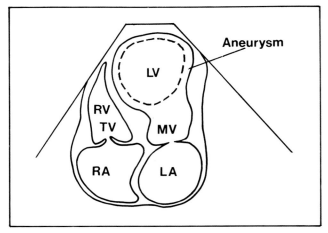

2-D echocardiographic apical four-chamber view of a large aneurysm containing thrombus.

49

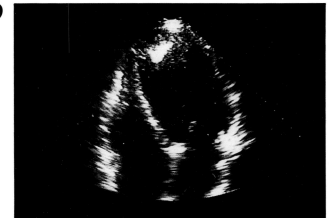
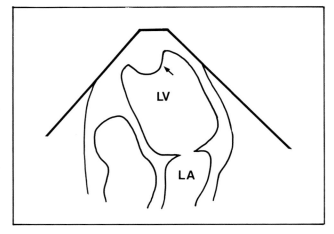

2-D echocardiographic apical four-chamber view of thrombus (arrow) in a patient with an old apical myocardial infarction.

50

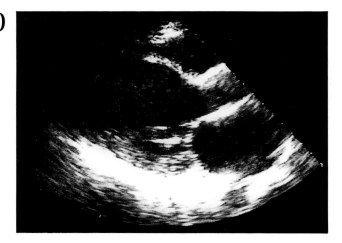
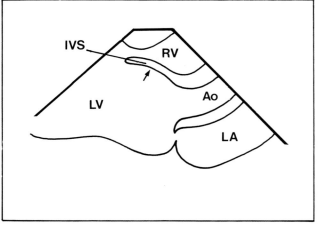

2-D echocardiographic systolic long axis view showing thinning of the septum (arrow) bulging into the right ventricle.

51

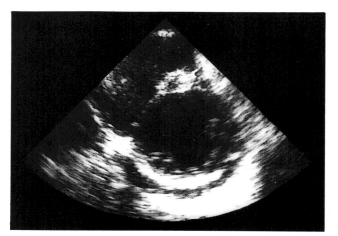
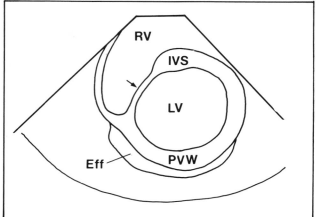

2-D echocardiographic systolic short axis view at level of papillary muscles in a patient with septal infarction. There is thinning of the septum (arrow) in relation to the anterior wall, and there is a pericardial effusion.

52

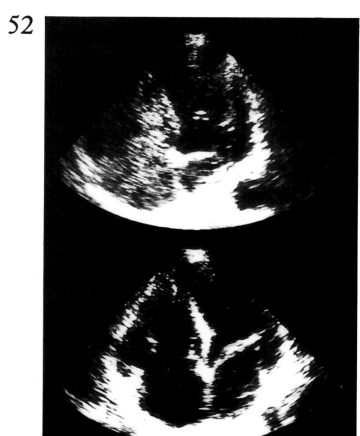
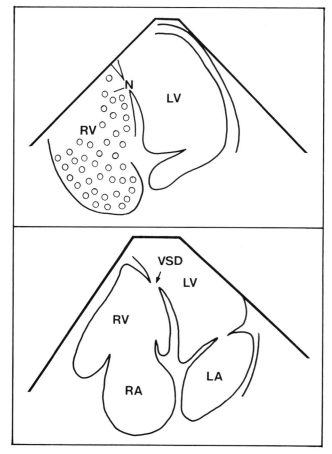

2-D echocardiographic four-chamber view in a patient with apico-septal ventricular septal defect after myocardial infarction. Above is a contrast injection into the right atrium and passing into the right ventricle. A negative contrast effect is seen in the right ventricle (N). Below is a non-contrast study in the same patient showing the ventricular septal defect (arrow) and a large right ventricle.

53

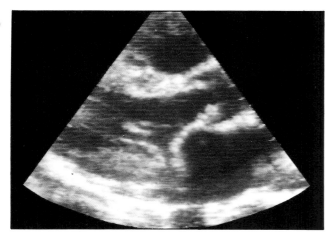
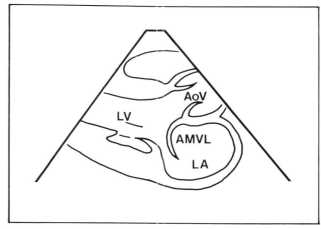

2-D echocardiographic parasternal long axis view showing 'flail' systolic motion of the anterior mitral valve leaflet into the left atrium.

54 Normal left coronary arteriogram in the right anterior oblique view.

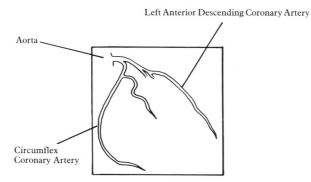
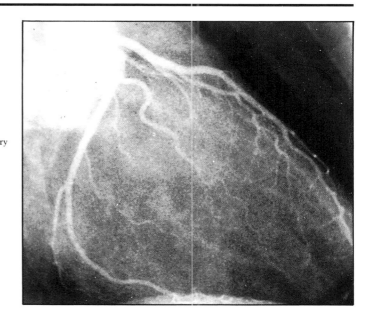

55 Angiogram in the left anterior oblique projection showing a normal left coronary artery.

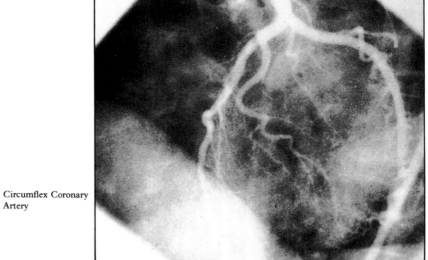

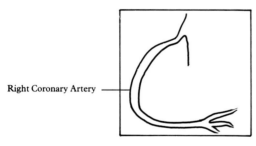

Left Anterior Descending Coronary Artery

Diagonal Branch of Left Anterior Descending Coronary Artery

Circumflex Coronary Artery

56 Angiogram in the left anterior oblique projection showing a normal right coronary artery.

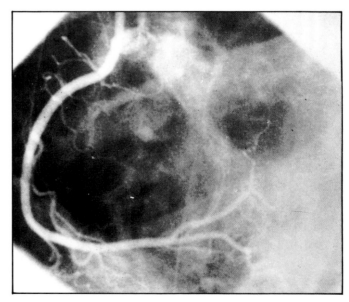

Right Coronary Artery

57 Angiogram showing atherosclerotic narrowing of the left anterior descending coronary artery (arrow).

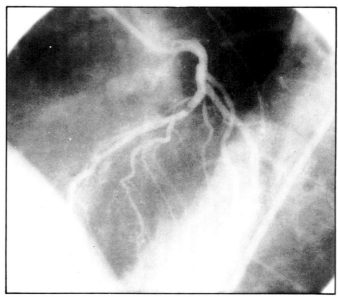

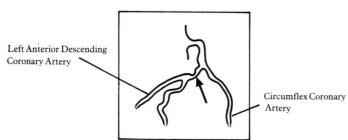

Left Anterior Descending Coronary Artery

Circumflex Coronary Artery

58 Angiogram showing atherosclerotic narrowing (arrow) of the left anterior descending coronary artery.

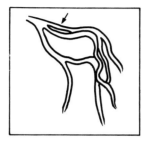

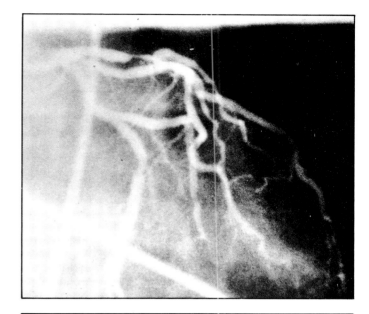

59 Right coronary angiogram viewed in the right anterior oblique projection showing obvious narrowing.

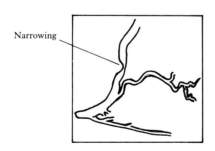

Narrowing

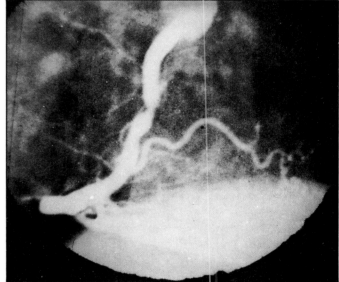

60 Right coronary angiogram viewed in the right anterior oblique projection showing diffuse disease of the artery with retrograde filling of the anterior descending coronary artery via septal collateral vessels.

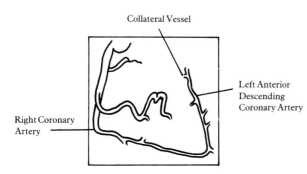

Collateral Vessel

Left Anterior Descending Coronary Artery

Right Coronary Artery

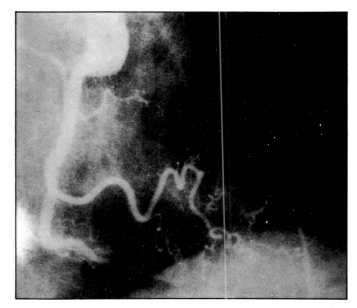

61

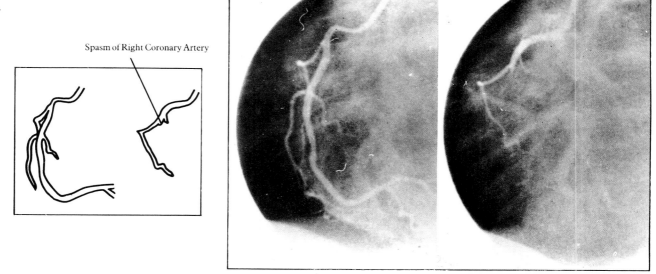

Coronary artery spasm. The angiogram on the left (left anterior oblique projection) shows normal blood flow in the right coronary artery. The angiogram on the right shows coronary artery spasm completely occluding the right coronary artery.

62

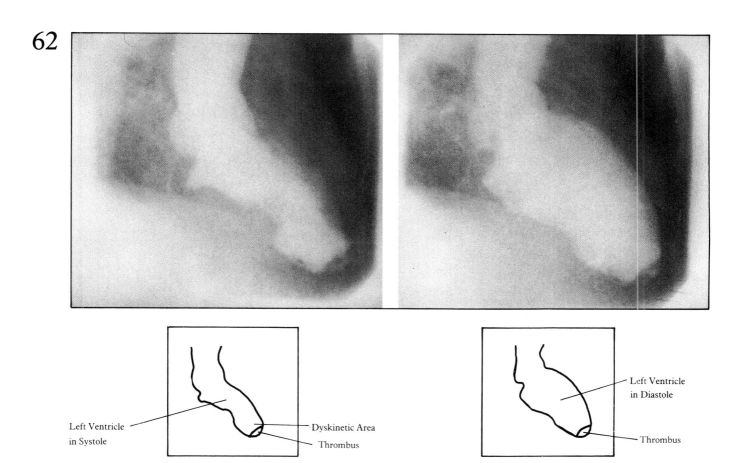

Left ventricular angiogram in the right anterior oblique projection. Systolic (left) and diastolic (right) frames reveal presence of apical dyskinesis and thrombus.

63

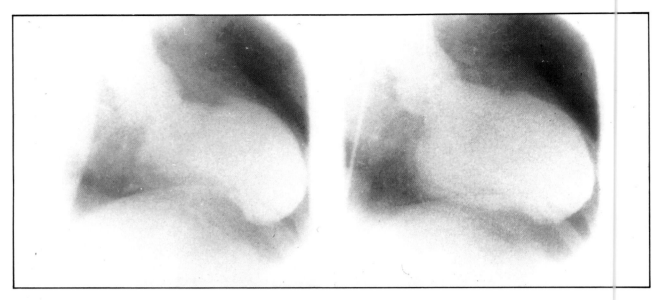

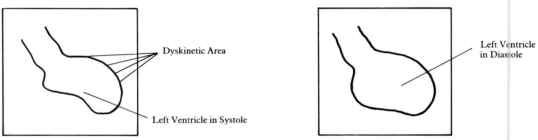

Left ventricular angiogram in the right anterior oblique projection with systolic (left) and diastolic (right) frames. It shows a large apical aneurysm with normal contraction of the remainder of the ventricle.

64

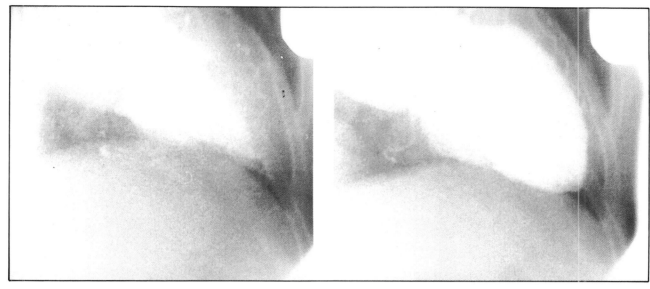

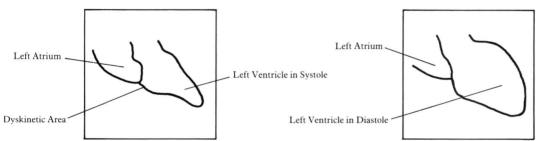

Left Atrium — Left Ventricle in Systole

Dyskinetic Area

Left Atrium — Left Ventricle in Diastole

Left ventricular angiogram in the right anterior oblique projection with systolic (left) and diastolic (right) frames. It shows reduced contraction of the inferior wall of the left ventricle and dense opacification of the left atrium due to mitral regurgitation.

65 Left ventricular angiogram in the left anterior oblique projection showing a shunt from the left ventricle into the right ventricle due to rupture of the muscular septum.

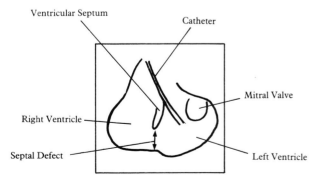

Ventricular Septum — Catheter

Mitral Valve

Right Ventricle

Septal Defect — Left Ventricle

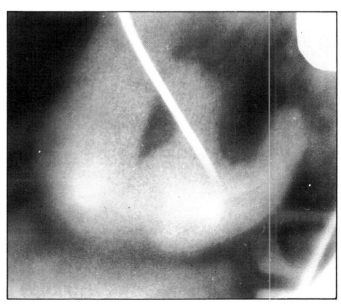

Chapter 2.
Heart Failure

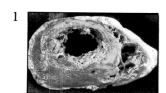

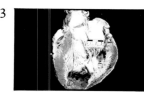

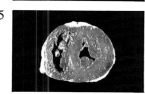

Pathology

The clinical syndrome of heart failure consists of breathlessness, evidence of poor tissue perfusion (fatigue, oliguria, drowsiness) and the consequences of stimulation of the sympathetic and renin-angiotensin-aldosterone systems (tachycardia, peripheral vasoconstriction, salt and water retention). The clinical features of heart failure may be caused by impairment of myocardial function or a structural abnormality. Investigation of the patient is necessary in order to determine the cardiac abnormality which has given rise to the clinical syndrome of heart failure.

The commonest pathologic abnormality of the heart which gives rise to the clinical syndrome of heart failure is disease of the myocardium. Other causes such as valvular heart disease, congenital heart disease and pericardial disease will not be discussed in this text. In ischemic heart disease (acute myocardial infarction [1] and chronic ischemic myocardial damage [2] including left ventricular aneurysm [3]) and dilated cardiomyopathy [4], left ventricular dysfunction may be both systolic and diastolic. Myocardial dysfunction is predominantly diastolic in hypertensive heart disease, hypertrophic cardiomyopathy [5,6] and restrictive cardiomyopathy (e.g. endomyocardial fibrosis [7]). Other causes include specific heart-muscle disease such as alcohol related cardiomyopathy, myocarditis and thyroid disease which cause clinical syndromes indistinguishable from dilated cardiomyopathy. Amyloidosis [8] causes a syndrome similar to restrictive cardiomyopathy. High output states such as Paget's disease, arteriovenous fistula, anemia and Beri-Beri can result in heart failure. Right ventricular dysfunction may accompany left ventricular dysfunction. Any cause of pulmonary hypertension, either acute (massive pulmonary embolism [9]) or chronic (chronic obstructive airways disease, primary pulmonary hypertension, chronic thromboembolic disease) may result in right ventricular myocardial dysfunction and clinical heart failure.

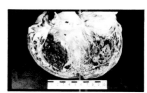

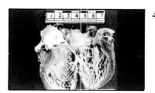

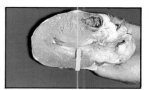

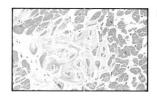

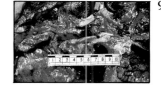

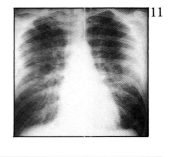

Symptoms

Acute heart failure presents with acute breathlessness and lack of perfusion of vital organs. Breathlessness is mainly caused by pulmonary congestion due to increased left ventricular filling pressure. Lying flat increases pulmonary venous pressure further and causes orthopnea; this may progress to the development of frank pulmonary edema causing attacks of breathlessness at night which wake the patient (paroxysmal nocturnal dyspnea). Unlike acute heart failure the cause of breathlessness in chronic heart failure is less well understood, but is probably more related to reduced perfusion of the tissues than to pulmonary congestion. Occasionally, a non-productive cough may be the only symptom in heart failure. Pulmonary edema is often incorrectly diagnosed as bronchitis. Fatigue in chronic heart failure is mainly due to the reduced cardiac reserve on exercise and inadequate blood flow to exercising muscles.

Acute heart failure may be precipitated by an alteration of cardiac rhythm in patients with pre-existing myocardial dysfunction, fresh damage to the myocardium (e.g. myocardial infarction or myocarditis), inappropriate alterations of therapy and rarely, infection or pulmonary infarction. Occasionally, no precipitating cause can be found.

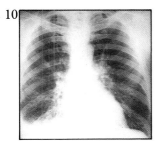

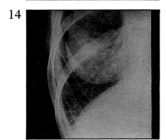

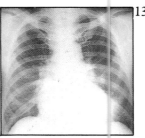

Patients with chronic heart failure may notice the development of fluid retention with swollen ankles and abdominal distention due to ascites or hepatic congestion. The patient with chronic heart failure may complain of nausea, vomiting and loss of weight due to gastrointestinal and hepatic congestion; such patients are frequently thought to have other abdominal pathology.

Acute right ventricular failure due to massive pulmonary embolism presents with circulatory collapse or acute breathlessness.

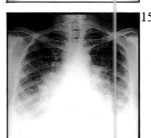

Signs

The physical signs may indicate whether heart failure is due to myocardial dysfunction or some other abnormality. Myocardial dysfunction renders the ventricles stiff and gives rise to a double apical impulse, a gallop rhythm (fourth and/or third heart sound) and secondary mitral or tricuspid regurgitation (pansystolic murmur); primary valvular abnormalities, congenital cardiac abnormalities or pericardial disease have distinctive clinical features.

Low cardiac output with stimulation of the sympathetic and renin-angiotensin-aldosterone systems will be associated with sinus tachycardia, peripheral vasoconstriction and fluid retention, causing a raised jugular venous pressure, pulmonary edema, hepatic congestion, ascites and peripheral edema. Renal, hepatic and cerebral impairment may also occur.

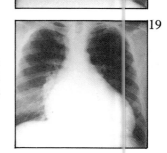

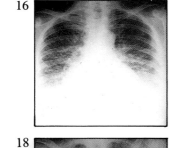

Investigations

Investigation of patients with clinical heart failure is essential in order to diagnose the cause. Valvular, congenital and pericardial disease may be detected but will not be discussed further in this section.

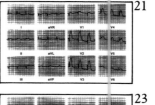

Radiology

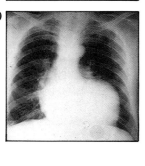

In patients presenting with 'acute' heart failure and breathlessness, the heart size may be normal [10,11] or enlarged. An enlarged heart implies pre-existing heart disease. The chest X-ray will show evidence of raised pulmonary venous pressure, such as dilatation of the upper zone pulmonary vessels, left atrial enlargement [12], Kerley B-lines (short horizontal lines in the peripheral lung fields [13,14]) and occasionally, unilateral or bilateral pleural effusions [15]; these findings correlate well with the elevation of left ventricular filling pressure and left atrial pressure and the consequent high pulmonary capillary wedge pressure. Pulmonary edema is usually bilateral [16] but, occasionally, may be unilateral [17]. In 'chronic' heart failure the heart is usually enlarged and there may [18] or may not [19] be radiologic features associated with raised pulmonary venous pressure. Characteristic radiologic abnormalities are seen in acute pulmonary embolism, cor pulmonale, primary pulmonary hypertension and chronic thromboembolic disease. Features suggestive of a left ventricular aneurysm may also be seen [20].

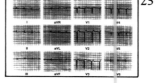

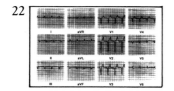

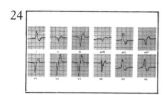

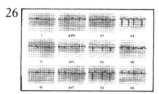

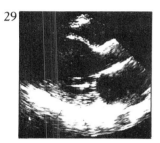

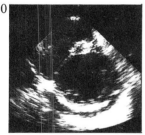

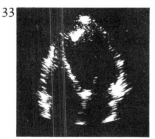

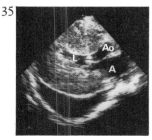

Electrocardiography

A normal ECG should alert the clinician to the possibility that the diagnosis of myocardial failure is incorrect. The ECG may show acute [21] or old [22] myocardial infarction, or evidence of left ventricular aneurysm [23]. Common abnormalities associated with chronic left ventricular dysfunction include left atrial configuration of the 'P' waves, left bundle branch block [24] or only ST/T abnormalities [25]. Patients with heart failure due to myocardial disease often have rhythm abnormalities which may be seen on the routine ECG [26,27] or may be detected only during 24 hour ambulatory monitoring [28]. Right ventricular dysfunction may be associated with right axis deviation and right bundle branch block or evidence of right ventricular hypertrophy.

Echocardiography

The echocardiographic features will reflect the underlying cardiac abnormality. In patients with ischemic heart disease, 2-dimensional echocardiography will show an increase in left ventricular dimensions and reduction in wall motion which may be either regional [29,30] or generalized [31]. Systolic wall thinning and/or dyskinesia are readily apparent from inspection of the systolic and diastolic images. A localized left ventricular aneurysm may be detected by 2-dimensional echocardiography [32] and thrombus within an abnormal ventricle may sometimes be seen [33]. In patients with dilated cardiomyopathy not due to ischemic heart disease, the left ventricular dimensions are again increased and amplitude of wall motion is reduced globally [34]. Slight enlargement of the left atrium, due to chronic elevation of the left ventricular filling pressure, is common.

In hypertrophic cardiomyopathy there is marked left ventricular hypertrophy which may be concentric [35] or predominantly affecting the septum [36] or only the apex. The left ventricular cavity is small and may become obliterated in systole. Systolic anterior motion (SAM) of the anterior mitral valve leaflet may be seen [36] and there may be left atrial enlargement.

In restrictive cardiomyopathy, 2-dimensional echocardiography is helpful in the early diagnosis. Specific cavity changes such as apical and endocardial thickening can be demonstrated. Myocardial infiltration (e.g. endomyocardial fibrosis) gives a particular diagnostic reflection pattern on the grey scale and this can be further enhanced by amplitude process, color-encoded tissue characterization techniques [37].

In patients with right heart failure due to pulmonary hypertension there may be evidence of paradoxical septal motion on M-mode echocardiography, and right ventricular hypertrophy and dilatation will be seen by 2-dimensional echocardiography.

In patients with hypertensive heart disease, 2-dimensional echocardiography may show a hypertrophied but normally contracting left ventricle with diastolic dysfunction, but in more advanced disease, hypertrophy with a dilated and poorly contracting ventricle is seen.

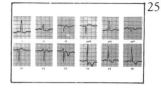

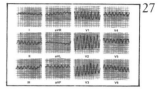

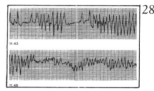

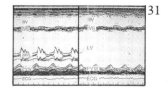

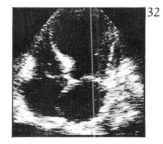

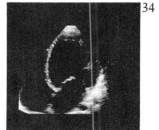

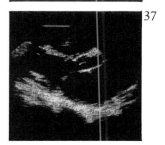

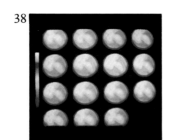

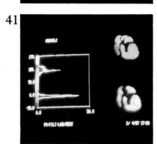

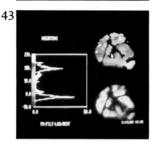

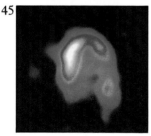

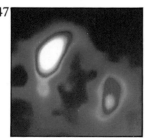

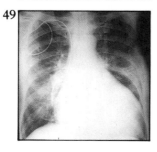

Nuclear Techniques

Nuclear techniques show functional information which complements the anatomical information provided by, for instance, coronary arteriography. An important nuclear cardiologic procedure in patients with congestive heart failure is radionuclide ventriculography using technetium-99m to label the intracardiac blood pools. Imaging is either performed during the first passage of the bolus through the central circulation or when it has reached equilibrium [38,39]. Left ventricular volumes, ejection fraction and parameters of diastolic function such as filling rates can be measured [40]. Unfortunately, the ejection fraction is only an approximate indicator of ventricular performance and is poorly related to the severity of symptoms in congestive heart failure. Many variables in addition to ventricular function influence the ejection fraction, including ventricular preload and afterload. Regional wall motion can also be assessed and helpful methods of displaying both the extent and the timing of contraction are the Fourier amplitude and phase images [41-43]. Imaging during stress allows the response to exercise to be measured and a fall in LVEF and/or new regional wall motion abnormalities are suggestive of exercise induced ischemia.

Regional myocardial perfusion abnormalities causing heart failure can be assessed by thallium-201 scintigraphy. It is possible to define normally perfused [44], reversibly ischemic [45], and infarcted myocardium [46] and to assess the site and extent of abnormalities. Planar images have traditionally been used, but a significant advance has been the use of rotating gamma cameras to acquire images from many angles from which to reconstruct emission tomograms. The three dimensional view of myocardial perfusion provided by tomographic imaging greatly increases the accuracy of assessment and hence the clinical value of the technique. A further development that has increased the scope of the technique is the use of intravenous dipyridamole, a coronary arterial dilator, to induce abnormalities of thallium uptake in patients with coronary artery disease without the need for dynamic exercise [47].

Positron emission tomography allows the imaging of radionuclides such as oxygen-15, nitrogen-13, fluorine-18, and carbon-11. Myocardial perfusion can be assessed quantitatively and myocardial metabolism can also be assessed with radiopharmaceuticals such as flourine-18 deoxyglucose (FDG). In patients with congestive heart failure, regions with reduced perfusion but preserved metabolism (a change from fatty acid uptake to glucose uptake) have been termed 'hibernating myocardium'. Function returns in such areas following revascularization and so positron emission tomography is likely to gain increasing importance in the assessment of patients with ischemic heart failure.

Cardiac Catheterization and Angiography

Bedside monitoring of right heart, hemodynamic variables can be useful in the management of patients with acute heart failure. A balloon-tipped thermodilution catheter [48] positioned with its tip in the pulmonary artery [49] allows accurate measurement of

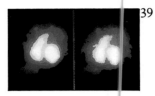

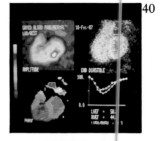

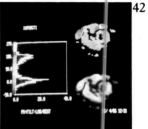

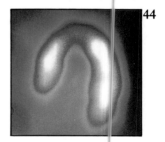

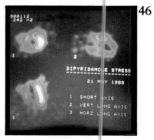

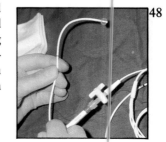

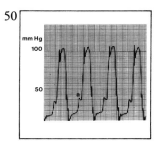

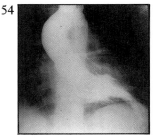

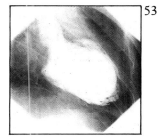

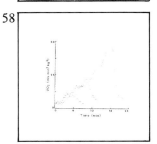

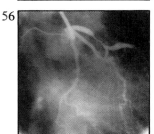

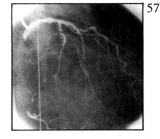

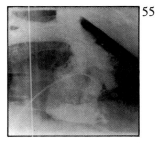

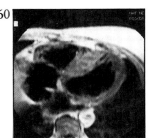

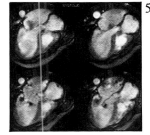

pulmonary artery and wedge pressure and cardiac output, facilitating accurate diagnosis.

In heart failure due to left ventricular disease, the left ventricular end-diastolic pressure is usually elevated, often with a prominent 'a' wave [50]. In hypertrophic cardiomyopathy, intracavity recordings may reveal left ventricular mid-cavity obstruction; restrictive cardiomyopathy causes characteristic hemodynamic abnormalities [51].

Left ventricular angiography is often unnecessary in patients with heart failure as non-invasive techniques will have defined the nature and degree of dysfunction. Localized hypokinesis [52] or left ventricular aneurysm may be seen following myocardial infarction. Alternatively, the left ventricle may be globally hypokinetic in generalized ischemic heart disease or dilated cardiomyopathy [53]. Gross hypertrophy and systolic cavity obliteration is seen in hypertrophic cardiomyopathy [54]. Cavity obliteration and atrioventricular valvar regurgitation is also seen in restrictive cardiomyopathy [55].

Coronary arteriography is performed to demonstrate whether heart failure is due to coronary artery disease and, if so, to assess the possibilities of treatment. Localized stenoses [56] or, more often, widespread coronary disease may be found [57] even in the absence of a history of myocardial infarction or angina.

Exercise Testing

All the investigations referred to above assess the type and degree of left ventricular dysfunction rather than the clinical state of the patient. Exercise testing proves an objective measure of functional impairment in heart failure. Maximal or submaximal tests on a treadmill or bicycle ergometer, with measurement of exercise time or oxygen consumption [58] can be useful in the diagnosis and follow up of symptomatic patients.

Magnetic Resonance Imaging

Magnetic resonance images are maps of the radio signals emitted by the photons within the body (mainly those in water and fat) under the influence of a powerful magnetic field. They reveal cardiac anatomy noninvasively and without the injection of contrast media. Accurate measurements of ventricular volumes [59], wall thickness [60a & 60b] and wall motion [61] can be made, and filling defects such as thrombus are readily detected. The images can be acquired as cine loops to demonstrate moving anatomy, and the turbulence of valvular disease and intracardiac shunting can be encoded in the phase of the magnetic resonance signal. Cine velocity mapping holds great potential for the assessment of vascular disease.

In patients with heart failure, the main application of magnetic resonance imaging is in the accurate measurement and follow up of ventricular function, the detection of thrombus, and the assessment of associated lesions such as mitral regurgitation.

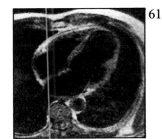

1   Transverse slice (fresh) of the ventricles. A recent (four-day-old) full-thickness myocardial infarction is present in the anterior wall of the left ventricle which extends into the interventricular septum.

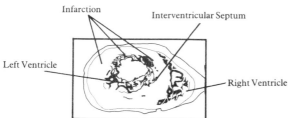

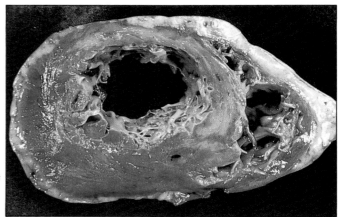

2   Widespread ischemic scarring of the myocardium producing a dilated thin-walled ventricle. A thrombus has formed in one area in relation to the aneurysmal bulge of the ventricular wall.

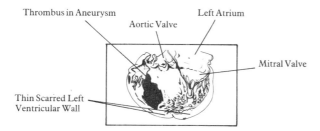

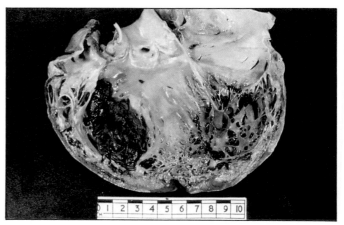

3   Localized left ventricular aneurysm due to previous myocardial infarction. The aneurysm does not contain more than a fine deposit of thrombus and has a larger central cavity opening into the ventricle.

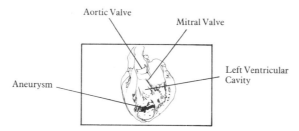

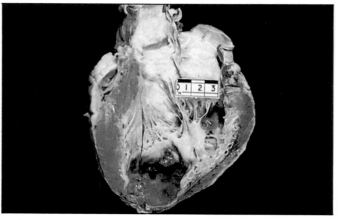

4   Dilated cardiomyopathy: the opened left ventricle has a large cavity and thin wall.

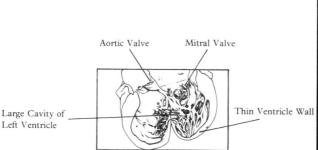

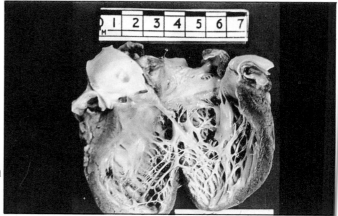

5   Transverse section through heart in hypertrophic cardiomyopathy showing concentric left ventricular hypertrophy.

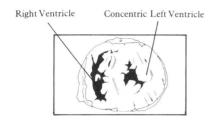

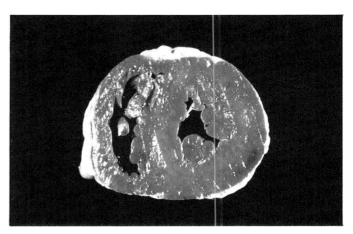

6   The left ventricle from a patient with hypertrophic cardiomyopathy showing a small cavity with very thick wall. The septal region is asymmetrically thickened being at least twice as thick as the parietal wall. The septum bulges into the outflow tract of the left ventricle and impinges onto the anterior cusp of the mitral valve (arrow).

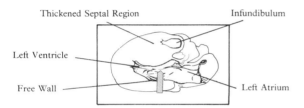

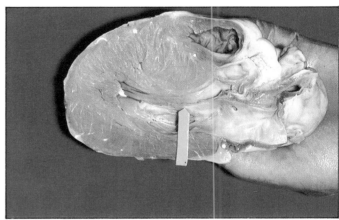

7   Section through the left ventricle in endomyocardial fibrosis. There is marked left ventricular apical obliteration with endocardial thickening and super-added thrombus.

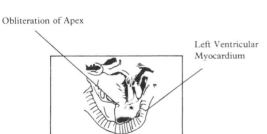

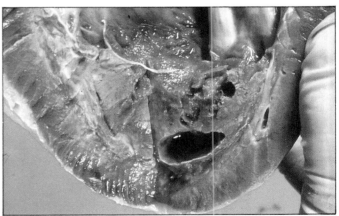

8   Amyloid deposition in the myocardium. In hematoxylin and eosin stained histologic sections amyloid is a pale pink homogeneous material. Amyloid (arrows) is laid down between myocardial cells and ultimately completely surrounds them leaving a lattice of amyloid within which a few residual muscle cells are embedded, staining a deeper pink colour.

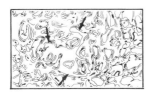

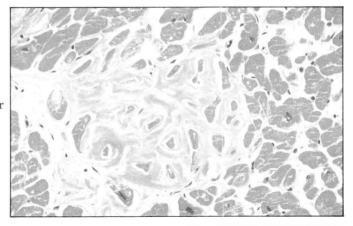

9   Large saddle embolus is seen astride both right and left pulmonary arteries.

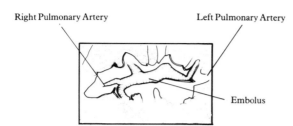

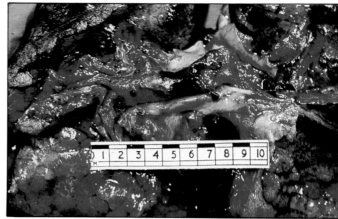

10   Chest radiograph showing a normal sized heart with upper lobe venous distention and a small right pleural effusion, due to recent myocardial infarction.

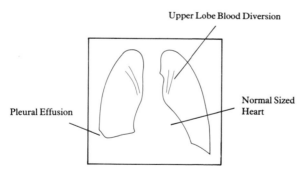

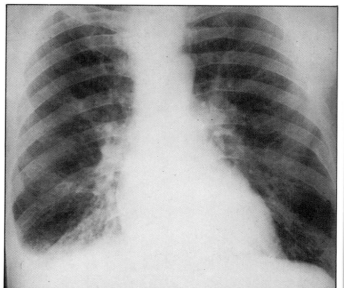

11 Chest radiograph showing a normal sized heart with pulmonary edema.

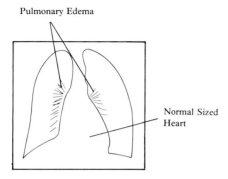

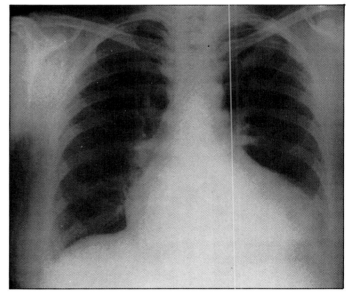

12 Chest radiograph showing large heart and left atrium with pulmonary venous hypertension.

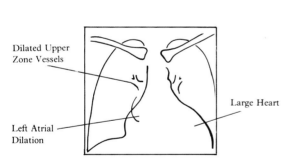

13 Chest radiograph showing cardiomegaly, upper lobe pulmonary venous distention and Kerley B-lines.

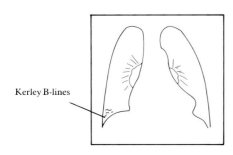

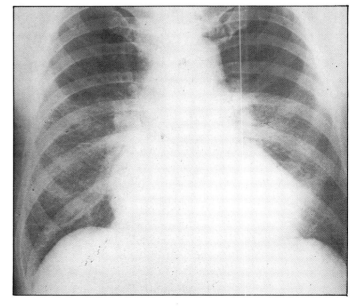

14 Detail from chest radiograph showing septal lines and pleural effusion.

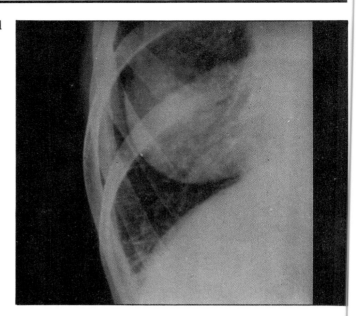

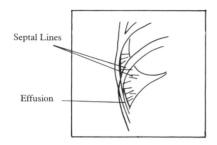

15 Chest radiograph showing pulmonary edema and bilateral pleural effusions following acute myocardial infarction.

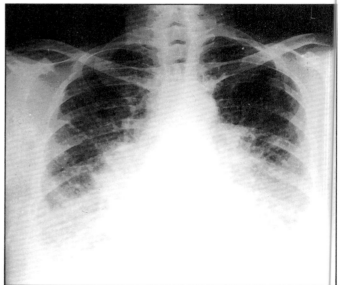

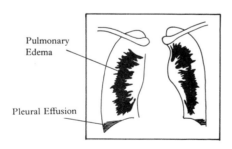

16 Chest radiograph in acute heart failure due to acute myocardial infarction. There is gross pulmonary edema.

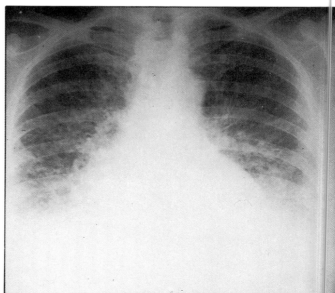

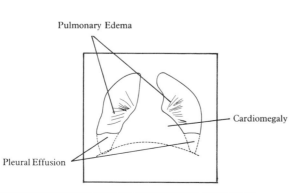

17 Chest radiograph showing cardiomegaly and pulmonary edema of the right lung only.

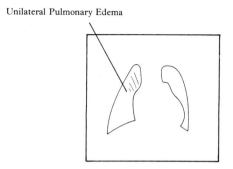

Unilateral Pulmonary Edema

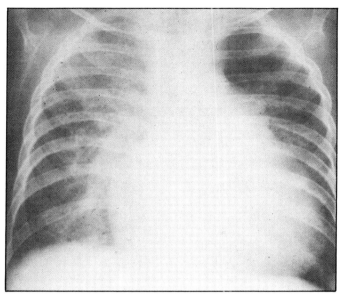

18 Chest radiograph showing cardiomegaly with features of raised pulmonary venous pressure (enlarged veins and upper zone blood diversion).

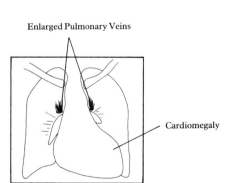

Enlarged Pulmonary Veins

Cardiomegaly

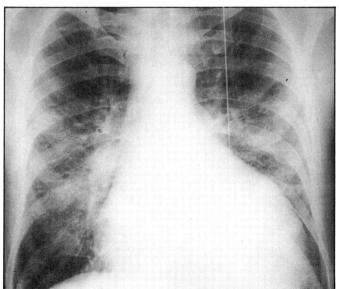

19 Chest radiograph showing an enlarged heart without upper zone blood diversion.

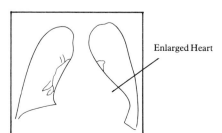

Enlarged Heart

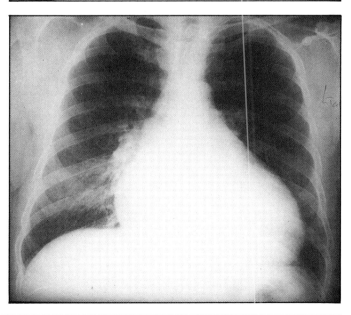

20 Chest radiograph showing a bulge on the left heart border suggestive of a left ventricular aneurysm.

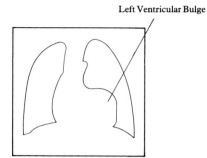

Left Ventricular Bulge

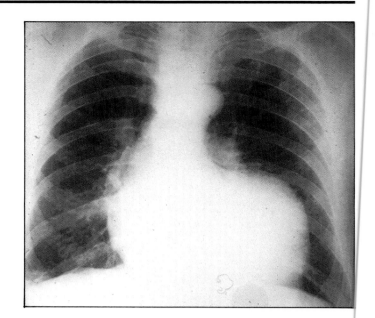

HEART FAILURE

Electrocardiography

21

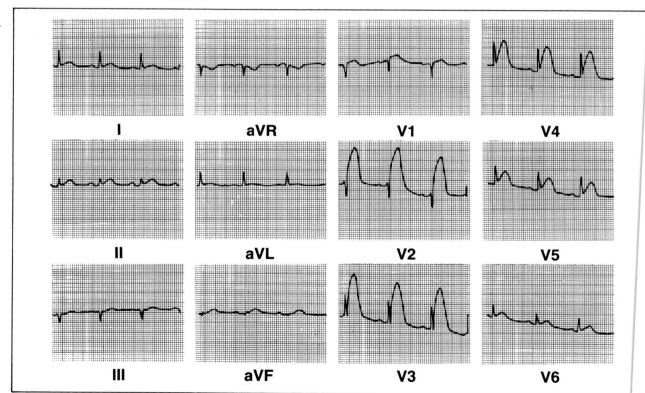

I	aVR	V1	V4
II	aVL	V2	V5
III	aVF	V3	V6

Electrocardiogram showing the very early changes of anterior myocardial infarction (30 min after onset of pain). There is ST elevation in leads I, II, and across all the V leads, but no Q wave development yet.

22

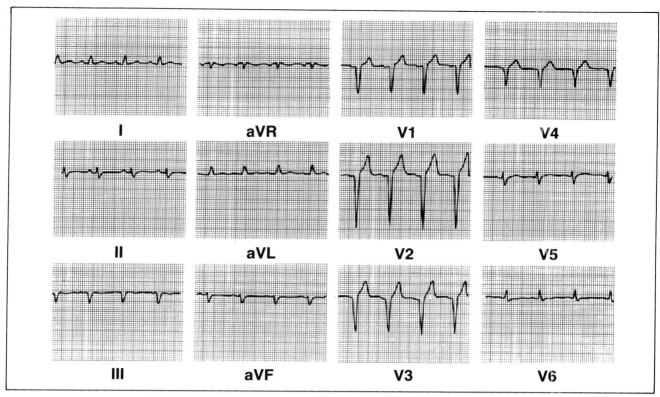

Electrocardiogram of a patient with chronic ischemic heart disease, showing old anterior infarction, with Q waves in V_{1-4} and poor R wave progression in V_{5-6}.

23

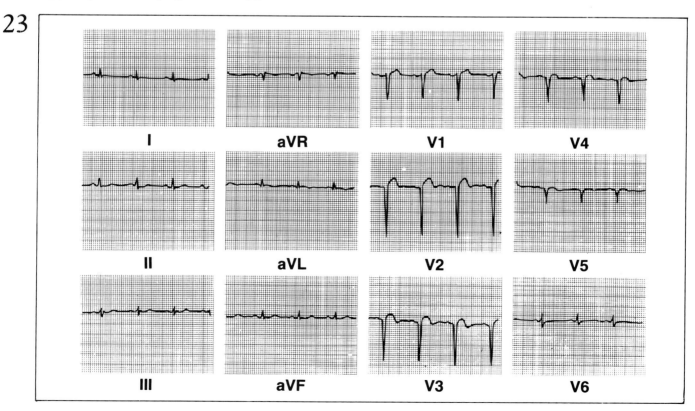

Electrocardiogram in a patient with left ventricular aneurysm, showing Q waves and persistent ST elevation in the anterior chest leads, six months after myocardial infarction.

24

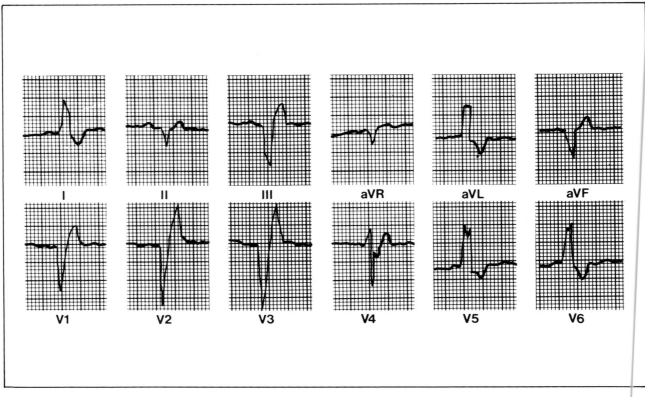

Electrocardiogram in a patient with dilated cardiomyopathy showing left bundle branch block.

25

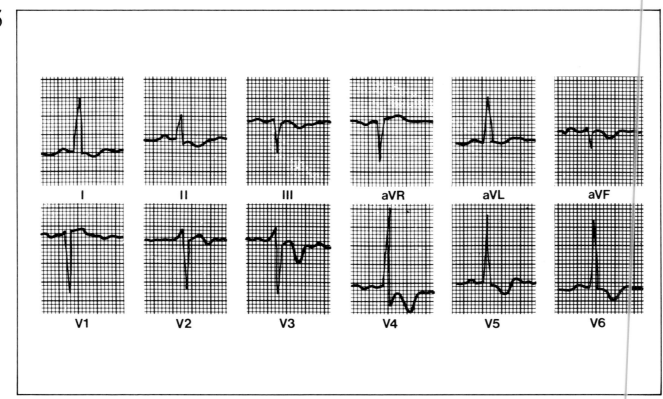

Electrocardiogram in a patient with dilated cardiomyopathy showing non-specific ST/T abnormalities.

26

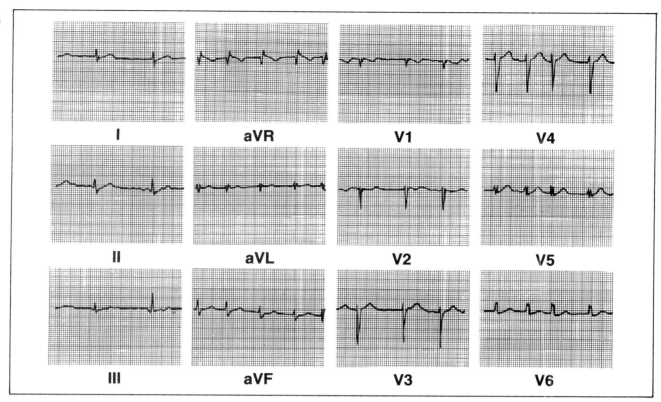

Electrocardiogram of a patient with dilated cardiomyopathy, showing atrial fibrillation, poor R wave progression in the chest leads, and partial left bundle branch block, but no Q waves.

27

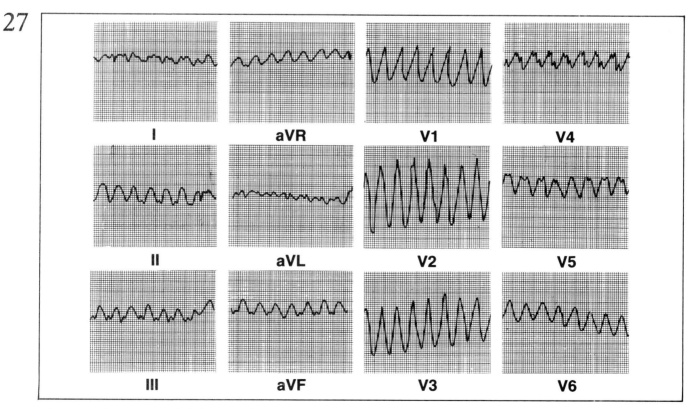

Electrocardiogram recorded from a patient with dilated cardiomyopathy, taken when he complained of dizziness. The 12 lead ECG shows ventricular tachycardia.

28

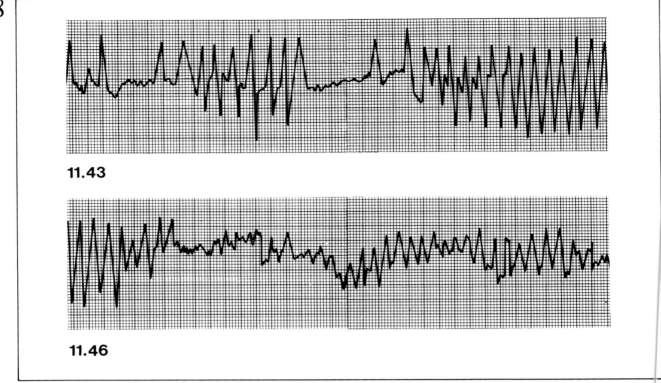

11.43

11.46

Ambulatory ECG recording from a patient with heart failure. On returning home with the recorder at 11.35, the patient sat down to drink a cup of coffee. At 11.43 he developed ventricular tachycardia and collapsed. At 11.46 ventricular fibrillation developed and the patient died.

29

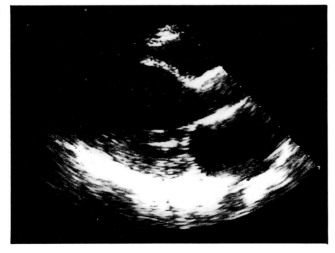 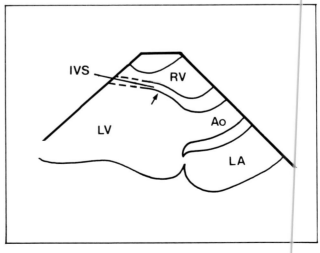

2-D echocardiographic systolic long axis view in a patient with septal infarction showing thinning of the septum (arrow) bulging into the right ventricle.

30

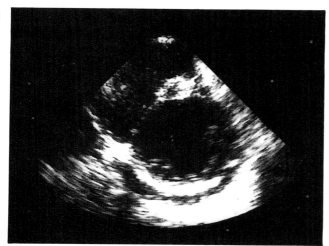
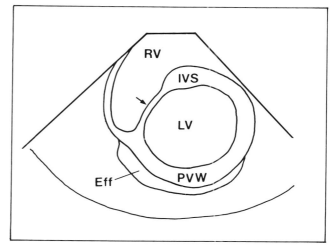

2-D echocardiographic systolic short axis view at level of papillary muscles in a patient with septal infarction. There is thinning of the septum (arrow) in relation to the anterior wall, and there is a pericardial effusion.

31

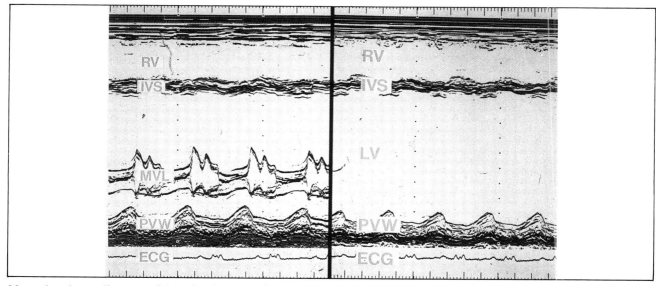

M-mode echocardiogram of the mitral valve (left) and left ventricle (right) in a patient with severe generalized left ventricular dysfunction due to coronary artery disease.

32

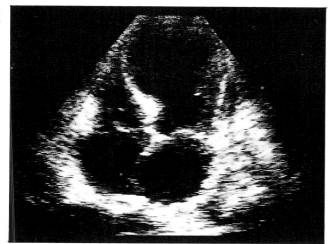
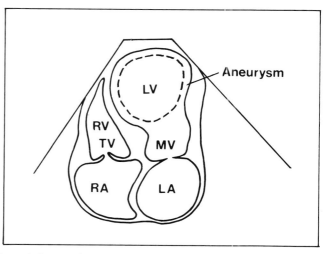

2-D echocardiographic apical four-chamber view showing a large left ventricular aneurysm.

33

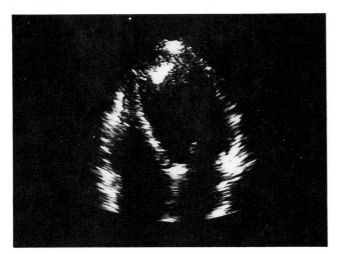 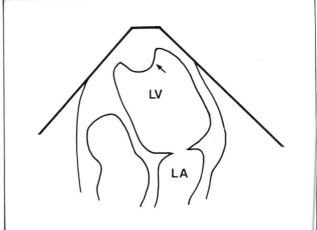

2-D echocardiographic apical four-chamber view showing apical thrombus (arrow) in a patient with an old apical myocardial infarction.

34

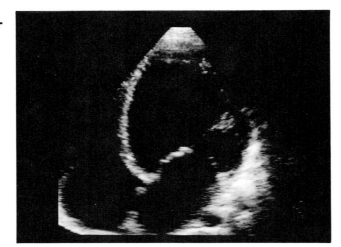 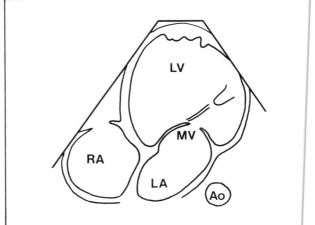

2-D echocardiographic apical four-chamber view showing left ventricular dilatation in dilated cardiomyopathy. Note the thin-walled globular left ventricle. The irregularities in the apex may be due to mural thrombus.

35

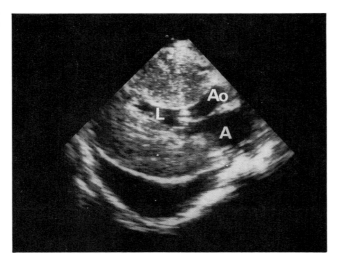 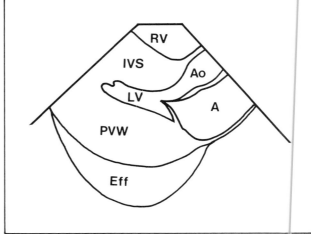

2-D echocardiographic parasternal long axis systolic view in hypertrophic cardiomyopathy with gross symmetric hypertrophy of the left ventricle and slit-like cavity. Note additional pericardial effusion.

36

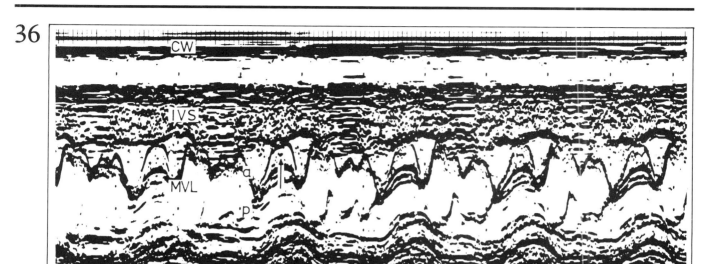

M-mode echocardiogram of hypertrophic cardiomyopathy with left ventricular outflow obstruction. The echocardiogram shows systolic anterior movement of the anterior leaflet (arrowed) which also strikes the septum at the onset of diastole.

37

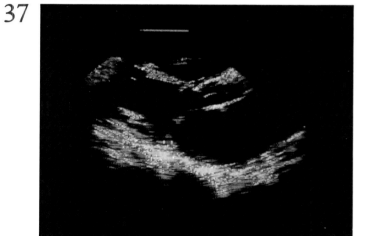

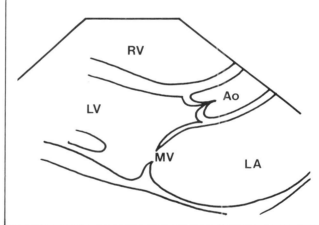

2-D echocardiographic amplitude processed color-encoded long axis parasternal view in endomyocardial fibrosis showing increased echo density and endocardial thickening on the posterior left ventricular wall, thickening and tethering of the posterior mitral valve leaflet and left atrial dilatation.

38 Gated blood pool scan in a normal subject : 16 frames have been acquired (end systole at frame 4, end diastole at frame 1).

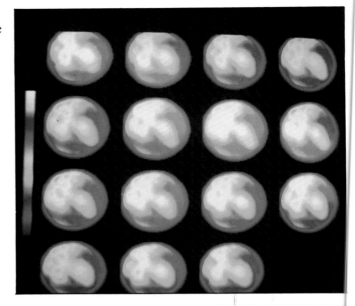

39 Gated blood pool scan in dilated cardiomyopathy showing little difference in the size of the ventricular cavities between end-diastole (left) and end-systole (right).

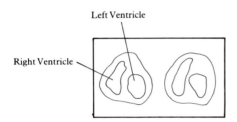

Left Ventricle

Right Ventricle

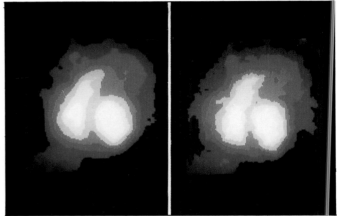

40 End-diastolic frames of equilibrium gated blood pool scans (top right) with regions of interest outlining the right and left ventricular cavities. By measuring the counts in these regions throughout the cardiac cycle, an accurate measure of the change in cavity volume can be made, to yield volume curves and calculated ejection fractions (EF) (bottom right);
a) Normal (LVEF 58%, RVEF 44%),
b) LV aneurysm (LVEF 23%, RVEF 24%),
c) Dilated cardiomyopathy (LVEF 10%, RVEF 11%).

(a)
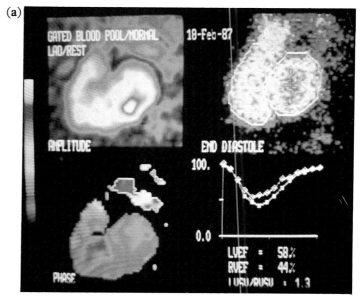

(b)
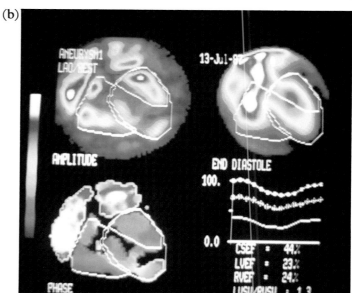

(c)
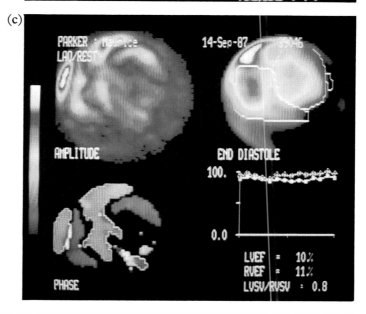

41 Parametric imaging. By constructing volume curves throughout the cardiac cycle from each pixel of a gated blood pool scan, the computer can generate color-encoded images of amplitude of regional wall motion, and phase of wall motion. In this normal heart the amplitude image (bottom right) shows vigorous left ventricular contraction. The phase image (top right) shows both ventricles contract uniformly and in synchrony (coded blue), with the atria 180° out of phase (i.e. contract in diastole) (coded red), giving two sharp peaks at 0° and 180° on the phase histogram.

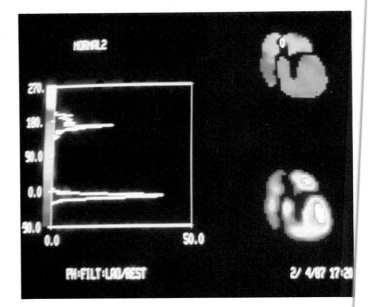

42 Parametric images following myocardial infarction. The amplitude image reveals poor amplitude of left ventricular wall motion. The phase image is fragmented, showing discoordinate ventricular contraction, giving poorly defined peaks on the phase histogram.

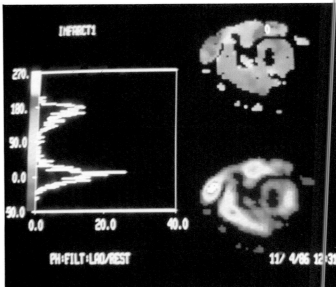

43 Parametric images from a patient with left ventricular aneurysm. The amplitude image shows reduced apical movement and the phase image shows clearly that motion of the apex is out of phase compared to the rest of the ventricle.

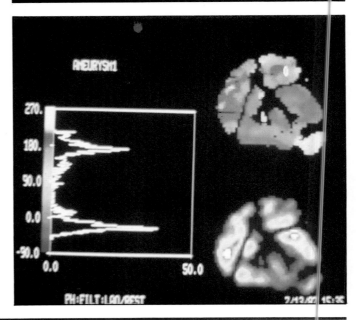

44 Normal thallium-201 myocardial perfusion emission tomograms in vertical and horizontal long axis and short axis planes. There is uniform uptake of thallium throughout the myocardium.

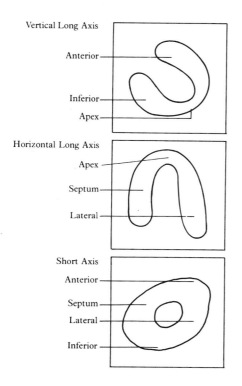

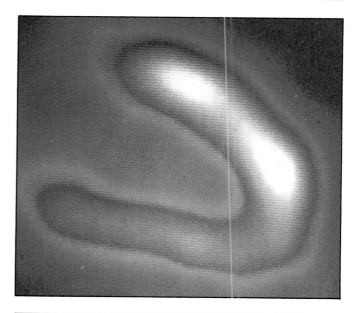

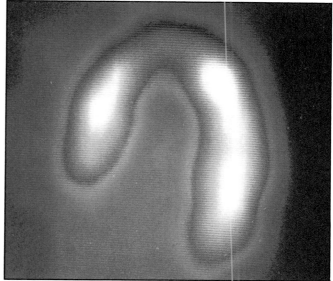

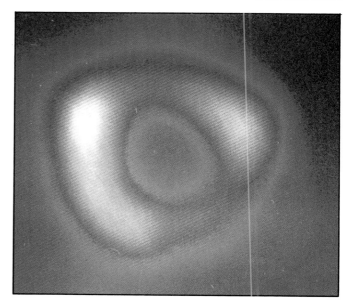

45 Stress and redistribution horizontal long axis tomograms showing reversible lateral wall ischemia in a patient with left circumflex coronary artery disease. The extent of ischemia is limited.

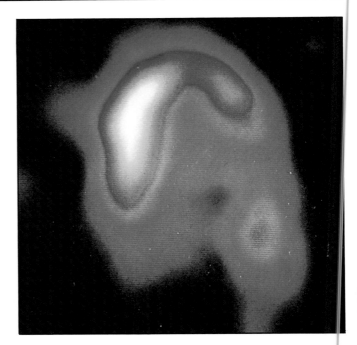

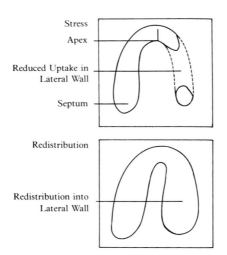

Stress

Apex

Reduced Uptake in Lateral Wall

Septum

Redistribution

Redistribution into Lateral Wall

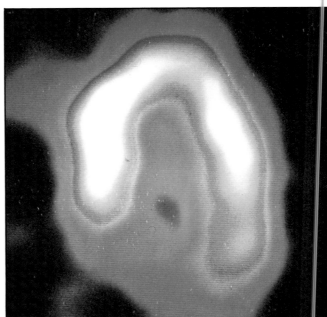

46 Stress and redistribution tomograms showing inferior infarction and reversible anteroseptal and apical ischemia. The patient presented with congestive heart failure.

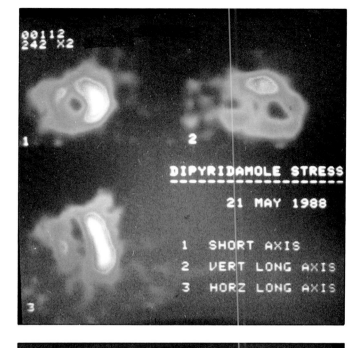

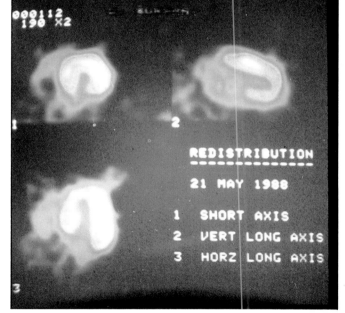

Stress

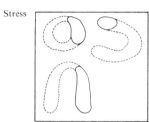

Redistribution

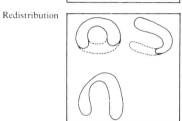

47

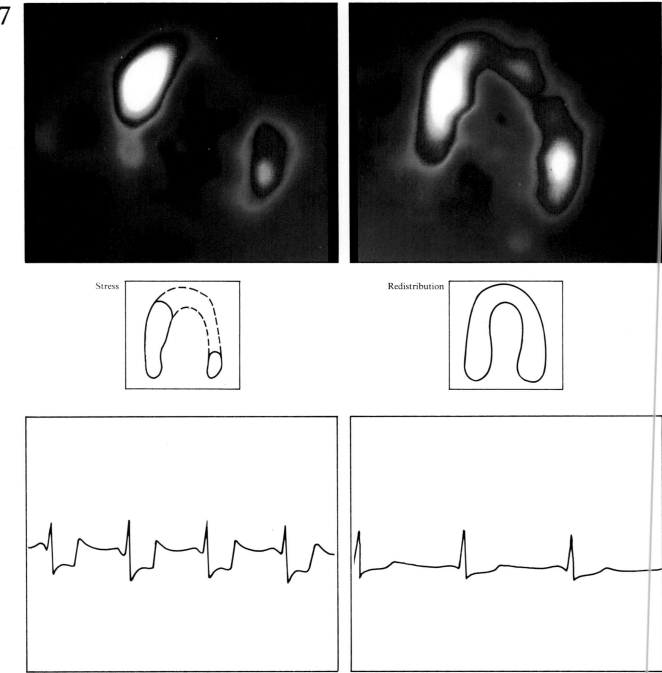

Stress and redistribution horizontal long axis tomograms with ECG showing reversible ischemia of the lateral wall and basal septum. In this case, the abnormality was induced by intravenous infusion of dipyridamole and no exercise was necessary.

48 A balloon-tipped thermodilution catheter for right heart hemodynamic monitoring.

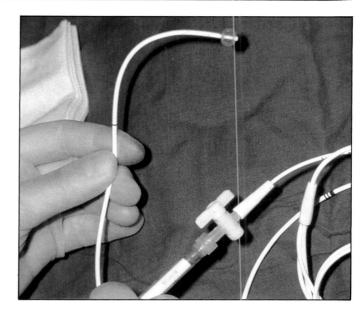

49 Chest radiograph showing a catheter inserted via the right subclavian vein, positioned with its tip in the right pulmonary artery for measurement of wedge pressure.

Balloon Tipped Catheter

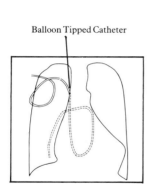

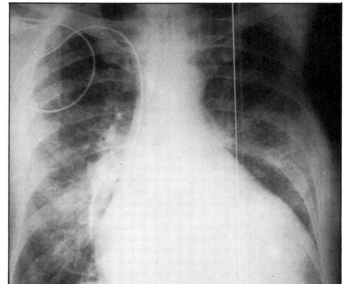

50 Pressure recording from the left ventricle in a patient with heart failure. The end-diastolic pressure is raised and there is a prominent 'a' wave.

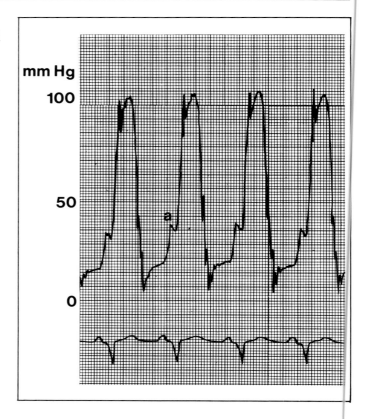

51 Pressure recordings taken from the right and left ventricles simultaneously in endomyocardial fibrosis showing the typical 'dip and plateau' and the elevated and different end diastolic pressure measurements.

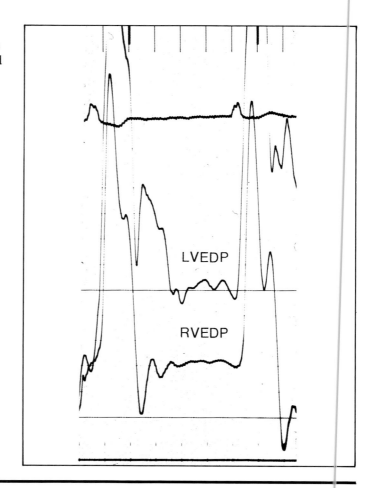

52

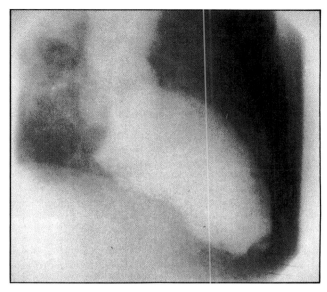

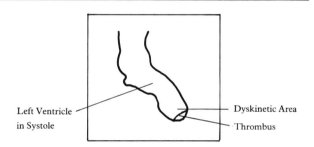

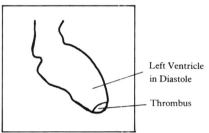

Left ventricular angiogram in the right anterior oblique projection. Systolic (left) and diastolic (right) frames reveal presence of apical dyskinesis and thrombus.

53

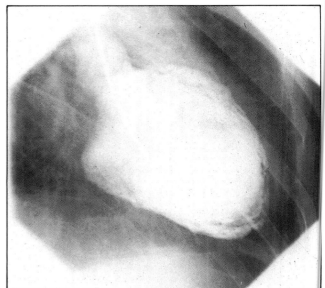
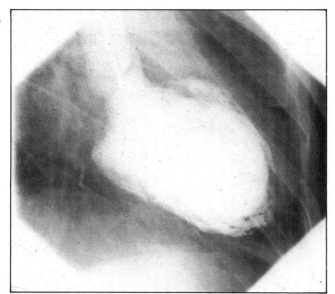

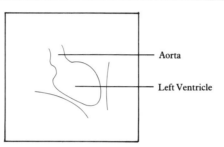
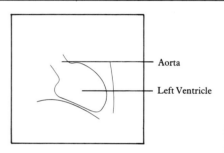

Left ventricular angiogram in the right anterior oblique projection with systolic (left) and diastolic (right) frames showing global hypokinesis and ventricular dilatation.

54 Left ventricular angiogram in hypertrophic cardiomyopathy showing in systole (antero-posterior projection) a small irregular cavity.

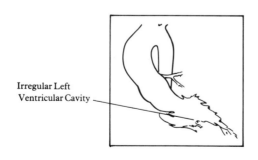

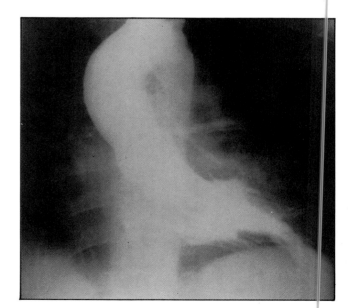

55 Right ventricular angiogram showing apical cavity obliteration and tricuspid regurgitation due to endomyocardial fibrosis.

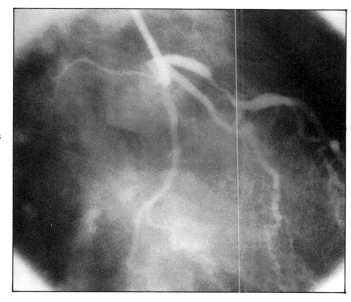

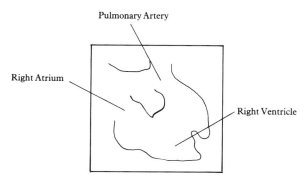

56 Coronary arteriogram (right anterior oblique projection) showing a long severe narrowing of the left anterior descending coronary artery.

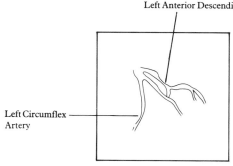

57 Coronary arteriogram (right anterior oblique projection) in three vessel coronary disease. The left coronary has been injected showing extensive disease, with retrograde filling of the right coronary artery.

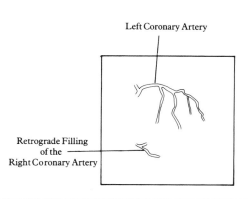

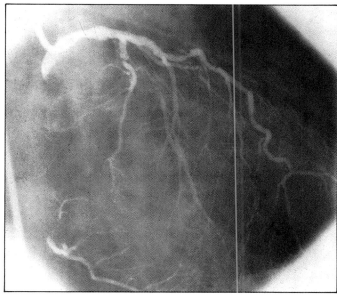

58 Oxygen consumption (VO_2) during symptom limited treadmill exercise and on recovery, in a normal subject (right), a patient with moderate heart failure (middle) and a patient with severe heart failure (left). At rest and during the first 5 minutes of exercise all three subjects have similar oxygen consumption, but peak VO_2 is progressively reduced with increasing heart failure.

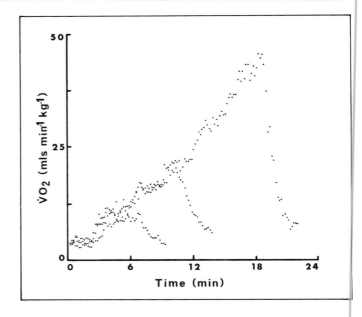

59 Magnetic resonance imaging in dilated cardiomyopathy. Four frames from a cine acquisition in the horizontal long axis plane using a field echo sequence where blood appears with high signal (white) except where there is turbulence. There is global left ventricular hypokinesia.

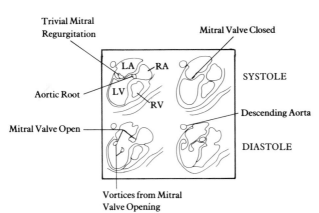

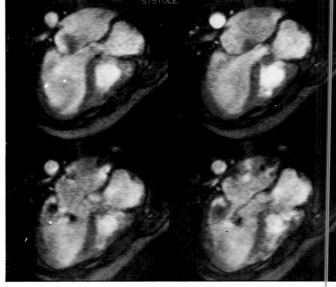

60 Magnetic resonance imaging in hypertrophic cardiomyopathy (HCM). Diastolic (a) and systolic (b) transverse sections showing asymmetric septal hypertrophy. The high signal from the septal myocardium is a consequence of altered relaxation times in the abnormal muscle.

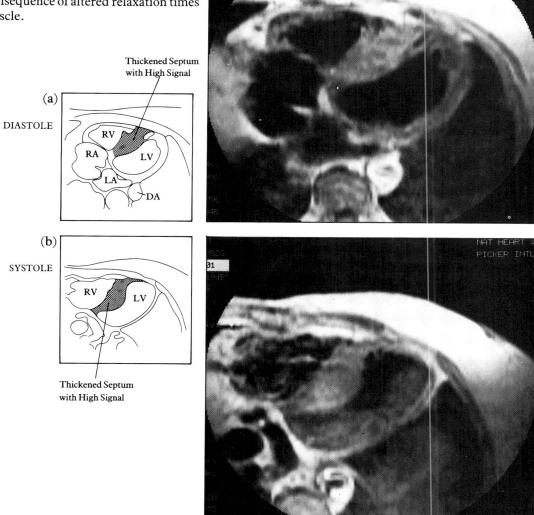

Thickened Septum with High Signal

(a) DIASTOLE — RV, RA, LV, RA, LA, DA

(b) SYSTOLE — RV, LV

Thickened Septum with High Signal

61

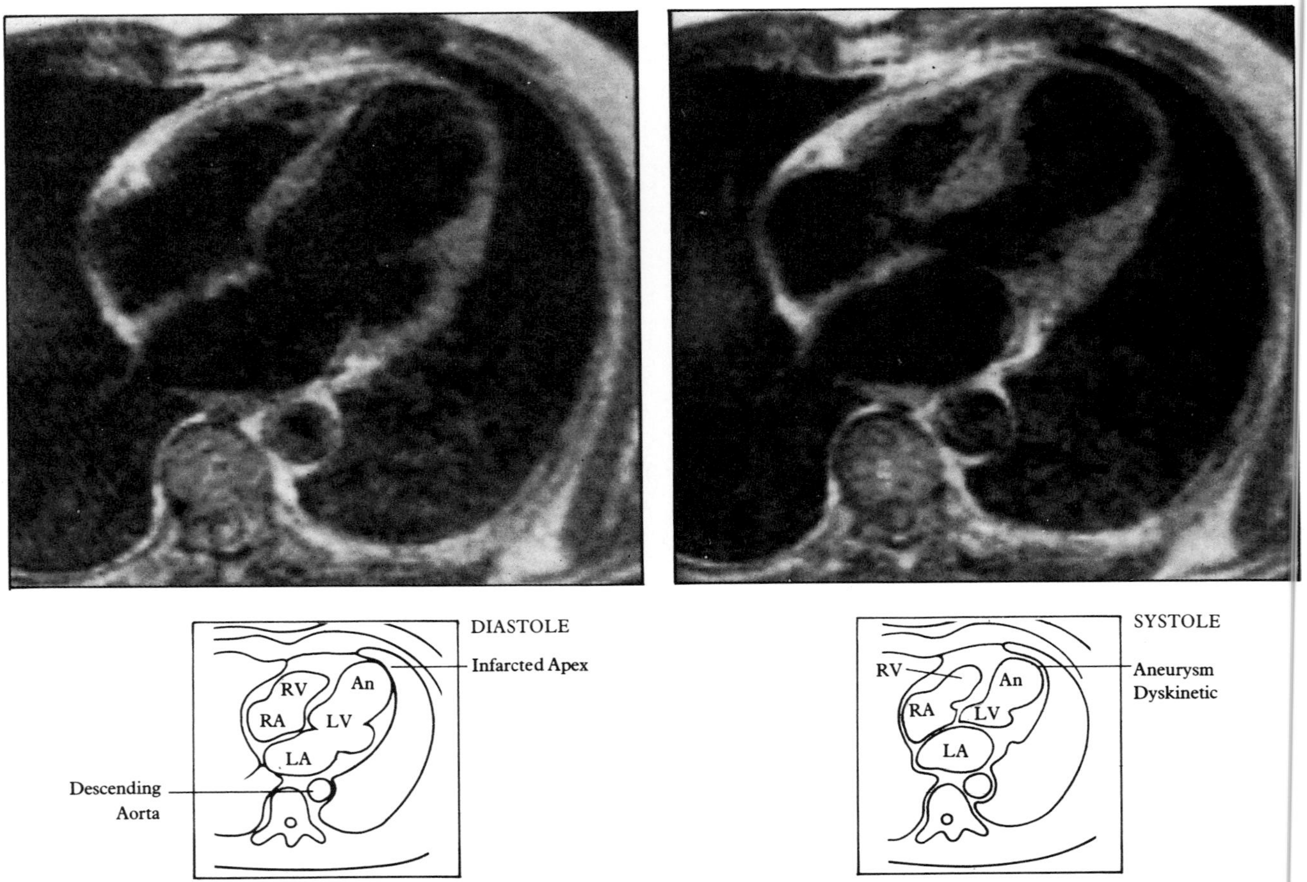

DIASTOLE

- Infarcted Apex

RV | An
RA | LV
LA

Descending Aorta

SYSTOLE

Aneurysm Dyskinetic

RV
RA | An
LV
LA

Magnetic resonance imaging in left ventricular aneurysm. Diastolic (left) and systolic (right) transverse sections in a patient with previous infarction and an apical left ventricular aneurysm. The basal myocardium contracts well whilst the apical myocardium is thin and dyskinetic.

Chapter 3.
Hypertension

Prevalence

Hypertension is defined by selecting an arbitrary cut-off point for systolic and diastolic blood pressures. Since there is no natural dividing line, the proportion of hypertensive patients in any population depends upon the judgement of the observer [1]. The most widely used criterion is that chosen by the Expert Sub-Committee of the World Health Organization i.e. 160/95 mmHg or above. Using this criterion the prevalence of hypertension ranges from about 3% in subjects below the age of 20 to over 40% of the male population in the older age groups. The overall prevalence on single readings lies between 15% and 20%. When repeated measurements are taken the observed blood pressure falls and therefore the observed prevalence of hypertension falls *pari passu*.

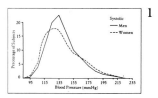

High blood pressure is a multifactorial condition in which both environmental and genetic factors play an important part. It is, for instance, more common in obese subjects, in those consuming large amounts of alcohol and in subjects with a strong family history of this condition. Hypertension is commonly classified according to its cause. Individuals in whom the only apparent factor is a genetic predisposition are regarded as having primary or essential hypertension whilst individuals in whom a specific cause can be identified are regarded as having secondary hypertension. This subdivision, whilst convenient, suffers from the disadvantage that the overwhelming majority of hypertensive patients in the given population will have essential hypertension. The true prevalence of the two classes of hypertension is difficult to establish as most specialists in the area deal with highly selected populations usually biased towards secondary hypertension. However, it is unlikely that more than 5% of hypertensive population suffer from secondary hypertension. When evident causes such as obesity, alcohol and the contraceptive pill are excluded, the true prevalence of secondary hypertension is probably less than 1%.

Hypertension can also be classified into so called 'benign' or 'accelerated' (malignant) hypertension. Although this is a clinically useful subdivision, the term 'benign' is a misnomer as any chronic elevation of blood pressure carries an increased risk of strokes, heart attacks and peripheral vascular disease. In addition, the same patient may show evidence of both benign and accelerated hypertension at different times. Accelerated hypertension is best considered as a phase in either essential or secondary hypertension characterized by certain clinical and pathologic features.

Pathology

Hypertension gives rise to changes throughout the arterial tree. Pathologic changes may also occur in organs supplied by those vessels ('target organs'). In addition, some of the conditions which cause hypertension may give rise to pathologic appearances in the relevant tissues. Such causes are shown in Table 1.

Table 1
Causes of Secondary Hypertension

Renovascular,	Renal Parenchymal,	Endocrine,
Pregnancy,	Medications,	Coarctation,
Neurologic,	Dietetic (alcohol and obesity)	

Renal Hypertension

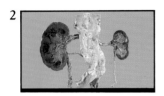

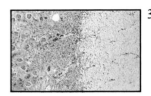

Diseases of the renal blood vessels may cause hypertension (renovascular hypertension) as may diseases of the kidney itself (renal parenchymal hypertension).

Renovascular hypertension is produced by unilateral or bilateral renal ischemia [2,3]. The two commonest causes of this are atheroma of the renal arteries and fibromuscular dysplasia. The former causes discrete areas of narrowing associated with atheromatous plaques, most commonly situated at the mouth of the renal artery. The most common form of fibromuscular dysplasia gives rise to regular fibromuscular ridges separated by thin segments of the vessel wall. The cause is unknown but it usually occurs in a younger age group than atheroma and is more common in female patients and smokers.

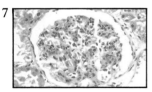

In addition to these intrinsic diseases of the renal artery, ischemia may be produced by fibrous bands compressing the vessel or by tumors [4].

The three commonest forms of renal parenchymal disease giving rise to hypertension are chronic pyelonephritis [5], chronic glomerulonephritis and polycystic kidney. Hypertension may also be seen in less common diseases affecting the kidney such as scleroderma [6], polyarteritis nodosa, disseminated lupus erythematosus and analgesic nephropathy.

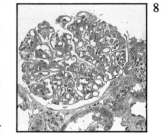

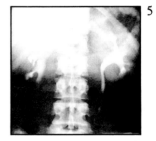

Hypertension is a common feature of acute glomerulonephritis and is seen in most patients with proliferative glomerulonephritis [7] at some stage in the course of their disease. It is less common in membranous glomerulonephritis [8] and not observed in minimal change nephropathy [9]. Macroscopically, in the acute stage of glomerulonephritis the kidneys may be swollen but as chronic glomerulonephritis proceeds they become shrunken. The more florid, proliferative glomerular changes are associated with more severe degrees of hypertension.

Endocrine Causes of Hypertension

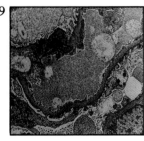

Both glucocorticoid and mineralocorticoid adrenal secretions produce hypertension. Glucocorticoids produce the characteristic appearances of Cushing's syndrome [10] which may be due to either adrenal tumors or hyperplasia. The latter may be secondary to stimulation of the adrenal glands as a result of a basophil pituitary tumor. Primary aldosteronism (Conn's syndrome [11]) results from hypersecretion of aldosterone which, in addition to producing hypertension, gives rise to a characteristic hypokalemic alkalosis. The majority of cases of primary aldosteronism are due to a tumor but a substantial minority are caused by bilateral multinodular hyperplasia. The biochemical changes are usually less marked in this condition. Adrenal medullary tumors produce hypertension through secretion of excessive amounts of the catecholamines, noradrenaline and adrenaline (pheochromocytoma) [12]. Occasionally, these tumors may lie outside the adrenal glands, developing in sympathetic tissue in, for instance, the urinary bladder, thorax, organ of Zuckerkandl or other situations within the abdomen. These tumors are loaded with stored catecholamines [13] and manipulation, i.e. during palpation of the abdomen or during surgery, may cause the release of catecholamines and disastrous paroxysmal hypertension.

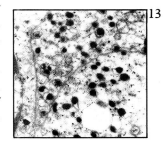

Hypertension is frequently seen in rare endocrine conditions such as acromegaly, myxedema or hyperparathyroidism. It frequently regresses when these conditions are treated medically or surgically.

Medication

Hypertension may be iatrogenic e.g. due to steroid treatment or as a result of the contraceptive pill. A slight elevation of blood pressure is produced by medication which causes fluid retention e.g. carbenoxolone or non-steroidal antiinflammatory drugs. It can also be produced by drugs which mimic the action of the sympathetic nervous system such as ephedrine, amphetamine and monoamine oxidase inhibitors taken with tyramine containing foods. Withdrawal of clonidine may cause hypertension through increased sympathetic activity.

Hypertension of Pregnancy

Hypertension may occur in pregnancy as a result of pre-existing renal disease or essential hypertension. In addition, hypertension may occur (particularly in first pregnancies) after the thirtieth week of gestation in association with proteinuria and edema (pre-eclamptic toxemia). Renal biopsy in such patients has shown enlarged edematous glomeruli with narrowing of the capillary lumina and swelling of endothelial cells [14].

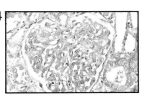

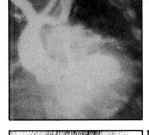

Coarctation

This is a congenital narrowing of the aorta usually just below the origin of the left subclavian artery, causing hypertension proximal to the lesion [15,16].

Large Arteries and Arterioles

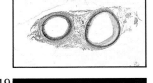

Increased perfusion pressure causes hypertrophy of the smooth muscle of the vascular media. The internal elastic lamina becomes duplicated and there is fibrous thickening of the sub-intimal part of the artery [17,18]. The aorta and larger vessels arising from it are slightly dilated and lose some of their elasticity. The peripheral large arteries may become elongated and tortuous [19] so that visible pulsations may be noticeable, particularly in older subjects. Atheroma is more frequently seen in hypertensive patients [20].

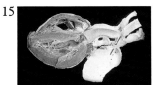

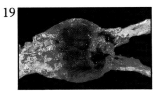

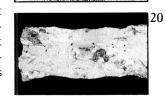

Small Arteries and Arterioles

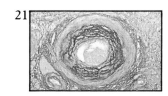

Medial hypertrophy occurs with an increased collagen content in the media [21]. Sub-intimal thickening is more pronounced and as a result the lumen of the vessel is narrowed. The increase in wall to lumen ratio in the smaller arteries and arterioles causes an increased resistance to flow and may therefore help to perpetuate and, indeed, amplify blood pressure elevation. Arterioles characteristically display hyaline thickening which develops gradually from patchy deposition until, in longstanding hypertension, it may replace the structure of the arteriolar wall leaving only the endothelium intact [22]. It is most frequently seen in the arterioles of the abdominal viscera and in the renal vessels. It is probably not of great functional significance.

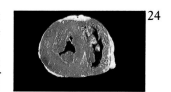

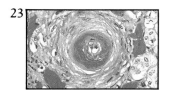

Patients with accelerated (malignant) hypertension usually have fibrinoid necrosis [23] of the smaller arteries; this arises because hypertensive damage results in increased permeability of the vascular endothelium to plasma proteins. The vessel wall is replaced by a structureless fibrin-like material containing plasma protein components. A distinct lesion, but often associated with fibrinoid necrosis, is progressive extreme intimal thickening by concentric collagenous rings (onion skinning).

The Heart

The need to contract against increased resistance produces left ventricular hypertrophy in hypertensive patients [24]. With the development of sensitive non-invasive methods such as echocardiography it has become apparent that a mild degree of left ventricular hypertrophy occurs quite early in the development of hypertension. This is not reflected in changes in the external cardiac profile but is associated with a slight reduction in cavity volume and in compliance of the left ventricle. This has important functional consequences since prognosis of hypertension is worse in patients with more marked degrees of left ventricular hypertrophy. Left ventricular failure [25] in hypertension is associated with dilatation of the left ventricle.

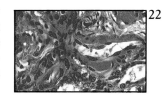

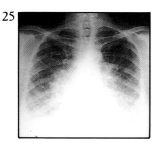

In addition to these direct consequences of increased afterload, coronary atheroma is much more frequent in hypertensive patients [26]. Myocardial infarction is the most frequent cause of death in hypertensive patients and is three times as common as stroke.

The Brain

Hypertension has both direct and indirect effects upon the brain. Increased prevalence of atheroma in both extracranial and intracranial vessels increases the risk of cerebral infarction either as a result of *in situ* thrombosis or embolization from a distant site.

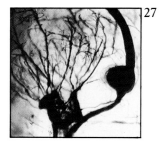

Intracerebral hemorrhage occurs as a result of rupture of a Charcot-Bouchard aneurysm [27]. These are small degenerative lesions occurring in the basal ganglia, thalamus and internal capsule. Thrombosis of these aneurysms may also give rise to small lacunar infarctions in the brain, causing minor strokes.

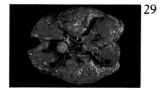

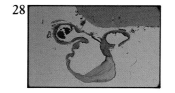

Aneurysms of the circle of Willis are congenital lesions giving rise to subarachnoid hemorrhage [28,29]. Whilst they are more

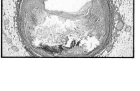

frequent in hypertensive patients, they also often cause subarachnoid hemorrhage in normotensive patients.

Sudden acute rises in cerebral perfusion pressure give rise to focal areas of vasodilatation in the smaller arteries and arterioles of the brain. The dilated areas are abnormally permeable and cause local cerebral edema. This is the pathologic basis of hypertensive encephalopathy.

The Kidneys

Renal failure is very rare in patients with essential hypertension unless they have entered the accelerated phase. Nevertheless, histologic changes are evident. Atheroma of the renal vessels or renal embolization from the aorta or renal arteries may cause infarction and scarring. The renal vessels show the changes of hypertension described above. Hyaline degeneration is particularly evident, often in the afferent glomerular arterioles. The normal loss of nephrons with ageing is accelerated in essential hypertension so that histologically nephrosclerosis becomes evident. There is frequently a moderate reduction in renal size with diffuse cortical thinning [30]. Scarring of the surface of the kidney leads to an adherent capsule with an irregular sub-capsular surface. Whilst vascular disease usually produces a slight reduction in renal blood flow, glomerular filtration rate is maintained.

Both renal blood flow and glomerular filtration rate are reduced in accelerated hypertension as a result of the vascular lesions of malignant hypertension. Renal failure may progress rapidly. The afferent renal arterioles are particularly susceptible to fibrinoid necrosis. The afferent arteriole wall is disrupted, the lumen is often completely obliterated and therefore the distal glomerulus is destroyed. Since this is a relatively acute process the kidneys are usually normal in size and the sub-capsular surface is spotted with tiny hemorrhages [31].

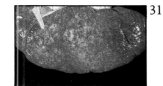

Symptoms

In the majority of patients hypertension gives rise to no symptoms until target organ damage occurs. There is, however, an increased incidence of nocturia and epistaxis in hypertensive patients. Hypertensive headaches are characteristically situated in the occiput, throbbing in character and occurring in the early morning. However, the vast majority of headaches in hypertensive patients are not attributable to high blood pressure.

Physical Signs

The pulse is usually normal in hypertensive patients. Marked left ventricular hypertrophy gives rise to a forceful displaced apex beat. The aortic component of the second sound may be accentuated and an ejection systolic murmur may be heard in the aortic area. Advanced hypertensive disease may give rise to signs of left ventricular failure or aortic regurgitation.

Fundal appearances give best assessment of the vascular tree during clinical examination. Thickening of the arterial wall gives rise to an increased reflection of light ('light reflex') and the appearance of silver wiring. The veins may be nipped at the point

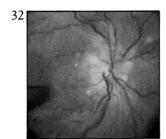

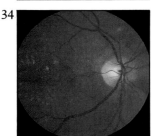

where they cross an artery (arteriovenous nipping) [32]. It should be emphasized that both these appearances occur in normotensive elderly patients and the presence of either sign is therefore of little significance in patients from their late fifties onwards. These appearances are frequently referred to as grade 1 and grade 2 retinopathy respectively. Grade 3 retinopathy is associated with hemorrhages and exudates [33]. The latter comprises two types. Hard exudates are small, discrete, white lesions caused by small amounts of denatured protein [34]. Cottonwool spots are larger white lesions with a less distinct outline. They are due to retinal infarction secondary to arterial blockage. Grade 4 changes are characterized by papilledema. Both grade 3 and grade 4 changes are associated with a bad prognosis in the untreated patient. Recent studies have suggested that there is no difference in prognosis between grade 3 and grade 4 changes.

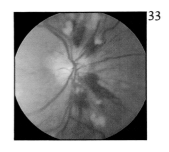

Investigations

Routine Tests

The vast majority of patients with essential hypertension have normal serum biochemistry. Renal impairment is usually evidence for either a renal cause of hypertension or hypertension which has entered the accelerated phase. Urine testing may also be normal. Abnormal proteinuria suggests either primary renal disease or accelerated hypertension. The latter is also associated with casts and red cells [35]. Increased numbers of white cells suggest renal parenchymal disease e.g. pyelonephritis.

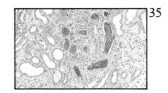

Electrocardiogram

The ECG may be normal or show left axis deviation in patients with mild hypertension in whom more sensitive investigations show significant left ventricular hypertrophy. More marked long-standing hypertension is associated with electrocardiographic evidence of left ventricular hypertrophy i.e. an increase in the R wave voltage in the left chest leads and in the S waves in the right chest leads so that the sum of the two exceeds 35 mm. Later T wave flattening, ST depression and T wave inversion occur in the antero-lateral chest leads (left ventricular strain) [36].

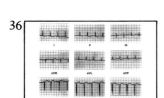

Chest X-ray

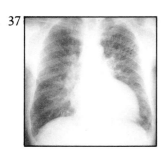

Mild to moderate hypertension is frequently associated with a normal chest X-ray. Left ventricular enlargement may be manifested by an increased cardiothoracic ratio although this is a comparatively insensitive measure. In addition, the aortic shadow becomes 'unfolded'. Left ventricular failure is manifested by a 'bats wing' appearance of the pulmonary vessels, cardiomegaly, small pleural effusions and Kerley's B-lines [37]. Rib notching may be visible in patients with coarctation of the aorta [38]. This is produced by collateral vessels by-passing the coarctation.

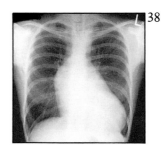

Renal Radiology

Intravenous urography is usually normal in patients with essen-

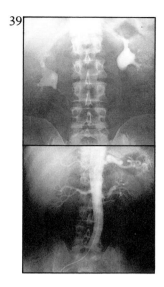

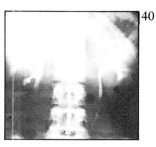

tial hypertension. In patients with renal artery stenosis [39a & b] the affected kidney may be smaller and there is delay in the appearance of the urogram which may persist longer on the affected side and be more dense. Rapid sequence films are therefore necessary to time the first appearance of the urogram on the two sides. Chronic pyelonephritis [40] may be associated with scarring of the renal cortex and clubbing of the calyces. Chronic glomerulonephritis causes bilateral smooth contraction of both kidneys [41] whilst polycystic kidneys [42] give rise to distortion and stretching of the calyces around the large cysts. Analgesic nephropathy may be apparent as distorted calyces: necrotic papillae cause characteristic ring shadows [43].

Renal angiography may be necessary to demonstrate the lesion in renal artery stenosis. Atheromatous plaques may be visible as small, discrete lesions causing luminal narrowing and poststenotic dilatation. Fibromuscular dysplasia causes a characteristic corkscrew appearance with alternate areas of narrowing and dilatation [44]. Pheochromocytoma can be demonstrated by arteriography. However, CAT scanning is a safer and preferable option.

Adrenal adenomata can be demonstrated by either arteriography or adrenal phlebography [45]. These lesions can also be seen on CAT scanning although they are more difficult to demonstrate.

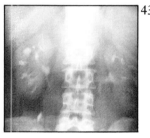

Echocardiography

This is now the preferred non-invasive method for demonstrating left ventricular hypertrophy. It allows for measurement of both cardiac dimensions and mass and helps in the diagnosis of associated lesions such as valvular heart disease.

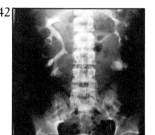

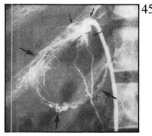

Ultrasonic Scanning

This may help to demonstrate transsonic renal cysts in polycystic renal disease [46] and may help in the assessment of renal size in patients with parenchymal disease.

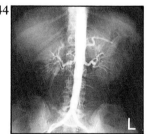

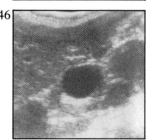

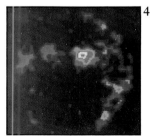

Isotope Scanning

Radiolabeled cholesterol is taken up preferentially by the adrenal gland and used in the synthesis of adrenal steroids. This provides an excellent method for demonstrating tumors in e.g. Conn's syndrome and lateralizing them for surgery [47]. I^{131} metaiodobenzylguanethidine localizes both intra- and extra-adrenal pheochromocytomata.

Isotope renography is useful in the demonstrating and lateralizing of renovascular disease. DTPA (technetium labeled diethylenetriamine pentaacetic acid) acts as a measure of glomerular filtration on the two sides, whilst DMSA (dimercaptosuccinic acid) or radiolabeled sodium iodohippurate serve as markers of renal plasma flow.

Nuclear Magnetic Resonance Techniques

Magnetic resonance images can be used to calculate atrial and

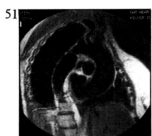

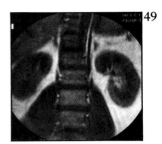

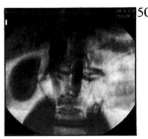

ventricular volumes and these measurements can be used to derive very accurate values for stroke volume and ejection fractions. The ventricular myocardium is well shown on magnetic resonance images and its thickness can be accurately measured [48a, 48b]. Some of the causes of hypertension, such as renal disease [49], renal artery stenosis [50] and coarctation [51] are clearly demonstrated. In addition, some of the sequelae are also seen [52]. The value of this technique in assessment of the hypertensive patient is currently a matter of research and techniques have not yet entered routine clinical practice.

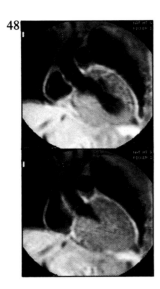

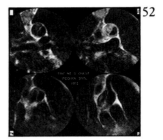

1 Systolic blood pressure distribution in healthy men and women.

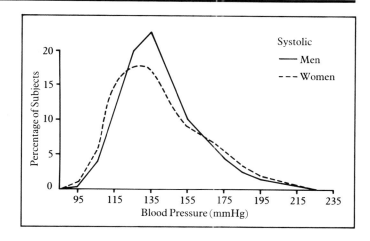

2 Left renal artery stenosis due to atheroma causing left renal atrophy and compensatory hypertrophy of the right kidney which has three patent arteries. There is mild aortic atheroma.

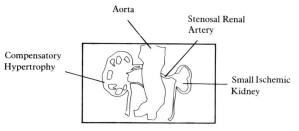

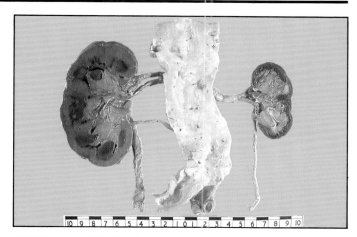

3 Long-standing renal artery stenosis has caused almost total tubular atrophy in the kidney with relative sparing of the glomeruli which are protected from the effects of systemic hypertension by the renal artery stenosis.

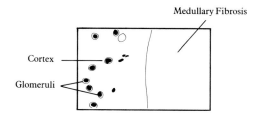

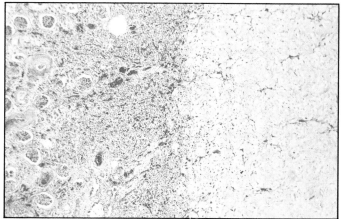

4 Large Wilm's tumor from five-year-old child compressing the kidney. The child presented with hypertension.

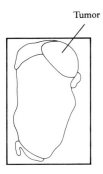

Tumor

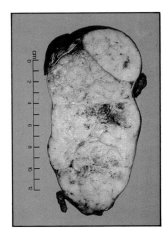

5 Intravenous urogram from hypertensive patient with contracted right kidney due to chronic pyelonephritis.

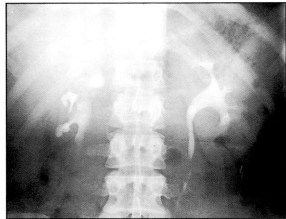

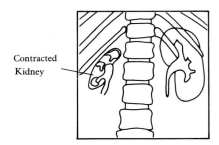

Contracted Kidney

6 Fingers of a patient with scleroderma. The patient had been treated for Raynaud's disease for several years when she presented with a fit secondary to malignant hypertension. The patient died of renal failure two weeks later.

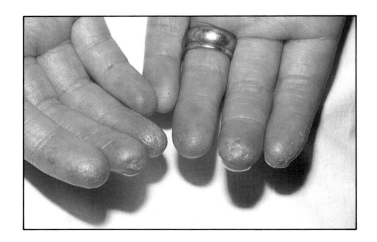

7 Proliferative glomerulonephritis. The glomerular tuft is hypercellular and swollen. Only a few glomerular capillary loops appear patent. The hypercellularity is due to increased numbers of mesangial and endothelial cells and to an infiltrate of neutrophil polymorphonuclear **leukocytes.** The latter are recognized by their lobed nuclei. There is no epithelial proliferation and Bowman's space remains clear.

Neutrophil Polymorphs

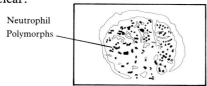

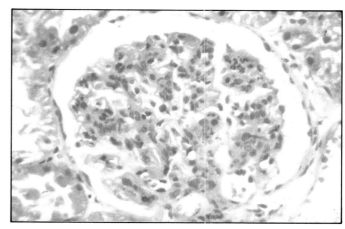

8 Advanced membranous glomerulonephritis. Resin section stained with hematoxylin and eosin shows uniform thickening of the glomerular capillaries on the edge of this biopsy. The glomerulus is of normal cellularity.

Thickened Glomerular Capillaries

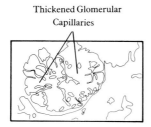

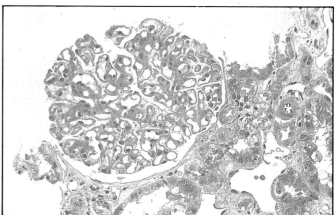

9 Minimal change glomerulonephritis. Electron micrograph from a male with nephrotic syndrome due to minimal change glomerulonephritis. There is total foot process fusion (arrows) of the epithelial cells on the outer surface of the glomerular capillary loops. There is no immune complex deposition or any other abnormality of the basement membrane.

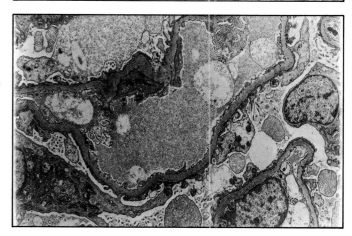

10 Facial appearance from patient who presented with moderate hypertension (BP180/110). She commented that her face had recently become rounded which had been noted by her friends. A diagnosis of Cushing's syndrome with bilateral adrenal hyperplasia was subsequently made.

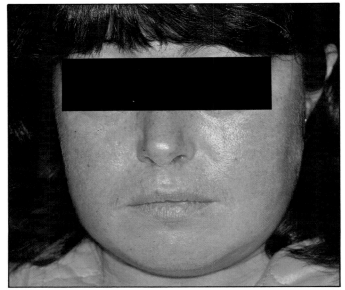

11 Adrenal gland removed at operation from a patient with primary aldosteronism. The orange tumor has been cut open.

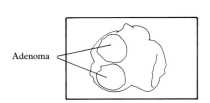

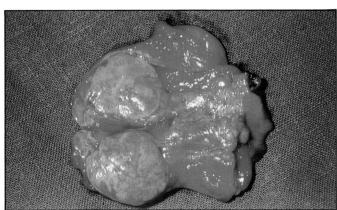

12 A typical adrenal pheochromocytoma forming a round brown nodule within the medulla and quite distinct from the yellow cortical layer.

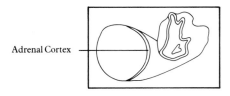

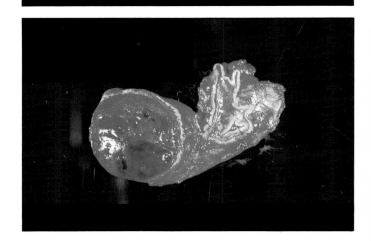

13 Electron micrograph (× 33,000) of pheochromocytoma showing stored secretory granules.

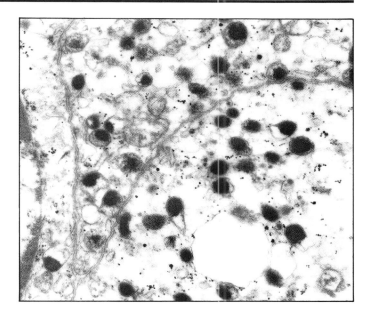

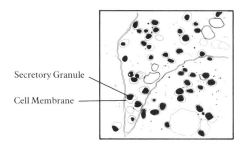

Secretory Granule

Cell Membrane

14 A swollen glomerulus from a patient dying from eclampsia shows thickening of the capillary walls due to cell swelling. The capillary loops are patent.

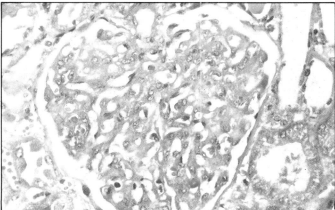

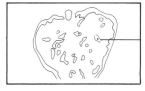

Swollen Endothelial Cells and Narrowing Capillary Lumen

15 Coarctation of the aorta just distal to the left subclavian artery. A red probe is present through the coarctation and also through a coincidental ventricular septal defect.

Aortic Arch

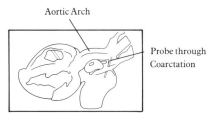

Probe through Coarctation

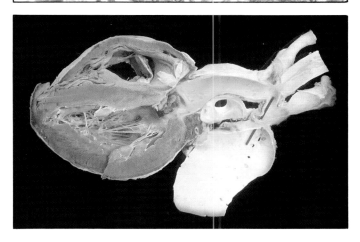

16 Left ventricular angiogram (antero-posterior projection) showing severe tubular hypoplasia of the aortic arch.

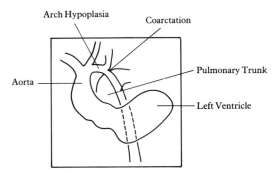

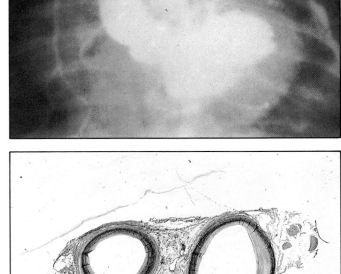

17 Carotid bifurcation showing marked intimal thickening in the sinus associated with hypertension.

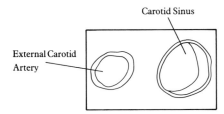

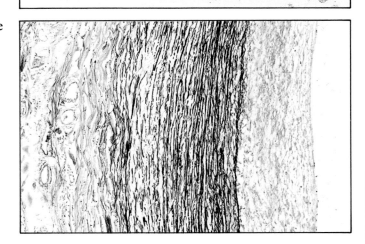

18 Higher magnification of carotid sinus wall from same patient confirming intimal thickening, irregular elastic laminae and some medial collagen increase.

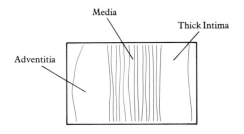

19 An atheromatous abdominal aortic aneurysm at the typical site below the renal arteries and proximal to the bifurcation. The aneurysm contains thrombus.

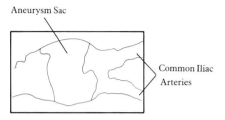

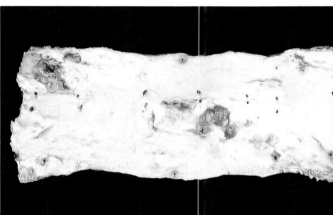

20 Aorta with severe atheroma. The plaques are ulcerated and calcified.

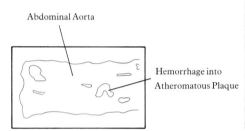

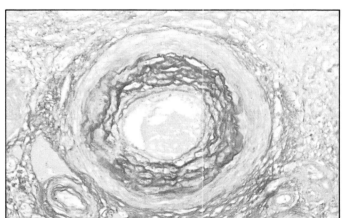

21 Section through a renal interlobular artery in essential hypertension showing reduplication of the internal elastic lamina. The lumen is reduced but patent.

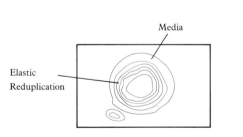

22 Microscopic appearance of hyaline arteriolar change in afferent glomerular arteriole due to essential hypertension. The hyaline deposit is sharply defined and the vessel lumen is patent.

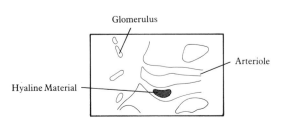

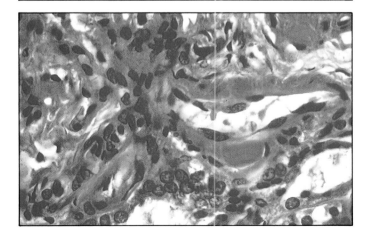

23 High power photomicrograph of renal arteriole showing fibrinoid necrosis in malignant hypertension. The fibrin deposits are blurred and poorly localized compared with the hyaline deposits in essential hypertension.

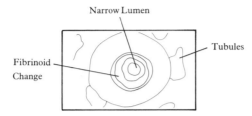

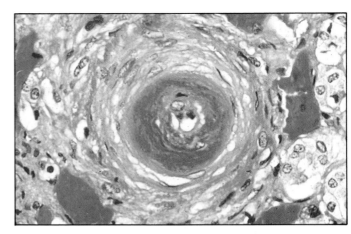

24 Transverse section of heart with concentric left ventricular hypertrophy due to hypertension. Small left ventricular cavity indicates absence of cardiac failure.

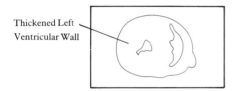

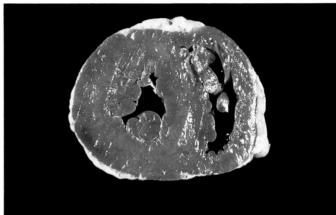

25 Chest radiograph showing pulmonary edema and bilateral pleural effusions following acute myocardial infarction.

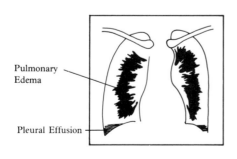

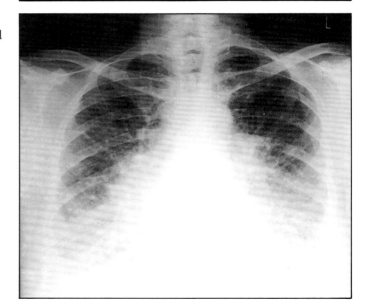

26 Transverse section of atheromatous coronary artery. The intima shows fibrous thickening with a large lipid deposit on one side leaving a reduced slit-like lumen.

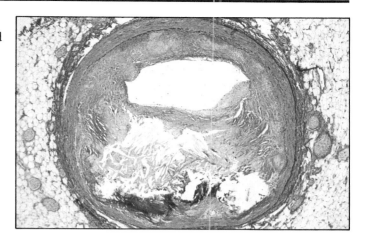

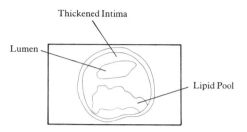

Thickened Intima

Lumen

Lipid Pool

27 Charcot Bouchard aneurysm laying along the course of a small intracerebral artery

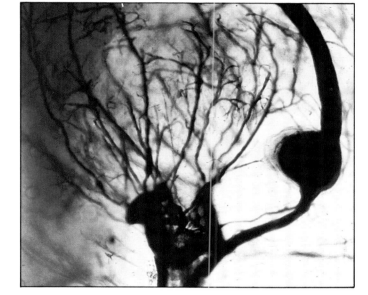

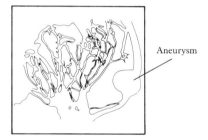

Aneurysm

28 Microscopic section through an intact berry aneurysm on the circle of Willis. The aneurysm has a fibrous wall with no elastic tissue present.

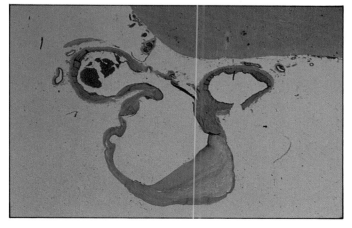

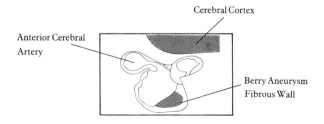

Cerebral Cortex

Anterior Cerebral Artery

Berry Aneurysm Fibrous Wall

29 Inferior surface of the brain from a patient dying after extensive subarachnoid hemorrhage due to rupture of a large berry aneurysm.

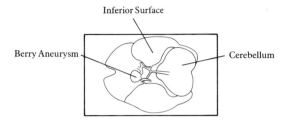

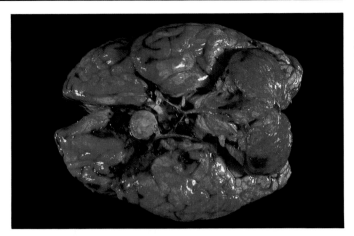

30 Nephrosclerosis due to essential hypertension causing cortical thinning with a granular capsular surface. The kidneys are atrophic due to ischemia.

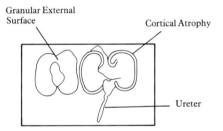

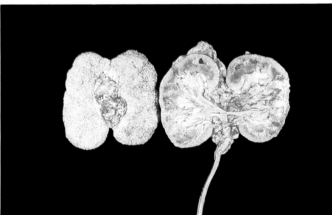

31 External surface of a kidney in malignant hypertension (BP 210/130) showing 'flea-bitten' appearance due to tiny subcapsular hemorrhages.

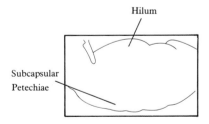

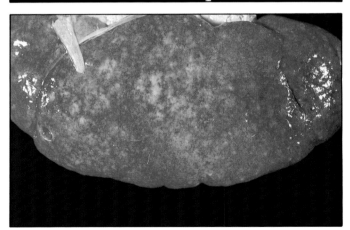

32 Fundus from a hypertensive patient presenting with a subarachnoid hemorrhage. A large sub-hyaloid hemorrhage with an upper fluid level is seen on the left. There is also silver wiring with arteriovenous nipping and hard and soft exudates.

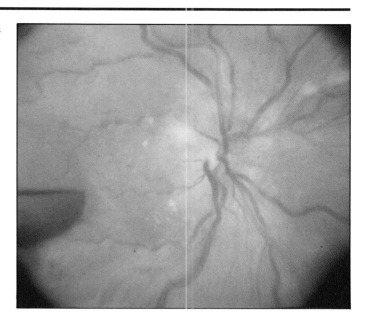

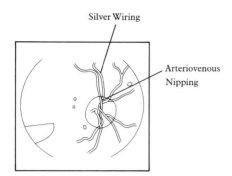

33 Fundus from a patient with malignant hypertension. Note presence of extensive hemorrhages, soft exudates and papilledema. Blood pressure was treated medically and the patient remains well.

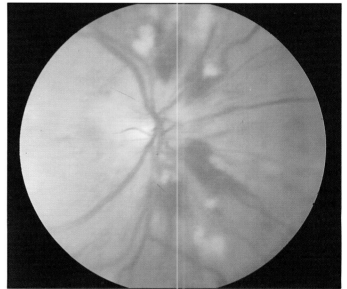

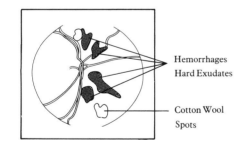

34 Fundus from a patient with accelerated hypertension. Note 'macular starring' of hard exudates and some small hemorrhages.

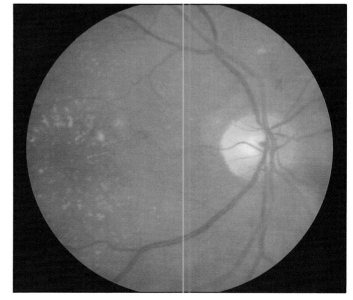

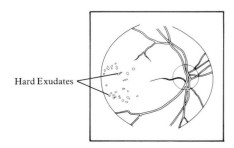

35 Red cell casts fill renal tubules and may be seen by microscopy of urine passed by patients with necrotizing glomerulonephritis and some cases of malignant hypertension which cause glomerular bleeding.

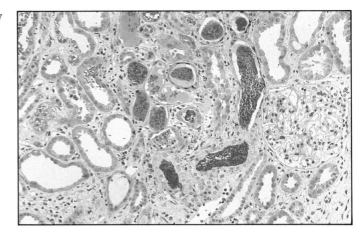

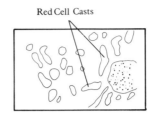

36

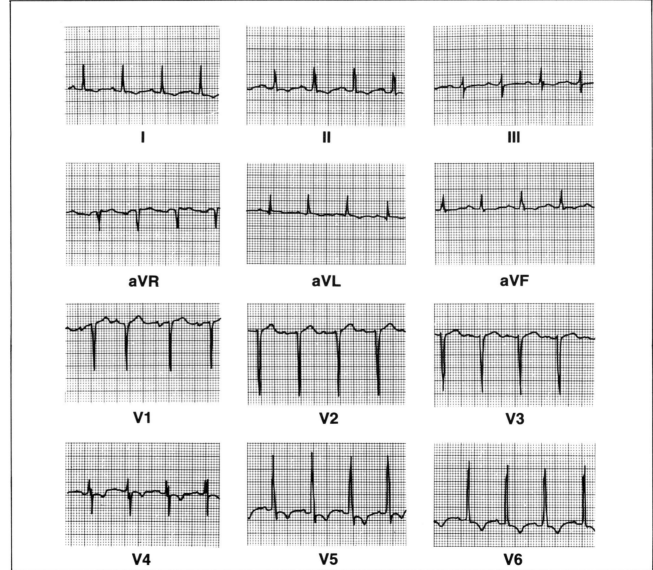

Electrocardiogram from patient with malignant hypertension. Voltage charges of left ventricular hypertrophy (deep S waves in the right ventricular leads and tall R waves in left ventricular leads) are seen together with a 'strain' pattern (inverted T waves in the left ventricular leads).

37 Chest X-ray from patient with left ventricular failure due to hypertension. Vascular engorgement gives rise to a 'bats wings' appearance and distended lymphatics cover Kerley B-lines.

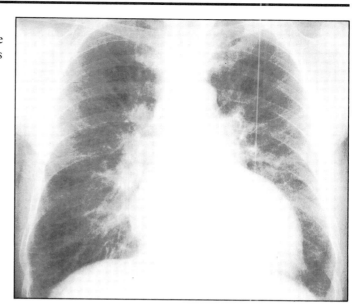

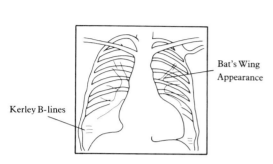

38 Chest X-ray from 20-year-old hypertensive patient. Coarctation is suggested by the rib-notching, bulging ascending aorta and absence of aorta knuckle.

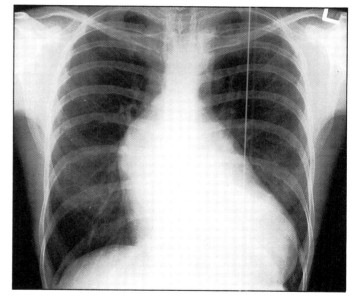

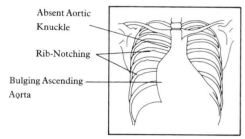

39a Intravenous urogram from patient with left renal artery stenosis at 20 minutes after injection. The dye is more concentrated in the pelvis of the left kidney.

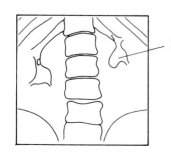

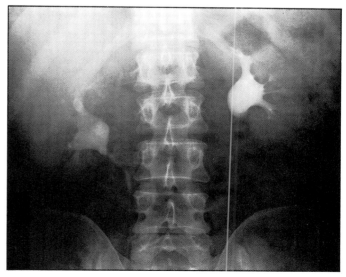

39b Renal angiogram from the same patient. A tight stenosis is seen at the mouth of the left renal artery.

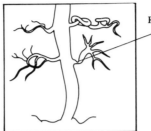

Renal Artery Stenosis

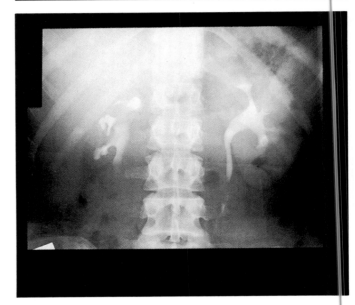

40 Intravenous urogram from hypertensive patient. Clubbing of the calyces is clearly visible on the contracted kidney.

Clubbed Calyces

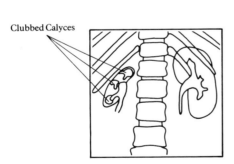

41 Intravenous urogram with tomography from hypertensive patient with contracted kidneys due to chronic glomerulonephritis.

Contracted Kidney

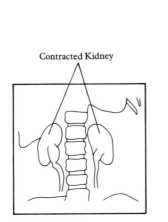

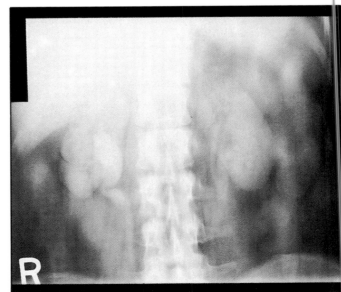

42 Intravenous urogram from patient with polycystic kidney showing calyces stretched over cysts.

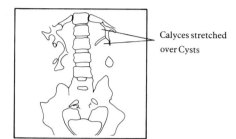

Calyces stretched over Cysts

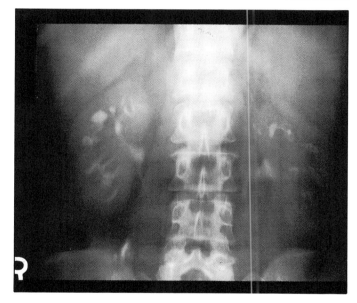

43 Intravenous urogram from patient with papillary necrosis due to analgesic nephropathy. Characteristic 'ring' shadows are caused by necrotic papillae.

'Ring' Shadow

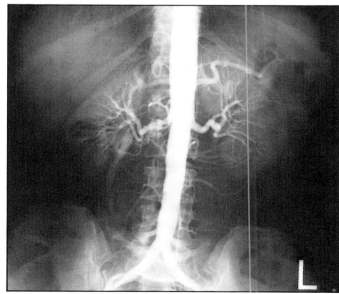

44 Arteriogram showing characteristic 'corkscrew' appearance from patient with fibromuscular dysplasia.

Fibromuscular Dysplasia

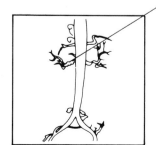

45 Right adrenal venogram from a patient with a pheochromocytoma. The vessels are displaced by the tumor.

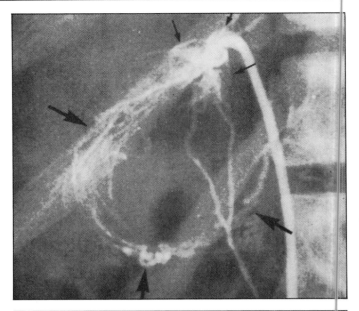

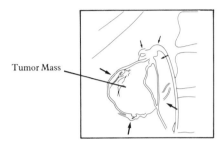

Tumor Mass

46 Ultrasound scan of kidney from patient with polycystic renal disease. Note the multiple large cysts.

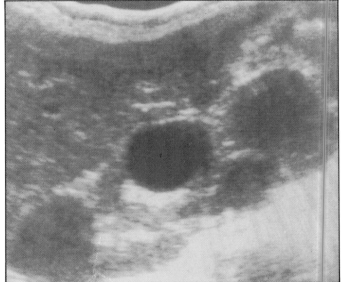

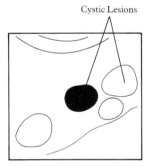

Cystic Lesions

47 Isotope scan from patient with a right adrenal adenoma. Note the high concentration of isotope (shown by a brown 'hot spot' over the right adrenal).

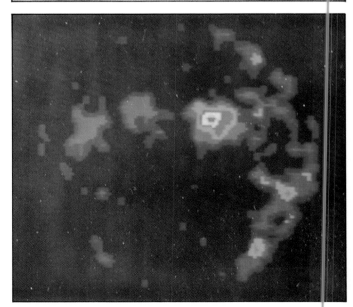

'Hot Spot'

48a Left ventricular hypertrophy. Coronal image through aortic valve and left ventricle in a patient with hypertension (diastole).

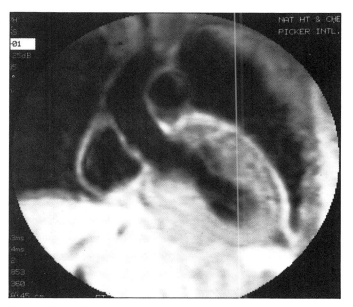

DIASTOLE

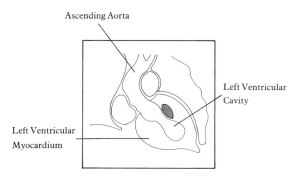

48b There is severe symmetrical hypertrophy with almost total obliteration of the left ventricular cavity at end systole (systole).

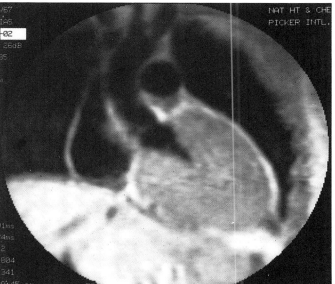

SYSTOLE

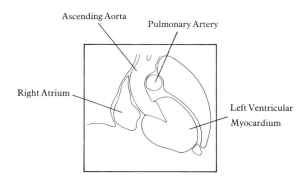

49 Normal kidneys. Coronal section through both kidneys. On the left the distinction between cortex and medulla can be seen.

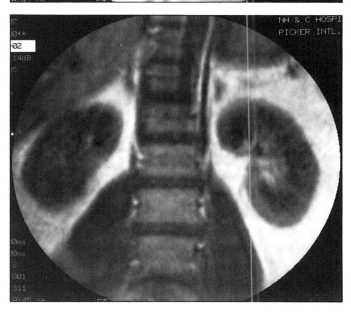

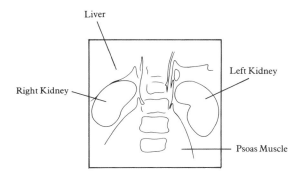

50 Renal arteries. Coronal section through the abdominal aorta showing the origins of both renal arteries. The inferior vena cava, the lower pole of the right kidney and the right ureter are also seen.

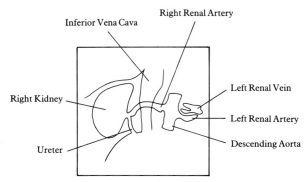

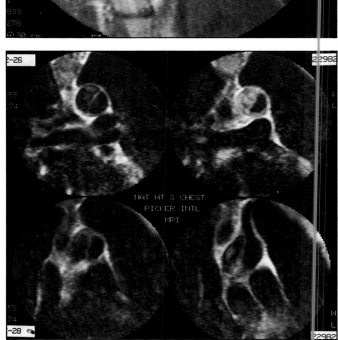

51 Coarctation. Oblique section through the aortic arch showing a coarctation just beyond the origin of the left subclavian artery.

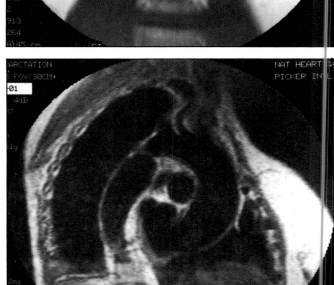

52 Dissection. Four coronal sections through the aortic arch from posterior (top left) to anterior (bottom right). There is an intimal flap dividing the lumen into true and false channels.

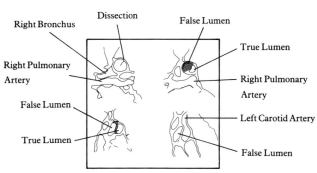

Chapter 4.

Valve Disease

Abbreviations

A	Left Atrium	FA	Femoral Artery	PE	Pericardial Effusion
a	Anterior Leaflet	IVS	Interventricular Septum	PVL	Pulmonary Valve Leaflets
Ao	Aorta	LA	Left Atrium	PVW	Posterior Ventricular Wall
Asc Ao	Ascending Aorta	LV	Left Ventricle	RA	Right Atrium
AV	Aortic Valve	LVOT	Left Ventricular Outflow Tract	RV	Right Ventricle
AVL	Aortic Valve Leaflets	MV	Mitral Valve	TV	Tricuspid Valve
CW	Chest Wall	MVL	Mitral Valve Leaflets	TVL	Tricuspid Valve Leaflets
Desc Ao	Descending Aorta	p	Posterior Leaflet	V	Left Ventricle
Eff	Effusion	P-A	Postero-Anterior	Veg	Vegetation
F	Flap	PAWP	Pulmonary Artery Wedge Pressure		

Pathology

Rheumatic fever in the acute phase is characterized by inflammation in all layers of the heart: pericarditis, myocarditis and endocarditis. The pericarditis is non-specific with an acute fibrinous exudate. Myocarditis has a specific histologic picture typified by the presence of Aschoff bodies, which are microscopic foci of degenerate collagen surrounded by giant cells. The pertinent features of endocarditis are small flat vegetations [1] on the closure lines of the mitral and aortic valve cusps. Microscopically the valve cusps are inflamed and thickened, the vegetations consisting largely of platelets.

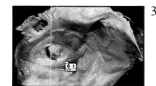

Patients who recover from the acute phase of rheumatic fever can develop chronic effects. These are seen most prominently in the endocardium. In some instances repeated sub-clinical attacks of rheumatic fever lead to progressive damage. In other patients, changes secondary to ageing and abnormal hemodynamics lead to progressive destruction of the damaged valve.

In chronic rheumatic mitral valve disease, fusion of the anterior and posterior commissures leads to a steady reduction in the area of the aperture of the fully open valve [2,3]. In some instances the valve cusps, although fused at the commissures, remain mobile. Other patients develop considerable cusp fibrosis or calcification with resultant rigidity [4]. Chronic rheumatic valve disease also produces chordal shortening and thickening. In some instances the chordae fuse into a solid fibrous mass attaching the cusps directly onto the papillary muscles. Chordal shortening decreases cusp mobility with resultant mitral regurgitation which is present in many cases of dominant stenosis. Pure regurgitation is unusual.

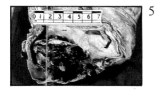

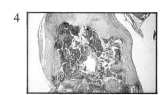

Increased left atrial pressure usually produces chamber enlargement, although there is considerable individual variation. Thrombosis may form in large atria particularly in the appendage [5]. This may be the source of systemic emboli.

Presentation

Symptoms

The main symptom is breathlessness on exertion which is caused by the rise in left atrial pressure with a consequent rise in pulmonary venous pressure. Breathlessness develops gradually in about 50% of patients. Some patients may remain asymptomatic for many years and then develop symptoms usually with the onset of atrial fibrillation. When the mitral stenosis is severe the patient may develop orthopnea and paroxysmal nocturnal dyspnea.

Hemoptysis occurs in about 15% of patients with mitral stenosis. There are several possible causes. The patient may bleed into the alveoli during an acute attack of pulmonary edema; the sputum may be bloodstained during the course of intercurrent bronchitis or pneumonia; a major pulmonary vein may rupture into a bronchus owing to a considerable rise in pulmonary venous pressure; finally, hemoptysis may be produced by pulmonary infarction as a result of pulmonary embolism.

Many patients with mitral stenosis first present when embolization from the left atrium into the systemic circulation leads to cerebral infarction, impairment of circulation to a limb, mesenteric infarction or infarction of the spleen, kidney or retina.

Palpitation may be a presenting feature in patients with rheumatic heart disease, usually when the rhythm of the heart has changed to atrial fibrillation.

Fatigue resulting from a low fixed cardiac output is a very common complaint of the patient with severe mitral stenosis.

Signs

The patient may have cyanotic patches over the cheeks - the so-called mitral facies. The arterial pulse is usually normal in quality and the rhythm is frequently atrial fibrillation. If sinus rhythm is present the jugular venous pulse may show an abnormal 'a' wave due to pulmonary hypertension. Severe pulmonary hypertension may give rise to right ventricular hypertrophy and subsequent dilatation with resultant tricuspid regurgitation characterized by a dominant systolic wave in the jugular venous pulse.

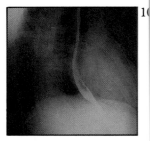

The loud first heart sound characteristic of mitral stenosis may be palpable giving rise to the 'tapping apex beat'. In addition right ventricular hypertrophy may be elicited by palpation at the left sternal edge.

In pure mitral stenosis in sinus rhythm the auscultatory findings include an atrial systolic murmur (pre-systolic murmur) a loud first heart sound, an opening snap and variable length mid diastolic murmur. The more severe the stenosis, the closer the interval between aortic valve closure and the opening snap and the longer the mid-diastolic murmur. If the valve is calcified and rigid the first heart sound and opening snap may not be heard. If there is additional mitral regurgitation a high frequency pansystolic murmur will be heard. The presence of severe pulmonary hypertension will give rise to a loud pulmonary valve closure sound best heard at the left sternal edge but this needs to be distinguished from the opening snap which may also be best heard at the left sternal edge. If there is additional aortic or tricuspid rheumatic valve disease the physical signs of these valve lesions will be superadded or even may dominate the clinical picture.

Radiology

The plain chest radiograph shows left atrial enlargement [6]. Typically in mitral stenosis a prominent left atrial appendage is also seen [7]. If pulmonary venous pressure is elevated (as is usual), the upper zone vessels are dilated [8]. A higher pressure in the pulmonary veins produces septal lines and pleural effusions [7,9]. With chronic disease the valve frequently becomes calcified [10]. In long-standing cases hemosiderin deposits may be found in the lungs, seen as wide-spread mottling [11]. In patients with mixed stenosis and regurgitation the left atrium may become very large and calcified [12,13]. Long-standing pulmonary venous hypertension gives rise to pulmonary arterial hypertension. This is reflected in a large pulmonary trunk and a greater discrepancy in size between the large upper zone and the smaller lower zone vessels [14].

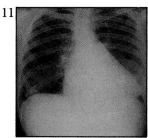
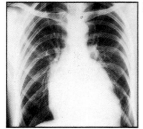
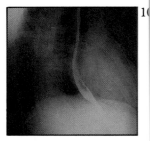
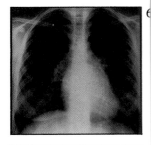
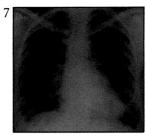
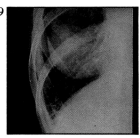
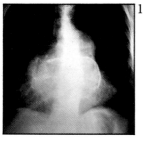
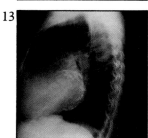
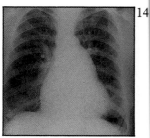

Electrocardiography

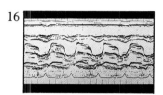

In sinus rhythm, the electrocardiogram usually shows a broad P wave in lead II, and a negative deflection in V1 reflecting left atrial enlargement [15]. Atrial fibrillation is common. Right axis deviation, tall R waves in V1 and deep S waves in V5 indicate right ventricular hypertrophy which may be present with sinus rhythm [15] or with atrial fibrillation.

Echocardiography

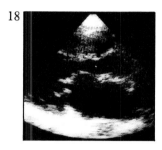

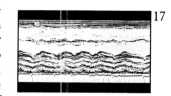

Commissural fusion produces abnormal movement of the posterior mitral valve cusp. On the M-mode echocardiogram it is seen to move forward in diastole, in the same direction as the anterior leaflet, instead of posteriorly and away from the anterior cusp [16]. The thickened leaflets return stronger echoes than normal and when calcification is present, characteristic multiple dense echoes are seen [17]. A mobile valve has a normal amplitude of excursion, but when fibrosed or calcified this is reduced. Heavy calcification and reduced mobility are reliable signs of severe disease. The two-dimensional echocardiogram enables direct visualization of the abnormal valve and its deranged movement [18].

The altered pattern of inflow of blood into the left ventricle is associated with a reduction in the diastolic closure rate of the anterior mitral valve leaflet seen on the M-mode. In clinically significant mitral stenosis the diastolic closure rate is almost invariably less than 30 mm/sec.

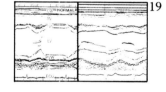

The left ventricular dimensions and septal motion are normal in mitral stenosis unless there is additional tricuspid incompetence, when septal motion may be neutral or reversed in association with an increased right ventricular dimension. In severe mitral stenosis left ventricular dimension increases in diastole more slowly than normal [19]. When there is significant mitral regurgitation the left ventricle is enlarged but fractional shortening in systole remains normal unless there is additional left ventricular disease.

Enlargement of the left atrium is also seen on the echocardiogram [20].

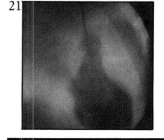

Cardiac Catheterization and Angiography

Unless information about the coronary arteries is required, cardiac catheterization is unnecessary in most cases of rheumatic mitral valve disease. An individual patient can be assessed on the basis of the clinical features and non-invasive investigation and the need for surgery so determined.

In a typical case of mitral stenosis left atrial pressure will be raised depending on the severity of the stenosis and the compliance of the left atrium. The elevation of the pulmonary artery pressure may reflect the rise in left atrial pressure or additional rise in pulmonary vascular resistance. The pressure difference across the mitral valve may be determined from simultaneous left atrial (or pulmonary capillary wedge pressure) and left ventricular diastolic pressures and knowledge of cardiac output will enable mitral valve orifice size to be calculated.

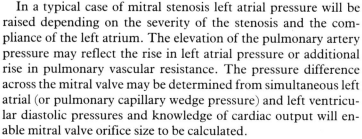

Mitral regurgitation when present can be roughly assessed by left ventricular angiography [21].

1 Mitral valve in the acute phase of rheumatic fever showing the characteristic row of small sessile vegetations along the line of closure.

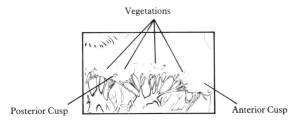

2 Fully open normal mitral and tricuspid valves viewed from left and right atria.

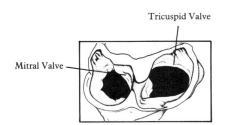

3 Rheumatic mitral stenosis viewed from left atrium. The valve orifice is a small crescentic fixed opening. The atrium is enlarged. Some calcification is present in the anterior cusp.

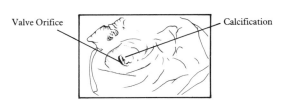

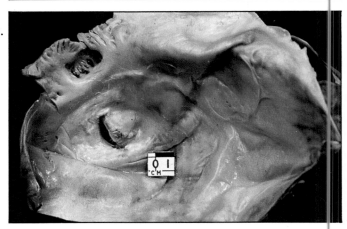

4 Histology of a rheumatic mitral valve. The valve is thickened with masses of dystrophic calcification.

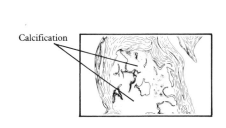

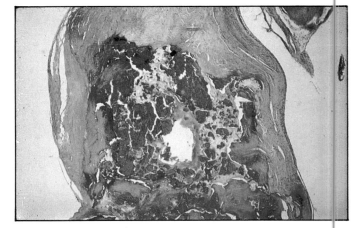

RHEUMATIC MITRAL VALVE DISEASE

5 Typical mitral stenosis viewed from left atrium. The valve orifice is a small oval. A large mass of thrombus almost fills the atrium arising from the left atrial appendage.

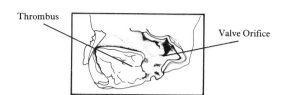

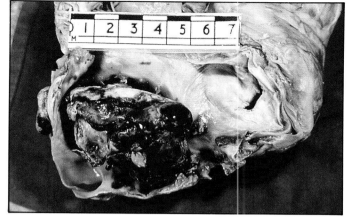

RHEUMATIC MITRAL VALVE DISEASE

6 Chest radiograph showing left atrial enlargement.

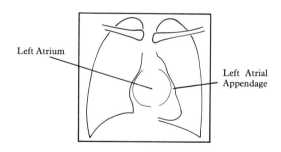

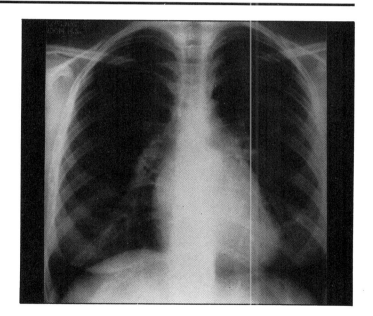

7 Chest radiograph showing small heart with a large left atrial appendage. There are bilateral pleural effusions.

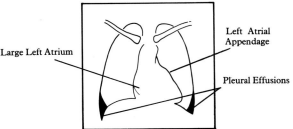

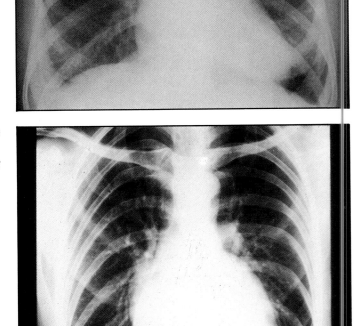

8 Chest radiograph of a patient with mitral valve disease showing [1] enlargement of left atrium, [2] distended upper lobe pulmonary veins, [3] constricted lower lobe veins.

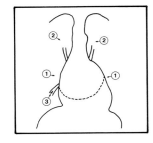

9 Detail from chest radiograph showing septal lines and pleural effusion.

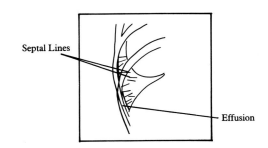

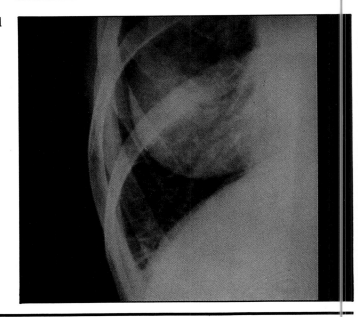

10 Chest radiograph (oblique projection) with barium outlining the esophagus showing calcification of the mitral valve.

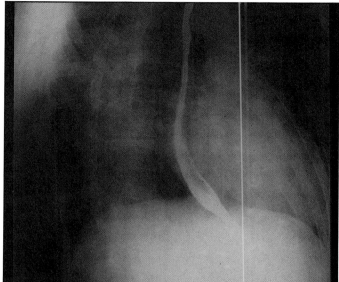

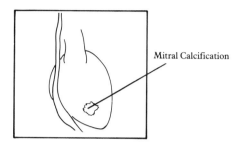

Mitral Calcification

11 Chest radiograph showing typical fine mottling of hemosiderosis.

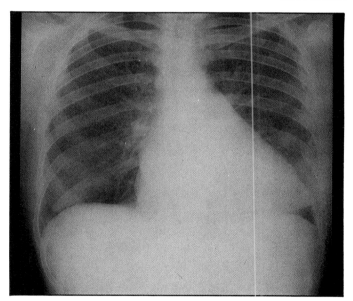

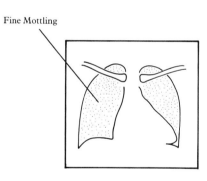

Fine Mottling

12 Chest radiograph (penetrated P-A view) showing a very large, calcified left atrium.

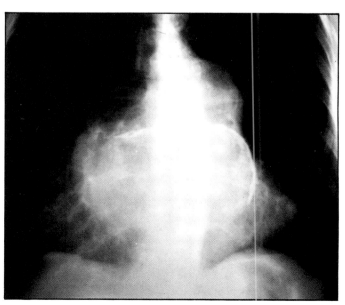

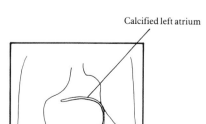

Calcified left atrium

13 Chest radiograph (lateral projection) from same patient as fig.12 showing calcified left atrium.

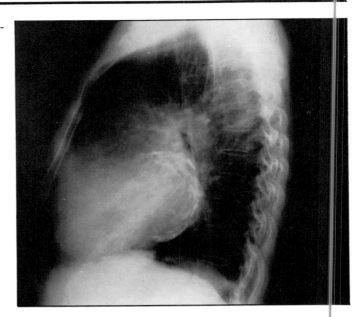

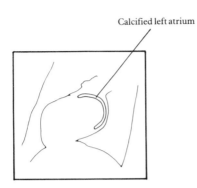

Calcified left atrium

14 Chest radiograph showing a large pulmonary trunk and upper zone vessels. Lower segmental vessels are small.

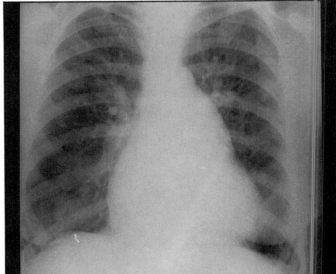

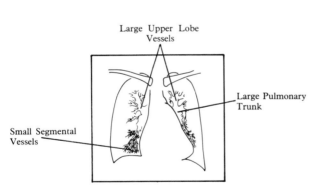

Large Upper Lobe Vessels

Large Pulmonary Trunk

Small Segmental Vessels

15

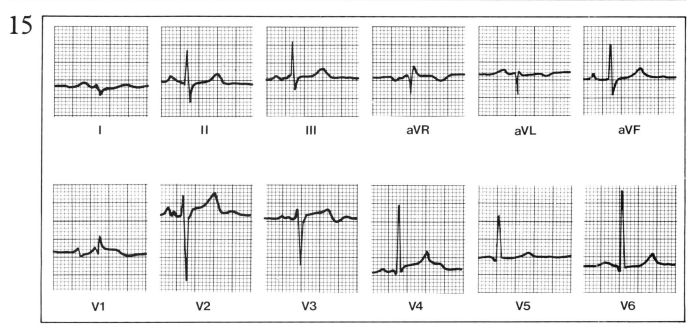

Electrocardiogram of moderately severe mitral stenosis showing the broad bifid P wave of left atrial enlargement (P mitrale), right ventricular hypertrophy as shown by a dominant R wave in lead V1. Note for V3 to V5 1mv = 0.5cm.

16

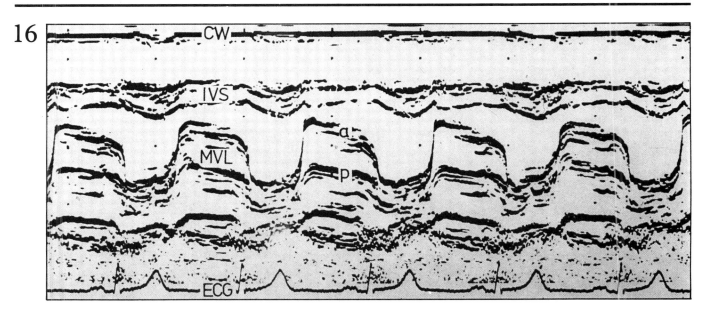

M-mode echocardiogram in moderately severe mitral stenosis showing reversed movement of the posterior cusp. The diastolic closure rate is reduced and no re-opening is seen after atrial systole.

17

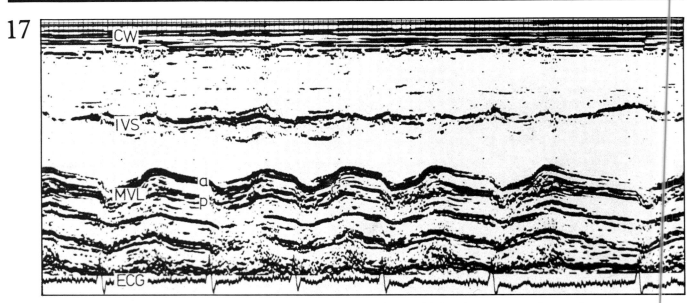

M-mode echocardiogram of heavily calcified mitral valve showing multiple echoes, reversed posterior cusp movement and reduced amplitude of movement of the anterior cusp.

18

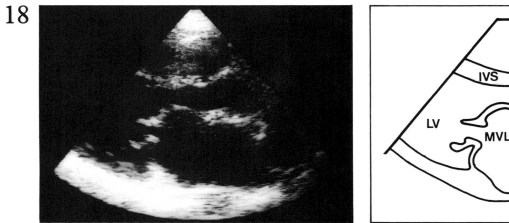
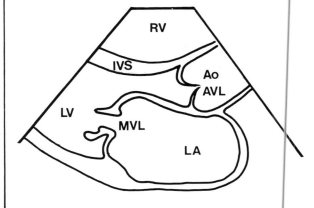

2-D echocardiographic parasternal long axis view of a stenotic mitral valve during diastole. Note the thickening of the leaflet tips and the doming of the anterior leaflet.

19

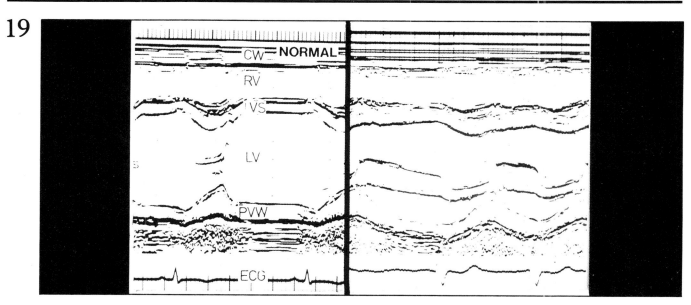

M-mode echocardiogram showing reduced rate of left ventricular dimension increase in diastole in a patient with mitral stenosis (right). Compare with normal (left).

20

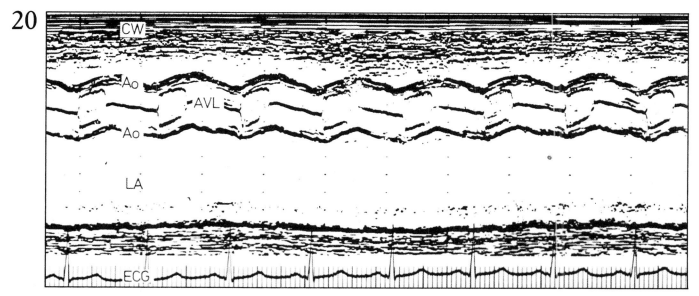

M-mode echocardiogram in mitral stenosis showing left atrial enlargement (6cm). The rate of posterior aortic root movement is reduced.

21 Left ventricular angiogram (right anterior oblique projection) showing slight mitral regurgitation through a stenotic valve.

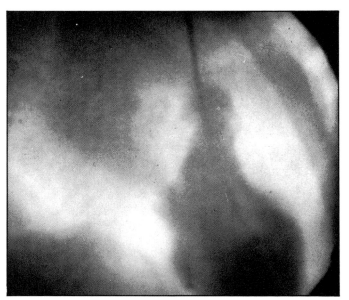

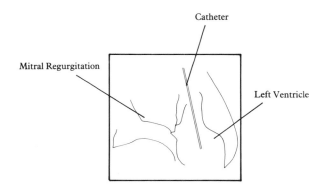

Pathology

The competence of the mitral valve depends upon the normal co-ordinated function of the left atrial wall, mitral annulus, leaflets, chordae tendineae, papillary muscles and left ventricular myocardium. Disease may affect any one or all of these structures and result in mitral regurgitation. Redundant cusp tissue and elongation of the chordae tendineae can result in a floppy mitral valve permitting slight mitral regurgitation to occur [1,2]. More severe regurgitation may develop over a long period or may occur acutely if there is chordal rupture spontaneously [3] or as a result of infective endocarditis [4].

In patients with coronary artery disease, infarction involving a papillary muscle may lead to its rupture with the development of sudden severe mitral regurgitation [5]. Ischemia of the papillary muscles can cause long standing disorganization of the subvalvular mitral apparatus with resultant mitral regurgitation [6]. Mitral regurgitation may be secondary to left ventricular myocardial disease, such as dilated cardiomyopathy, as a result of stretching the mitral annulus. It may also occur in left ventricular myocardial disease due to coronary atheroma when regional abnormalities of left ventricular function develop, which interfere with the subvalvular apparatus.

Presentation

Symptoms

Patients with slight mitral regurgitation, due for example to floppy mitral valve, are usually asymptomatic although rarely patients will complain of non-specific chest pain or palpitation due to various arrhythmias. When long-standing mitral regurgitation is severe and pulmonary venous pressure significantly raised, the patient will develop dyspnea due to the marked rise in pulmonary venous pressure.

Signs

Unless mitral regurgitation is severe the carotid pulse will be normal. With long-standing significant mitral regurgitation, atrial fibrillation may develop. The reduction in cardiac output in severe cases will result in a small carotid pulse with a sharp upstroke. With the development of pulmonary hypertension and the retention of sinus rhythm the jugular venous pressure may show a dominant 'a' wave. In chronic, moderate or severe mitral regurgitation the apical impulse is hyperdynamic due to the increased stroke volume of the left ventricle unless the cause of the regurgitation is left ventricular myocardial disease.

Prolapse of a leaflet of the mitral valve into the left atrium at peak left ventricular systolic pressure gives rise to a mid or late systolic click. The subsequent slight mitral regurgitation will give rise to a late systolic murmur. Irrespective of cause, if the valve is incompetent throughout the whole of systole there will be a pansystolic murmur. Shortening of left ventricular ejection results in an abnormally wide but physiologically split second heart sound. The pulmonary component will be accentuated if there is additional pulmonary hypertension. Rapid left ventricular filling of an increased volume of blood is associated with a third heart sound.

Investigations

Radiology

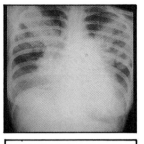

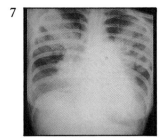

Acute severe mitral regurgitation due to chordal rupture results in pulmonary edema which is evident on the chest radiograph often with little or no cardiac enlargement [7]. If mitral regurgitation is long-standing, the chest radiograph shows cardiac enlargement with left atrial dilatation indistinguishable from chronic rheumatic mitral valve disease [8]. Dilatation of the upper lobe pulmonary veins will reflect long-standing elevation in pulmonary venous pressure.

Electrocardiography

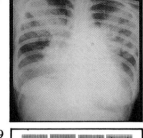

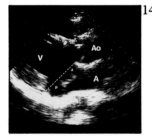

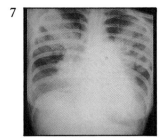

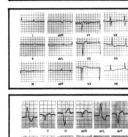

In a patient with a floppy mitral valve with only slight regurgitation or in acute severe regurgitation due to chordal rupture, the electrocardiogram may be normal or show minor ST-T abnormalities in the infero-lateral leads [9]. In chronic severe regurgitation there may be atrial fibrillation and increased left ventricular voltage with or without ST-T changes [10]. In acute rupture of the papillary muscle the ECG may show acute inferior myocardial infarction [11]. In patients with secondary mitral regurgitation from left ventricular myocardial disease, the ECG often shows left bundle branch block [12].

Echocardiography

Echocardiography allows the motion of the mitral valve to be visualized and consequently distinguishes between valvular abnormalities due to rheumatic involvement and mitral regurgitation of non-rheumatic etiology. Prolapse of the posterior or anterior leaflet of the mitral valve is often detected by echocardiography [13,14]. More severe mitral regurgitation with a flail leaflet may also be identified [15,16]. In infective endocarditis leading to mitral regurgitation, vegetations may be seen on the mitral valve leaflets [17,18].

It is important to examine left ventricular systolic function in patients with mitral regurgitation; the large left ventricular stroke volume with normal ventricular contraction of the patient with long-standing severe regurgitation due to mitral valve leaflet and chordal abnormalities [19] can be distinguished from the dilated but poorly contracting ventricle of the patient who has left ventricular myocardial disease such as a dilated cardiomyopathy with secondary mitral regurgitation [20,21].

Cardiac Catheterization and Angiography

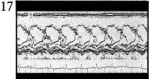

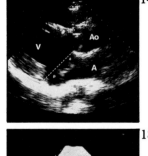

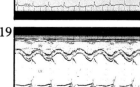

In acute severe mitral regurgitation the left atrial or pulmonary capillary wedge pressure pulse shows a large systolic 'V' wave [22]. Left ventricular angiography may demonstrate an abnormality of the mitral leaflets [23]. Chordal rupture may also be inferred if excessive movement of the leaflet is seen. In chronic severe mitral regurgitation, left ventricular dilatation may be

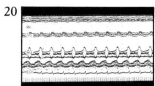

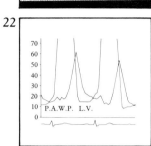

seen. Systolic function will be preserved if the cause of the regurgitation is a chordal or leaflet abnormality, but it will be impaired if the cause is left ventricular myocardial disease which may be generalized in dilated cardiomyopathy, or show regional functional abnormalities in coronary artery disease.

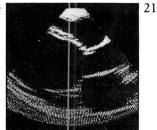

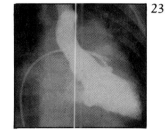

1 Mitral valve in Marfan's syndrome. Both anterior and posterior cusps are increased in area and the surface appears folded. Chordae are elongated.

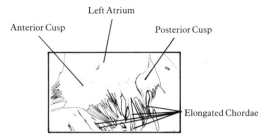

2 Floppy mitral valve viewed from the left atrium. A portion of the posterior cusp is domed into the atrium (prolapsed cusp).

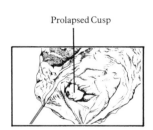

3 Floppy mitral valve with ruptured chordae. The posterior cusp is domed upward into the atrium. Stumps of ruptured chordae are present.

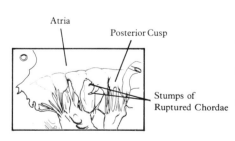

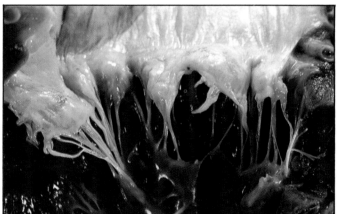

4 Mitral valve with ruptured chordae due to infective endocarditis. The posterior cusp is covered by a mass of thrombotic vegetations. Stumps of ruptured chordae are present.

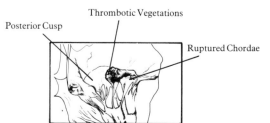

5 Partial avulsion of a papillary muscle during acute myocardial infarction producing mitral regurgitation. One head of the postero-medial papillary muscle is torn from the ventricular wall.

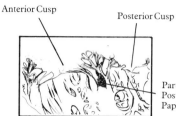

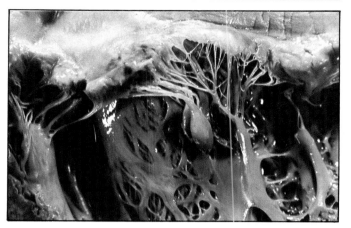

6 Fibrosis and shrinkage of the papillary muscles resulting in mitral regurgitation following myocardial infarction. The apex of the postero-medial papillary muscle is elongated and the body of the muscle is shrunken. A small chord has avulsed from the papillary muscle.

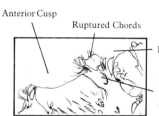

MITRAL REGURGITATION (NON-RHEUMATIC)   **Radiology**

7 Chest radiograph in acute chordal rupture. The heart is normal in size but there is gross pulmonary edema.

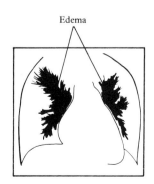

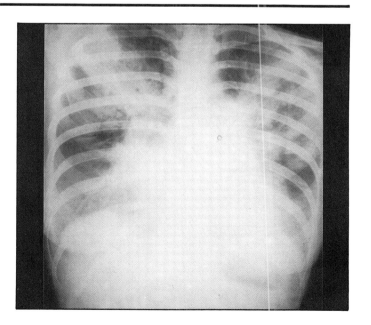

8 Chest radiograph in chronic mitral regurgitation showing cardiac enlargement, dilatation of the left atrium and the upper lobe pulmonary veins.

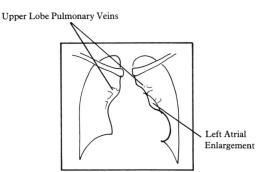

Upper Lobe Pulmonary Veins

Left Atrial
Enlargement

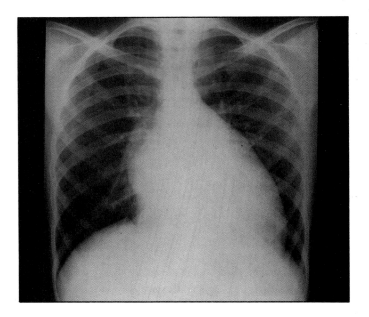

MITRAL REGURGITATION (NON-RHEUMATIC)

Electrocardiography

9

I aVR V1 V4

II aVL V2 V5

III aVF V3 V6

Electrocardiogram from a patient with mitral valve prolapse showing infero-lateral ST-T wave abnormalities.

10

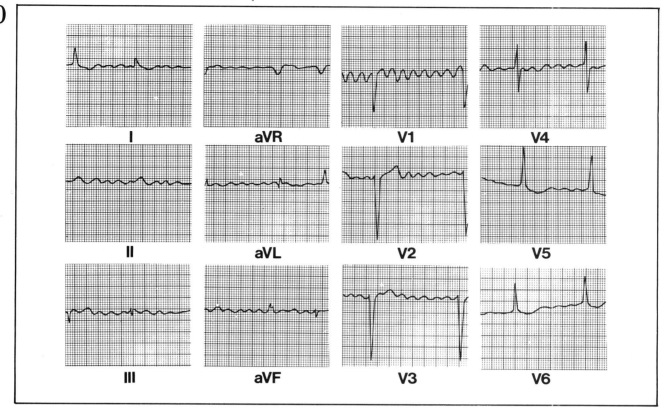

Electrocardiogram from a patient with long standing non-rheumatic mitral regurgitation showing atrial fibrillation and left ventricular hypertrophy.

11

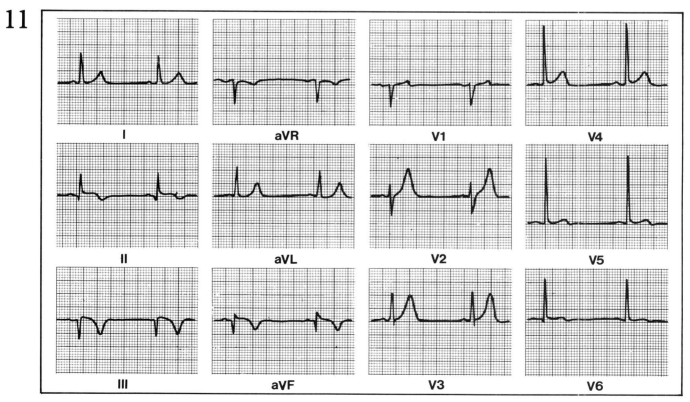

Electrocardiogram from a patient with acute papillary muscle rupture showing inferior myocardial infarction.

12

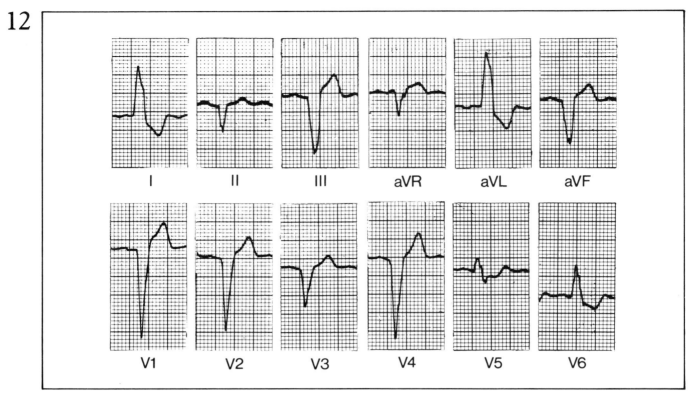

Electrocardiogram showing left bundle branch block in a patient with chronic mitral regurgitation due to dilated cardiomyopathy.

MITRAL REGURGITATION (NON-RHEUMATIC)

Echocardiography

13

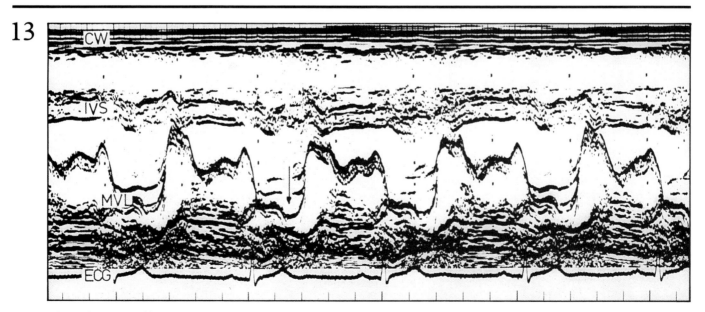

M-mode echocardiogram showing mid-systolic prolapse of the posterior leaflet of the mitral valve (arrowed).

14

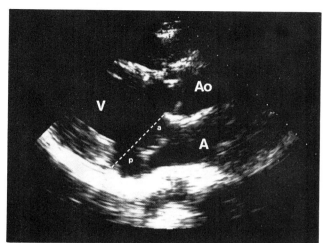
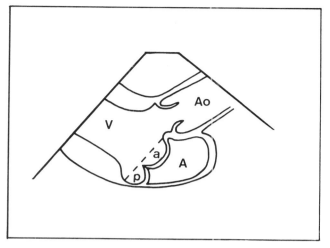

Systolic long axis 2-D echocardiographic view in mitral valve prolapse. The dotted line indicates the plane of mitral valve ring with prolapse of both anterior (a) and posterior (p) leaflets into the left atrium.

15

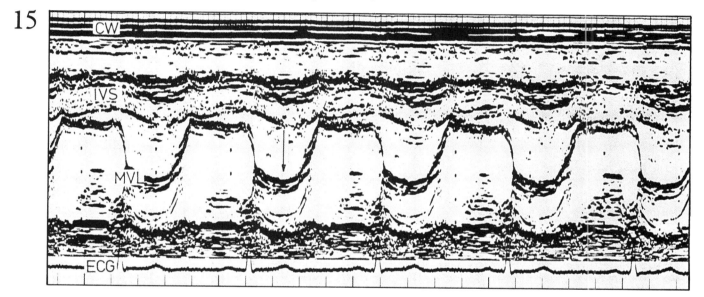

M-mode echocardiogram showing a 'hammock' prolapse of the posterior leaflet of the mitral valve (arrowed).

16

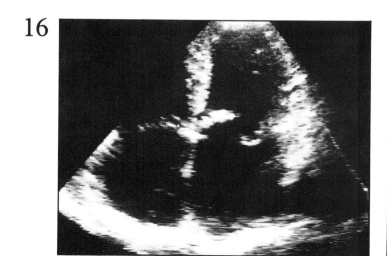
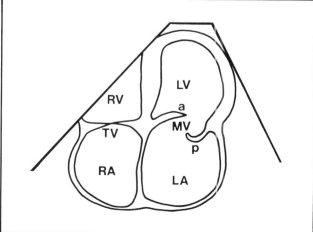

Four-chamber 2-D echocardiographic view, showing failure of coaptation of anterior and posterior leaflets of the mitral valve in systole with prolapse of the posterior leaflet into the left atrium.

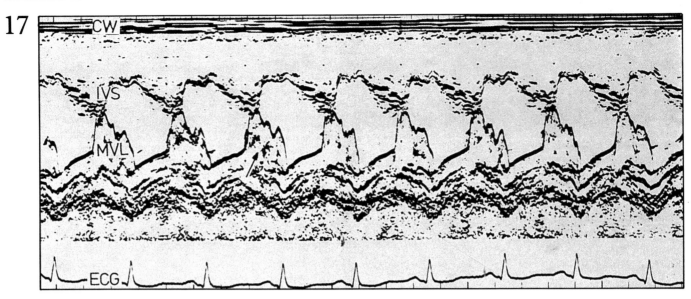

M-mode echocardiogram showing echoes (arrowed) arising from vegetations on the mitral valve in infective endocarditis.

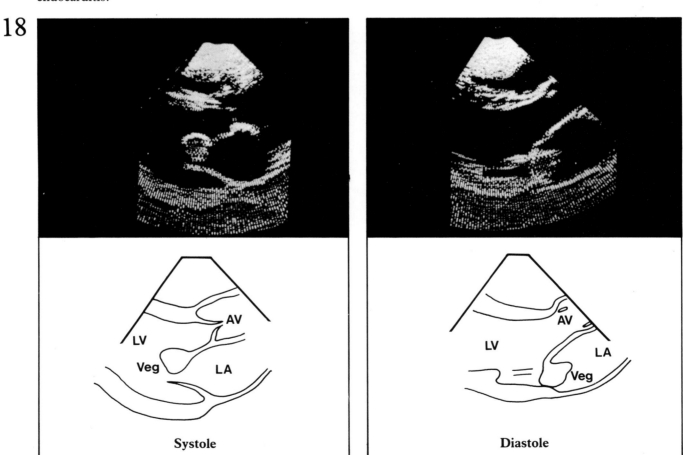

2-D echocardiographic parasternal long axis views of a vegetation attached to the mitral valve leaflet.

19

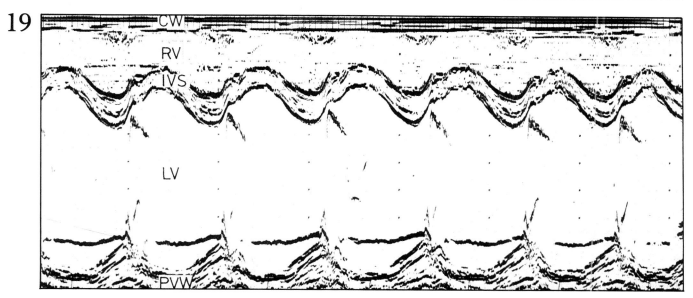

M-mode echocardiogram showing increased end-systolic and end-diastolic dimensions of the left ventricle in pure mitral regurgitation. Ejection fraction is normal.

20

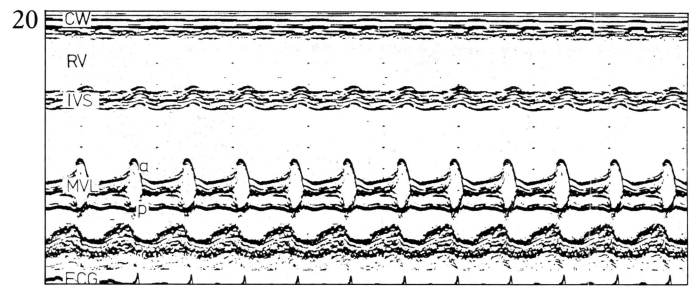

M-mode echocardiogram in dilated cardiomyopathy with secondary mitral regurgitation. Left ventricular dimensions are increased in systole and diastole, but the ejection fraction is reduced.

21

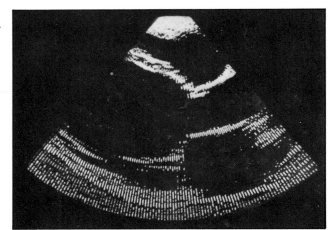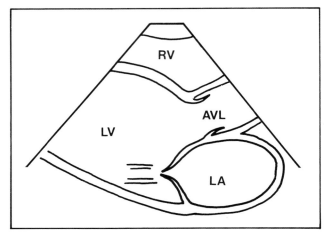

2-D echocardiographic parasternal long axis view showing left ventricular dilatation in a case of dilated cardiomyopathy. Note the thin-walled globular shape of the left ventricle. The left atrium is also enlarged.

22 A prominent 'V' wave is recorded in the pulmonary capillary wedge pressure in a patient with mitral regurgitation.

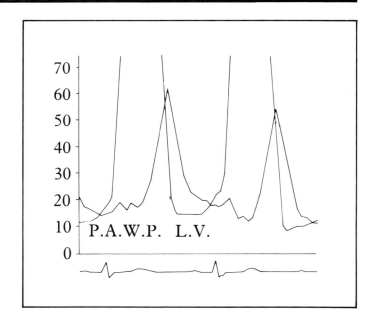

23 Left ventricular angiogram (antero-posterior projection) showing a ballooned posterior mitral leaflet.

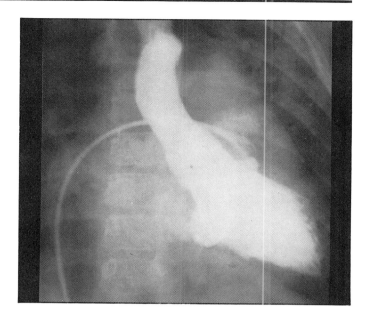

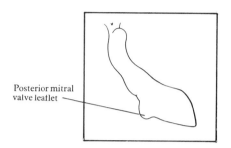

Posterior mitral
valve leaflet

Fixed obstruction to left ventricular outflow can occur at 3 levels. Most frequently it is at valve level (aortic valve stenosis), but it may also be found above or beneath the valve (supravalvular aortic stenosis and subvalvular aortic stenosis respectively). This section deals with these 3 conditions; muscular, dynamic outflow tract obstruction which forms part of the spectrum of hypertrophic cardiomyopathy is considered elsewhere.

Pathology

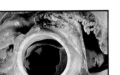

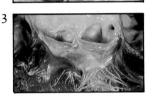

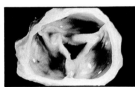

Aortic Valve Stenosis

The normal aortic valve is tricuspid [1,2]. The commonest cause of isolated aortic stenosis in the adult is a congenitally bicuspid valve [3]. Dystrophic calcification of the biscupid valve only develops with time and is rarely present before the age of 45 [4]. Up to 1% of the population are born with bicuspid aortic valves, but in only a proportion of these will the valve calcify and produce stenosis.

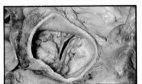

Rheumatic aortic stenosis is characterized by fusion of all 3 commissures to produce a central triangular aperture [5]. In the majority of these patients, co-existent mitral valve disease is also present.

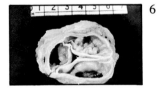

Senile calcific aortic stenosis occurs as a result of dystrophic calcification in the normal tricuspid aortic valve [6]. It is essentially an accelerated or exaggerated ageing change and is unusual below 65 years of age.

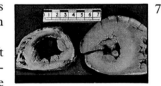

Mixed forms of aortic valve stenosis also occur. Patients with bicuspid valves may develop rheumatic disease resulting in commissural fusion or infective endocarditis which usually produces aortic regurgitation. Dystrophic calcification may also occur in mildly affected rheumatic aortic valves.

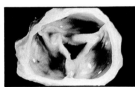

All forms of aortic valve stenosis cause obstruction to left ventricular outflow and therefore produce left ventricular hypertrophy characterized by a small cavity and thick wall [7]. In the end-stage, considerable subendocardial fibrosis may occur leading to papillary muscle dysfunction and a dilated left ventricular cavity.

Supravalvular Aortic Stenosis

Supravalvular aortic stenosis occurs as a fibrous shelf or diaphragm across the aortic root above the aortic valve. The lesion is congenital and may be associated with hypercalcemia and a characteristic facies.

Subvalvular Aortic Stenosis

In fixed subvalvular aortic stenosis, the obstruction lies immediately below the aortic valve in the left ventricular outflow tract. The obstruction to outflow has diaphragmatic and fibromuscular components. The diaphragmatic portion, which is attached to the anterior leaflet of the mitral valve, consists of cusp-like tissue and extends forward to insert just below the right coronary cusp of the aortic valve [8]. The fibromuscular component protrudes anteriorly from the ventricular septum opposite the anterior mitral cusp. Cases of fixed subvalvular aortic stenosis may develop muscular hypertrophy causing the septum to bulge.

Presentation

In childhood, patients with asymptomatic aortic stenosis may present at a routine clinical examination during which a cardiac murmur is heard. Furthermore, even in later life certain patients with severe aortic stenosis may remain symptom free.

Symptoms

Some patients with severe aortic stenosis suffer from angina pectoris. Various factors may contribute to the development of this symptom: the hypertrophied left ventricle requires an increased coronary blood flow which is not met, or patients with aortic stenosis may have co-existing coronary artery disease. Exertional syncope may occur as a result of impaired cerebral perfusion due either to relatively fixed cardiac output on exercise or to transient ventricular arrhythmias. Exertional dyspnea may also be a presenting symptom.

Signs

Fixed obstruction to left ventricular outflow due either to aortic valve stenosis or subvalvular aortic stenosis results in a slow rise of the aortic pressure pulse which can be detected clinically as a slow rise in the carotid pulse. In supravalvular aortic stenosis, the arterial pulses in the neck are asymmetric with usually the right carotid having a sharp upstroke while the left is slow-rising due to preferential propagation of the high velocity jet into the innominate artery. Turbulence created at the site of obstruction to left ventricular outflow gives rise to an ejection systolic murmur.

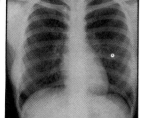

In aortic valve stenosis the abrupt halting of the abnormal domed valve gives rise to an aortic ejection sound which is not a feature of subvalvular or supravalvular aortic stenosis. Obstruction to left ventricular outflow results in prolongation of left ventricular ejection. This causes a delay in closure of the aortic valve and, consequently, reversed splitting of the second heart sound may be heard. If the obstruction is due to valvular aortic stenosis and the valve is rigid and immobile, then neither the ejection sound nor the aortic component of the second heart sound may be heard.

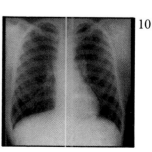

The hypertrophied stiff left ventricle gives rise to two abnormal palpatory findings. The apical impulse is usually sustained in quality during systole, but is not markedly exaggerated. In addition, the abnormally powerful left atrial contraction can be palpated as a separate atrial (double) impulse and may be audible as a fourth heart sound.

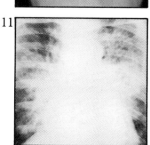

Investigations

Radiology

Valvular Aortic Stenosis

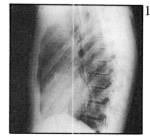

In uncomplicated aortic valve stenosis, the heart size remains

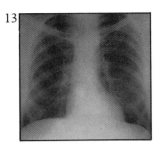

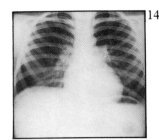

within normal limits [9], but the ascending aorta shows post-stenotic dilatation [10]. Although all cases of severe aortic stenosis develop left ventricular hypertrophy, in the later stages dilatation of the left ventricle may also occur leading to left ventricular failure [11]. The aortic cusps become irregular, disorganized and calcified [12].

Supravalvular and Subvalvular Aortic Stenosis

In supravalvular aortic stenosis the chest radiograph shows a normal sized heart with an inconspicuous aorta [13]. There may also be evidence of associated pulmonary artery stenoses [14].

In subvalvular aortic stenosis the chest radiograph is usually normal, although occasionally post-stenotic dilatation of the aorta may be present.

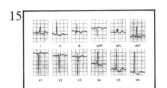

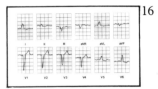

Electrocardiography

The electrocardiogram may remain normal even in severe left ventricular outflow obstruction, but it is more usual for it to reflect left ventricular hypertrophy with ST-segment and T-wave abnormalities in the left ventricular leads [15]. Left bundle branch block may also be seen [16].

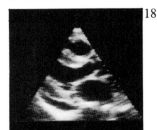

Echocardiography

Valvular Aortic Stenosis

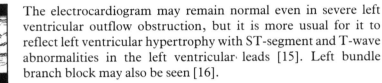

Although it may appear normal, the M-mode echocardiogram of a bicuspid non-calcified aortic valve typically has an eccentric diastolic closure line; almost invariably it is displaced anteriorly [17]. The bicuspid valve usually domes during systole [18]. In calcified aortic stenosis, dense parallel echoes are seen in the aortic root due to multiple re-reflection of the ultrasound beam at the interfaces of the calcific material. In mild cases, it is still possible to visualize some cusp movement or at least to appreciate clearing of the echoes as the calcified leaflets separate in systole [19], but, as the pathologic process progresses, the echoes obliterate the space of the aortic root and are present throughout the cardiac cycle [20].

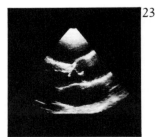

It is usually easier to visualize the aortic valve and its abnormal structure and movement by 2-dimensional echocardiography than from M-mode recordings [21].

Supravalvular and Subvalvular Aortic Stenosis

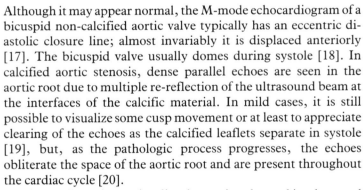

The region of narrowing in supravalvular aortic stenosis may be demonstrated echocardiographically by scanning upwards from the aortic root [22]. If a definite increase in diameter is seen, this provides strong evidence of a reduction in aortic size.

It is often possible to visualize the obstruction in subvalvular aortic stenosis in the long axis view [23]. Occasionally, M-mode echocardiography shows that the aortic valve leaflets close progressively throughout systole with a coarse fluttering motion indistinguishable from that seen in hypertrophic cardiomyopathy. Subvalvular aortic stenosis is commonly associated with minor

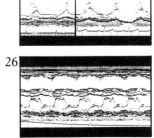

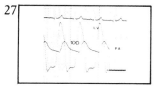

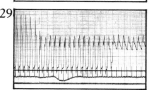

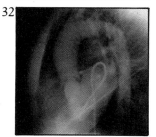

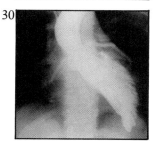

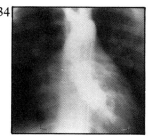

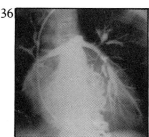

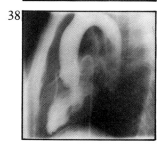

valvular incompetence which is detected by the fluttering of the anterior mitral valve cusp in diastole.

In fixed left ventricular outflow obstruction, the left ventricle is usually symmetrically hypertrophied and this is reflected echocardiographically as an increased thickness of both the septum and posterior wall and a reduction in ventricular diameter [24,25]. Although the hypertrophy is usually symmetric, the septum may be thicker than the free wall as in cases of hypertrophic cardiomyopathy. On M-mode echocardiography, the anterior mitral valve leaflet may show a decreased diastolic closure rate in severe left ventricular hypertrophy from any cause [26] and it is important to distinguish this appearance from rheumatic mitral stenosis by demonstration of the normal opposite movement of the posterior cusp or by 2-dimensional echocardiography.

Cardiac Catheterization and Angiography

In valvular aortic stenosis, there is a systolic pressure difference across the valve [27] while in supravalvular stenosis the pressure difference is between the supravalvular chamber and the aorta [28] and in subvalvular aortic stenosis it is within the left ventricle [29].

Left ventricular hypertrophy may be seen by left ventriculography [30]. In valvular aortic stenosis the typical change is the thickening of the cusps, with doming in systole, and a central ejection jet may be seen [31,32,33].

In supravalvular stenosis, angiography shows the obstructive lesion above the sinuses of Valsalva [34,35]. If additional pulmonary artery stenoses are present, they may be seen on right ventricular angiograms [36].

In subvalvular aortic stenosis, the left ventricular angiogram shows the subvalvular obstruction [37,38] or a more diffuse fibromuscular lesion [39]. Associated aortic valve regurgitation may be demonstrated by aortography.

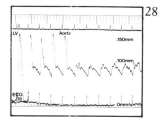

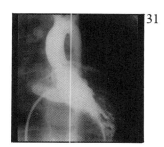

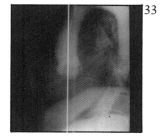

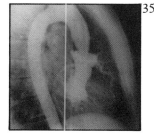

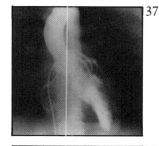

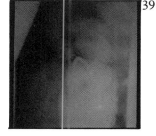

1 Fully open normal aortic valve. The cusps fold back into the aortic sinuses to leave a large central opening.

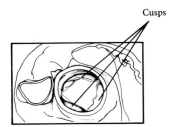

Cusps

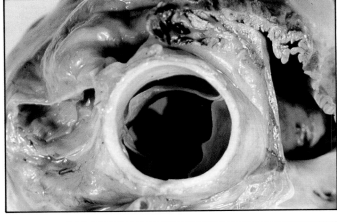

2 Fully closed normal aortic valve. The cusps meet and overlap providing support for each other in the closed position.

Cusp

Cusp

Cusp

3 A bicuspid aortic valve. The opened valve has only two cusps which at this age have not undergone calcification.

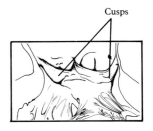

Cusps

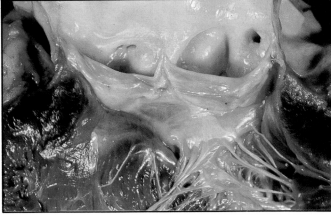

4 Calcific bicuspid aortic stenosis. The aperture of the valve is a transverse slit across the aortic root between two cusps. Masses of calcium bulge from each cusp.

Aperture of Valve

Cusp

Cusp

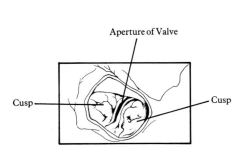

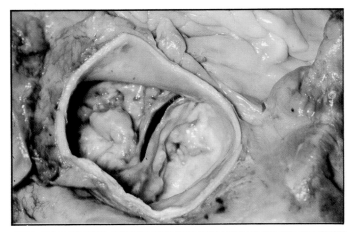

5 Rheumatic aortic stenosis in a patient with co-existent mitral disease. The aortic valve aperture is triangular due to fusion of all three commissures.

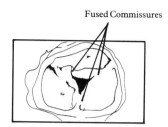

Fused Commissures

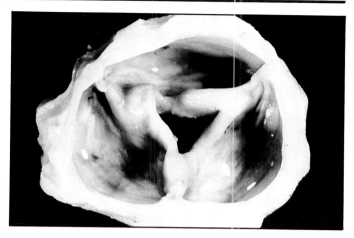

6 Pure 'senile' aortic stenosis in a tricuspid aortic valve due to extreme age-related dystrophic calcification in the cusps.

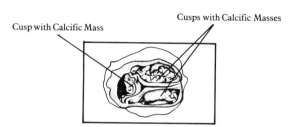

Cusp with Calcific Mass   Cusps with Calcific Masses

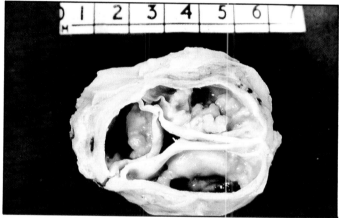

7 Transverse slice of left ventricle from a patient with a normal heart compared with a patient with aortic stenosis. In aortic stenosis the ventricular wall is thick and the cavity is small.

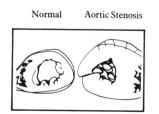

Normal   Aortic Stenosis

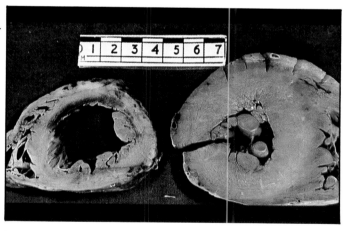

8 The aortic outflow tract in a case with subvalvular aortic stenosis. A membrane joins the anterior cusp of the mitral valve to the interventricular septum beneath the aortic valve.

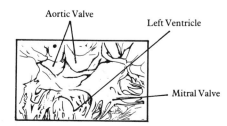

Aortic Valve   Left Ventricle

Mitral Valve

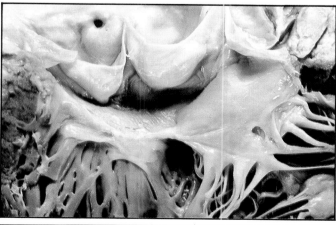

9 Chest radiograph of uncomplicated aortic valve stenosis, showing normal heart size.

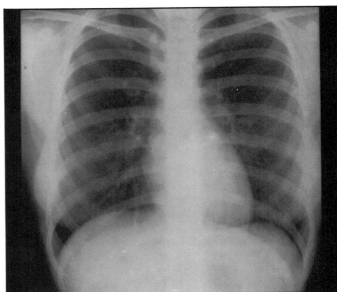

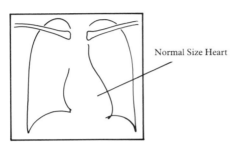

Normal Size Heart

10 Chest radiograph of aortic valve stenosis showing post-stenotic dilatation of the ascending aorta.

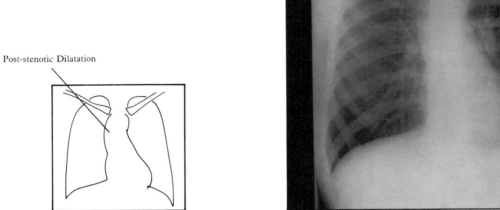

Post-stenotic Dilatation

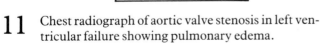

11 Chest radiograph of aortic valve stenosis in left ventricular failure showing pulmonary edema.

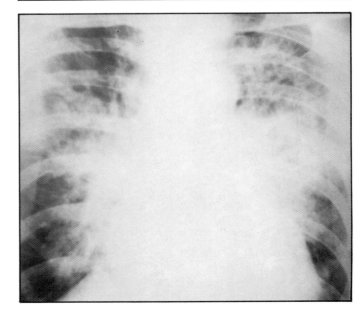

Edema

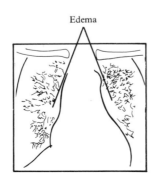

12 Chest radiograph (lateral projection) in aortic valve stenosis showing a calcified aortic valve.

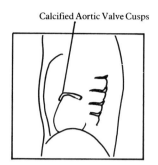

Calcified Aortic Valve Cusps

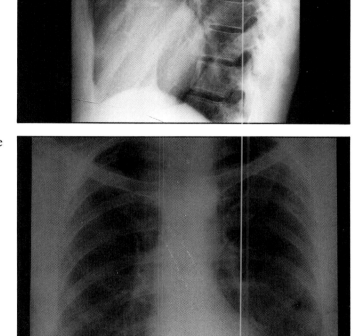

13 Chest radiograph in supravalvular aortic stenosis. The heart size is normal and the ascending aorta inconspicuous.

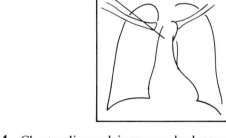

Aorta

14 Chest radiograph in supravalvular aortic stenosis associated with central pulmonary artery stenosis. The aortic arch is inconspicuous; there is post-stenotic dilatation of the pulmonary arteries.

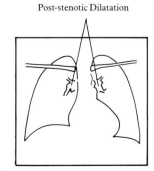

Post-stenotic Dilatation

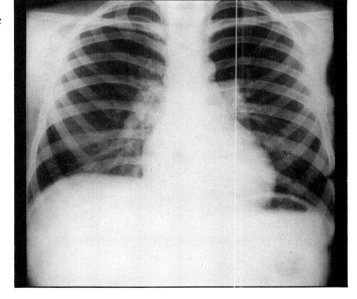

15

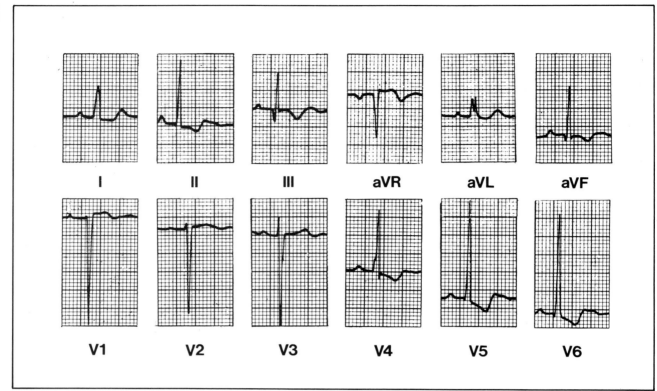

Electrocardiogram in severe aortic stenosis showing deep S wave in V1 and tall R wave in V5 with ST and T-wave changes indicating left ventricular hypertrophy.

16

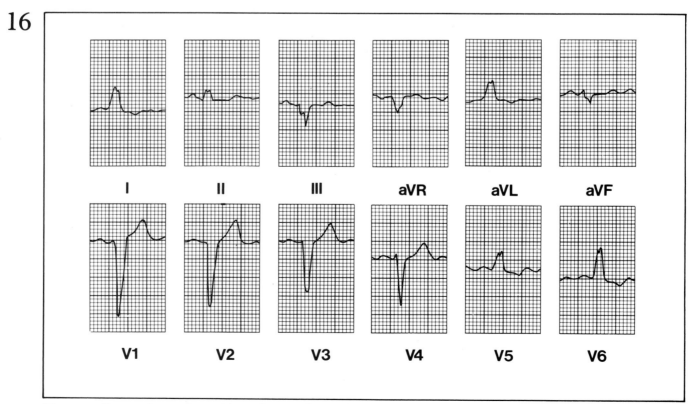

Electrocardiogram in a patient with aortic stenosis showing left bundle branch block.

17

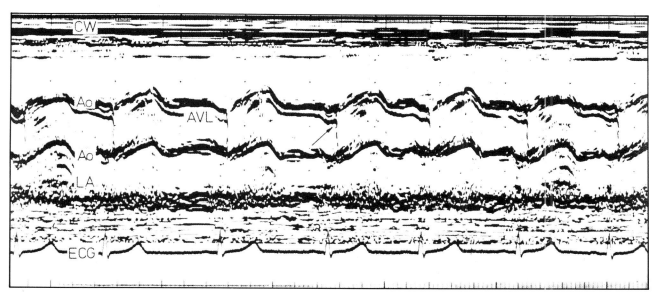

M-mode echocardiogram of a patient with a bicuspid aortic valve showing anterior displacement of the diastolic closure line (arrowed).

18

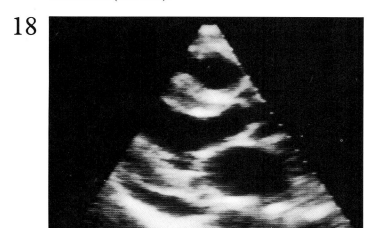 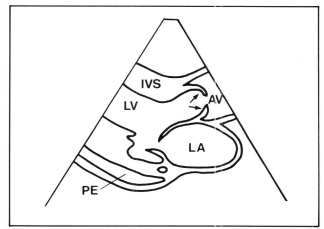

2-D parasternal long axis echocardiographic view showing doming of the aortic valve leaflets in systole (arrows). A pericardial effusion is also present.

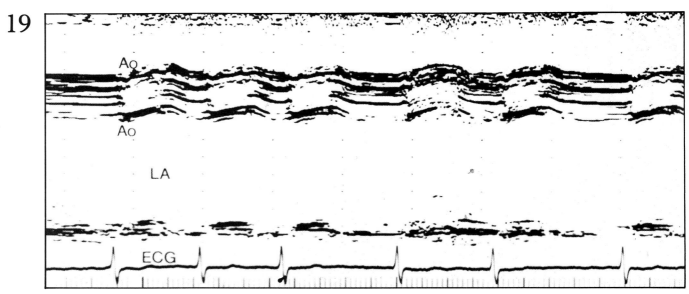

M-mode echocardiogram in calcific aortic stenosis showing multiple echoes in the aortic root which partially clear during systole.

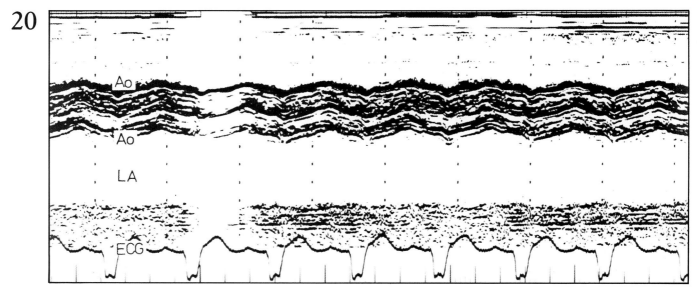

M-mode echocardiograms in calcific aortic stenosis showing obliteration of the aortic root by dense echoes through the cardiac cycle.

21

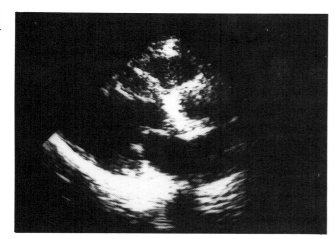
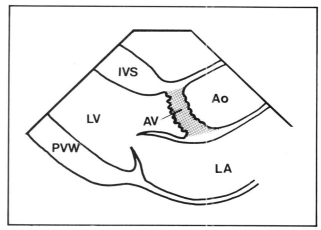

2-D parasternal long axis echocardiographic view showing a thickened calcified aortic valve.

22

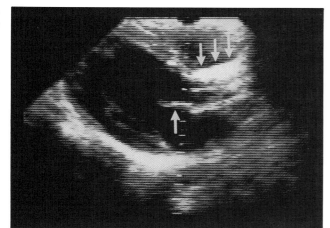
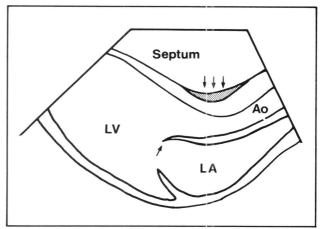

2-D echocardiographic parasternal long axis view showing supravalvular aortic stenosis (arrowed).

23

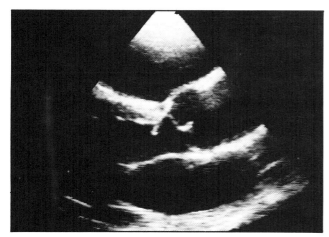
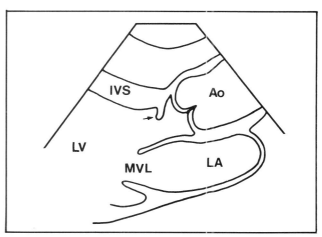

2-D parasternal long axis echocardiographic view of the left ventricle and outflow tract showing discrete subaortic membrane obstructing the outflow tract (arrowed).

24

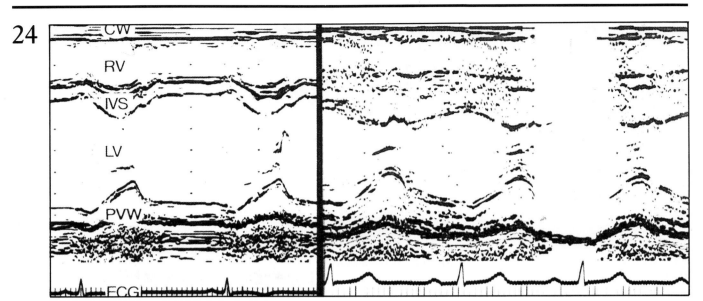

M-mode echocardiogram of a normal left ventricle [left], and left ventricular hypertrophy [right], showing symmetric thickening of the septum and left ventricular posterior wall and reduction of cavity size.

25

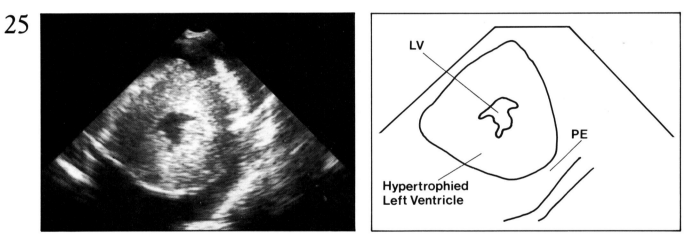

2-D short axis echocardiographic view showing concentric hypertrophy of the left ventricle with a small left ventricular cavity. There is an additional pericardial effusion.

26

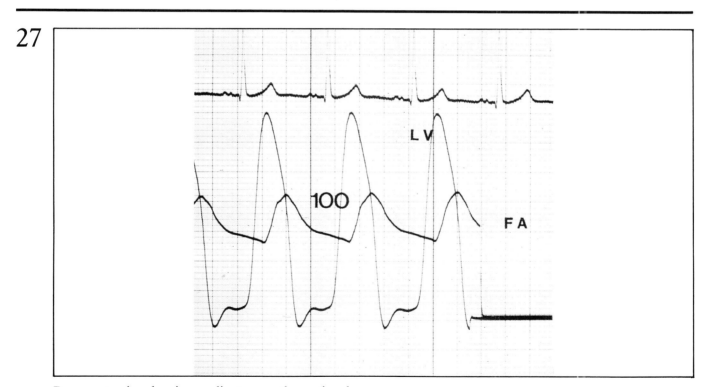

M-mode echocardiogram in aortic stenosis showing reduction in diastolic closure rate of the anterior leaflet of the mitral valve (arrow), but normal posterior cusp movement indicating a normal mitral valve.

AORTIC STENOSIS

Cardiac Catheterization & Angiography

27

Pressure tracing showing gradient across the aortic valve.

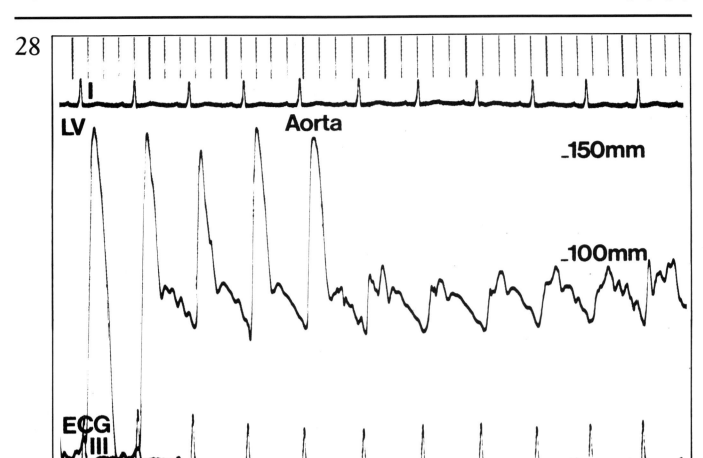

Withdrawal pressure tracing showing gradient across the supravalvular stenosis.

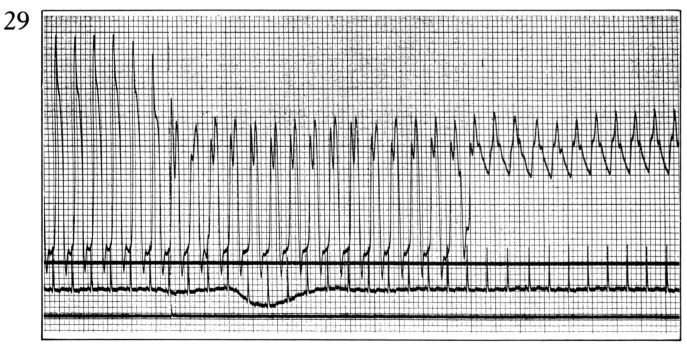

Withdrawal pressure tracing showing gradient across a subvalvular stenosis.

30 Left ventricular angiogram (right anterior oblique projection) in aortic valve stenosis showing gross left ventricular hypertrophy.

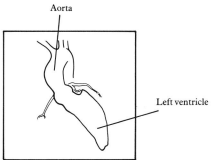

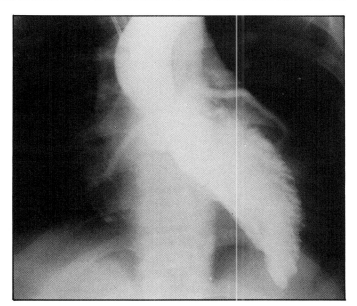

31 Systolic frame from the same patient as [30] showing a thick domed valve.

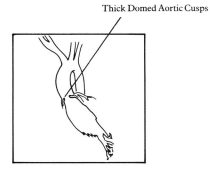

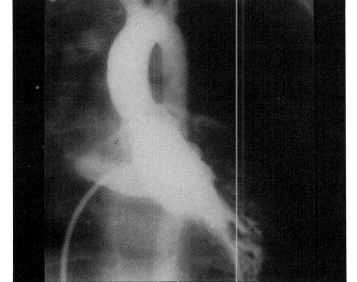

32 Lateral view of a ventricular angiogram in aortic stenosis showing a thick domed valve with post-stenotic dilatation of the aorta.

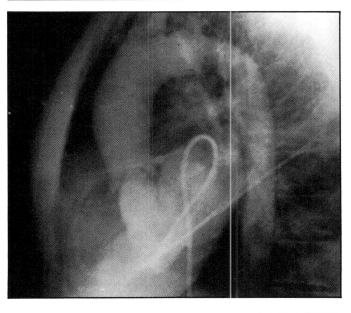

33 Lateral view of an aortogram in aortic stenosis, showing thick irregular rigid cusps of the aortic valve.

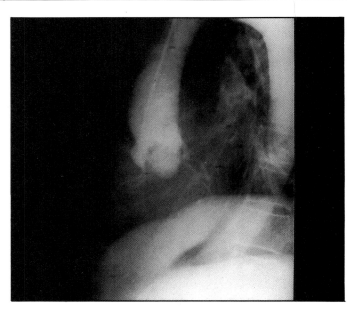

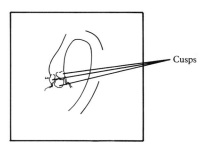

Cusps

34 Left ventricular angiogram (antero-posterior projection) showing supravalvular stenosis and left ventricular hypertrophy.

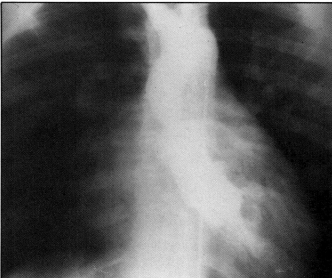

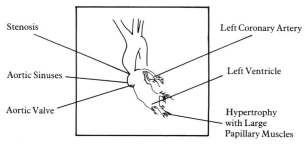

Stenosis

Aortic Sinuses

Aortic Valve

Left Coronary Artery

Left Ventricle

Hypertrophy with Large Papillary Muscles

35 Lateral view of [34].

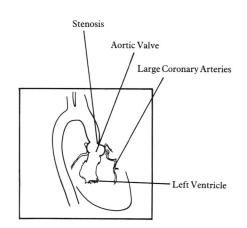

Stenosis

Aortic Valve

Large Coronary Arteries

Left Ventricle

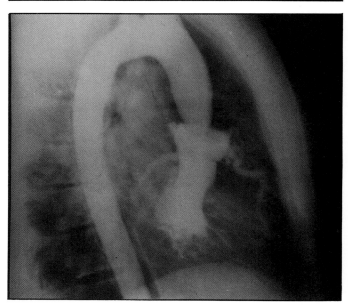

36 Right ventricular angiogram (antero-posterior projection) in the same patient as [34,35] showing pulmonary artery stenosis.

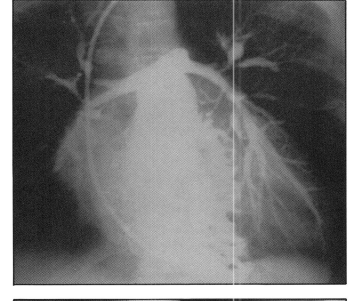

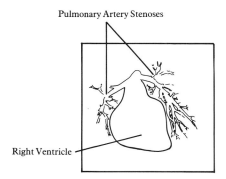

37 Left ventricular angiogram (antero-posterior projection) showing diaphragmatic subvalvular aortic stenosis and left ventricular hypertrophy.

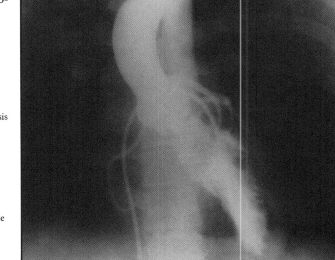

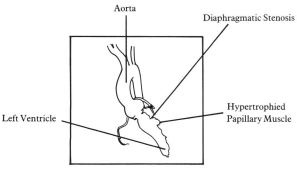

38 Lateral view of [37].

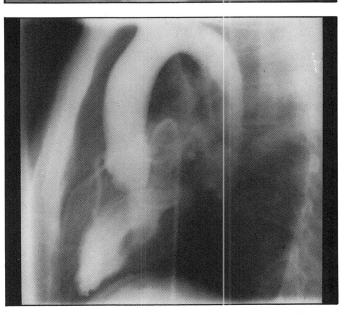

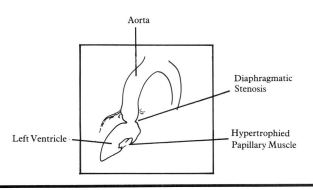

39 Left ventricular angiogram (lateral projection) with tunnel subvalvular aortic stenosis.

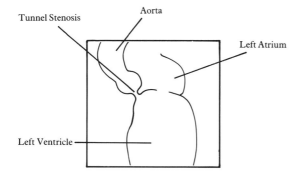

Pathology

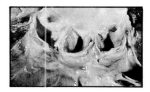

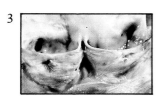

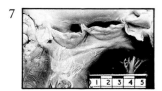

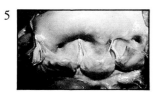

Aortic regurgitation results either from disease of the aortic cusps or disease of the aortic wall leading to aortic root dilatation. Infective endocarditis involving either the bicuspid or tricuspid aortic valve may result in perforation of a cusp and consequent aortic regurgitation [1]. Other causes of aortic regurgitation due to cusp disease include a chronic rheumatic process [2] and even rheumatoid granulomata.

Aortic root dilatation occurs in both inflammatory aortitis and medial aortic degeneration. The causes of aortitis include syphilis [3] and ankylosing spondylitis [4]. Syphilis produces characteristic widening, i.e. separation of the cusp edges at the commissures. Ankylosing spondylitis in contrast produces a more distorted aortic root but commissure widening is less marked. In all forms of aortitis the intima is often wrinkled and scarred (tree barking) expressing underlying medial destruction. Distinction of the various types of aortitis without serology and clinical history is usually impossible, as the histology is uniform. Aortic medial degeneration is characterized by loss of muscle and elastic tissue in the aortic root. In some instances focal accumulation of acid mucopolysaccharide is found. Such changes occur in Marfan's syndrome [5 & 6]. It is more common for these changes to be an isolated finding without other skeletal stigmata of Marfan's syndrome than to have a greater degree of mucin accumulation in the media (cystic medial necrosis).

Chronic aortic regurgitation leads to left ventricular dilatation often with associated hypertrophy. Regurgitant jets across the valve may hit the interventricular septum [7] or the ventricular aspect of the anterior cusp of the mitral valve [8] producing patches of endocardial thickening.

Presentation

Symptoms

Patients with slight aortic regurgitation may present following the finding of a cardiac murmur at routine medical examination. Symptoms are rare in chronic aortic regurgitation unless the lesion is severe. Patients who complain of exertional dyspnea, or dyspnea at rest, do so because the pulmonary venous pressure is raised — a change which occurs late in the natural history of the disease. Angina occurs occasionally in patients with aortic regurgitation. This may be the result of aortitis affecting the origin of the coronary arteries, or because of coronary atheroma. Angina can also occur without coronary artery narrowing because coronary perfusion is inadequate to meet the demands of the enlarged left ventricle.

In contrast severe aortic regurgitation developing acutely (due to aortic dissection) or over a short period (as in infective endocarditis) is poorly tolerated. Pulmonary edema in these circumstances develops rapidly because there is a rapid increase in left ventricular diastolic pressure (and hence pulmonary venous pressure) in the presence of a previously normal left ventricle.

Signs

The constant physical sign of aortic regurgitation is the presence of an early diastolic murmur. This may be accompanied by a systolic murmur due to increased stroke volume through a normal aortic valve or one with abnormal leaflets. The presence of an ejection sound may be associated either with a bicuspid aortic valve or with aortic root dilatation. In slight aortic regurgitation there will be no other abnormality. In moderate or severe chronic aortic regurgitation there will be a wide pulse pressure with a rapid upstroke and downstroke in the arterial pulses. The apical impulse will be hyperdynamic reflecting the large stroke volume of the left ventricle. A mid-diastolic murmur may be heard in the mitral area (Austin-Flint murmur). In acute severe aortic regurgitation the clinical picture will be dominated by pulmonary edema.

Investigations

Radiology

If aortic regurgitation is due to abnormalities of the aortic wall then the ascending aorta on the chest X-ray may be seen to be enlarged. Usually there is generalized dilatation of the ascending aorta [9], but in syphilis a localized aneurysm may be seen [10]. If aortic regurgitation is due to a leaflet abnormality, the ascending aorta may appear normal.

In long-standing aortic regurgitation, the left ventricle dilates producing cardiac enlargement in the chest X-ray [11]. In acute aortic regurgitation as from perforation of a cusp there may be pulmonary edema but the cardiac silhouette remains normal [12].

Electrocardiography

The electrocardiogram usually reflects left ventricular enlargement. Large voltages may be present in V1 (deep S wave) and V5 (tall R wave) [13]. There may be associated ST-T changes [14]. In acute aortic regurgitation the electrocardiogram may be normal even though the aortic regurgitation may be severe.

Echocardiography

In aortic wall disease the aortic valve leaflets are usually normal. However, dilatation of the aorta may be detected by echocardiography [15,16,17]. In aortic regurgitation due to acute dissection of the aortic root it is frequently possible to visualize the intra mural separation [18]. Most patients with dissection extending back to the aortic root have an increased amount of pericardial fluid which is readily detected by echocardiography.

Where aortic regurgitation is due to a leaflet abnormality, such as prolapse of the leaflet, calcification or a vegetation, it may be visualized directly [19,20].

Dilatation of the left ventricle occurs as a consequence of moderate or severe aortic regurgitation and can be detected echocardiographically [21]. The severity of chronic aortic regurgita-

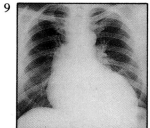

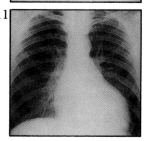

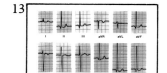

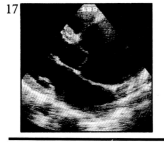

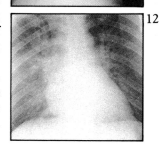

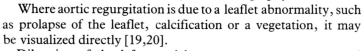

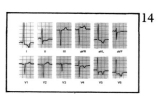

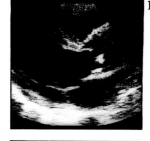

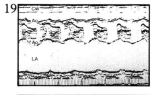

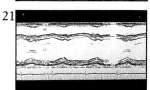

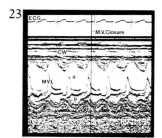

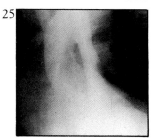

tion can be assessed by calculation of the left ventricular stroke volume. It is possible to estimate left ventricular stroke volume from the echocardiogram by reference to end-diastolic and end-systolic dimensions. Calculated fractional shortening remains normal until left ventricular failure supervenes.

The regurgitant jet of blood impinging on the anterior mitral valve leaflet causes fluttering in diastole [22]. This sign is not related to the severity of the regurgitation but is a very sensitive method of detecting aortic regurgitation. Sometimes the jet is directed at the septal endocardium and this may then be seen to flutter.

In acute severe aortic regurgitation (as occurs in endocarditis) premature closure of the mitral valve detected echocardiographically indicates severe hemodynamic disturbance [23]. However left ventricular dimensions may remain close to normal.

Cardiac Catheterization and Angiography

Elevation of the left ventricular end-diastolic pressure is often present in patients with moderate or severe aortic regurgitation. The highest end-diastolic pressures are seen in patients with acute severe aortic regurgitation and this may exceed left atrial pressure causing premature closure of the mitral valve.

Aortic regurgitation can be demonstrated by aortography which also demonstrates the anatomy of the aortic root [24]. An ascending aortogram is the best method of diagnosing dissection of the aorta [25].

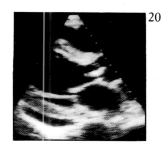

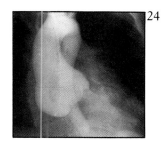

1 Infective endocarditis of the aortic valve with perforation of a cusp (arrowed) producing incompetence. Vegetation present on the valve.

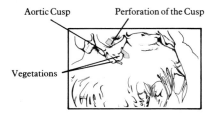

2 Rheumatic aortic incompetence: all three cusps are fibrotic and retracted. Note the coexistent thickening of mitral chordae.

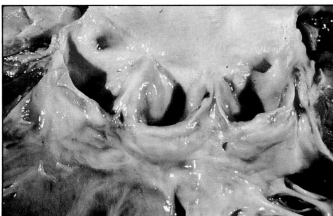

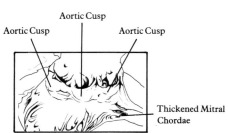

3 Mild syphilitic aortic valve disease. The commissure is widened, the two cusps not meeting. The ascending aorta shows pearly yellow flat plaques.

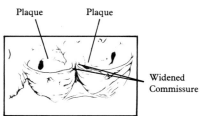

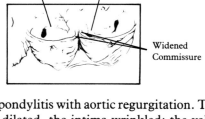

4 Ankylosing spondylitis with aortic regurgitation. The aortic root is dilated, the intima wrinkled; the valve cusps are distorted and shrunken.

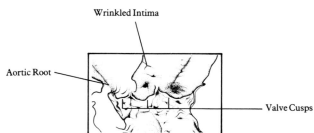

5 Dilated aortic root with ballooned thin aortic cusps producing aortic incompetence in Marfan's syndrome.

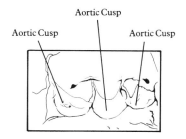

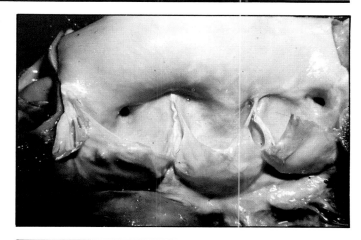

6 Aorta in Marfan's syndrome. The aortic root is dilated and there are two healed dissection tears (arrowed).

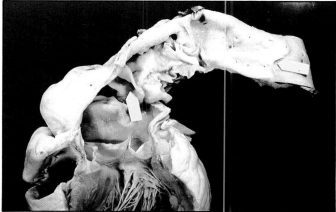

7 Aortic root dilatation with a patch of endocardial thickening on the ventricular septum due to impingement of a regurgitant jet.

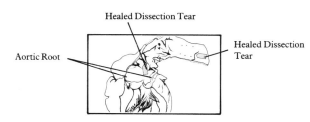

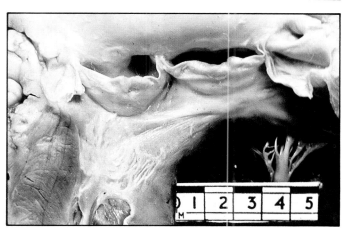

8 Biscupid aortic valve with a cleft in the largest cusp producing mild aortic regurgitation. Jet lesion on the ventricular surface of the anterior cusp of the mitral valve (arrow).

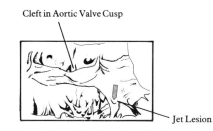

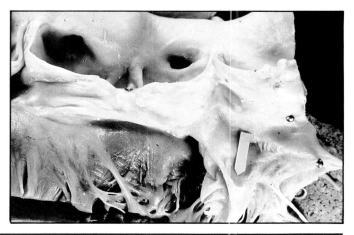

9 Chest radiograph showing dilatation of the ascending aorta due to Marfan's syndrome with cardiac enlargement from resultant aortic regurgitation.

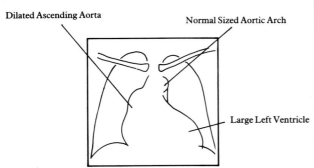

Dilated Ascending Aorta

Normal Sized Aortic Arch

Large Left Ventricle

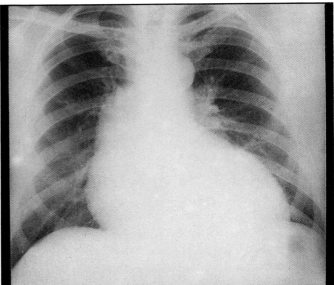

10 Chest radiograph showing a localized aneurysm of the ascending aorta due to syphilis.

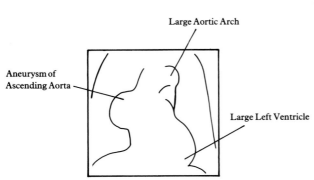

Large Aortic Arch

Aneurysm of Ascending Aorta

Large Left Ventricle

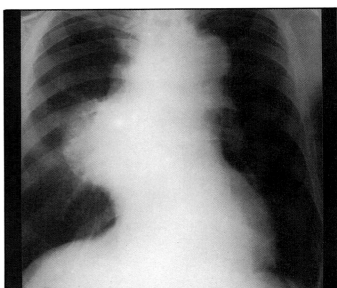

11 Chest radiograph showing cardiac enlargement in chronic aortic regurgitation.

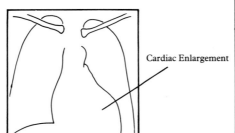

Cardiac Enlargement

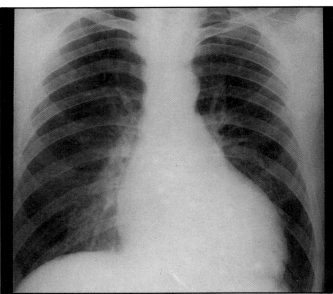

12 Chest radiograph showing pulmonary edema with normal heart size due to acute aortic regurgitation from a ruptured cusp.

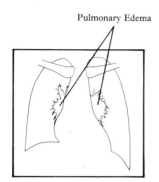

Pulmonary Edema

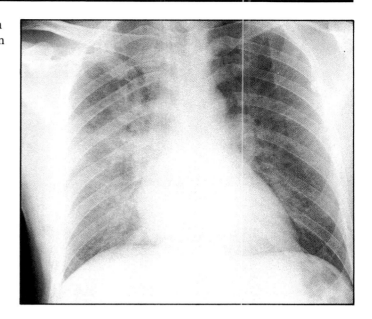

AORTIC REGURGITATION

Electrocardiography

13

| I | II | III | aVR | aVL | aVF |

| V1 | V2 | V3 | V4 | V5 | V6 |

The electrocardiogram in chronic aortic regurgitation showing increased left ventricular voltage (deep S wave V1, tall R wave V6).

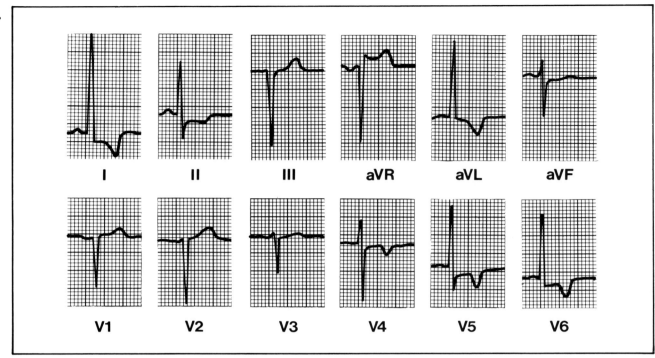

The electrocardiogram in chronic aortic regurgitation showing severe left ventricular hypertrophy (i.e. increased voltage and ST-T wave abnormalities in the lateral leads).

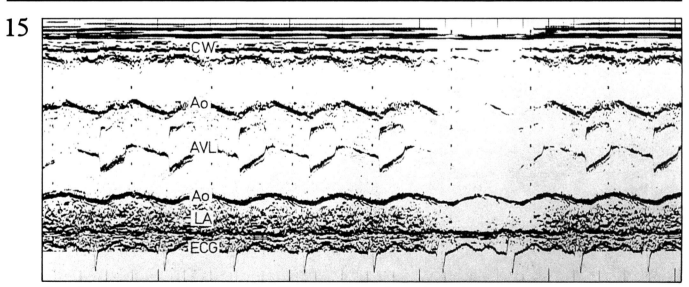

M-mode echocardiogram showing massive dilatation of the aortic root in Marfan's syndrome with aortic regurgitation.

16

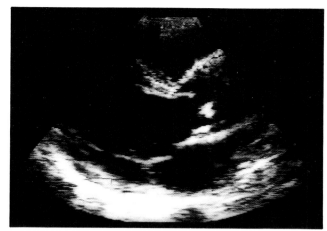
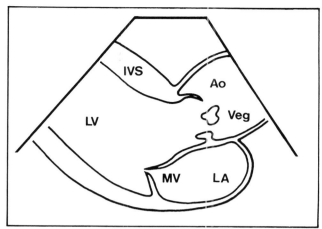

2-D echocardiographic parasternal long axis systolic frame in aortic regurgitation due to infective endocarditis showing the vegetation being carried up the ascending aorta during ejection. The vegetation is attached to the non-coronary aortic cusp. Note the shape of the right coronary cusp suggesting that the valve is bicuspid.

17

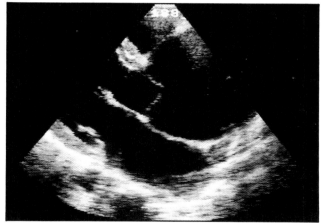
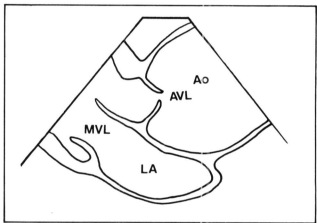

2-D echocardiographic parasternal long axis view in a case of aortic regurgitation secondary to aneurysmal dilatation of the aortic root. This is a diastolic frame, as shown by the wide open mitral valve, yet the aortic cusps fail to appose and one is prolapsing below the other.

18

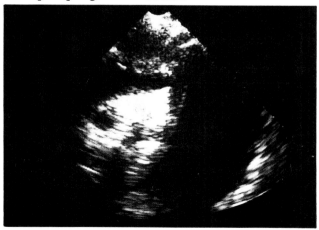
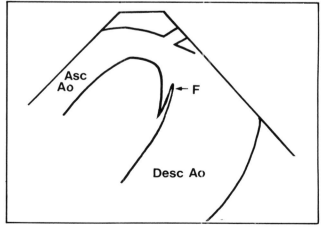

2-D echocardiographic suprasternal long axis view of the aortic arch showing the intimal flap in a patient with Marfan's syndrome and aortic dissection.

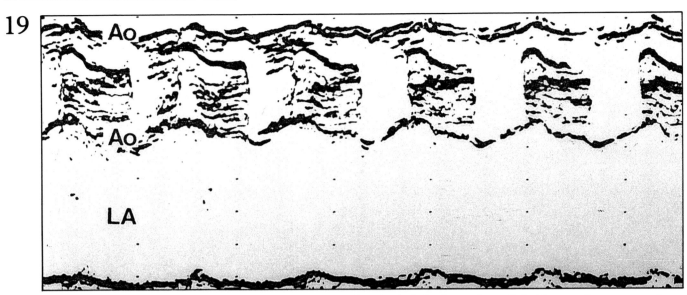

M-mode echocardiogram showing vegetations on the aortic valve in infective endocarditis. Dense echoes are seen in diastole with clearing in systole.

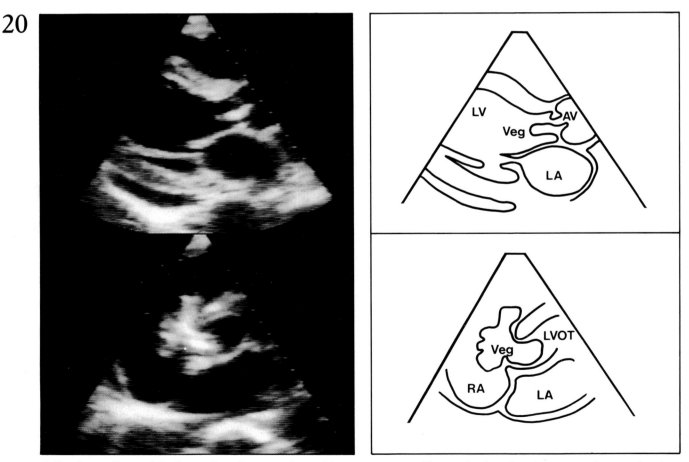

2-D echocardiographic views of aortic vegetations. Above, parasternal long axis view showing vegetations prolapsing into the left ventricular outflow tract. Below, modified parasternal short axis view of the aortic root showing the aortic vegetation invading across the aortic wall to the tricuspid valve.

21

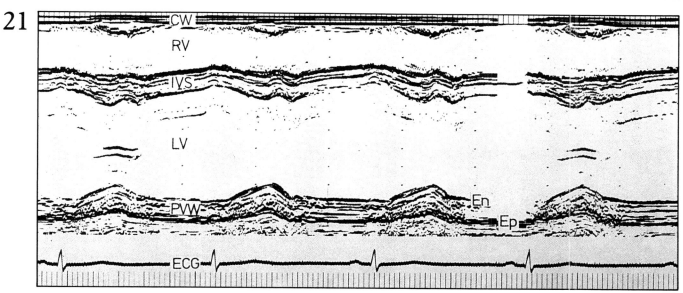

M-mode echocardiogram showing left ventricular dimensions in chronic severe aortic regurgitation. The diastolic diameter is greatly increased (6.4 cms) but fractional shortening is normal.

22

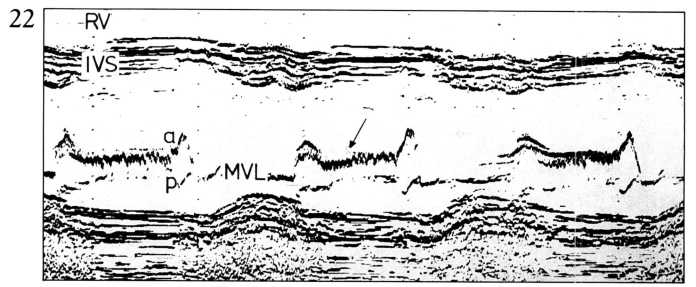

M-mode echocardiogram of the mitral valve in aortic regurgitation showing fluttering of its anterior leaflet in diastole (arrowed).

23 M-mode echocardiogram showing premature closure of the mitral valve in acute severe aortic regurgitation.

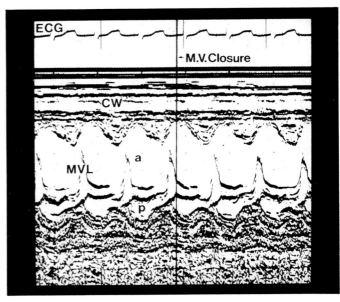

AORTIC REGURGITATION   Cardiac Catheterization & Angiography

24 Aortogram (antero-posterior projection) showing aortic root dilatation in Marfan's syndrome.

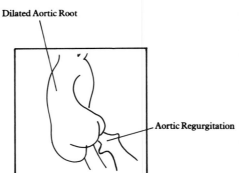

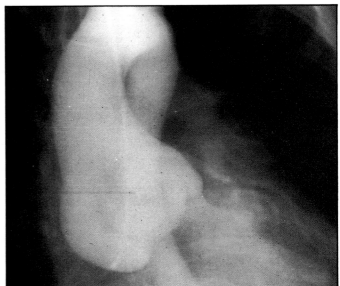

25 Aortogram (antero-posterior projection) of aortic dissection. The true lumen is compressed by the nonopaque false lumen.

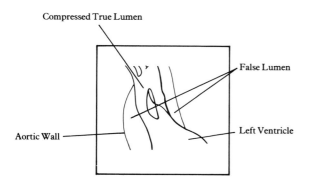

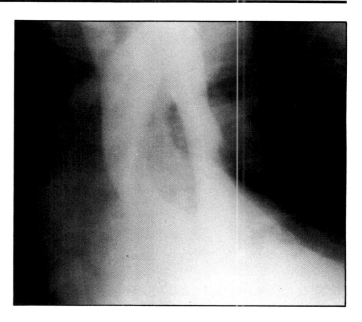

TRICUSPID VALVE DISEASE

Although there are several congenital malformations that may involve the tricuspid valve (e.g. tricuspid atresia) only Ebstein's anomaly, and acquired tricuspid valve disease, will be considered here.

Pathology

In Ebstein's anomaly the tricuspid valve is patent. In its most severe form, the valve orifice is displaced into the right ventricle down to the junction of the inlet and outlet portions [1]. The valve leaflets are dysplastic and the inlet portion of the ventricle becomes considerably thinned (atrialization).

Acquired tricuspid valve disease is unusual. A small proportion of patients with chronic rheumatic valve disease develop involvement of the tricuspid valve in addition to aortic and mitral disease. This produces fusion of the commissures in a manner analogous to mitral valve disease [2]. Acute infective endocarditis of the tricuspid valve is a complication in drug addicts who use intravenous injections. Carcinoid tumors may produce large amounts of vaso-active amines resulting in white fibrous thickening of the surfaces of the tricuspid and pulmonary valves [3]. This leads to tricuspid and pulmonary stenosis and incompetence.

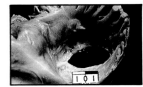

Presentation

Symptoms

Paroxysmal supraventricular tachycardia is the usual presenting feature of an adult with Ebstein's anomaly, though some may have no symptoms at all and are detected as a result of a routine chest X-ray.

The average patient with rheumatic tricuspid valvular disease usually presents with symptoms attributable to the co-existence of rheumatic mitral valve disease. Thus, breathlessness on exertion is not due to tricuspid valve disease but due to the associated mitral valve disease. However when tricuspid stenosis is severe the dypsnea which normally accompanies severe mitral stenosis may be absent. Tricuspid involvement may cause in addition venous distention resulting in hepatic enlargement, ascites and peripheral edema.

Fatigue resulting from a low fixed cardiac output is a very common symptom in the patient with severe tricuspid valve disease. Isolated tricuspid regurgitation occurs most frequently as a result of infective endocarditis in drug addicts. The presenting features will be those of infective endocarditis. Right atrial thrombosis or endocarditis of the valve may result in pulmonary embolism.

Signs

Most patients with Ebstein's anomaly are cyanosed. The atria and venous pulses are usually normal but prominent systolic waves in the venous pulse may be seen. The first heart sound may be widely split due to delayed tricuspid closure and the second heart sound is also abnormally wide but moves with respiration. An extra sound characteristically occurs after the two components of the second heart sound; in addition there may be the murmur of tricuspid regurgitation.

The most important clinical clue to the diagnosis of tricuspid valve disease is the alteration in the venous pulse. If tricuspid stenosis is dominant and the patient is in sinus rhythm the abnormally powerful right atrial contraction results in a striking increase in the 'a' wave of the venous pulse. Because there is an obstruction to right atrial emptying the rate of fall of the elevated pressure in diastole is reduced giving rise to a slow 'y' descent. By contrast, in dominant or pure tricuspid regurgitation the right atrial pressure in systole reflects the right ventricular systolic pressure with a marked increase in the 'v' or systolic wave of the venous pulse in the neck. The systolic venous expansion may be transmitted to the liver causing a systolic expansile pulsation. The descent of the venous pulse (y) is prominent and rapid. Peripheral edema and ascites are common findings in severe tricuspid valve disease due to the high venous pressure.

Tricuspid regurgitation results in a pan-systolic murmur usually best heard at the left sternal edge, the intensity of which is increased by inspiration. In pure tricuspid regurgitation a third heart sound will also be heard at the left sternal edge. With tricuspid stenosis there may be an opening snap and a mid-diastolic murmur both best heard at the left sternal edge during inspiration.

Investigations

Radiology

In Ebstein's anomaly the chest radiograph often shows a large globular heart. There may be a bulge on the left heart border due to displacement of the right ventricular outflow tract [4]. The right heart border may also be prominent and there is frequently pulmonary oligemia [5].

In rheumatic tricuspid valve disease the radiographic features are often dominated by the associated rheumatic involvement of the mitral or aortic valves. In severe tricuspid stenosis the right atrium may be very large [6]. The normal radiographic features of mitral valve disease may be limited by the presence of tricuspid valve disease. Thus, upper lobe pulmonary venous dilatation due to mitral involvement may be less obvious if there is additional severe tricuspid valve disease [7].

Electrocardiography

In Ebstein's anomaly, the typical features include tall P waves and right bundle branch block [8]. In acquired tricuspid valve disease right atrial hypertrophy may be the only electrocardiographic feature [9].

Echocardiography

In Ebstein's anomaly the tricuspid valve is seen to be large and displaced [10]. The abnormal position of the tricuspid valve causes it to be always seen in the same M-mode view as the mitral valve. In most cases of Ebstein's anomaly the tricuspid valve closes

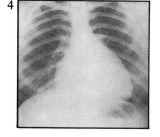

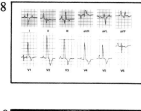

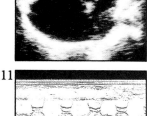

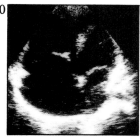

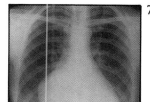

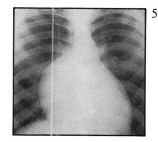

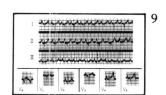

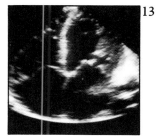

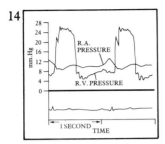

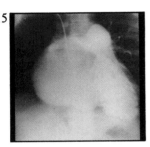

significantly later than the mitral valve [11]. In rheumatic tricuspid valve disease similar abnormalities are seen in the mobility and structure of the tricuspid valve as are seen in rheumatic mitral valve disease [12,13]. The large right atrium may be visualized directly and in pure tricuspid regurgitation the large right ventricle will be seen.

Contrast echocardiography may be useful in the diagnosis of both Ebstein's anomaly and tricuspid regurgitation. The bubbles may be seen to pass from right to left across the atrial septum in Ebstein's anomaly, while in tricuspid regurgitation the bubbles may pass back and forth across the tricuspid valve.

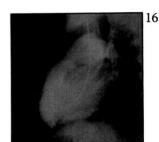

Cardiac Catheterization and Angiography

In Ebstein's anomaly it may be evident at cardiac catheterization that a right atrial pressure trace is obtained in a position when an endocardial electrode shows right ventricular configuration. Tricuspid regurgitation will result in an elevation of mean right atrial pressure with a dominant 'v' wave; the presence of tricuspid stenosis will be detected by simultaneous pressure tracings in the right atrium and right ventricle showing a diastolic pressure difference [14].

Angiography in Ebstein's anomaly will show displacement of the effective right atrioventricular orifice into the cavity of the right ventricle, frequently with atrialization of the ventricular inlet portion. This results in tricuspid regurgitation and a very large right atrium and atrialized portion [15,16].

1 Heart with Ebstein's anomaly of the tricuspid valve viewed from the outlet portion of the right ventricle. The valve is a fenestrated curtain which is attached in such a way as to separate the inlet and outlet portions of the right ventricle. The cavity of the inlet portion (atrialized right ventricle) is behind the valve.

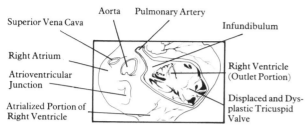

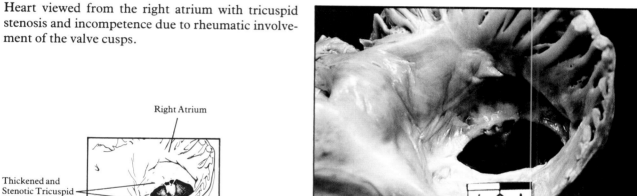

2 Heart viewed from the right atrium with tricuspid stenosis and incompetence due to rheumatic involvement of the valve cusps.

3 Heart in carcinoid disease showing fibrous thickening of the tricuspid valve.

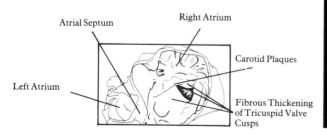

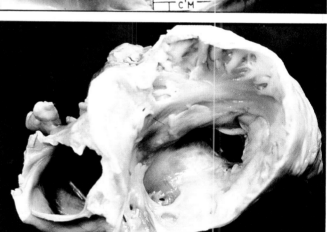

4 Chest radiograph in Ebstein's anomaly. The heart is enlarged and globular. There is a prominent bulge on the left heart border due to the displaced right ventricular outflow tract.

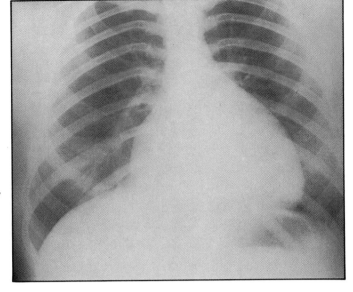

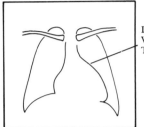

Displaced Right Ventricular Outflow Tract

5 Chest radiograph in Ebstein's anomaly showing pulmonary oligemia and a prominent right atrial border.

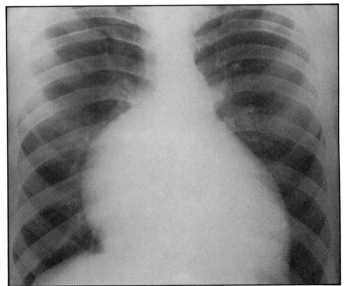

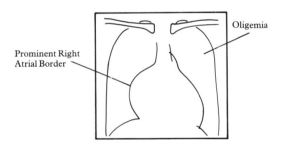

Oligemia

Prominent Right Atrial Border

6 Chest radiograph in rheumatic tricuspid stenosis showing an enormous right atrium.

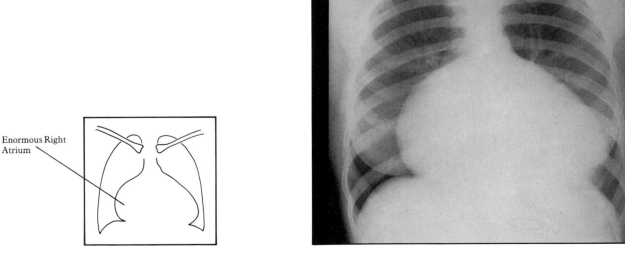

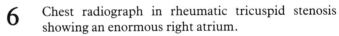

Enormous Right Atrium

7 Chest radiograph in rheumatic tricuspid and mitral disease showing a large right atrium. Upper lobe blood diversion is inconspicuous.

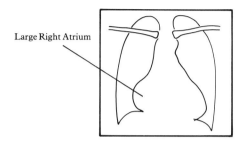

Large Right Atrium

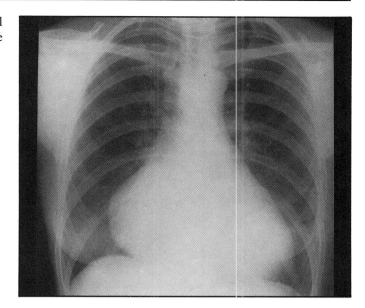

8

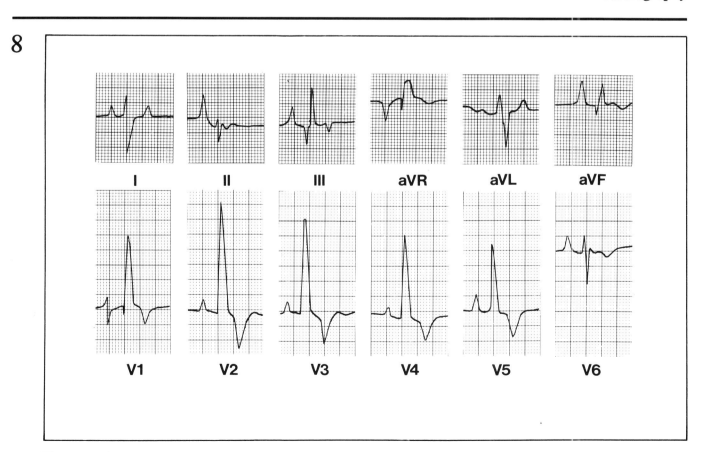

Electrocardiogram in Ebstein's anomaly showing tall P waves and right bundle branch block.

9

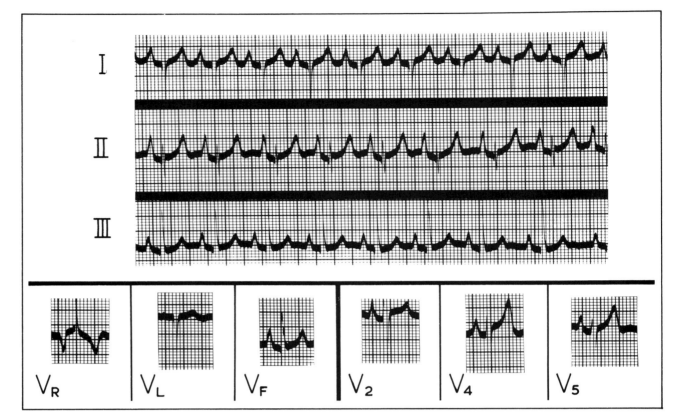

Electrocardiogram in tricuspid stenosis showing right atrial hypertrophy (tall P wave in lead II).

10

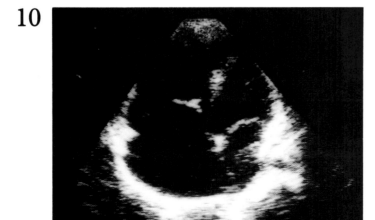
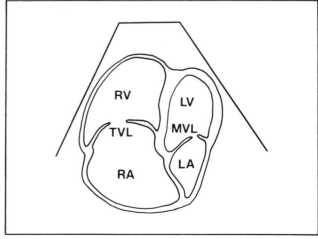

2-D echocardiographic apical four-chamber view of Ebstein's anomaly. The tricuspid valve is greatly displaced into the right ventricle.

11

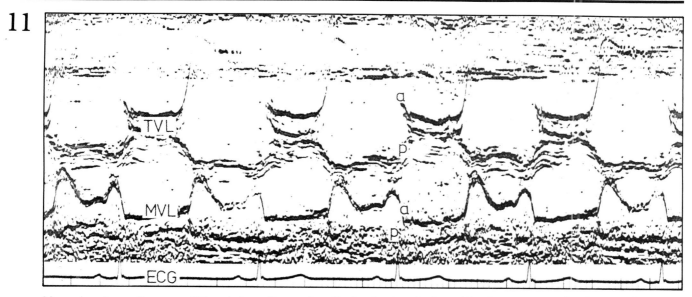

M-mode echocardiogram of Ebstein's malformation. Both mitral and tricuspid valves are seen simultaneously with tricuspid valve closure occurring after mitral valve closure.

12

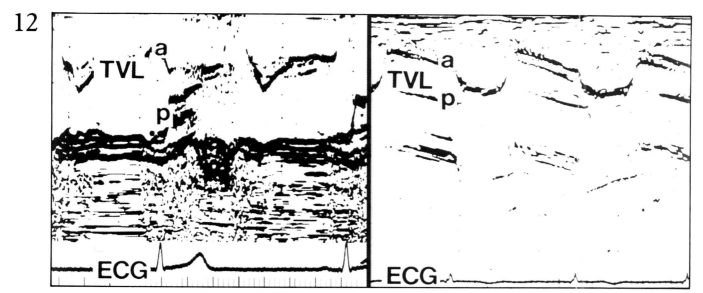

M-mode echocardiogram of tricuspid stenosis (right hand panel) showing reduced diastolic closure rate. A normal tricuspid valve is shown in the left hand panel for comparison.

13

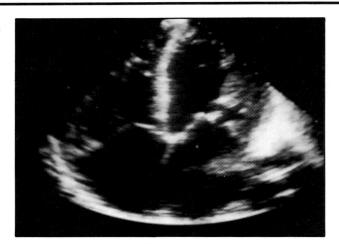 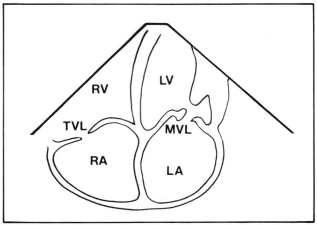

Apical four-chamber 2-D echocardiographic view in rheumatic mitral and tricuspid valve disease. The leaflet tips **hardly** separate.

14 Pressure tracings from a patient with tricuspid stenosis showing a diastolic gradient between right atrium and right ventricle.

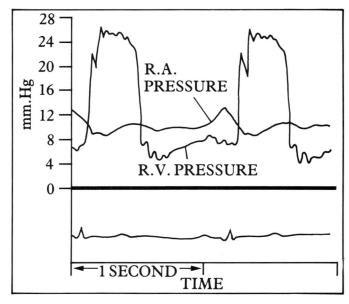

15 Right ventricular angiogram (antero-posterior projection) in Ebstein's anomaly. The injection is in the outlet portion. Both the true atrioventricular annulus and the effective orifice are outlined by regurgitation through the downwardly displaced tricuspid valve. The right atrium is dilated. In this patient there was additional pulmonary valve stenosis.

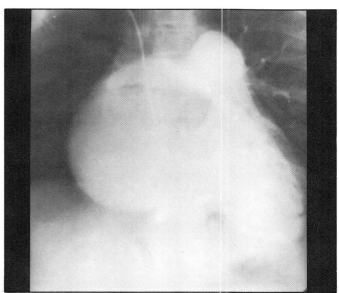

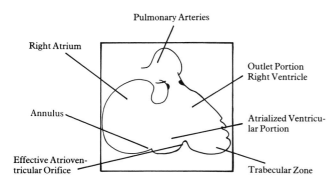

16 Lateral projection of [14]. The effective orifice of the tricuspid valve is seen between the inlet and outlet portions of the right ventricle. The thickened pulmonary valve is also seen.

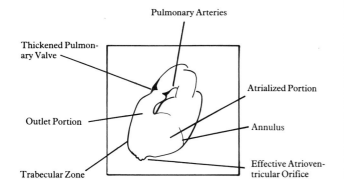

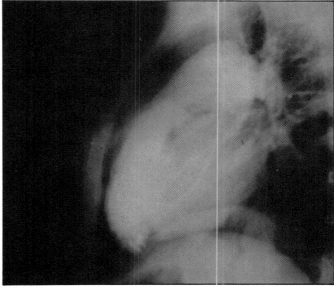

Chapter 5.

Congenital Heart Disease

Abbreviations

Ao	Aorta	LCCA	Left Common Carotid Artery	PVW	Posterior Ventricular Wall
Asc Ao	Ascending Aorta	LPA	Left Pulmonary Artery	RA	Right Atrium
ASD	Atrial Septal Defect	LSA	Left Subclavian Artery	RAVL	Right Atrioventricular Valve Leaflet
AV	Aortic Valve	LV	Left Ventricle		
CW	Chest Wall	MV	Mitral Valve	RPA	Right Pulmonary Artery
Desc Ao	Descending Aorta	MVL	Mitral Valve Leaflet	RV	Right Ventricle
En	Endocardium	PA	Pulmonary Artery	RVOT	Right Ventricular Outflow Tract
Ep	Epicardium	PDA	Persistent Ductus Arteriosus		
Inn	Innominate Artery			S	Septum
IS	Infundibular Stenosis	PT	Pulmonary Trunk	TV	Tricuspid Valve
IVS	Interventricular Septum	PV	Pulmonary Valve	VSD	Ventricular Septal Defect
LA	Left Atrium	PVL	Pulmonary Valve Leaflet		
LAVL	Left Atrioventricular Valve Leaflet				

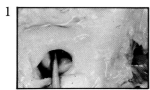

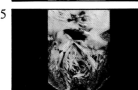

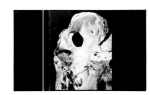

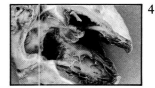

Pathology

In up to 25% of all normal hearts there is a patent foramen ovale [1]. However a shunt from left atrium to right atrium is prevented by a flap valve and a right to left shunt will only occur if the right atrial pressure is raised. A secundum atrial septal defect results from a deficiency of the flap valve of the foramen ovale [2]. Other types of atrial septal defect include 'sinus venosus' defect which lies superior to the fossa ovalis; this is usually associated with partial anomalous pulmonary venous return either into the superior vena cava or into the right atrium [3]. Rarely a defect in the postero-inferior portion of the atrium results in the inferior vena cava draining directly into the left atrium. The ostium primum atrial septal defect usually presenting in childhood involves the lowermost part of the atrial septum [4] and is characteristically associated with a defect of the ventricular septum and cleft in the atrioventricular valves [5].

Presentation

Symptoms

Whereas most children with an atrial septal defect are asymptomatic, patients presenting over the age of 40 will often complain of breathlessness on exertion, palpitation or fatigue. Rarely the elderly patient presents not only in atrial fibrillation but with frank heart failure. At any age the lesion may be initially discovered by routine chest X-ray.

Signs

The diagnostic hallmark of an atrial septal defect is the fixed wide splitting of the second heart sound virtually always associated with an ejection systolic murmur in the pulmonary area. Irrespective of the level of the pulmonary artery pressure or the direction of the shunt, pulmonary valve closure is as loud or louder than aortic valve closure. With a large left to right shunt at atrial level there may be an additional mid-diastolic murmur increased by inspiration at the left sternal edge. This is due to increased flow through the normal tricuspid valve. A pan-systolic murmur due to mitral valve regurgitation may suggest ostium primum defect although the electrocardiogram showing left axis deviation will be more helpful. A mid-systolic click and a late systolic murmur suggest mitral valve prolapse; this sometimes occurs with a secundum atrial septal defect.

In an atrial septal defect with the Eisenmenger complex, central cyanosis may be present. The auscultatory signs are similar to those of a secundum atrial septal defect with a large left to right shunt except that a pulmonary ejection sound is frequently heard, pulmonary valve closure is very loud and a tricuspid flow murmur is not present.

The quality of the arterial pulse in an atrial septal defect is usually normal but the jugular venous pulse is frequently visible with a normal wave form unless there is additional tricuspid

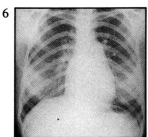

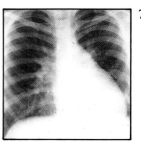

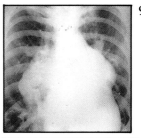

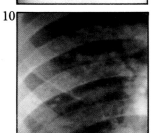

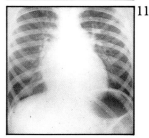

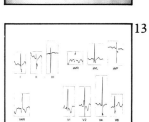

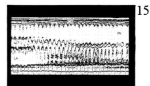

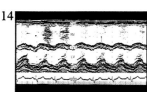

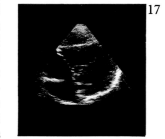

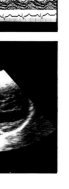

regurgitation. There may be a hyperdynamic impulse at the left sternal edge due to increased right ventricular stroke volume but this finding is often obscured in the elderly patient.

Investigations

Radiology

Both the central and peripheral pulmonary vessels in a left to right shunting atrial septal defect are dilated due to increased pulmonary blood flow (pulmonary plethora) [6]. The aortic knuckle is usually small. Most adults also show cardiac enlargement as a result of right ventricular and right atrial dilatation [7]. If there is marked pulmonary hypertension with a left to right shunt all these features become more obvious [8]. If the Eisenmenger reaction has occurred the central pulmonary arteries may become very large while the distal vessels are reduced in caliber [9]. There may be calcified atheroma in the pulmonary artery. The presence of partial anomalous pulmonary venous drainage may be indicated by the anomalous veins lying in an abnormal anatomic position [10]. Although the chest radiograph of an ostium primum atrial septal defect may be indistinguishable from that of a secundum defect, upper zone vessel dilatation and left atrial enlargment may be apparent, reflecting mitral regurgitation [11].

Electrocardiography

The typical ECG of a secundum atrial septal defect shows a normal QRS axis with complete or incomplete right bundle branch block [12]. There may be frank right ventricular hypertrophy recognized from the ECG in an atrial septal defect with severe pulmonary hypertension. Left axis deviation in the ECG suggests that the atrial septal defect is of the ostium primum variety [13].

Echocardiography

M-mode echocardiography in atrial septal defect shows a dilated right ventricle relative to the left due to the volume overload [14]. This usually results in reversed septal motion [15]. Two-dimensional echocardiography can directly visualize the defects in the majority of cases. The atrial septum is best viewed from the subcostal position and when a secundum defect is present it is seen to lie centrally bounded superiorly and inferiorly by atrial septal tissue and the atrioventricular septum is always intact with a clear separation of the septal insertion of the mitral and tricuspid valves [16]. In an ostium primum defect both mitral and tricuspid valves insert onto the crest of the ventricular septum at the same level without any atrioventricular septum. The abnormal position of the mitral valve in the left ventricular outflow tract can be seen [17]. Sinus venosus defects are difficult to detect and careful exploration of the atrial septum is necessary. The anomalous drainage of the right upper pulmonary vein to the right side of the atrial septum is best appreciated from the suprasternal position.

Echocardiography using a contrast injection may be helpful in the diagnosis of atrial septal defect. A right to left shunt at atrial level will be readily detected by the passage of microbubbles from the right to the left atrium [18].

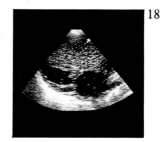

Cardiac Catheterization and Angiography

If cardiac catheterization is carried out in patients with atrial septal defects the size of the shunt and its direction will be identified. The level of the pulmonary artery pressure and pulmonary vascular resistance can be measured.

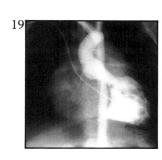

Additional anomalous pulmonary venous drainage can be demonstrated by pulmonary arteriography. In an ostium primum atrial septal defect, left ventricular angiography shows a characteristic abnormality in the left ventricular outflow tract. This is the 'goose-neck' deformity due to the abnormal position of the mitral valve [19].

1 The probe is passed between the flap valve and the limbus. When the probe is removed the flap valve will close the defect.

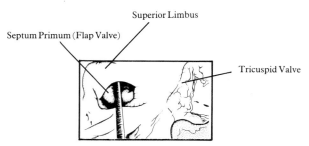

2 Secundum atrial septal defect. A single round defect occupies the site of the foramen ovale. The coronary sinus lies below and the tricuspid valve is separated from the defect by several centimeters of muscle tissue.

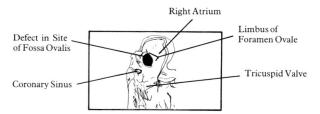

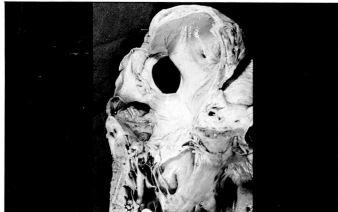

3 Sinus venosus defect. The defect is high in the wall of the superior vena cava and the right pulmonary veins drain to the right atrium via the defect.

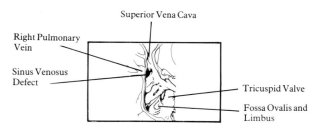

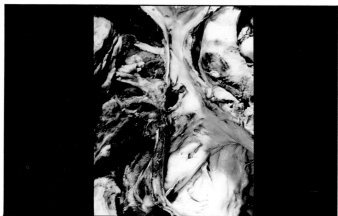

4 The right atrium and ventricle in a heart with an ostium primum atrial septal defect. There is a deficiency in the base of the atrial septum, but separate annuli of the mitral and tricuspid valves.

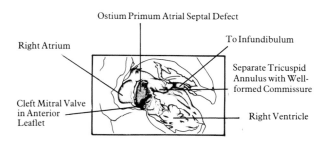

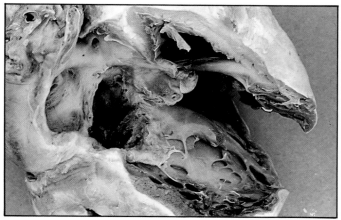

5 The left atrium and ventricle in a heart following operation, with an ostium primum atrial septal defect. There is a cleft in the mitral valve.

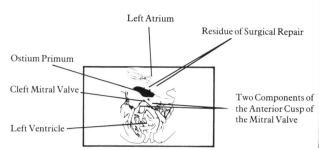

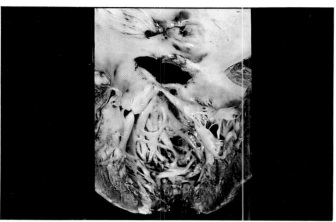

6 Chest radiograph in secundum atrial septal defect. There is pulmonary plethora, a large pulmonary trunk and a small aortic knuckle.

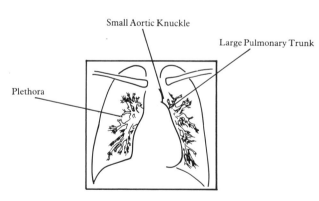

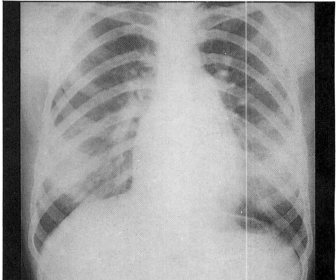

7 Chest radiograph in a secundum atrial septal defect showing cardiac enlargement.

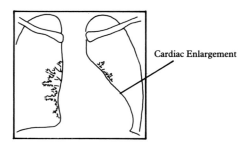

Cardiac Enlargement

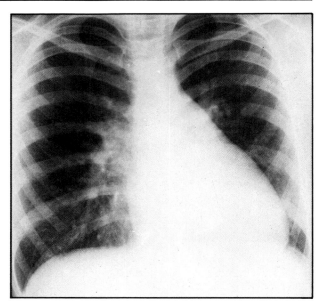

8 Chest radiograph in an atrial septal defect with pulmonary hypertension showing a large heart, a grossly dilated pulmonary trunk and more obvious plethora.

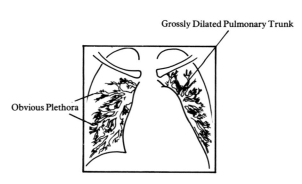

Grossly Dilated Pulmonary Trunk

Obvious Plethora

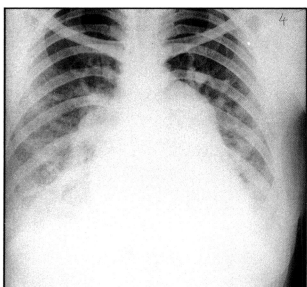

9 Chest radiograph in an atrial septal defect complicated by the Eisenmenger reaction. There is a grossly dilated pulmonary trunk.

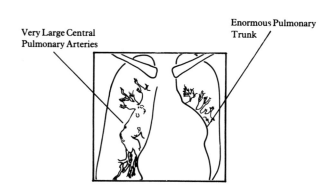

Very Large Central Pulmonary Arteries

Enormous Pulmonary Trunk

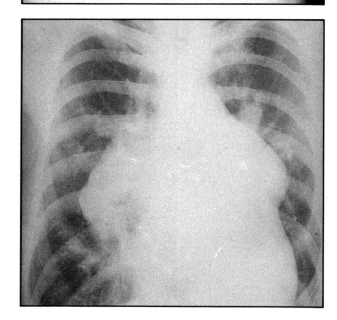

10 Chest radiograph showing a horizontal vessel above the right hilum representing an anomalous pulmonary vein.

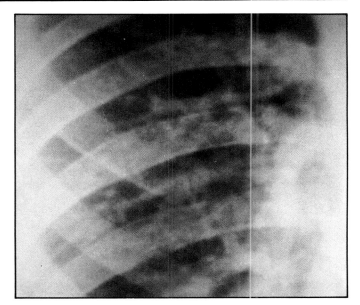

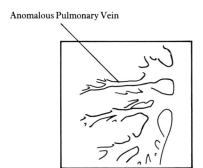

Anomalous Pulmonary Vein

11 Chest radiograph of a primum atrial septal defect with mitral regurgitation showing slight enlargement of the heart, a prominent pulmonary trunk, pulmonary plethora and upper zone vessel dilatation.

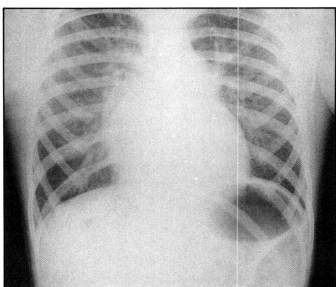

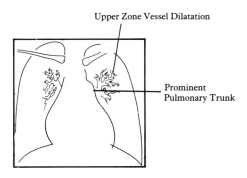

Upper Zone Vessel Dilatation

Prominent Pulmonary Trunk

12

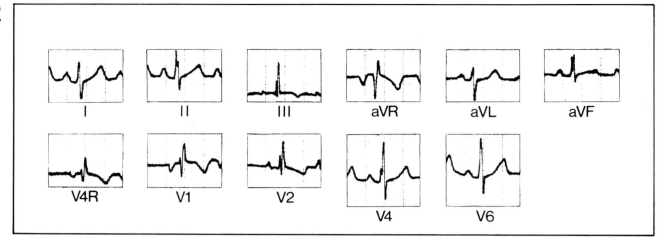

Electrocardiogram of a patient with a secundum atrial septal defect showing sinus rhythm, right axis deviation, and rsR complexes from V4R to V4 indicating incomplete right bundle branch block.

13

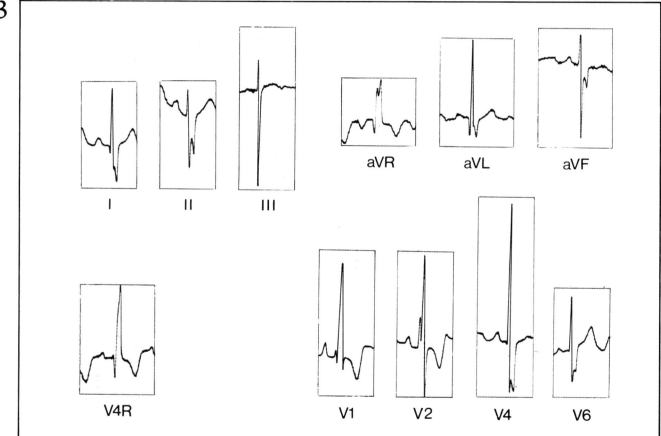

Electrocardiogram of a patient with ostium primum atrial septal defect showing left axis deviation and right bundle branch block.

14

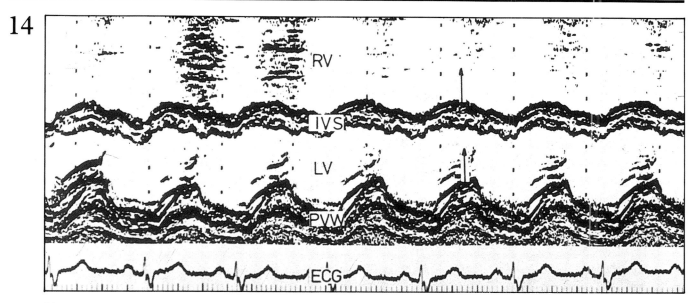

Slow M-mode scan in an atrial septal defect showing the right ventricular enlargement.

15

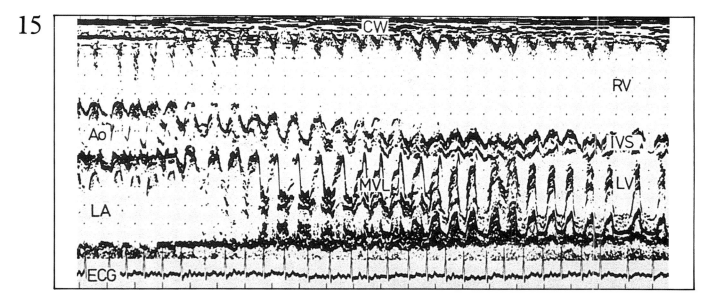

M-mode echocardiogram of a heart with atrial septal defect showing increased right ventricular internal dimension. Left ventricular dimension is smaller than right. Paradoxical septal motion is seen.

16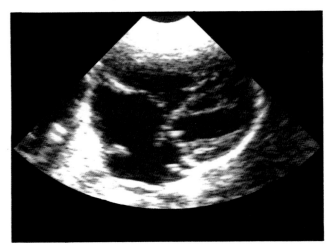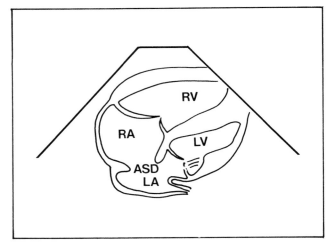

2-D echocardiographic subcostal view showing a secundum atrial septal defect. The defect lies in the central region of the atrial septum and is separated both from the atrioventricular valves and the atrial roof by septal tissue.

17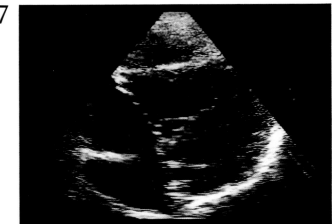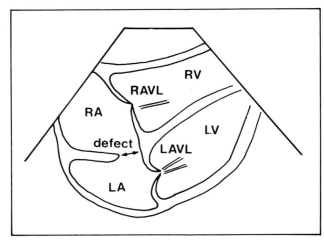

2-D echocardiographic subcostal four-chamber view of an ostium primum atrial septal defect. The defect extends right down to the atrioventricular valve.

18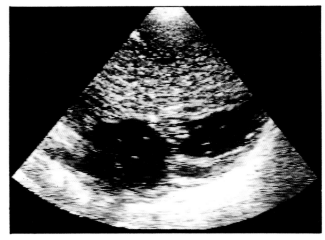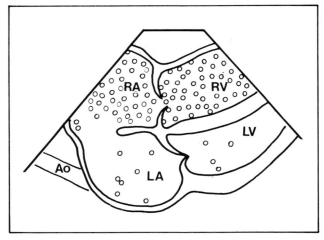

2-D echocardiographic subcostal four-chamber view using a contrast injection. The microbubbles injected into a systemic vein fill the right atrium and right ventricle. Blood shunting left to right shows as an un-opacified region in the right atrium. A few microbubbles are transferred into the left heart indicating that there is also a small right to left shunt.

19 Left ventricular angiogram (antero-posterior projection) in an ostium primum atrial septal defect showing the 'goose-neck' deformity.

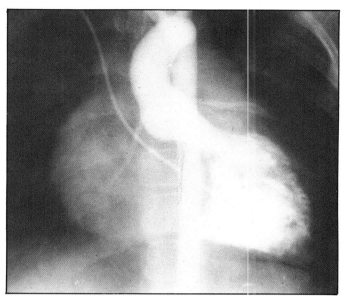

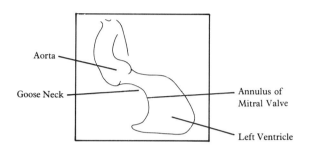

The incidence of ventricular septal defects is 2/1000 live births and constitutes about 20–30% of all congenital cardiac malformations. Its prevalence in school age children is about 1/1000 and in adults approximately 0.5/1000. In the adult it may be a part of a complex congenital cardiac malformation such as Fallot's tetralogy but in this section it will be considered as an isolated abnormality.

Pathology

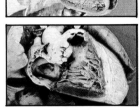

Ventricular septal defects can occur in the membranous septum [1] or in any part of the muscular septum. The defects may be single [2] or multiple [3]. Usually the defect permits communication between the two ventricles, but rarely when the defect is in the atrioventricular component of the membranous septum there will be a communication between the left ventricle and right atrium (Gerbode defect). The most common defects exist in and around the ventricular component of the membranous septum [4]. The size of the defect is variable and the hemodynamic consequences will therefore vary. Defects in the membranous septum are particularly likely to lead to aortic regurgitation due to aortic cusp prolapse [5]. Many of the ventricular septal defects which are present at birth close spontaneously. Later in life, if there has been longstanding left-to-right shunting, pulmonary vascular disease may develop [6].

Infective endocarditis is an important complication even if the lesion is hemodynamically insignificant.

Presentation

Symptoms

The patient with a small left-to-right shunting ventricular septal defect and a normal pulmonary artery pressure (Maladie de Roger) is usually asymptomatic, the condition being diagnosed on routine clinical examination. The child or young adult with a large left-to-right shunt and elevation of the pulmonary artery pressure may complain of breathlessness and fatigue. If pulmonary vascular disease has developed (Eisenmenger ventricular septal defect) then patients may be asymptomatic or complain of breathlessness, fatigue or may even be noticed to be cyanosed.

Signs

The patient with a 'Roger' ventricular septal defect has only a pan-systolic murmur usually accompanied by a thrill at the left sternal edge. The second heart sound may be abnormally widely split in expiration but moves normally in inspiration.

The patient with a large left-to-right shunt and pulmonary hypertension will have a hyperdynamic apical impulse reflecting the increased stroke volume of the left ventricle. On auscultation, in addition to the pan-systolic murmur, the pulmonary valve closure sound is accentuated although the splitting is physiologic. There is often an additional mid-diastolic murmur reflecting the increased flow through the normal mitral valve.

The patient with the Eisenmenger ventricular septal defect

may be cyanosed and clubbed. The jugular venous pulse may show abnormal dominance of the 'a' wave while the arterial pulse is usually normal. On auscultation the characteristic finding is that the second heart sound is single although incorporating both components (aortic closure and pulmonary closure) which have become fused. The second heart sound is accentuated due to the loud pulmonary closure sound. There may be no murmurs but a pulmonary ejection sound and a short ejection systolic murmur are common.

Investigations

Radiology

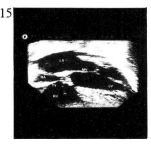

A small ventricular defect does not cause cardiac enlargement, but the central pulmonary arteries are usually slightly enlarged in the plain chest radiograph [7]. With a larger defect there is cardiac enlargement. The increased pulmonary flow and pressure is reflected in left atrial dilatation, a large pulmonary trunk and obvious pulmonary plethora [8]. If pulmonary vascular disease has developed (Eisenmenger situation) there is enlargement of the pulmonary trunk and central pulmonary vessels [9], while the peripheral vessels are constricted.

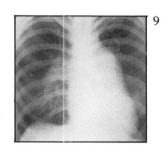

Electrocardiography

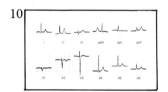

In a small left-to-right shunting defect the electrocardiogram may be normal. The adult with a moderately large left-to-right shunting defect may show voltage increases (tall R-waves in V5 and S-waves in V1) indicating left ventricular enlargement [10]. The electrocardiogram in a defect complicated by the Eisenmenger reaction shows right ventricular hypertrophy [11] although additional left ventricular hypertrophy is often also seen.

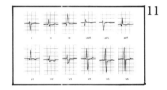

Echocardiography

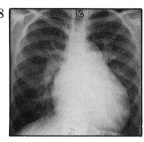

Although M-mode echocardiography provides information about the dimensions of the ventricles it does not enable the ventricular septal defect to be visualized directly. Thus in small defects the M-mode echocardiogram is frequently normal. With larger shunts the M-mode features are those of left ventricular volume overload (increased left ventricular end-diastolic and left atrial dimensions) [12]. In the presence of the Eisenmenger situation the right ventricular dimension is also increased and the pulmonary valve echocardiogram is abnormal. Abnormalities of the pulmonary valve which suggest pulmonary hypertension include flattening of the diastolic line, absence of the 'a' dip, large amplitude of systolic opening and mid-systolic vibration and partial collapse [13]. While none of these features taken in isolation are diagnostic, the presence of all strongly suggest significant pulmonary hypertension.

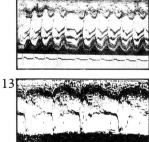

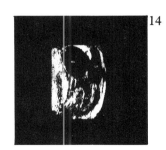

Two-dimensional echocardiography has proved extremely valuable in the identification of ventricular septal defects. Careful use of various views show characteristic features in many of the different anatomic locations of the defects. Thus a subcostal four-chamber view enables a perimembranous [14] or inlet

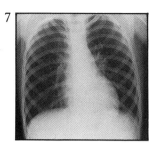

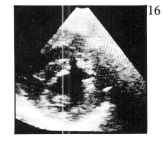

muscular [15] ventricular septal defect to be visualized. A parasternal short axis view may enable an anterior trabecular muscular defect to be seen [16].

Cardiac Catheterization and Angiography

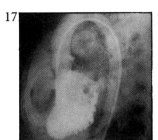

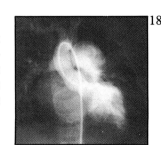

The left-to-right shunt or bi-directional shunt can be detected at cardiac catheterization and the pulmonary artery pressure measured. Pulmonary vascular resistance and pulmonary to systemic flow ratios may be calculated. A left ventricular angiogram shows the position of the ventricular septal defect and whether multiple defects are present [17,18,19].

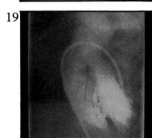

1 Heart from which the parietal wall of the right ventricle has been removed showing a slit-like defect at the site of the membranous septum.

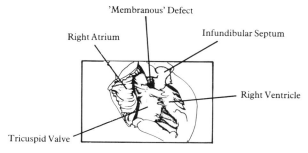

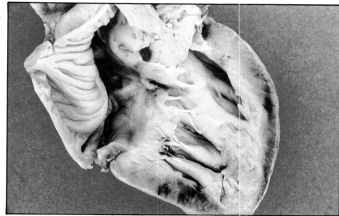

2 Posterior muscular septal defect.

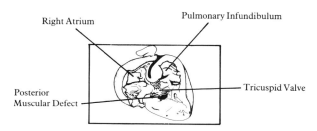

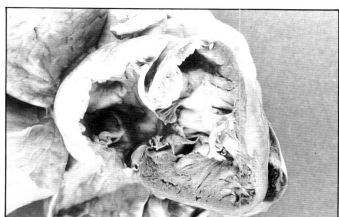

3 Multiple muscular defects in trabecular septum.

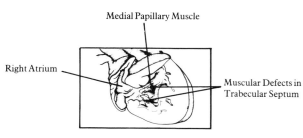

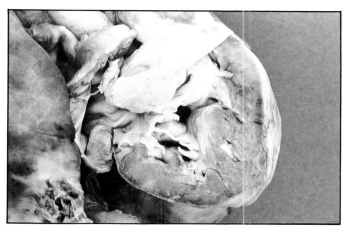

4 Heart opened in a similar fashion to [1] showing a large defect of the muscle surrounding the membranous septum.

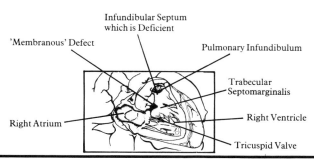

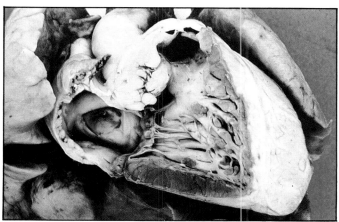

5 Infundibular septal defect with prolapsing aortic valve leaflet.

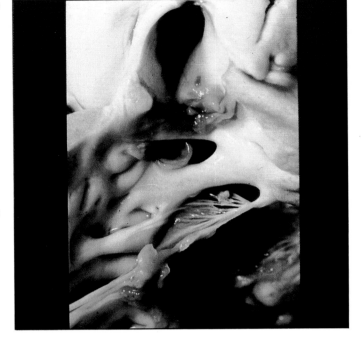

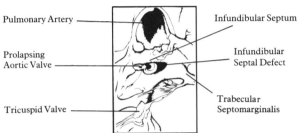

- Pulmonary Artery
- Infundibular Septum
- Prolapsing Aortic Valve
- Infundibular Septal Defect
- Tricuspid Valve
- Trabecular Septomarginalis

6 Pulmonary vascular disease secondary to a ventricular septal defect.

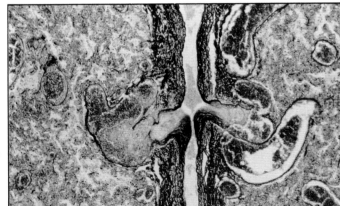

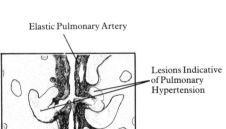

- Elastic Pulmonary Artery
- Lesions Indicative of Pulmonary Hypertension

7 Chest radiograph showing normal sized heart with slight enlargement of the central pulmonary arteries in a small ventricular septal defect.

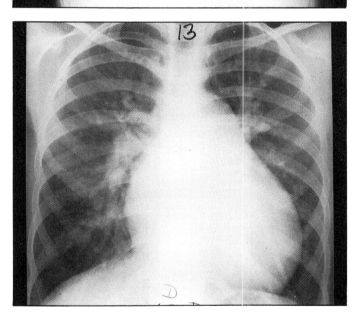

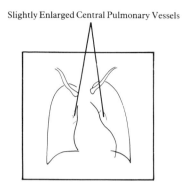

Slightly Enlarged Central Pulmonary Vessels

8 Chest radiograph showing increased cardiac size with dilatation of the left atrium, pulmonary trunk and pulmonary plethora in a ventricular septal defect with pulmonary hypertension.

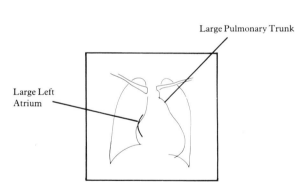

Large Pulmonary Trunk

Large Left Atrium

9 Chest radiograph in Eisenmenger ventricular septal defect showing slight enlargement of the heart and gross enlargement of the central pulmonary vessels.

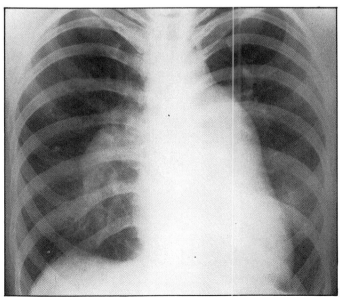

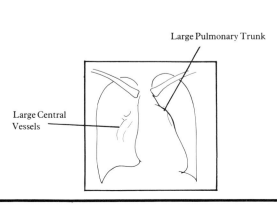

Large Pulmonary Trunk

Large Central Vessels

10

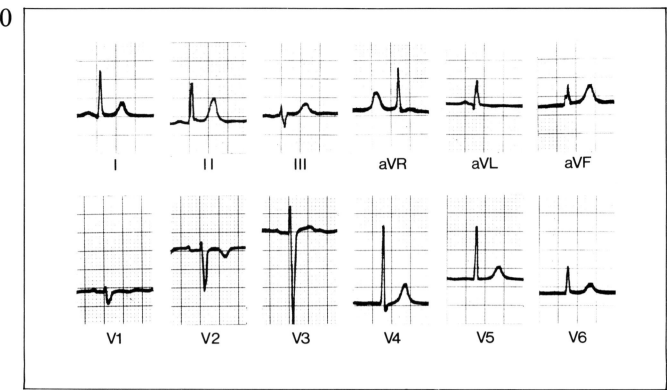

Electrocardiogram of a 10-year-old patient with ventricular septal defect. The pulmonary systemic flow ratio was 2:1 and the pulmonary vascular resistance normal. There is evidence of slight left ventricular hypertrophy as shown by the increased voltage of R-waves in the left precordial leads. Note: V4 to V6, 1mV = 0.5 cm.

11

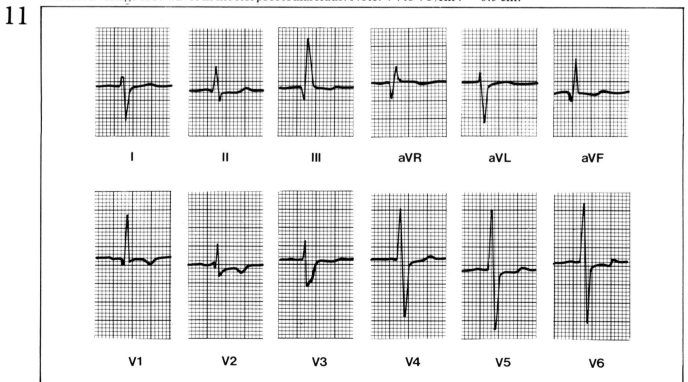

Electrocardiogram of a patient aged 21 with Eisenmenger ventricular septal defect, showing right axis deviation, with dominant R-waves, inverted T-waves in right chest leads and deep S-waves in V5 and V6. Note: 1mV = 0.5 cm.

12

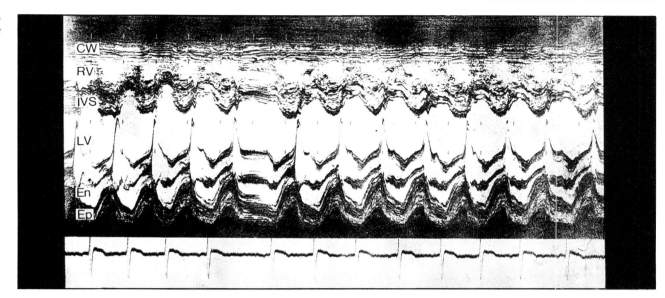

M-mode echocardiogram showing increased left ventricular dimensions and exaggerated movement of the septum and posterior wall in a case of ventricular septal defect with a large shunt.

13

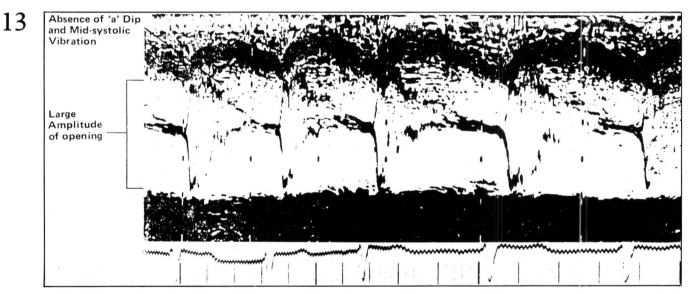

M-mode echocardiogram in ventricular septal defect with severe pulmonary hypertension showing the pulmonary valve. Note the absence of the 'a' dip, large amplitude of systolic opening and partial collapse and vibration of the pulmonary valve in mid-systole.

14

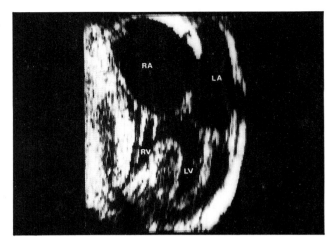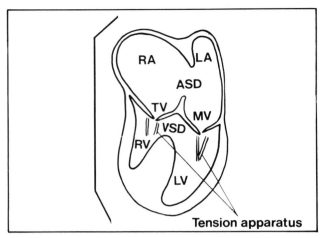

2-D echocardiographic subcostal four-chamber section close to the crux of the heart showing a perimembranous defect situated between the ventricular inlet components. The defect is roofed by the tricuspid and mitral valves in fibrous continuity, the hallmark of this type of defect. There is also an atrial septal defect within the fossa ovalis. Note that the tension apparatus is also seen.

15

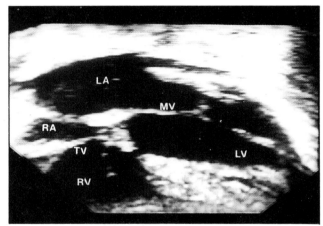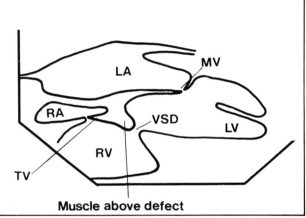

2-D echocardiographic subcostal four-chamber section showing a muscular inlet defect. It is distinguished from the perimembranous defect shown in [14] because it is surrounded by muscle and does not border on the valve annuli. The valve leaflets show the normal off-setting which is lacking in the perimembranous defect.

16

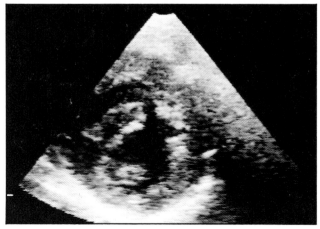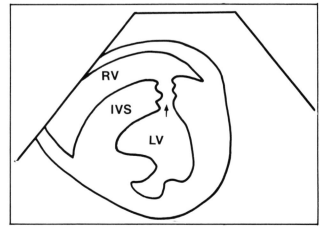

2-D echocardiographic parasternal short axis view showing an anterior trabecular ventricular septal defect (arrowed).

17   Left ventriculogram (lateral projection) showing membranous ventricular septal defect.

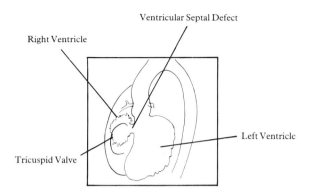

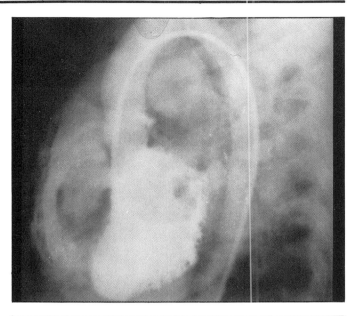

18   Left ventriculogram (antero-posterior projection) showing infundibular septal defect with shunt directly into the pulmonary trunk. The body of the right ventricle is not filled.

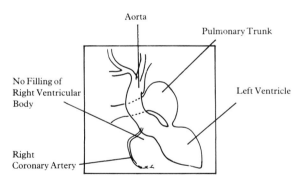

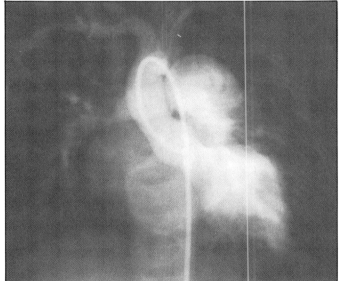

19   Left ventriculogram viewed in a projection which profiles the septum showing multiple defects in the trabecular septum.

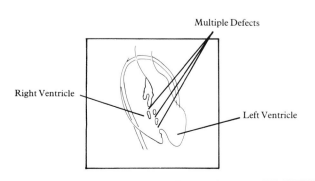

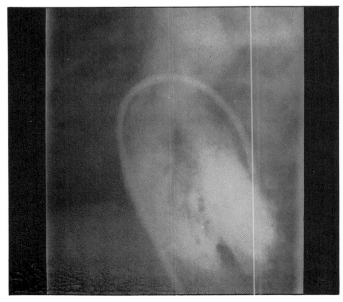

Pathology

The ductus arteriosus connects the proximal left pulmonary artery to the arch of the aorta just distal to the origin of the left subclavian artery and forms a communication between the pulmonary and systemic circulation which persists throughout the whole of fetal life and into the neonatal period [1]. Normally it closes shortly after birth but it may, for reasons which are not fully understood, remain patent throughout life. In children who have a persistent ductus arteriosus a small proportion will have an additional cardiac abnormality.

Presentation

Symptoms

The lesion is rare in adults because it has usually been corrected by surgery in childhood. Adults presenting with isolated persistent ductus arteriosus are usually asymptomatic and discovered by the chance finding of a murmur. Patients with a longstanding large left-to-right shunt may complain of breathlessness and even develop frank heart failure particularly following the development of atrial fibrillation.

Signs

The physical signs of a left-to-right shunting persistent ductus arteriosus include a continuous murmur best heard in the left infraclavicular area. If the shunt is small there may be no other abnormal physical signs; if the shunt is large there may be a sharp upstroke to the carotid pulse and a hyperdynamic left ventricle on palpation. Additionally there may be a mid-diastolic flow murmur in the mitral area. If pulmonary hypertension is present, the pulmonary valve closure sound will be accentuated.

The patient presenting with the Eisenmenger reaction and a persistent ductus arteriosus may be cyanosed particularly in the lower limbs with clubbing of the toes. The remaining physical signs include a physiologic splitting of the second heart sound but with an accentuated pulmonary valve closure sound, and right ventricular hypertrophy on palpation. There may be abnormal dominance of the 'a' wave in the jugular venous pulse. There may be either a short ejection systolic murmur or no murmur at all, but a pulmonary ejection sound may be present. An early diastolic murmur due to pulmonary regurgitation may be heard in those patients with the greatest dilatation of the central pulmonary arteries.

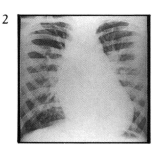

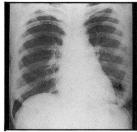

Investigations

Radiology

The patient with the large left-to-right shunt may show pulmonary plethora together with cardiac enlargement [2]. Characteristically the aorta is dilated at the site of the ductus [3]. The older patient may show calcification in the region of the ductus [4].

The patient with the Eisenmenger persistent ductus arteriosus

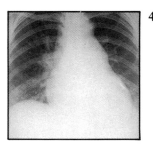

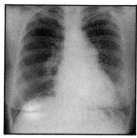

may have a normal sized heart but with dilated central pulmonary arteries and reduction in caliber of the peripheral pulmonary arteries [5].

Electrocardiography

If the ductus is small, the electrocardiogram will be normal. If the shunt is large, the left ventricle dilates and the electrocardiogram may show tall R-waves in V5 and deep S-waves in V1 (voltage changes of left ventricular hypertrophy) [6]. With the development of severe pulmonary vascular disease, the electrocardiogram reflects increasing right ventricular hypertrophy with tall R-waves and T-wave inversion in right ventricular leads and deep S-waves in the left ventricular leads [7]. Right axis deviation and right bundle-branch block are also common features in persistent ductus with severe pulmonary vascular disease.

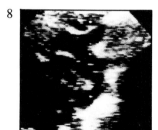

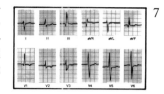

Echocardiography

It is possible to identify a persistent ductus arteriosus directly using two-dimensional echocardiography from the suprasternal position [8]. Patients with a large left-to-right shunt will show increase in left ventricular end-diastolic dimension consistent with an increase in stroke volume. The older patient may also show a large left atrium.

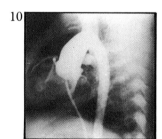

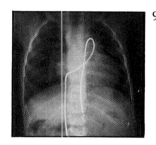

Cardiac Catheterization and Angiography

Evidence of a left-to-right shunt can be detected by a step up in oxygen saturation in the pulmonary artery. The catheter can usually be passed directly from the left pulmonary artery into the descending aorta via the ductus arteriosus [9]. The presence of increased pulmonary artery pressure or increased pulmonary vascular resistance can be measured directly.

The aortogram is used to show the anatomy of the ductus [10,11].

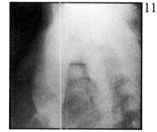

1   Pathologic specimen showing a persistent ductus arteriosus.

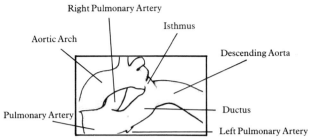

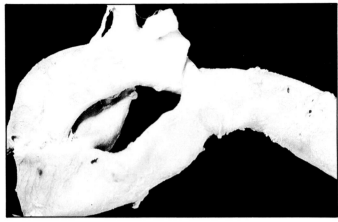

PERSISTENT DUCTUS ARTERIOSUS

2   Chest radiograph in persistent ductus arteriosus with a large left-to-right shunt showing a large heart and pulmonary trunk, prominent aortic knuckle and obvious pulmonary plethora.

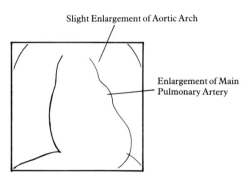

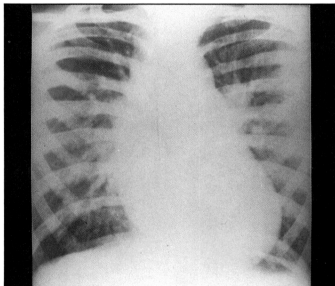

3 Chest radiograph showing a dilated aorta at the site of the persistent ductus.

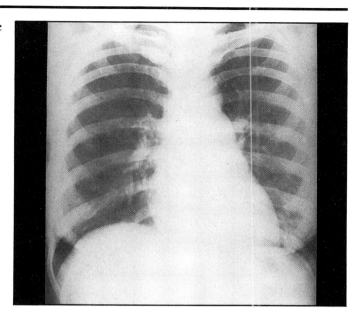

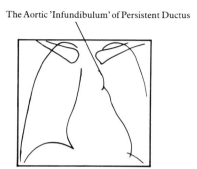

The Aortic 'Infundibulum' of Persistent Ductus

4 Chest radiograph showing calcification in the aorta at the orifice of a persistent ductus.

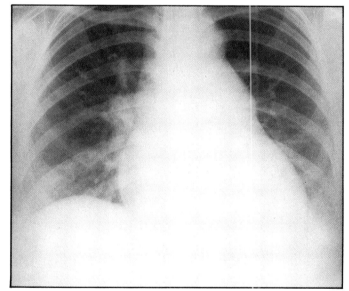

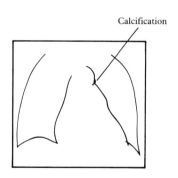

Calcification

5 Chest radiograph in persistent ductus with the Eisenmenger situation showing a slightly enlarged heart, very large pulmonary trunk and prominent aortic knuckle. The hilar vessels are large and the peripheral pulmonary vessels normal.

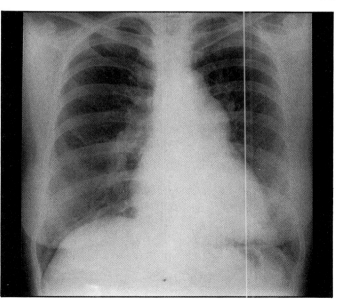

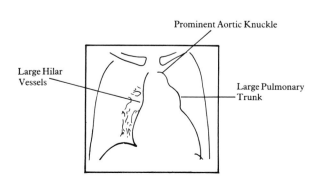

Prominent Aortic Knuckle

Large Hilar Vessels

Large Pulmonary Trunk

6

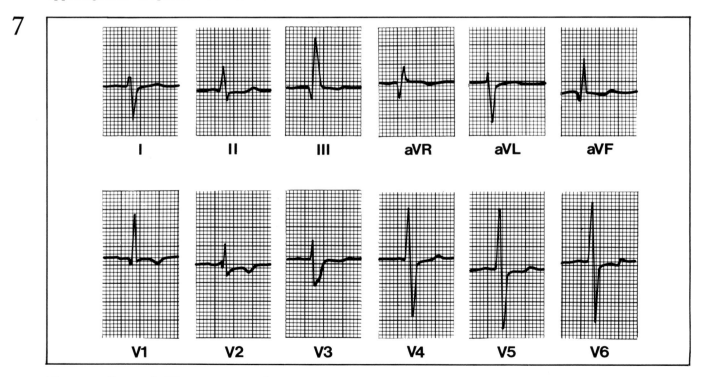

Electrocardiogram in persistent ductus arteriosus showing tall R-waves in left ventricular leads and deep S waves in opposing leads - the pattern of diastolic overload.

7

Electrocardiogram in Eisenmenger persistent ductus arteriosus, showing right axis deviation, dominant R-waves, inverted T-waves in right chest leads and deep S-waves in V5 and V6. Note 1 mV = 0.5 cm.

8

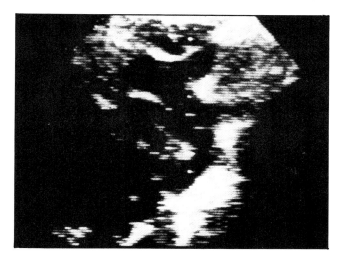 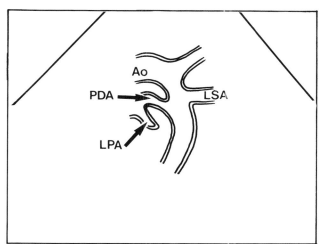

Suprasternal 2-D echocardiographic view of a persistent ductus arteriosus. The duct originates at the level of the left subclavian artery (LSA) and inserts into the main pulmonary artery.

9 Chest radiograph showing typical position of a cardiac catheter passed across a persistent ductus from the pulmonary trunk to the descending aorta.

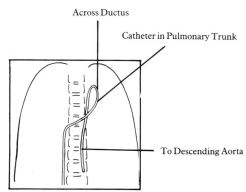 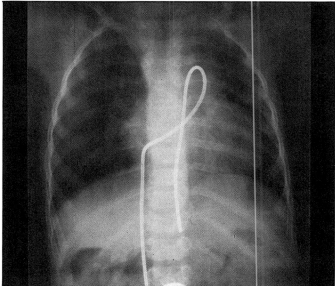

10   Aortogram (lateral projection) showing a small persistent ductus.

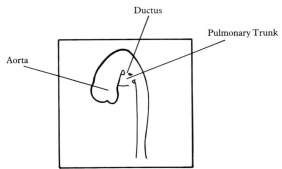

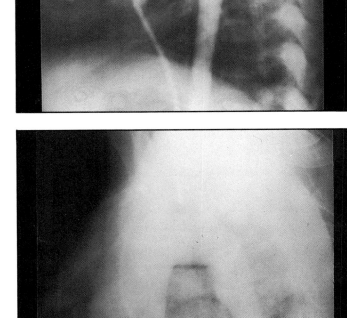

11   Aortogram (lateral projection) showing a large ductus.

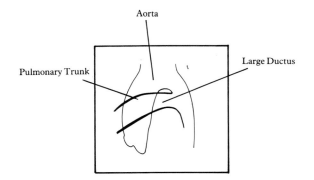

Pathology

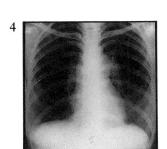

Right ventricular outflow tract obstruction can occur either at pulmonary valve level or due to narrowing of the infundibular portion of the right ventricle or both. In pulmonary valve stenosis the valve is usually tricuspid and the valve cusps are fused along the margins to form an obstructing diaphragm [1]. The valve orifice size may vary from 2–10 mm in diameter [2]. The valve may tend to become thickened and calcified. Right ventricular hypertrophy will develop with time even if the orifice is mildly narrowed [3]. Dilatation of the pulmonary arteries beyond the valve occurs gradually. Rarely, pulmonary valve stenosis may be due to the carcinoid syndrome.

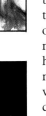

Infundibular stenosis may be due to hypertrophy of the outflow tract [3]. Obstruction may rarely occur if there is a compression externally from a tumor or aberrant muscle bundle within the right ventricle. Infundibular stenosis may develop in patients with a large left to right shunt due to ventricular septal defect, or may be present in hypertrophic cardiomyopathy.

Presentation

Symptoms

The majority of adults with pulmonary valve stenosis, even with significant obstruction, deny symptoms. Occasionally patients may complain of fatigue or dyspnea. The presence of angina or syncope would indicate severe obstruction as would the development of right heart failure.

Signs

Most patients with right ventricular outflow obstruction presenting in adult life are detected because of the chance finding of a murmur. The murmur is ejection in type and finishes before pulmonary valve closure. In mild or moderate pulmonary valve stenosis, the second heart sound is abnormally widely split in expiration, though the split widens further on inspiration as would occur in normal patients. The severity of the stenosis determines the width of splitting: the wider the expiratory split, the more severe the stenosis. Pulmonary valve closure becomes inaudible when the stenosis is very severe. The abrupt halting of the abnormal pulmonary valve at the onset of systole gives rise to a pulmonary ejection sound. In infundibular stenosis the ejection sound will be absent. Associated right ventricular hypertrophy may be detected by palpation and would give rise to abnormal dominance of the 'a' wave in the venous pulse.

Investigations

Radiology

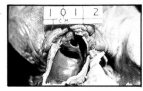

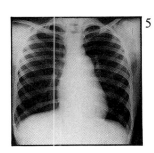

Pulmonary valve stenosis is characterized on the chest X-ray by a normal sized heart with post-stenotic dilatation of the pulmonary trunk, characteristically extending into the left branch [4]. Pulmonary artery dilatation in some cases may be gross [5]. Pulmonary oligemia may sometimes be visible.

Electrocardiography

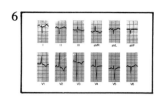

The electrocardiogram in mild or moderate pulmonary stenosis may be normal. In severe pulmonary stenosis, right ventricular hypertrophy is usually present [6]. In severe cases with right heart dilatation, right atrial enlargement may be present in addition to right ventricular hypertrophy.

Echocardiography

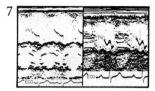

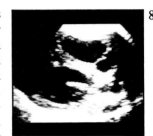

In mild pulmonary valve stenosis, the M-mode echocardiogram is normal. With moderate or severe obstruction the pulmonary valve echo shows marked exaggeration of its 'a' dip [7,8] and in extreme cases the valve may appear to open completely after atrial contraction and before the R wave of the electrocardiogram. In most cases of pulmonary valve stenosis even when it is severe, there is no M-mode echocardiographic evidence of right ventricular hypertrophy but occasionally the septum is thickened and echoes from the anterior wall of the right ventricle are unusually prominent. The septal motion is normal in direction unless the right ventricle fails with secondary tricuspid incompetence. Using two-dimensional echocardiography it may be possible to visualize the thickened restricted domed pulmonary valve. Right ventricular hypertrophy and infundibular obstruction, if present, may also be seen.

Cardiac Catheterization and Angiography

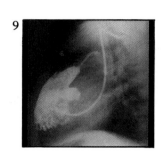

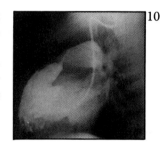

The right ventricular outflow tract obstruction is detected at cardiac catheterization by a systolic pressure difference. The site of obstruction will also be determined.

On right ventricular angiography the site of the outflow obstruction can be seen when it is at valve level [9], infundibular level or in the right ventricular cavity. In pulmonary valve stenosis the cusps will be thickened, domed in systole, with a central jet and post-stenotic dilatation of the pulmonary artery [10].

1 Moderate pulmonary valve stenosis viewed from above, through the opened pulmonary artery.

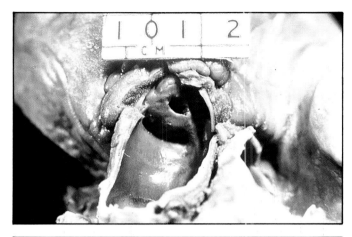

Pulmonary Valve

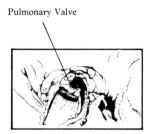

2 Severe pulmonary valve stenosis viewed from above, through the opened pulmonary artery.

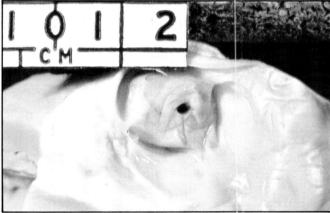

Pulmonary Valve

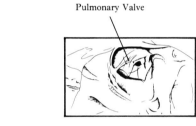

3 Critical pulmonary valve stenosis (red arrow) and secondary infundibular stenosis (white arrow) due to gross right ventricular hypertrophy, the wall being over 1 cm in thickness.

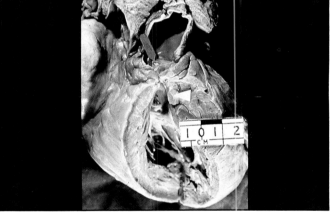

Pulmonary Artery

Critical Pulmonary
Valve Stenosis

Secondary Infundibular
Stenosis

Hypertrophied Right
Ventricle

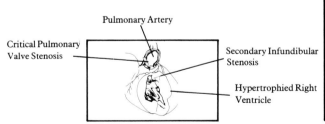

4 Chest radiograph in mild pulmonary stenosis showing post-stenotic dilatation of the pulmonary trunk and a prominent left pulmonary artery.

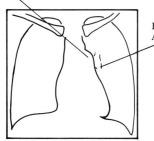

Large Pulmonary Trunk

Large Left Pulmonary Artery

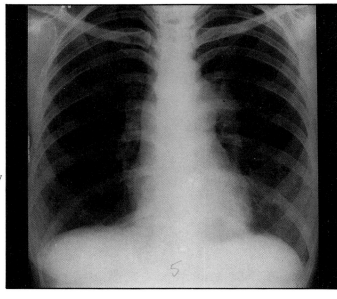

5 Chest radiograph showing obvious post-stenotic dilatation of the left pulmonary artery in pulmonary valve stenosis.

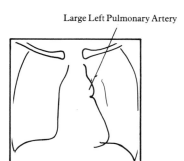

Large Left Pulmonary Artery

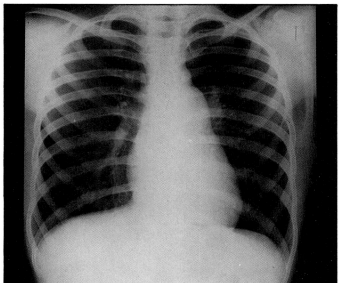

6

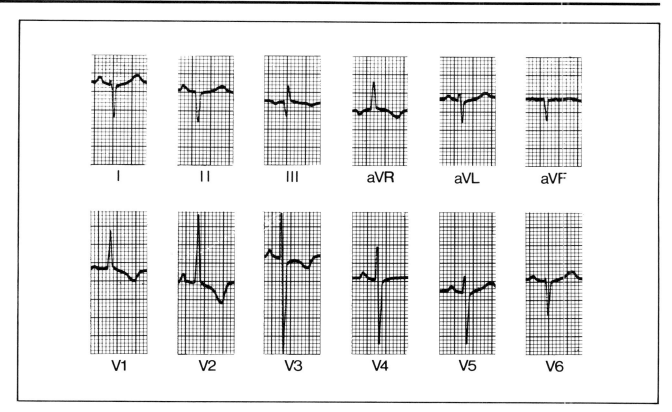

Electrocardiogram in severe pulmonary valve stenosis, showing deep S-wave in lead 1, a dominant R-wave in V1 and T-wave inversion in right chest leads.

7

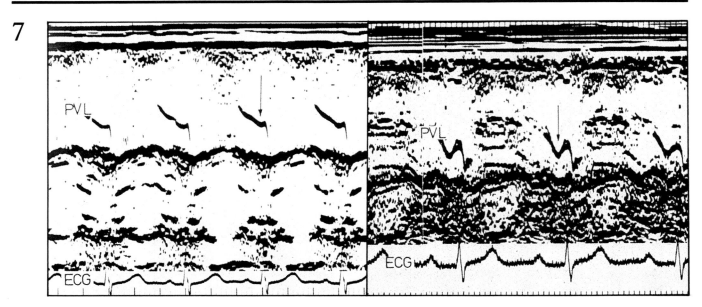

M-mode echocardiogram of the pulmonary valve showing normal atrial dip (Left hand panel; arrowed) and exaggerated atrial dip (arrowed) in pulmonary valve stenosis (right hand panel).

8

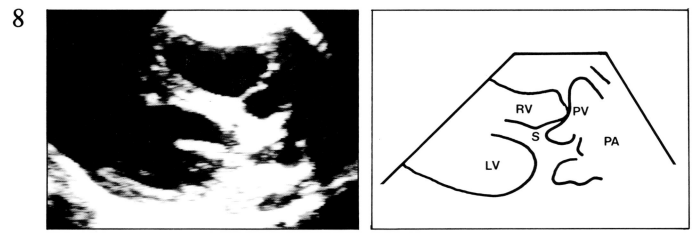

2-D echocardiographic view showing thickened pulmonary valve in mild pulmonary stenosis.

9 Right ventricular angiogram (lateral projection) in pulmonary valve stenosis showing a thickened and domed valve with a central systolic jet.

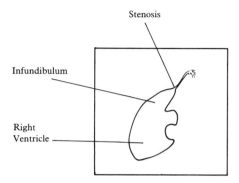

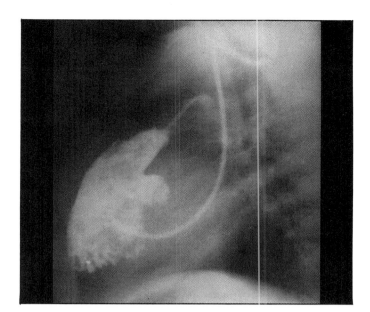

10 Another frame from the same patient as above, showing post-stenotic dilatation of the pulmonary artery.

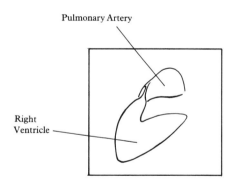

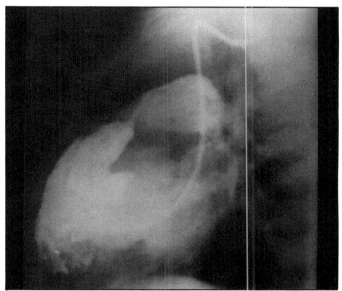

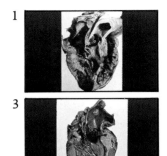

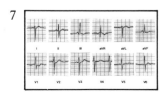

Pathology

Fallot's tetralogy consists of 4 discrete anatomical lesions: pulmonary infundibular stenosis with or without valvular stenosis, a ventricular septal defect, an aorta which overrides the ventricular septum and right ventricular hypertrophy [1,2,3]. The foramen ovale frequently remains patent although contributing little to the main right-to-left shunt which occurs at ventricular level. A right-sided aortic arch persists in 25% of patients.

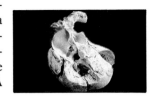

Presentation

Symptoms

Fallot's tetralogy will invariably present and be diagnosed in childhood. In adult life the major complications include cerebral thrombosis (associated with polycythemia), cerebral abscess, infective endocarditis and rarely cyanotic spells. Paradoxical embolism may occur in Fallot's tetralogy.

Signs

In Fallot's tetralogy the 'a' wave in the venous pulse is not exaggerated because of the associated ventricular septal defect. Usually, there is an ejection systolic murmur which may become abbreviated with severe obstruction. The pulmonary ejection sound and the pulmonary valve closure sound are often not heard as the valve is immobile. Central cyanosis and clubbing are an integral part of the condition.

Investigations

Radiology

The radiologic features of Fallot's tetralogy are a cardiac silhouette of normal size and lung fields which are either normally vascularized or under-vascularized[4]. The cardiac silhouette will not be enlarged in this condition since chamber dilatation is negligible. The shape of the cardiac silhouette is normal in about half the cases and the remainder show a 'boot shape' [5]. This is produced by the hypertrophy of the right ventricle in the absence of left ventricular enlargement leading to a lifting of the apex away from the left dome of the diaphragm, combined with an absence of shadow normally produced by the pulmonary artery (the pulmonary artery in Fallot's tetralogy being small). The absence of shadows in this area may be even more striking when a right-sided aortic arch is present [6].

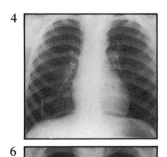

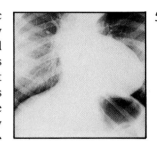

Electrocardiography

In Fallot's tetralogy the electrocardiogram will show moderate right ventricular hypertrophy usually less striking than in severe pulmonary valve stenosis without ventricular septal defect. Right atrial hypertrophy is also less common in Fallot's tetralogy than in pulmonary valve stenosis [7].

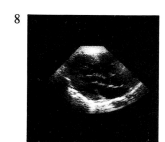

Echocardiography

The characteristic echocardiographic feature of Fallot's tetralogy is overriding of the interventricular septum by the aortic root. This is usually recognizable from the echocardiogram and represents a defect of the infundibular septum. Using 2-dimensional echocardiography both the valvar and infundibular obstruction and the aortic override can be visualized directly as can the ventricular septal defect [8,9].

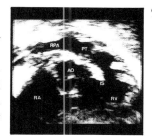

Cardiac Catheterization and Angiography

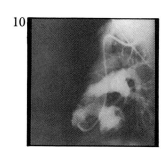

Evidence of a right-to-left shunt at ventricular level will be seen from the desaturation of the left ventricular and aortic blood. A systolic pressure difference will be seen between the right ventricular outflow tract and pulmonary artery.

On right ventricular angiography the outflow tract obstruction can be seen as can the right-to-left shunt across the ventricular septal defect by the passage of contrast from right ventricle to left ventricle [10]. The aortic override infundibular stenosis will also be seen [10,11].

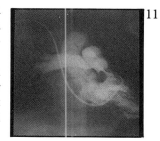

1   Right ventricular view of a specimen with Fallot's tetralogy. The aorta is seen overriding the ventricular septal defect and the infundibular septum is deviated anteriorly to produce infundibular pulmonary stenosis.

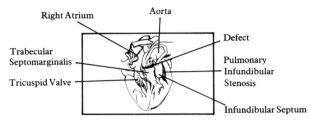

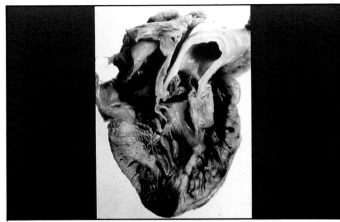

2   Fallot's tetralogy viewed from the anterior aspect with the anterior wall of the right ventricle cut away. Due to extreme aortic override, the great arteries have a side-by-side relationship.

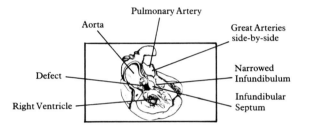

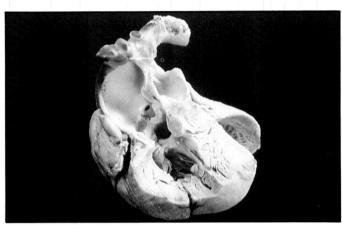

3   Fallot's tetralogy viewed from the right aspect showing extreme anterior deviation of the infundibular septum. The right ventricular outflow tract is a slit (arrowed).

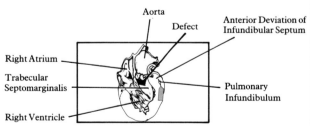

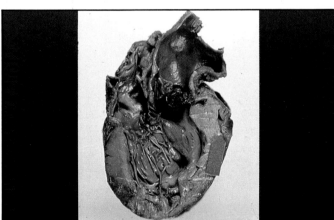

4 Chest radiograph in Fallot's tetralogy showing normal appearance apart from a slightly prominent aorta.

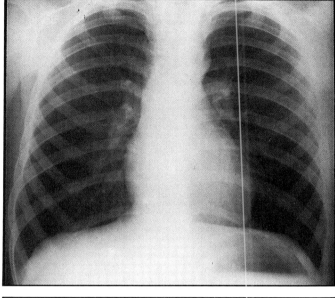

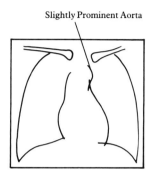

Slightly Prominent Aorta

5 Chest radiograph of Fallot's tetralogy showing a typical cardiac silhouette produced by 1) the tipped-up apex, 2) prominent pulmonary bay due to a small pulmonary artery and 3) underfilling of the pulmonary vasculature.

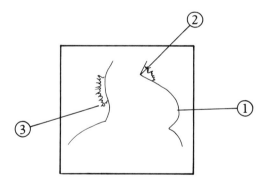

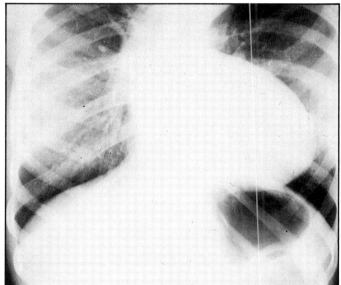

6 Chest radiograph showing right-sided aortic arch.

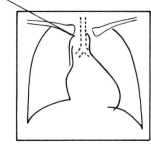

Right-Sided Aortic Arch

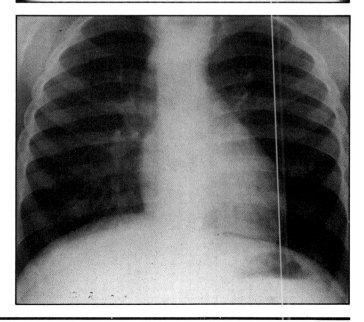

7

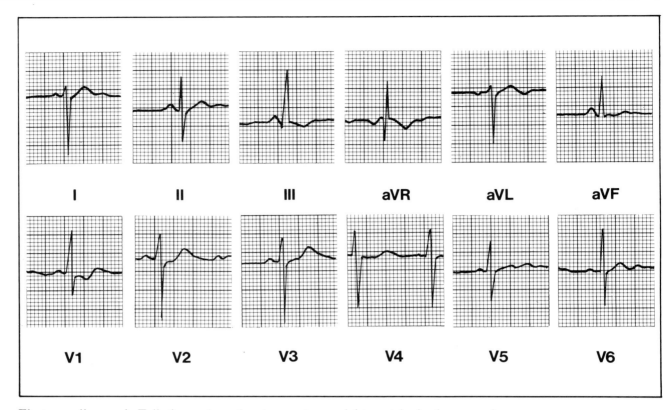

Electrocardiogram in Fallot's tetralogy showing moderate right ventricular hypertrophy.

8

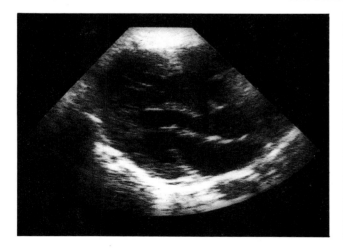 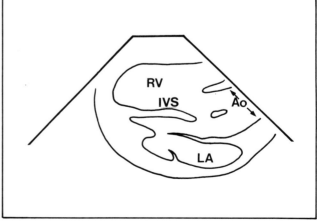

Parasternal 2-D echocardiographic long axis view showing aortic valve override of the septum. In this view the override appears to be more than 50%.

9

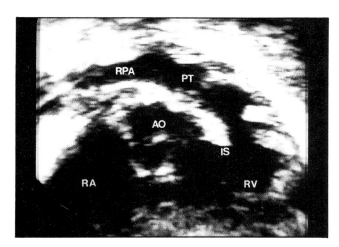

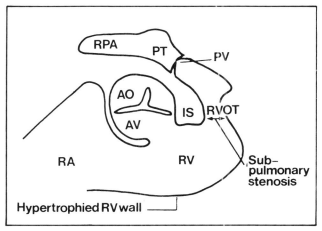

2-D echocardiographic subcostal anatomically orientated section. It shows three of the four features of Fallot's tetralogy, namely, overriding of the aortic valve, sub-pulmonary infundibular stenosis and right ventricular hypertrophy. The aorta overrides the ventricular septal defect (the fourth feature of tetralogy) not seen in this projection.

FALLOT'S TETRALOGY   Cardiac Catheterization & Angiography

10   Right ventriculogram (lateral projection) showing right-to-left shunt across the ventricular septal defect.

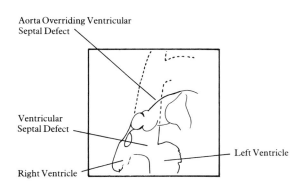

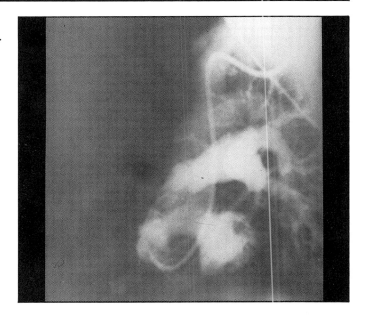

11 Right ventricular angiogram (antero-posterior projection) showing infundibular stenosis with aortic override.

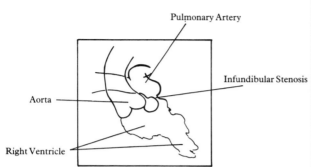

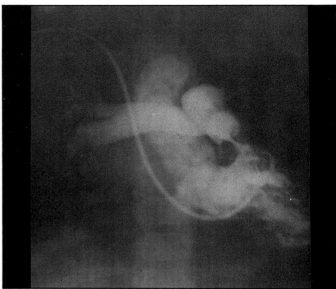

Pathology

Coarctation of the aorta is a congenital constriction or narrowing of the aortic arch or descending aorta. It is of variable position, extent and severity and may be associated with other congenital abnormalities such as bicuspid aortic valve. Acquired coarctation of the aorta occurs at variable and multiple sites (Takayasu disease).

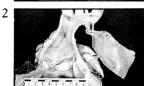

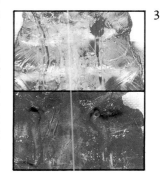

When coarctation of the aorta presents in adult life the lesion is usually a sharply localized constriction just beyond the origin of the left subclavian artery and proximal to the insertion of the ligamentum arteriosum [1]. In less than 10% of cases the coarctation extends over several centimeters. An associated bicuspid aortic valve is present in about 85% of cases [2]. In the presence of isolated coarctation a collateral circulation usually develops between the upper and lower parts of the body [3].

Presentation

Symptoms

Usually adults presenting with coarctation have no symptoms. The lesion is discovered at routine examination when hypertension is found or a murmur is heard. Occasionally patients present with complications e.g. angina, endocarditis, myocardial infarction or dissection of the aorta. Cerebrovascular complications are not infrequent and are usually due to cerebral hemorrhage often with rupture of a berry aneurysm.

Signs

The blood pressure is usually elevated. The pulses in the legs are often weak and the femoral pulse delayed by comparison with the right brachial pulse. Prominent arterial pulsation in the suprasternal notch may be present. The development of the collateral circulation between the upper and lower parts of the body may be revealed by palpating arterial pulsations around the scapulae. The left ventricle becomes hypertrophied in response to hypertension and this may be clinically obvious on palpation with a double apical impulse. A classic auscultatory finding is an ejection systolic murmur arising at the site of the coarctation which may be best heard high up on the back over the spine. This murmur is delayed relative to an aortic valve ejection murmur and consequently appears to spill through the aortic valve closure sound. Additional auscultatory findings may be due to a coexistent bicuspid aortic valve with an ejection sound and an ejection systolic murmur. Other murmurs may be produced by turbulent blood flow in the dilated and anastomotic arteries around the scapulae. These also sound like delayed ejection or sometimes continuous murmurs.

Investigations

Radiology

The characteristic features in the chest radiograph of a discrete

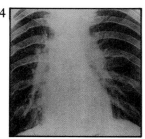

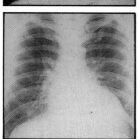

coarctation are rib notching [4], abnormalities of the aortic knuckle [5] and cardiac enlargement [6]. Rib notching is usually seen after puberty. The aortic knuckle may be flat, high or low or more rarely double. Post-stenotic dilatation of the descending aorta is a common feature.

Electrocardiography

The electrocardiogram in coarctation may be normal or show features of left ventricular hypertrophy with ST-T abnormalities in the left ventricular leads [7].

Echocardiography

The 2-dimensional echocardiogram can provide a qualitative if not quantitative assessment of the lesion from the suprasternal notch [8]. The severity of the coarctation is more readily determined by abnormalities of the left ventricle, notably hypertrophy, which can be detected by echocardiography. Another use of echocardiography is to identify the frequently associated intracardiac malformations.

Cardiac Catheterization and Angiography

There will be a systolic pressure difference between the region above the site of coarctation and the region below. The aortogram of a typical discrete coarctation shows a shelf-like narrowing at the junction between the isthmus and descending aorta [9]. With long standing severe coarctation there is visible dilatation of the internal mammary and other collateral arteries.

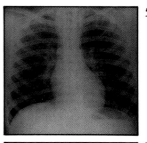

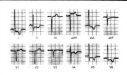

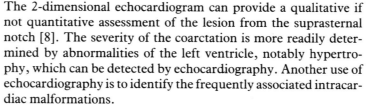

1 Arch arteries showing coarctation of the aorta (arrow) just beyond the left subclavian artery. The orifices of the intercostal arteries in the descending aorta are greatly enlarged.

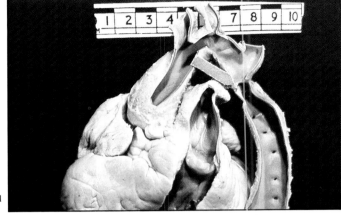

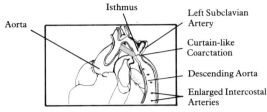

2 Arch arteries showing coarctation of the aorta with dilatation of the ascending aorta and bicuspid aortic valve.

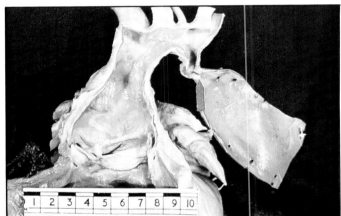

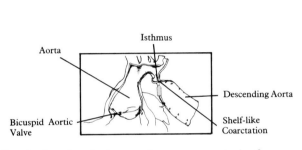

3 Panels showing the internal mammary arteries from a normal patient and a patient with coarctation. The patient with coarctation has gross dilatation of the arteries due to collateral flow.

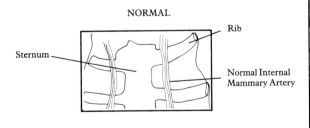

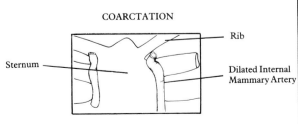

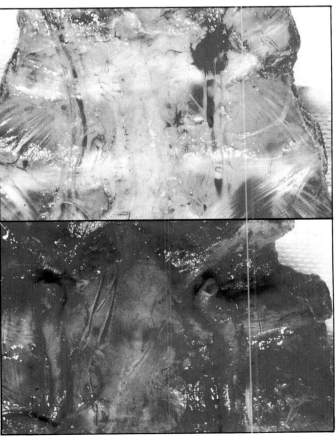

4 Chest radiograph in coarctation showing marked rib notching.

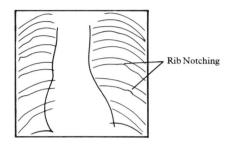

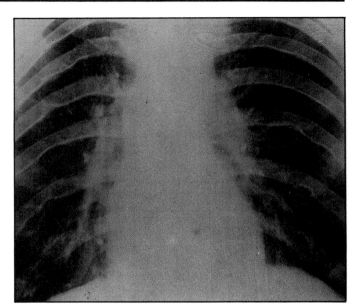

5 Chest radiograph in coarctation showing a flat aortic knuckle and rib notching.

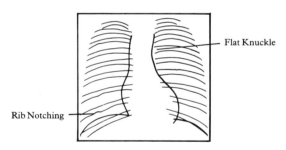

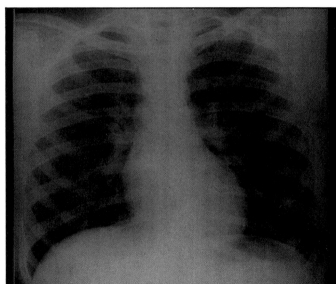

6 Chest radiograph in coarctation showing a large heart with left atrial and upper lobe vessel dilatation which indicates pulmonary venous hypertension.

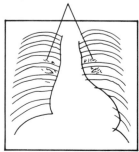

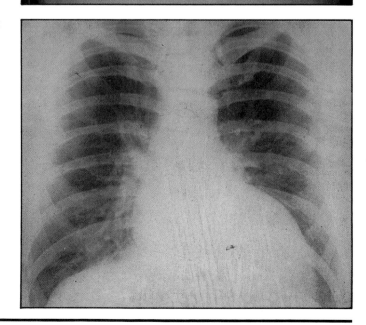

7

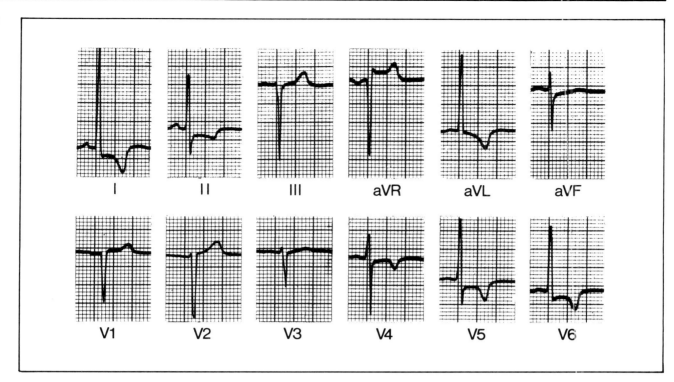

Electrocardiogram of a patient with coarctation of the aorta. Note high-voltage QRS complexes and ST-T changes in leads I, II, aVL and V4–V6 indicating left ventricular hypertrophy. Note for V1 to V6, 1 mV = 0.5 cm.

COARCTATION OF THE AORTA

Echocardiography

8

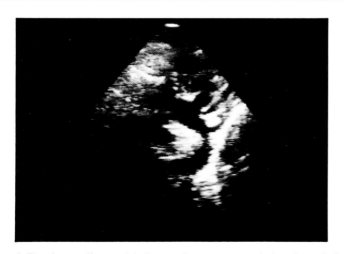 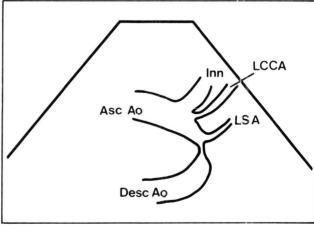

2-D echocardiographic long axis suprasternal view in an infant, showing a tight coarctation of the aorta just distal to the left subclavian artery.

9 Aortogram (antero-posterior projection) showing a shelf-like narrowing at the junction of the isthmus with the descending aorta. Note the dilated internal mammary artery.

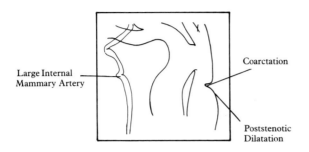

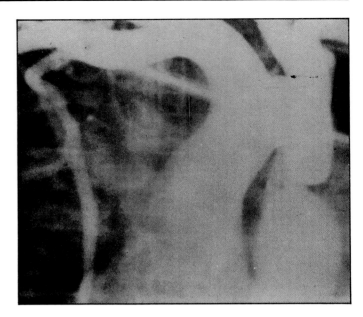

Chapter 6.

Myocardial and Pericardial Disease

Abbreviations

a	Anterior	LA	Left Atrium	Per	Pericardium
A	Atrium	LV	Left Ventricle	PVW	Posterior Ventricular
AVL	Aortic Valve Leaflet	LVEDP	Left Ventricular End		Wall
CW	Chest Wall		Diastolic Pressure	RA	Right Atrium
Eff	Effusion	MV	Mitral Valve	RV	Right Ventricle
En	Endocardium	MVL	Mitral Valve Leaflet	RVEDP	Right Ventricular End
Ep	Epicardium	p	Posterior		Diastolic Pressure
IVS	Intraventricular Septum	PE	Pericardial Effusion		

226

DILATED CARDIOMYOPATHY

Pathology

Dilated cardiomyopathy represents end stage left ventricular muscle disease with failure of emptying in systole not due to coronary artery disease or systemic hypertension. A number of etiologic factors have been associated with the development of a dilated cardiomyopathy such as alcohol or following a viral infection, but usually no clear etiology can be determined. The pathologic features are a dilated, globular, thin walled left ventricle with a large cavity [1]. Mural thrombus frequently develops in the ventricles. Histologic examination of virtually all forms of dilated cardiomyopathy reveals interstitial fibrosis and vacuolated muscle fibers [2].

Presentation

Symptoms

Patients with dilated cardiomyopathy may be asymptomatic and present with cardiomegaly on routine chest X-ray. The symptoms include breathlessness and fatigue or even frank fluid retention due to heart failure. Occasionally, presentation is the result of systemic emboli, perhaps with associated transient arrhythmia.

Signs

The signs are those of left ventricular dysfunction with a double apical impulse and gallop rhythm on auscultation. Sinus tachycardia is common with a small, sharp upstroke arterial pulse reflecting a low cardiac output. A pansystolic murmur due to secondary mitral or tricuspid regurgitation may be present. The jugular venous pressure may show an increased 'v' wave or systolic wave if there is additional tricuspid regurgitation. Patients with fluid retention usually show frank elevation of venous pressure.

Investigations

Radiology

In dilated cardiomyopathy the chest radiograph shows non-specific cardiac enlargement and the changes in the lungs reflect the elevation of pulmonary venous pressure [3]. These include upper lobe blood divertion, Kerley's B lines and frank pulmonary edema.

Electrocardiography

Cardiomyopathy is not associated with specific electrocardiographic abnormalities. Usually the electrocardiogram shows non-specific ST-T abnormalities [4] and sometimes left bundle branch block [5]. Some patients may show Q waves in mid precordial leads simulating myocardial infarction [6].

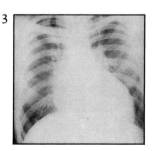

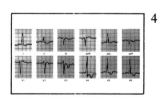

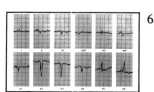

7
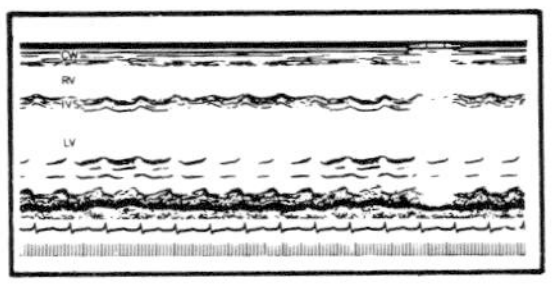

8
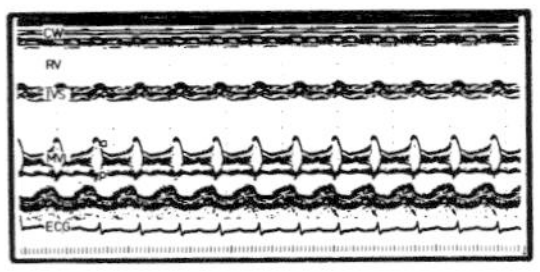

9
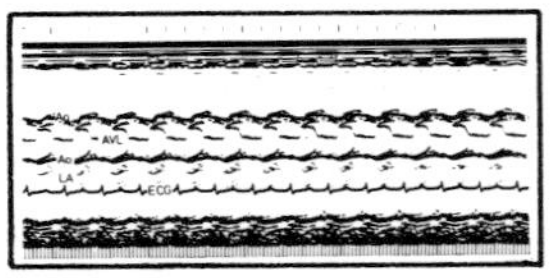

10
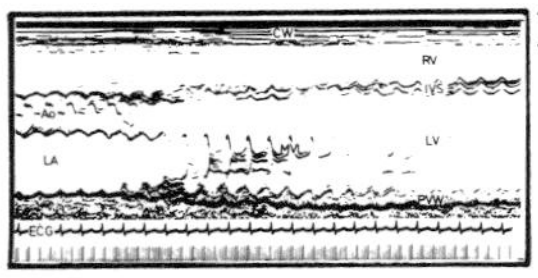

11
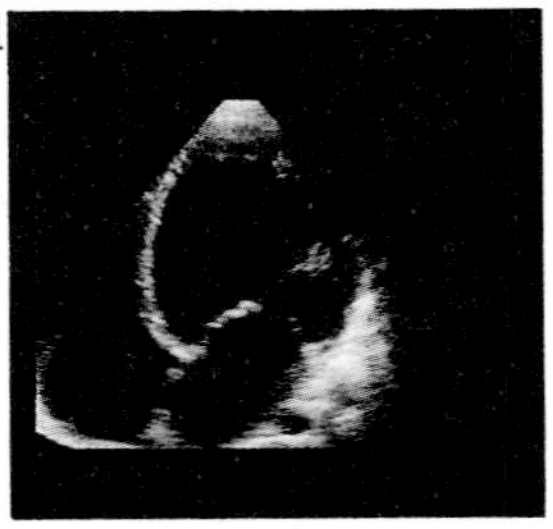

12
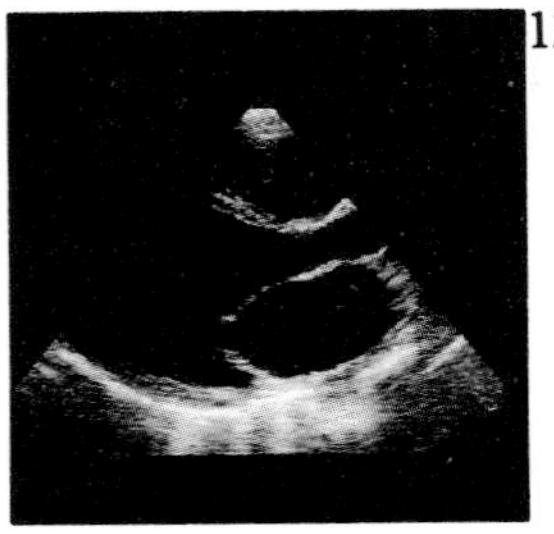

13
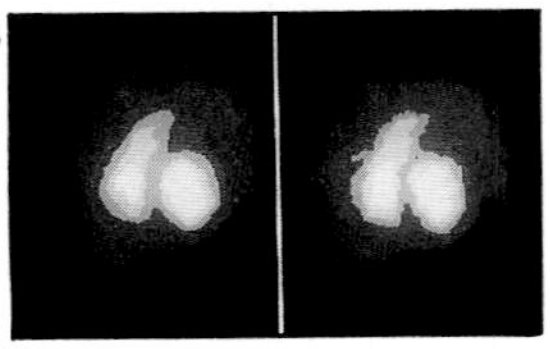

14
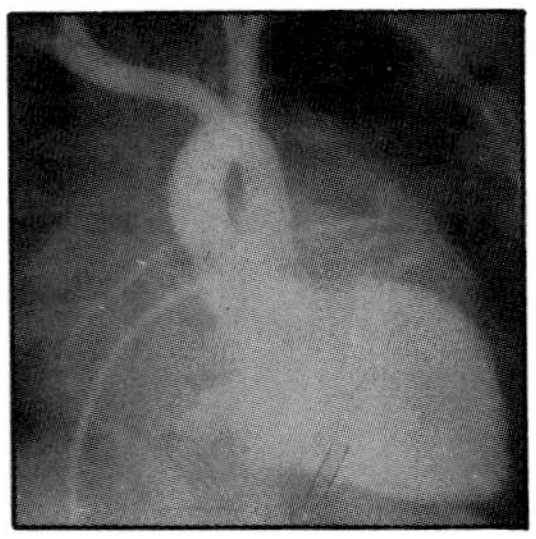

Echocardiography

The left ventricular dimensions are increased and amplitude of wall movement is reduced (i.e. reduced fractional shortening) [7]. As the stroke volume falls, the amplitude of diastolic separation of the mitral valve leaflets is reduced. A very characteristic appearance is of a low amplitude mitral echo 'floating' in a dilated ventricle [8]. Aortic root motion is also reduced so that the entire heart has a generally hypokinetic appearance [9] which is best appreciated on the slow scan from aorta to the ventricles [10], or on two-dimensional echocardiography [11,12]. Right ventricular dimension is often also increased. Slight enlargement of the left atrium due to chronic elevation of left ventricular end diastolic pressure is common.

Nuclear Techniques

Generalized abnormalities of left ventricular function may also be demonstrated using either first pass studies or gated blood pool imaging [13]. Such abnormalities may be distinguished from a left ventricular aneurysm due to coronary artery disease.

Cardiac Catheterization and Angiography

Echocardiography is so characteristic in dilated cardiomyopathy that cardiac catheterization is usually unnecessary except to exclude associated coronary artery disease. Left ventricular angiography will show a large volume left ventricle with a grossly reduced ejection fraction [14].

1 Dilated cardiomyopathy: the opened left ventricle has a large cavity and thin wall.

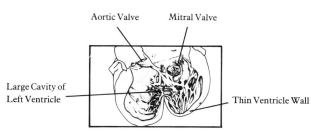

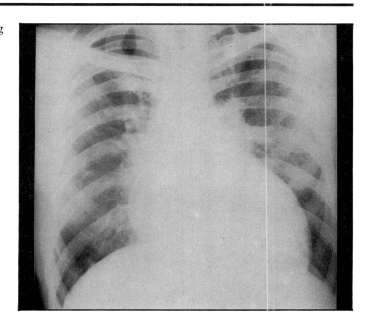

2 Histologic appearance of non-specific dilated cardiomyopathy. The muscle fibers vary in size and are vacuolated. Fibrosis is increased between the muscle fibers.

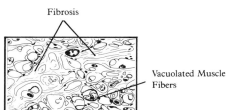

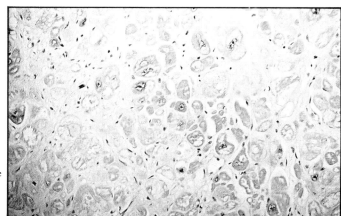

DILATED CARDIOMYOPATHY

Radiology

3 Chest radiograph in dilated cardiomyopathy showing a large heart with pulmonary venous hypertension.

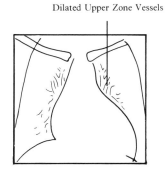

4

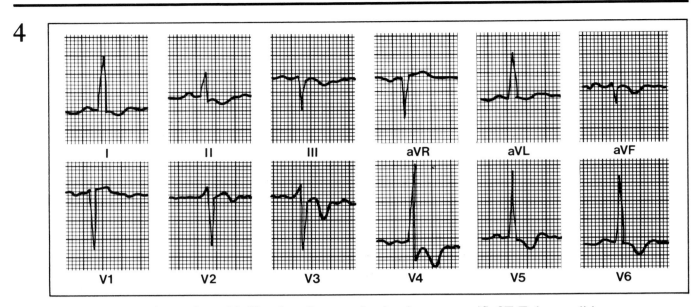

Electrocardiogram in a patient with dilated cardiomyopathy showing non-specific ST-T abnormalities.

5

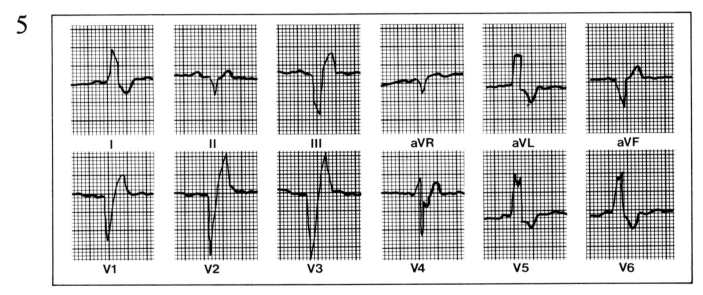

Electrocardiogram in a patient with dilated cardiomyopathy showing left bundle branch block.

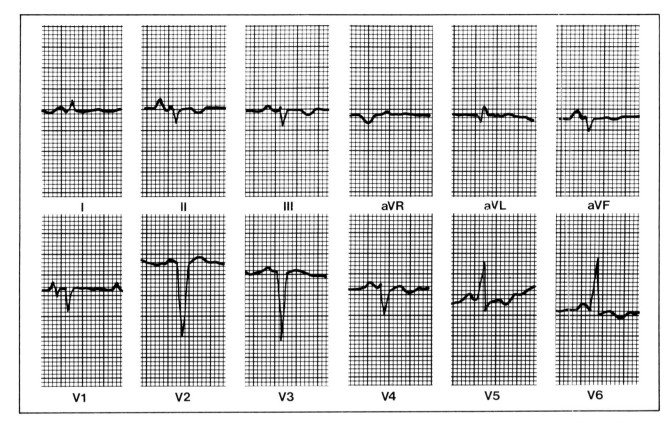

Electrocardiogram in a patient with dilated cardiomyopathy with septal Q-waves simulating myocardial infarction.

DILATED CARDIOMYOPATHY

Echocardiography

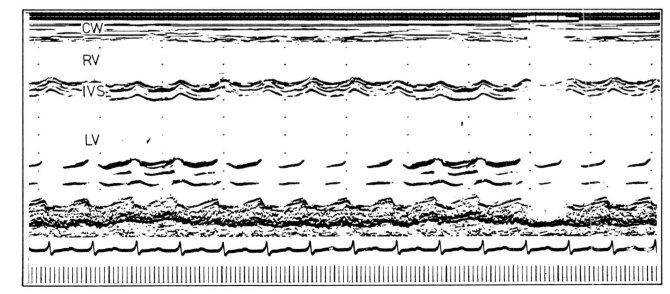

M-mode echocardiogram of dilated cardiomyopathy showing large ventricular dimensions and marked reduction in wall movement.

8

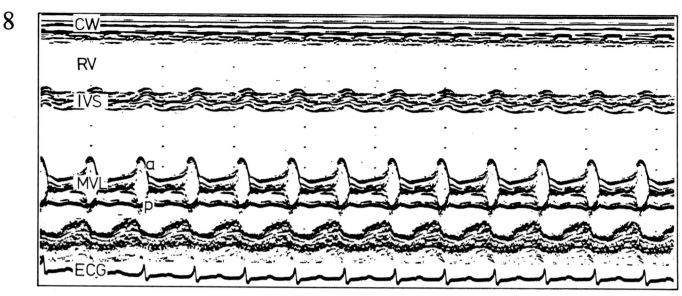

M-mode echocardiogram in dilated cardiomyopathy showing reduction in amplitude of the anterior leaflet of the mitral valve.

9

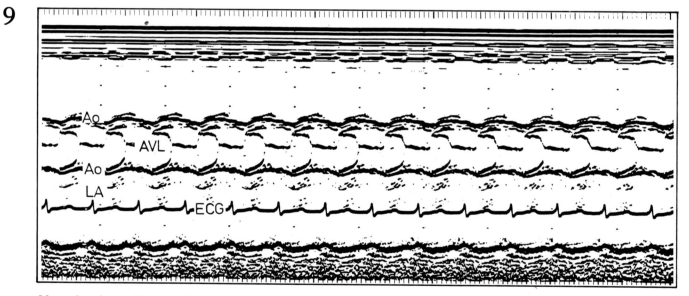

M-mode echocardiogram of dilated cardiomyopathy showing reduced aortic root motion.

10

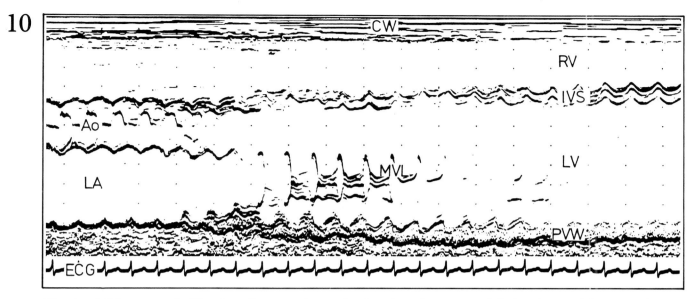

The slow left heart scan in dilated cardiomyopathy emphasizes the enlargement of all chambers and the generalized hypokinesia.

11

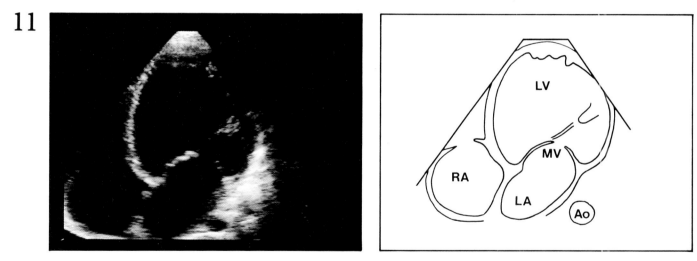

2-D echocardiographic apical four-chamber view showing left ventricular dilatation cardiomyopathy. Note the thin-walled globular left ventricle. The irregularities in the apex may be due to thrombus.

12

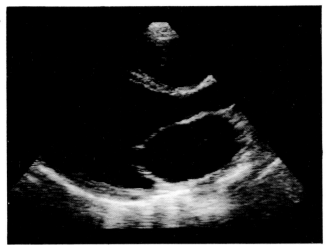 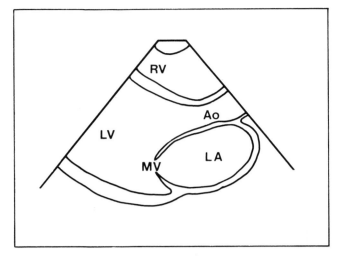

2-D echocardiographic parasternal long axis diastolic view showing left atrial and left ventricular enlargement. The small separation of the mitral valve leaflets indicates the low blood flow through the valve.

13 Gated blood pool scan showing little difference in the size of the ventricular cavities between end diastole (left) and end systole (right).

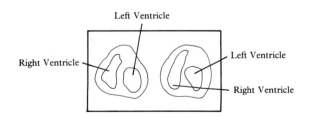 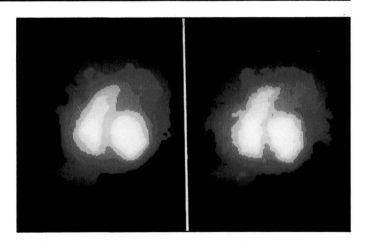

14 Left ventricular angiogram (antero-posterior projection) showing a dilated left ventricle in systole.

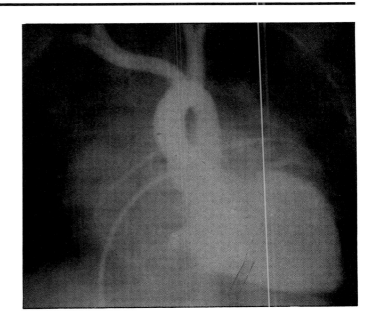

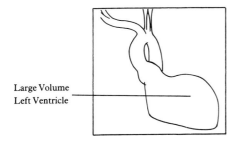

Large Volume Left Ventricle

HYPERTROPHIC CARDIOMYOPATHY

Pathology

Hypertrophic cardiomyopathy is a condition in which there is hypertrophy of the left ventricle without obvious cause. This pathologic process includes a spectrum ranging from a left ventricle which is concentrically hypertrophied [1] to septal hypertrophy disproportionate to the hypertrophy of the left ventricular free wall [2], or there may be localized hypertrophy of the apex of the left ventricle. Where there is asymmetrical septal hypertrophy, the septum may project into the left or right ventricles [3] or both. In cases where left ventricular obstruction occurs, a patch of endocardial thickening develops over the septum due to contact with the anterior cusp of the mitral valve [4].

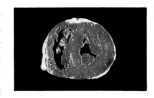

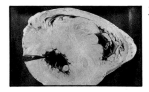

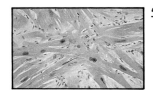

Histologic examination will often reveal only non-specific hypertrophied muscle bundles. Alternatively, some areas of abnormal muscle may show fibers arranged in circular whorls or in clusters with fibers radiating out from a central point [5]; examination at ultrastructural level shows myofibrillar disorganization within individual cells.

Presentation

Symptoms

There may be no symptoms and patients may present with a chance finding of left ventricular hypertrophy without an obvious cause. Patients with septal hypertrophy may also be asymptomatic and may be identified because a murmur is heard at a routine clinical examination. Symptomatic patients complain of angina, exertional syncope or dyspnea. Tachycardia induced by exercise results in a shortening of ventricular diastole which reduces the time available for coronary filling with consequent myocardial ischemia and angina. Myocardial ischemia may lead to ventricular fibrillation and sudden death. Incomplete left atrial emptying during exercise tachycardia leads to a rise in left atrial and pulmonary venous pressure resulting in breathlessness. Incomplete left ventricular filling due to a tachycardia can lead to a reduction in left ventricular stroke volume and systemic hypotension which may cause syncope.

Signs

Hypertrophy of the left ventricle makes it stiff; this results in an augmented left atrial contraction which may be palpable as a separate (double) impulse and audible as a fourth heart sound. In the presence of obstruction, the carotid pulse is jerky or sharp in its upstroke. This may be due to increased velocity of contraction and the increased rate of rise of left ventricular and aortic pressures early in systole. The jugular venous pulse may show abnormal 'a' wave dominance due to enhanced right atrial contraction as a result of either generalized right ventricular hypertrophy or hypertrophy of the septum encroaching on the right ventricular cavity. The systolic murmur may be due to turbulence created in the left ventricular outflow tract or due to mitral regurgitation as the anterior cusp of the closed mitral valve moves forward to meet the bulging hypertrophied septum. In either case the murmur will be delayed in systole. The second heart sound may be split physiologically or it may be reversed due to prolongation of left ventricular systole.

Investigations

Radiology

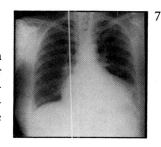

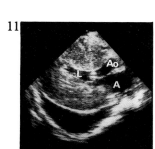

The heart is often enlarged and the diagnosis may be suggested on the chest radiograph by a slight bulge on the high left ventricular border due to septal hypertrophy [6]. In severe cases the pulmonary venous pressure may be raised; this is reflected by cardiomegaly, left atrial dilatation, and dilatation of the upper zone pulmonary vessels [7].

Electrocardiography

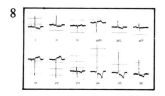

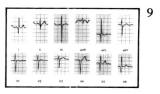

The electrocardiographic features of hypertrophic cardiomyopathy are variable. The electrocardiogram may be normal or strikingly abnormal without reflecting the severity of the pathologic abnormality or hemodynamic derangement. Left ventricular hypertrophy usually with marked T wave inversion may be seen [8]. In some patients the initial Q wave in the left precordial leads is absent. Steep QR or QRS waves simulating myocardial infarction may be seen in other patients [9]. These features have been attributed to septal hypertrophy and fibrosis. Atrial fibrillation may develop in advanced cases. The PR interval may be short with features suggestive of pre-excitation (Wolff-Parkinson-White syndrome) [10]. Left bundle branch block is uncommon.

Echocardiography

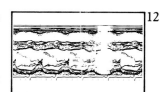

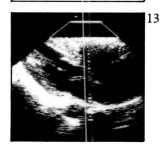

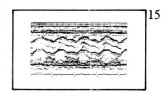

The echocardiogram permits direct visualization of the thickness of the ventricular walls and interventricular septum.

There may be concentric hypertrophy of the left ventricle [11]. Septal thickness may or may not exceed that of the free wall [12], but in many cases it is gross and it appears to obliterate the right ventricular cavity making definition of its right sided endocardial surface difficult. The left ventricular cavity is usually small and despite the immobile septum fractional shortening is normal or increased due to vigorous movement of the posterior wall. Apical hypertrophy will be visible on 2-D echocardiography [13].

Movement of the mitral valve appears to be restricted by the small ventricular cavity and the anterior leaflet appears to hit the ventricular septum as it opens in diastole [14]. A characteristic part of the mitral valve echo is the so called 'systolic anterior movement' (SAM). Soon after mitral valve closure, a group of echoes moves forwards from the closure line towards the septum, the anterior of which comes to close approximation to the septal endocardium. At the end of systole the echoes return to the closure line.

At the onset of ventricular ejection the aortic valve opens normally. If obstruction develops in mid systole the valve leaflets show a coarse fluttering motion and begin to come together [15].

Finally, complete closure of the valve occurs at the normal time or is even delayed if left ventricular ejection is prolonged.

Cardiac Catheterization and Angiography

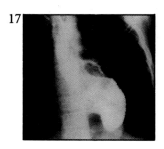

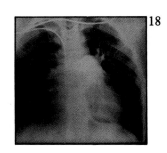

The characteristic hemodynamic abnormality is an elevation of left ventricular end-diastolic pressure due to the stiffness of the left ventricle. The presence of obstruction may be detected either as a resting systolic pressure difference between the cavity and outflow portion of the left ventricle or as a result of various maneuvers which reduce left ventricular cavity size (e.g. amyl nitrate or Valsalva maneuver). In contrast to aortic valve stenosis, following a premature ventricular beat aortic pressure may fall while left ventricular systolic pressure increases; this either results in an augmented pressure difference or the development of a pressure difference if none was present at rest.

Left ventricular angiography shows a small cavity, apical obliteration and prominent papillary muscles [16,17]. The ventricle often has an irregular outline and there may be mitral regurgitation. Right ventricular angiography may show infundibular obstruction due to septal hypertrophy [18].

1 Transverse section through the heart in cardiomyopathy showing concentric left ventricular hypertrophy.

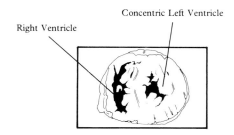

Right Ventricle
Concentric Left Ventricle

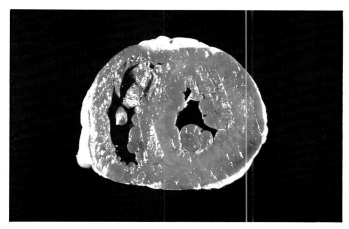

2 The left ventricle from a patient with hypertrophic cardiomyopathy showing a small cavity with very thick wall. The septal region is asymmetrically thickened being at least twice as thick as the parietal wall. The septum bulges into the outflow tract of the left ventricle and impinges onto the anterior cusp of the mitral valve (arrow).

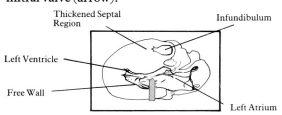

Thickened Septal Region
Infundibulum
Left Ventricle
Free Wall
Left Atrium

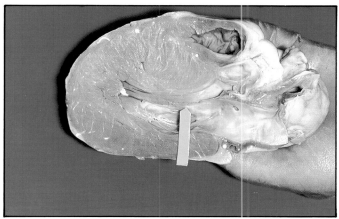

3 Transverse section across the left and right ventricles in hypertrophic cardiomyopathy. The septum is approximately two and a half times the thickness of the left ventricular free wall and bulges into the right ventricular outflow tract.

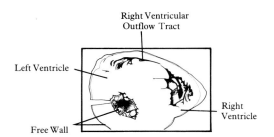

Right Ventricular Outflow Tract
Left Ventricle
Free Wall
Right Ventricle

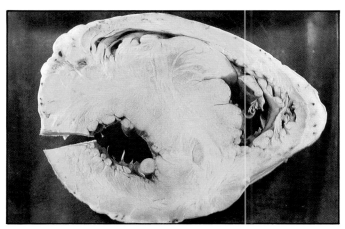

4 Pathologic specimen showing thickening of the anterior leaflet of the mitral valve with a corresponding thickening on the ventricular septum opposite (arrowed), indicating contact in life with an obstruction to ventricular outflow.

5 Histologic section of the myocardium in hypertrophic cardiomyopathy. The muscle fibers are arranged in a characteristic cross-over pattern radiating out in all directions rather than being arranged in parallel fashion.

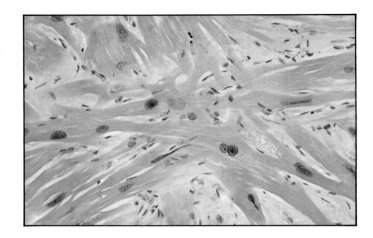

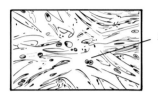

Muscle Fibers

6 Chest radiograph showing large heart with bulge on high left ventricular border characteristic of septal hypertrophy.

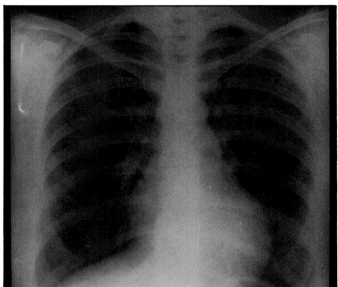

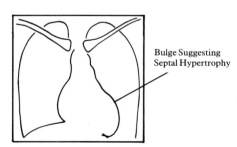

Bulge Suggesting Septal Hypertrophy

7 Chest radiograph showing large heart and left atrium with pulmonary venous hypertension.

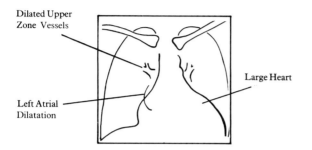

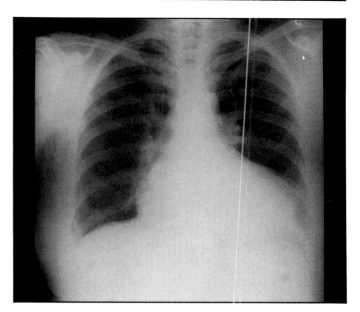

HYPERTROPHIC CARDIOMYOPATHY

Electrocardiography

8

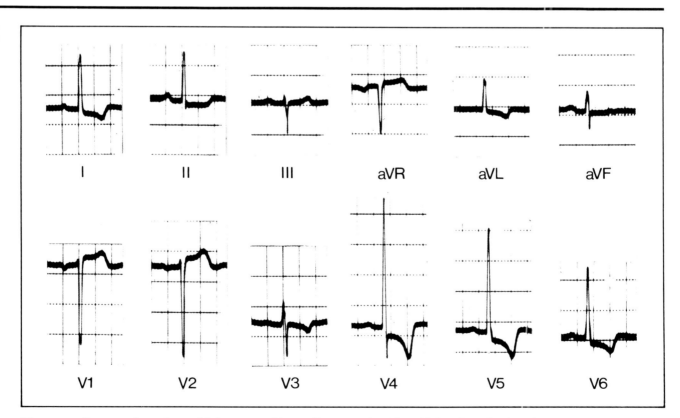

Electrocardiogram of a patient with hypertrophic cardiomyopathy. Note high voltage in chest leads and T-wave inversion in left ventricular leads. All chest leads 1mV = 0.5cm.

9

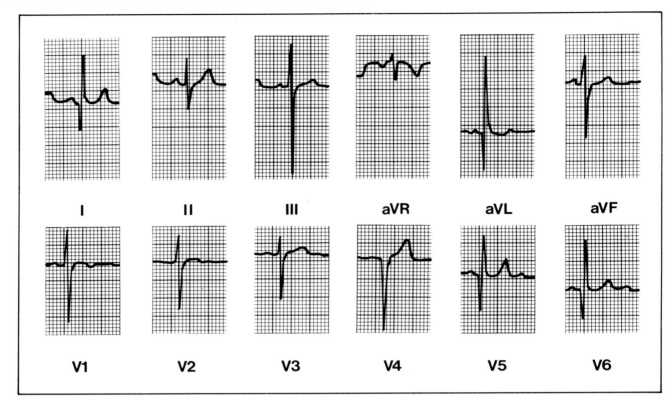

Electrocardiogram of a patient with hypertrophic cardiomyopathy, showing well developed Q-waves in lead 1, aVL and V4 to V6, simulating myocardial infarction.

10

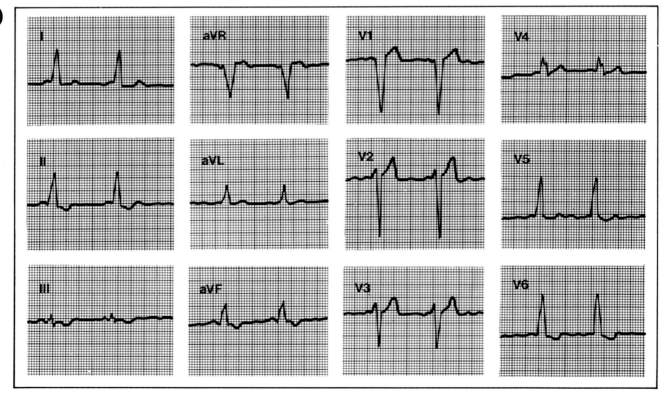

Electrocardiogram showing shortening of the PR interval, widening of the QRS complex and a delta wave indicative of pre-excitation. This is an occasional feature of hypertrophic cardiomyopathy.

11

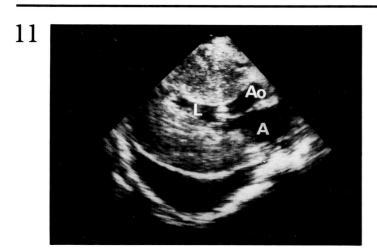
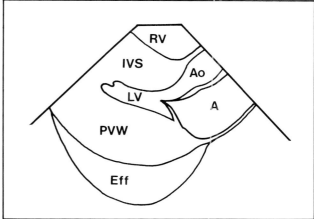

2-D echocardiographic parasternal long axis systolic view in hypertrophic cardiomyopathy with gross symmetrical hypertrophy of the left ventricle with slit-like cavity. Note additional pericardial effusion.

12

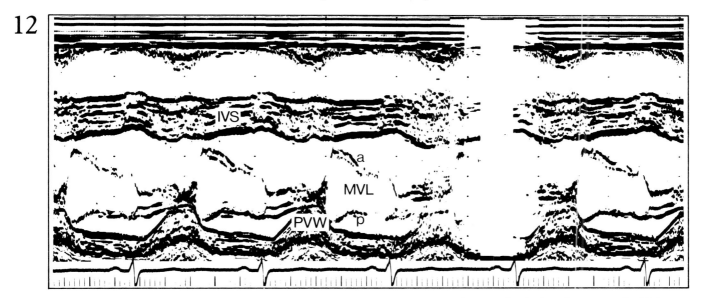

M-mode echocardiogram of mild hypertrophic cardiomyopathy. The only abnormality is that the septum is thicker than the posterior left ventricular wall.

13

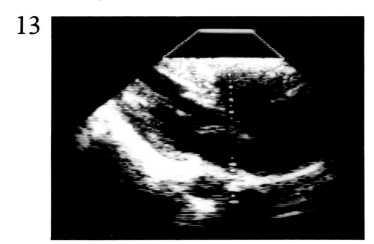
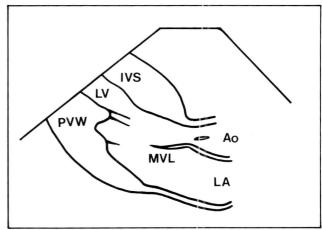

2-D echocardiographic parasternal long axis view showing hypertrophy, particularly in the apical region.

14

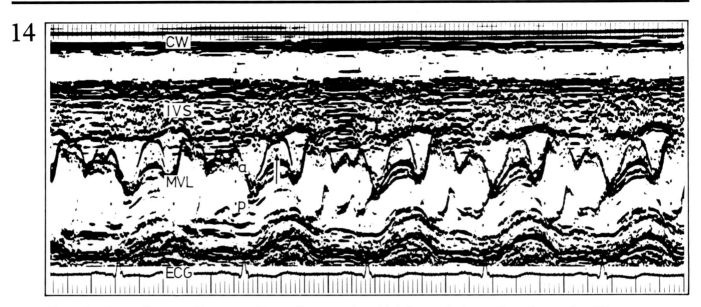

M-mode echocardiogram of hypertrophic cardiomyopathy with left ventricular outflow obstruction. The echocardiogram shows systolic anterior movement of the anterior leaflet (arrowed) which also strikes the septum at the onset of diastole.

15

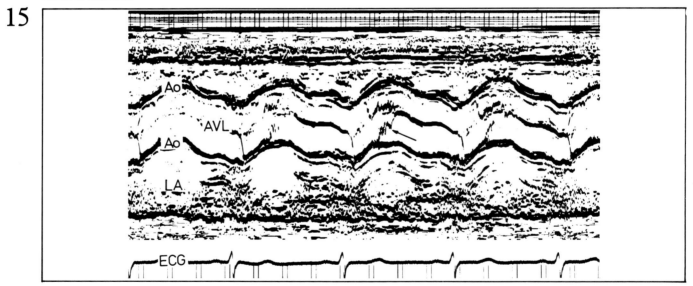

M-mode echocardiogram of the aortic valve showing mid-systolic closure and fluttering (arrowed). This may be seen in hypertrophic cardiomyopathy but it is a non-specific feature.

16 Left ventricular angiogram in systole (antero-posterior projection) showing a small irregular cavity.

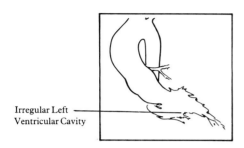

Irregular Left Ventricular Cavity

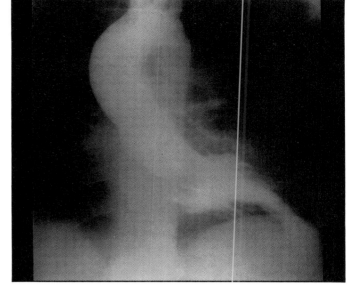

17 Left ventricular angiogram in diastole (antero-posterior projection) showing an irregular outline and inferior indentation from asymmetric septal hypertrophy.

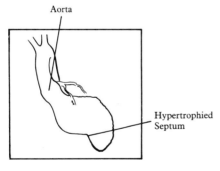

Aorta

Hypertrophied Septum

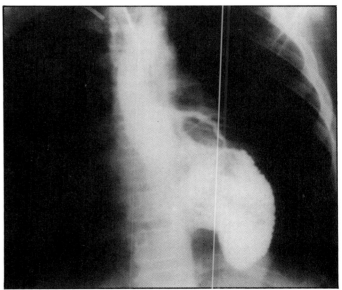

18 Right ventricular angiogram (antero-posterior projection) showing infundibular obstruction due to septal hypertrophy.

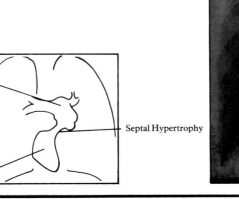

Pulmonary Artery

Septal Hypertrophy

Right Ventricle

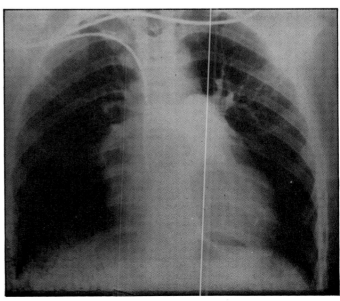

Pathology

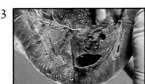

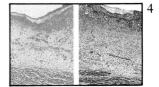

Restrictive cardiomyopathy is characterized by a restriction to diastolic filling and ventricular distensibility which can be brought about by endocardial and/or myocardial lesions. Signs of 'heart failure' which result are not related to abnormal systolic myocardial function but are the result of back pressure due to impaired diastolic filling. When this process becomes extensive, often due to super-added thrombus on top of endocardial scarring, the already small ventricular cavity may become 'obliterated'. Systolic function is usually well preserved.

Amyloid infiltration is probably the commonest cause of restrictive cardiomyopathy seen in the United Kingdom [1,2] but, throughout the world, the most common cause is endomyocardial fibrosis with or without eosinophilia [3,4]. Other rarer causes include hemochromatosis, glycogen storage disease, mucopolysaccharidosis and neoplastic infiltration. Restrictive cardiomyopathy can also occur without a specific pathologic basis.

Presentation

Symptoms

Patients usually present with dyspnea, ankle and abdominal swelling. There may be marked fluid retention while paroxysmal nocturnal dyspnea or orthopnea are absent. Although the reasons are not known, ascites may be much more marked than peripheral edema. Occasionally patients may present with palpitations due to atrial or ventricular arrhythmias. They may present with syncope due to conducting tissue involvement. Orthostatic hypotension may occur due to over-dehydration with diuretics, or due to amyloid infiltration of the autonomic nervous system.

Signs

Physical examination reveals evidence of restrictive filling of the right ventricle with an elevated jugular venous pressure, which may be further elevated by deep inspiration (Kussmaul's sign), peripheral edema and ascites. The liver is often enlarged. There may be signs of a low cardiac output. Auscultation often reveals a gallop rhythm and systolic murmurs due to atrio-ventricular valvular regurgitation.

Investigations

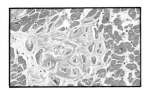

Radiology

The chest X-ray is generally unremarkable but there may be cardiomegaly usually due to bi-atrial dilatation [5]. Pulmonary edema may be present particularly when mitral regurgitation, due to tethering of the posterior leaflet of the mitral valve is the main hemodynamic lesion.

Pericardial calcification is absent in restrictive cardiomyopathy and when present enables the diagnosis of constrictive pericardi-

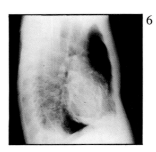

tis to be made [6]. The distinction between the two conditions is a common problem in differential diagnosis.

Electrocardiography

The electrocardiogram may show sinus rhythm, supraventricular arrhythmias (usually atrial fibrillation), or heart block due to conducting tissue involvement by fibrosis. Low voltage may be seen particularly in the presence of an accompanying pericardial effusion. ST-segment depression and T-wave inversion changes (in the absence of voltage criteria of left ventricular hypertrophy) may be seen and are thought to be due to myocardial fibrosis.

Echocardiography

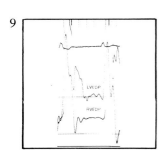

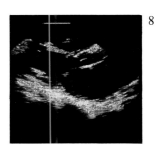

M-mode echocardiography reveals non-specific changes, including right ventricular dilatation with a normal-sized or small left ventricle [7]. Two-dimensional echocardiography is extremely helpful in the early diagnosis of restrictive cardiomyopathy and specific cavity changes such as apical obliteration and endocardial thickening can be easily demonstrated. Amyloid infiltration gives a particular and diagnostic reflection pattern on grey scale and this can be further characterized by amplitude processed color-coded tissue characterization techniques [8]. A highly specific feature of endomyocardial fibrosis well seen on the long axis 2-dimensional view is that of tethering of the posterior mitral valve leaflet.

Cardiac Catheterization and Angiography

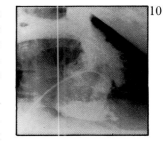

Catheterization reveals elevated ventricular filling pressures in both right and left ventricles and the filling pressures in the two ventricles differ with higher pressure in the left ventricle, unlike constrictive pericarditis where the pressures are usually equal. A prominent early diastolic dip and mid-late diastolic plateau is characteristically noted in both ventricular pressure pulses [9].

If the etiology is endomyocardial fibrosis left ventricular angiography frequently reveals cavity obliteration and mitral regurgitation. Left ventricular systolic function is generally intact and right ventricular angiography shows tricuspid regurgitation and right ventricular apical cavity obliteration [10]. The coronary arteries are normal. If the etiology is amyloid, left ventricular systolic function may be normal or slightly impaired, while the right ventricular cavity is dilated with tricuspid regurgitation. Endomyocardial biopsy will be needed to confirm the diagnosis histologically.

1 Amyloid deposition in the myocardium. In hematoxylin and eosin stained histologic sections amyloid is a pale pink homogenous material. Amyloid [arrows] is laid down between myocardial cells and ultimately completely surrounds them leaving a lattice of amyloid within which are embedded a few residual muscle cells staining a deeper pink colour.

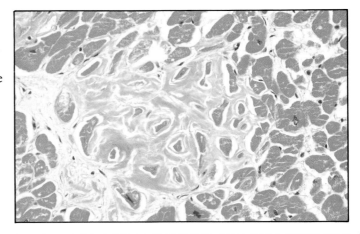

2 Macroscopic view of heart with cardiac amyloid showing amyloid deposits in the left atrium. After fixation in formalin, inspection of the surface of the left atrium shows deposits of amyloid as brown translucent nodules, 1–2 mm in diameter, just beneath the endocardium. Similar deposits are present in this specimen within the posterior cusp of the mitral valve but not in the anterior cusp.

Posterior Mitral Valve Cusp — Amyloid Deposits
Anterior Mitral Valve Cusp

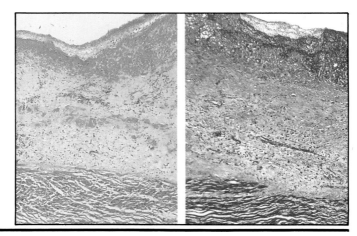

3 Section through the left ventricle in endomyocardial fibrosis. There is marked left ventricular apical obliteration with endocardial thickening and super-added thrombus.

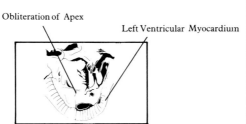

Obliteration of Apex — Left Ventricular Myocardium

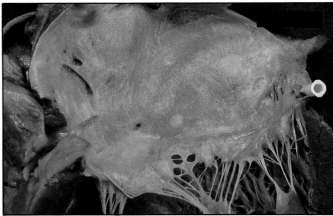

4 Endomyocardial fibrosis. The endocardium is markedly thickened and using hematoxylin and eosin (left hand panel) it is not easy to distinguish the cause of this thickening. However staining by a trichrome method (right panel) reveals that the endocardial thickening is due to a deep layer of collagen, staining blue, and a more superficial layer of fibrin.

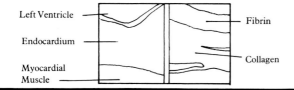

Left Ventricle — Fibrin
Endocardium — Collagen
Myocardial Muscle

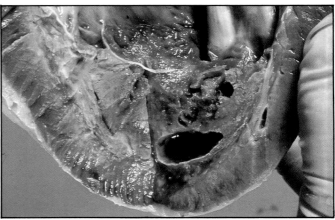

5 Chest radiograph showing cardiomegaly due to bi-atrial enlargement.

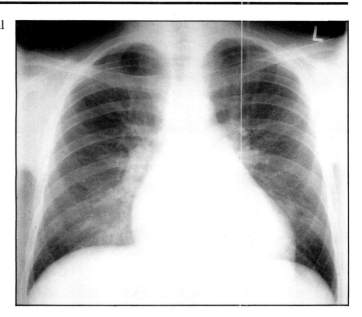

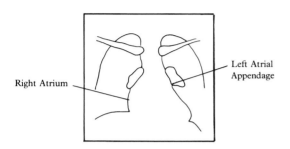

6 Lateral chest radiograph showing marked pericardial calcification.

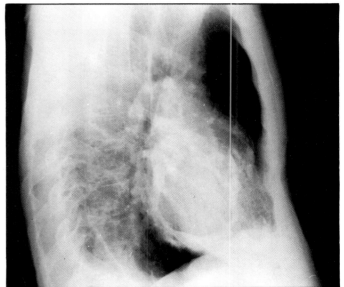

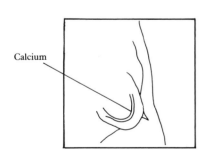

7

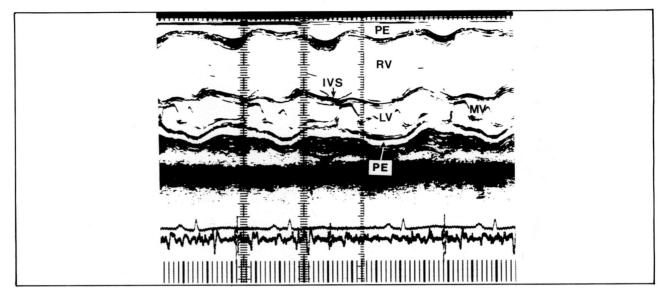

M-mode echocardiogram of endomyocardial fibrosis showing a dilated right ventricle, a small left ventricle and a pericardial effusion.

8

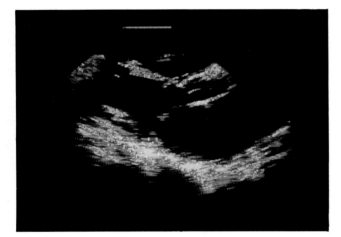
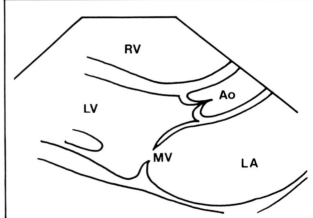

2-D echocardiographic amplitude process color-coded long axis parasternal view in endomyocardial fibrosis showing increased echo density and endocardial thickening on the posterior left ventricular wall, thickening and tethering of the posterior mitral valve leaflet and left atrial cavity dilatation.

9 Pressure recordings taken from the right and left ventricles simultaneously in endomyocardial fibrosis showing the typical 'dip and plateau' and the elevated and *different* end diastolic pressure measurements.

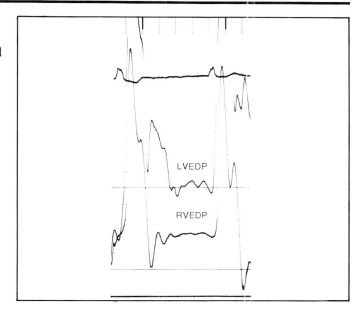

10 Right ventricular angiogram showing apical cavity obliteration and tricuspid regurgitation due to endomyocardial fibrosis.

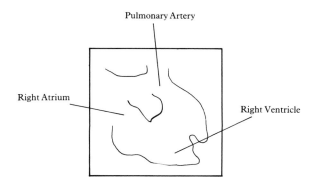

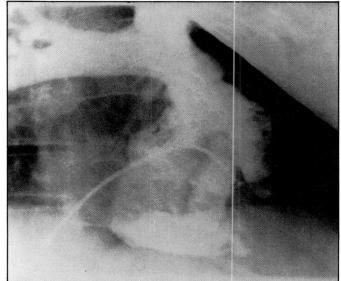

Pathology

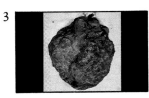

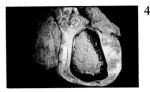

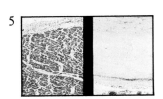

Acute pericarditis is characterized by a fibrinous exudate [1] over the visceral and parietal pericardium with varying amounts of rather turbid yellow fluid found in the pericardial cavity. Histologic examination shows strands of fibrin deposited on the serosa with dilated blood vessels and an acute inflammatory infiltrate.

The commonest causes of acute pericarditis are viral infection [2] and acute myocardial infarction. The pericardial reaction is non-specific, although clinical data usually allow the causes to be distinguished. Viral (Coxsackie) pericarditis in fatal cases is usually associated with myocarditis. Rarely bacterial infection of the pericardium gives rise to purulent pericarditis [3].

Chronic fibrosing constrictive pericarditis is usually due to tuberculosis [4]. The typical histology of giant cell granulomata may be found. However, many cases of constrictive pericarditis are due to a simple sheet of fibrous tissue in which a few lymphocytic foci are present [5]. The etiology cannot be established: some may be due to rheumatoid disease, some to organization of uremic pericarditis. The majority are assumed to be post-viral.

Secondary carcinoma commonly involves the pericardium [6]. The tumor may appear as white nodules over the visceral pericardium or as a more diffuse sheet of tumor.

Presentation

Symptoms

The presenting symptom of acute pericarditis is stabbing chest pain that is characteristically worse on movement. It should be distinguished from pleuritic chest pain but the distinction may be difficult. Fever and malaise are common accompaniments. Severe breathlessness may suggest the development of cardiac tamponade.

In long standing constrictive pericarditis patients may complain of abdominal distention and peripheral edema due to the high venous pressure.

Signs

The hallmark of acute pericarditis is a pericardial rub, but this may come and go. With the accumulation of pericardial fluid, signs of tamponade may occur. On inspiration there is a marked fall in systolic blood pressure (pulsus paradoxus) and a rise in venous pressure with a dominant systolic descent. A third heart sound will not be heard.

In chronic constrictive pericarditis the physical signs will be the same as with tamponade unless the disease process has significantly involved the myocardium. Myocardial involvement is distinguished by diastolic collapse in the venous pressure and the presence of a third heart sound. Hepatomegaly, ascites and peripheral edema may be present.

Investigations

Radiology

In acute pericarditis in which there is no effusion, the chest X-ray will be normal. Non-specific enlargement of the cardiac silhouette will be seen if the pericardial effusion is sufficiently large [7].

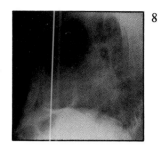

Constrictive pericarditis is calcified in approximately 50% of cases. The calcification is most commonly confined to the atrioventricular groove as seen in the penetrated and lateral chest X-rays [8]. Often, however, no abnormality is seen on the chest X-ray even though constriction is present.

Electrocardiography

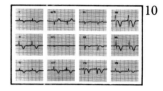

The electrocardiogram in pericardial disease usually shows non-specific ST-T abnormalities. Typically there is concave ST elevation in the acute phase [9] while T-wave inversion occurs later [10].

Echocardiography

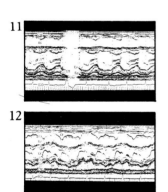

Echocardiography is the most reliable and sensitive method for making the diagnosis of a pericardial effusion. Some broad classification of the size of a pericardial effusion is possible from M mode studies. Normally visceral and parietal pericardial layers are in apposition and posteriorly return a single dense echo which moves with the endocardial echo. In pericardial effusion the two pericardial layers are separated by the fluid with the visceral pericardium moving normally with the posterior left ventricular wall, and the parietal layer immobile and separated from it by an echo free space [11]. Most frequently an echo free space can be visualized posteriorly. However, when fluid is present anteriorly, a space between the static chest wall echoes and those from the mobile right ventricular anterior wall may be observed [12]. With small amounts of fluid the gap is seen in systole, but with larger collections it is apparent throughout the cardiac cycle.

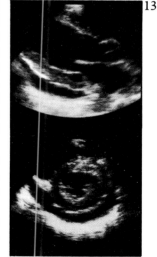

The extent and distribution of fluid surrounding the heart are much better assessed by 2-dimensional echocardiography [13]. The heart may take on a characteristic swinging motion within the bag of fluid if the effusion is large.

There are no diagnostic echocardiographic features of chronic pericardial disease without effusion. Even if calcification is present it cannot be visualized.

Cardiac Catheterization and Angiography

Cardiac catheterization and angiocardiography play little part in the diagnosis or management of patients with pericardial disease. If constriction or tamponade is present then the diastolic pressures in all the cardiac chambers will be equal. A characteristic dip and plateau is seen in the diastolic pressure but in contrast to restrictive cardiomyopathy the diastolic pressure in the two ventricles are the same.

1 Acute pericarditis. A thick fibrinous exudate covers the surface of the heart.

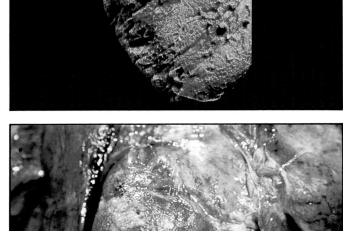

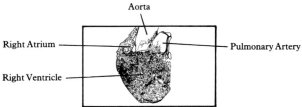

2 Viral pericarditis. The visceral pericardium is red and inflamed with a roughened surface due to deposition of fibrin.

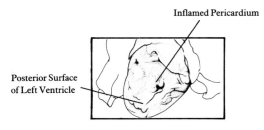

3 Bacterial pericarditis. Purulent exudate on visceral pericardium.

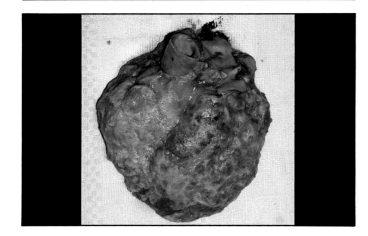

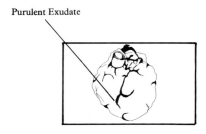

4 Chronic constrictive pericarditis. A window has been cut through the thickened parietal pericardium which forms a rough constrictive membrane. Note also the shaggy exudate on the visceral pericardium.

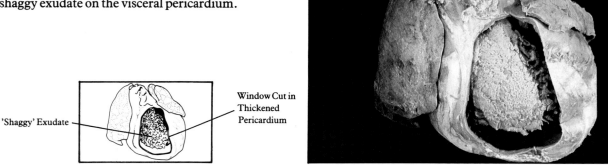

5 Histologic section of normal pericardium [left]. The pericardium forms a thin layer on the myocardium. Histologic section of grossly thickened pericardium [right] in chronic constrictive pericarditis. (Both sections are taken at the same magnification.)

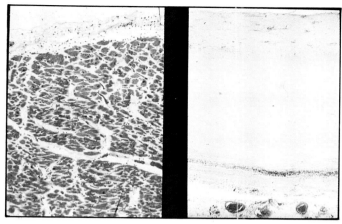

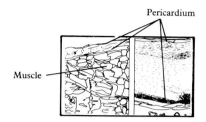

6 Secondary pericardial tumor. The pericardial cavity is opened to show the wide dissemination of tumor on the visceral pericardium of the right ventricle.

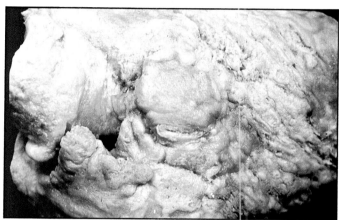

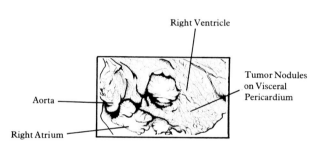

7 Chest radiography showing non-specific cardiac enlargement in pericardial effusion.

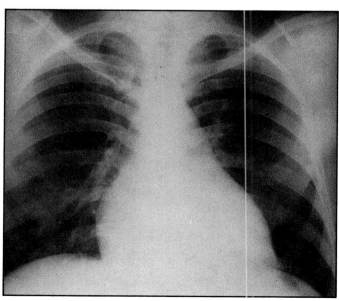

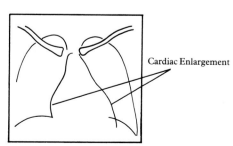

8   Lateral chest X-ray showing calcification in the atrioventricular groove in a patient with chronic constrictive pericarditis.

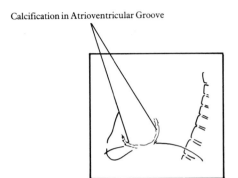

Calcification in Atrioventricular Groove

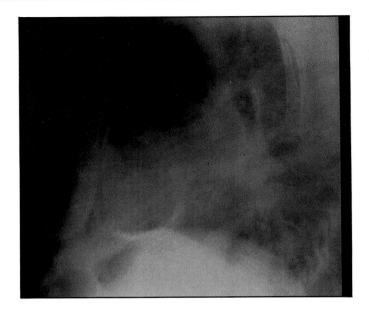

9

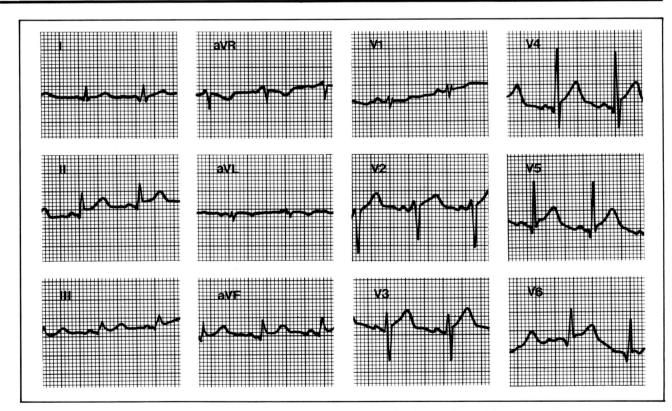

Electrocardiogram showing widespread concave ST-segment elevation in a patient with acute pericarditis.

10

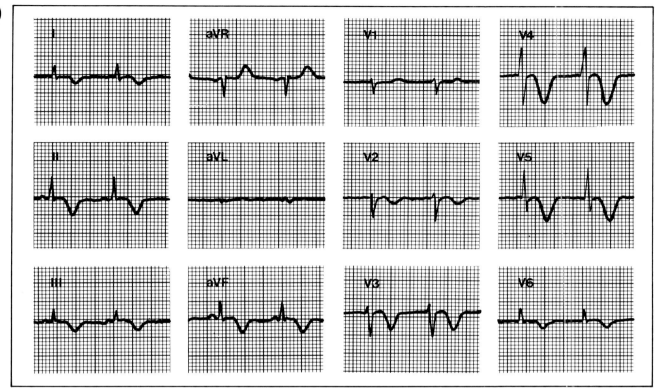

Electrocardiogram showing widespread T-wave inversion following acute pericarditis.

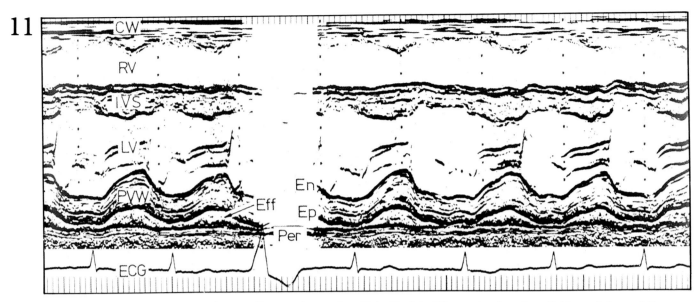

M-mode echocardiogram showing small posterior pericardial effusion. The parietal pericardial layer is immobile while the visceral layer moves with the posterior left ventricular endocardium

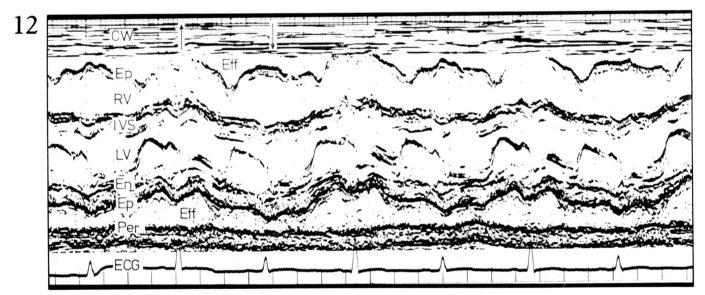

M-mode echocardiogram showing both anterior and posterior pericardial effusion.

13

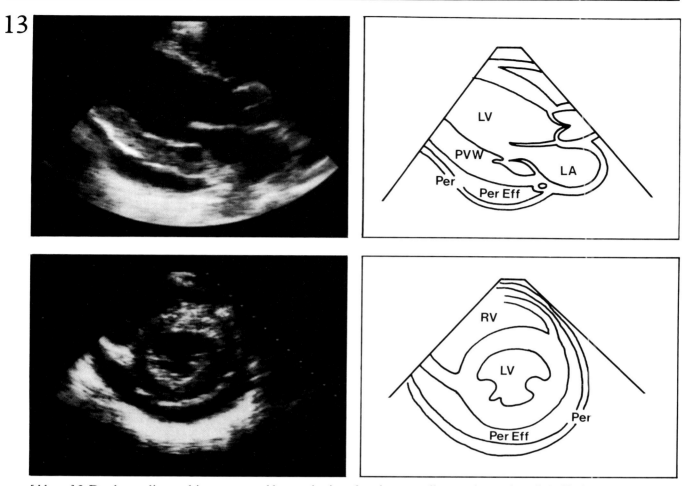

[Above] 2-D echocardiographic parasternal long axis view showing a small posterior pericardial effusion. [Below] 2-D echocardiographic parasternal short axis view showing a moderate pericardial effusion. The uneven distribution of the fluid can be seen in both views.

Chapter 7.

Miscellaneous Cardiac Conditions

Abbreviations

a	Anterior	LA	Left Atrium	p	Posterior
AP	Antero-Posterior	LL	Left Lateral	PA	Postero-Anterior
CW	Chest Wall	LV	Left Ventricle	RA	Right Atrium
Eff	Effusion	MV	Mitral Valve	RL	Right Lateral
IVS	Interventricular Septum	MVL	Mitral Valve Leaflet	RV	Right Ventricle

CARDIAC TUMORS

Pathology

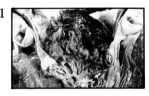

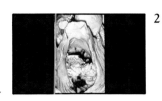

The most common primary cardiac tumor is the atrial myxoma; all others are very rare. Atrial myxomata arise on the interatrial septum around the site of the foramen ovale; 90% project into the left atrium [1] and 10% into the right atrium [2]. The myxoma is a shining gelatinous multicolored mass. Some myxomata extend into the mitral or tricuspid valve orifice producing obstruction, and with time the valve may be destroyed by direct mechanical trauma. Thrombus forms over the tumor and embolization of thrombus or actual tumor fragments is common. Histologically the tumor consists of nests of epithelial ('lipidic') cells in a myxomatous stroma. The tumor is not malignant but recurrence following partial removal occurs. Other primary tumors are rare, but include rhabdomyosarcoma [3] and hemangiosarcoma.

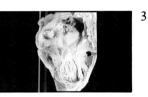

Children with tuberose sclerosis develop multiple rhabdomyomata consisting of large clear cells often interpreted as being masses of Purkinje cells. Occasionally isolated masses of fibrous tissue (fibromata or rhabdomyomata) are found in otherwise normal children [4].

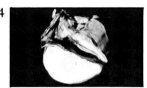

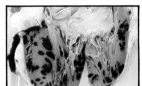

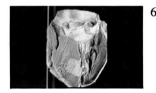

Secondary cardiac tumors are more common than primary neoplasms. Multiple small nodules may occur throughout the myocardium in carcinoma of the breast, malignant melanoma [5] or bronchial tumors. More rarely, single large tumor deposits occur [6]. Occasionally, renal carcinoma or hepatoma spreads to the right atrium via the vena cava, or bronchial carcinoma may spread to the left atrium via the pulmonary veins.

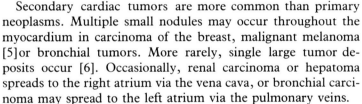

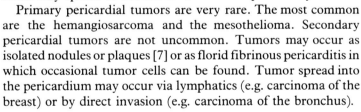

Primary pericardial tumors are very rare. The most common are the hemangiosarcoma and the mesothelioma. Secondary pericardial tumors are not uncommon. Tumors may occur as isolated nodules or plaques [7] or as florid fibrinous pericarditis in which occasional tumor cells can be found. Tumor spread into the pericardium may occur via lymphatics (e.g. carcinoma of the breast) or by direct invasion (e.g. carcinoma of the bronchus).

Presentation

Symptoms

Any cardiac tumor may present with a non-specific illness including a pyrexia and a high ESR. Tumors on the left side of the heart may present with single or multiple systemic emboli. Left atrial myxoma often presents with features indistinguishable from mitral valve disease. Similarly, right atrial myxomata mimic tricuspid valve disease and may present with embolism into the pulmonary circulation. Intermittent obstruction of the atrioventricular valves may result in syncope.

Signs

The physical signs of a left atrial myxoma may be indistinguishable from those of rheumatic mitral valve disease in sinus rhythm, including the same auscultatory features and the signs of pulmonary hypertension. Occasionally, a characteristic tumor 'plop' may distinguish left atrial myxoma from rheumatic mitral valve disease. Similarly, right atrial myxoma will closely mimic the physical signs of tricuspid valve disease.

Tumors involving the pericardium may present as a pericardial effusion or as cardiac tamponade. Where tumors extensively involve cardiac muscle the clinical features will be those of a restrictive cardiomyopathy.

Investigations

Radiology

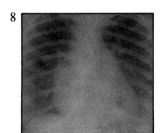

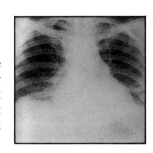

In left atrial myxoma, the chest X-ray may be normal or the appearances may reflect mitral valve obstruction with pulmonary venous hypertension [8]. With a right atrial myxoma the chest radiograph may show evidence of pulmonary infarcts - the result of tumor emboli [9]. An increased cardiac silhouette may be seen if there is a pericardial effusion.

Electrocardiography

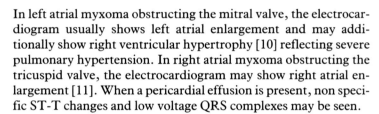

In left atrial myxoma obstructing the mitral valve, the electrocardiogram usually shows left atrial enlargement and may additionally show right ventricular hypertrophy [10] reflecting severe pulmonary hypertension. In right atrial myxoma obstructing the tricuspid valve, the electrocardiogram may show right atrial enlargement [11]. When a pericardial effusion is present, non specific ST-T changes and low voltage QRS complexes may be seen.

Echocardiography

Mobile tumors in the left atrium produce very characteristic echo recordings, which are diagnostic of the condition and preclude the need for further investigation.

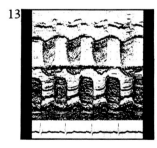

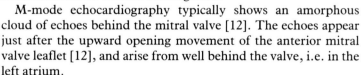

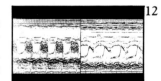

M-mode echocardiography typically shows an amorphous cloud of echoes behind the mitral valve [12]. The echoes appear just after the upward opening movement of the anterior mitral valve leaflet [12], and arise from well behind the valve, i.e. in the left atrium.

If the tumor is very mobile, it descends through the mitral orifice into the left ventricle during diastole, and returns to the left atrium during systole [13]. In other cases, the tumor stays mainly within the left atrium, and the echoes are only seen behind the mitral valve.

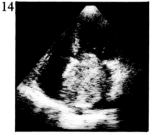

Two-dimensional echocardiography is an ideal technique for visualizing tumors within either atrium directly [14]. The mobility of an atrial myxoma usually enables it to be distinguished from the static thrombus. However, even large thrombi may not be seen at all since generally thrombus has the same echocardiographic appearance as blood.

No specific appearances are associated with intramural cardiac tumors, but any localized thickening of one of the chamber walls should raise the possibility of a tumor.

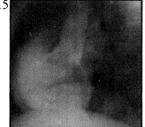

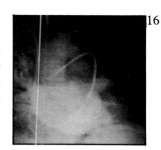

Cardiac Catheterization and Angiography

In patients with atrial myxomata the hemodynamics may reflect obstruction of the atrioventricular valves. Although rarely necessary for diagnostic purposes, particularly with the development of 2-D echocardiography, angiography when performed may show filling defects in the atria [15,16].

Where tumors involve the myocardium the hemodynamics may mimic restrictive cardiomyopathy while angiography may reveal encroachment on normal cardiac chambers [17]. Sometimes distortion of the normal coronary arterial pattern or even a pathologic tumor circulation may be seen.

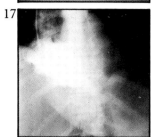

1 Left atrial myxoma. The tumor extends down into the mitral valve. Fibrous thickening is seen on the anterior cusp of the valve due to mechanical trauma from the tumor mass.

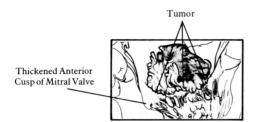

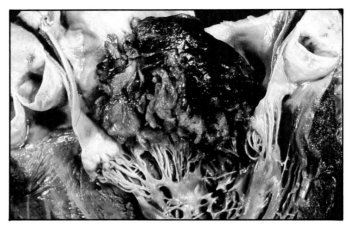

2 Right atrial myxoma. The tumor is a lobulated mass filling the cavity.

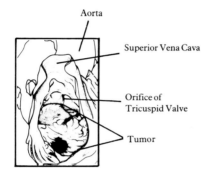

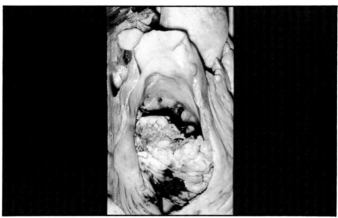

3 Rhabdomyosarcoma in the atrial septum. The right atrium is opened to show the bulging tumor mass which occupies the septum.

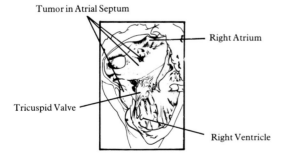

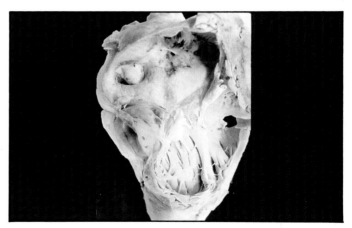

4 Right ventricular rhabdomyoma. A large solid white mass of tumor replaces most of the normal ventricular muscle.

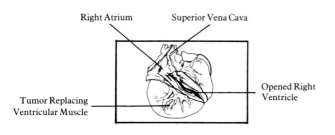

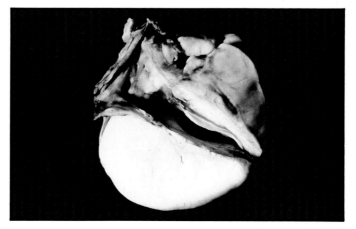

5 Secondary deposits of tumor in the heart. Multiple black deposits are seen in the myocardium secondary to malignant melanoma of the skin.

6 Single deposit of secondary carcinoma in the heart. The large tumor mass lies in the interventricular septum. The primary tumor site was in the kidney.

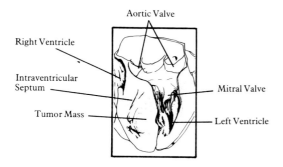

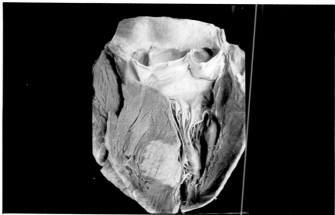

7 Secondary pericardial tumor. The pericardial cavity is opened to show the wide dissemination of tumor on the visceral pericardium of the right ventricle.

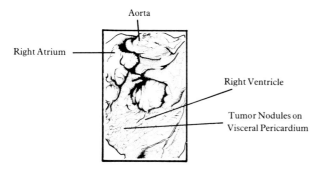

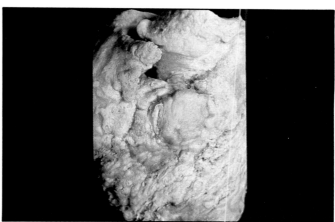

8 Chest radiograph in left atrial myxoma showing slight cardiac enlargement, prominent left atrial appendix and upper zone vessel dilatation indistinguishable from mitral valve disease.

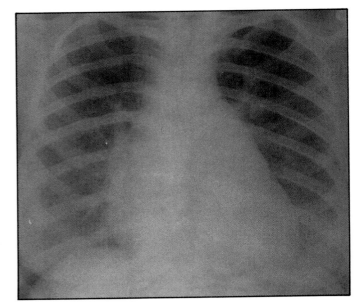

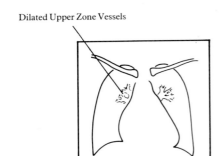

Dilated Upper Zone Vessels

9 Chest radiograph in right atrial myxoma showing pulmonary infarcts in the left lung field.

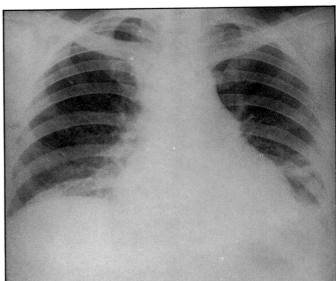

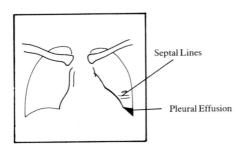

Septal Lines

Pleural Effusion

10

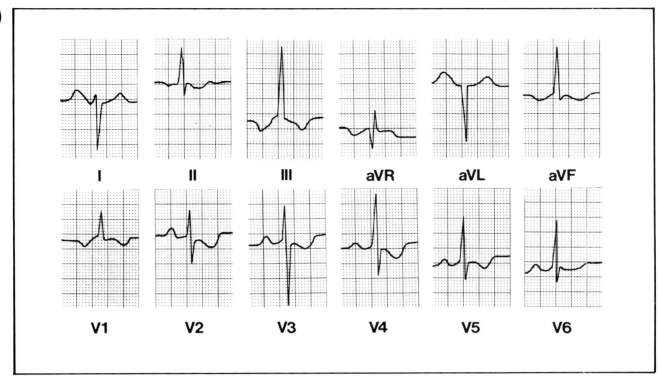

Electrocardiogram of a patient showing broad P wave of left atrial enlargement , with widespread T-wave inversion, dominant R wave in V_1 with deep S wave in V_5 indicating right ventricular hypertrophy.

11

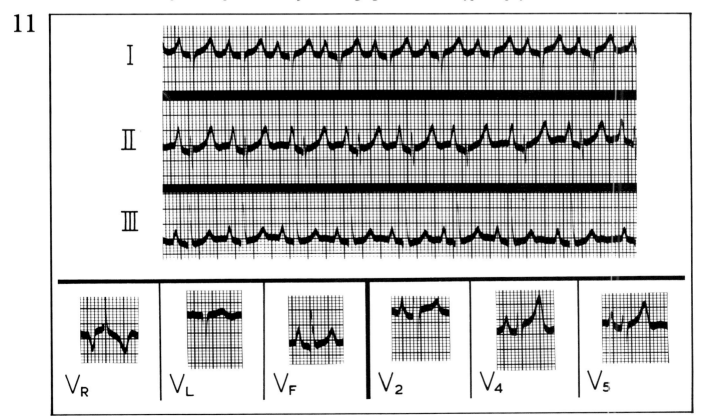

Electrocardiogram with tall P waves in lead II indicating right atrial enlargement.

12

Echocardiogram of a left atrial myxoma. There is a short interval between mitral valve opening and the appearance of the tumor echoes [left]. After surgical removal of the myxoma, a normal mitral valve is seen [right].

13

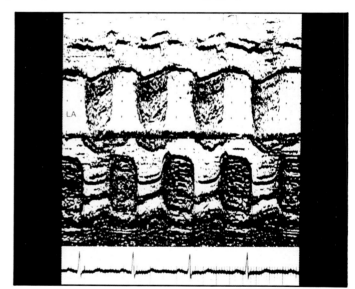

Echocardiogram of a mobile tumor seen in the left atrium during systole [top] and moving into the left ventricle behind the mitral valve during diastole [bottom]. The two recordings have been aligned using the electrocardiogram as a timing reference.

14

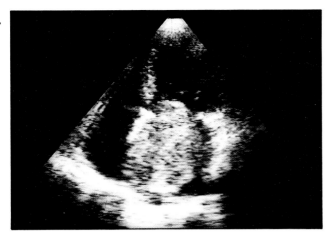 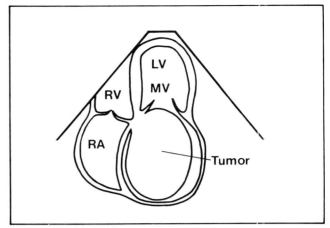

2-D echocardiographic apical four-chamber view showing a very large mass filling the left atrium. On the moving image it showed a rocking motion, indicating attachment to the interatrial septum behind the mitral valve. The mass was shown to be a myxoma at surgery.

15 Right atrial angiogram (lateral projection) showing large filling defect caused by myxoma.

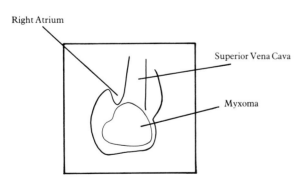 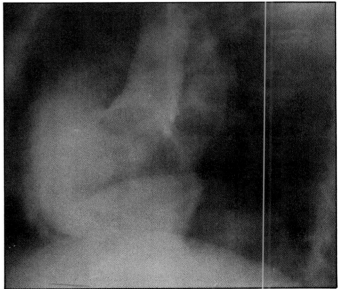

16 Pulmonary arteriogram showing pulmonary venous phase. The left atrium contains an extensive filling defect due to myxoma.

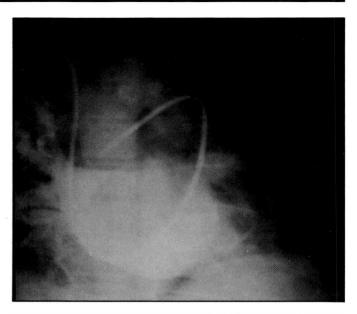

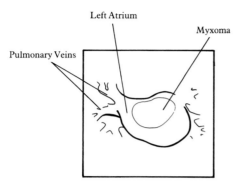

17 Right atrial angiogram showing gross distortion of the normal cavity due to infiltration of the right atrial wall by tumor.

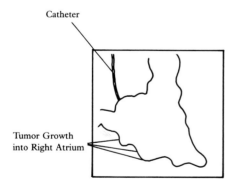

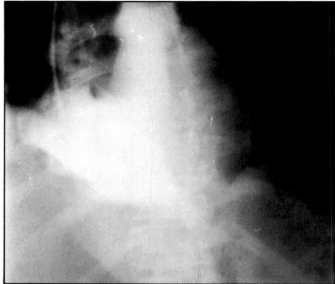

Pulmonary hypertension may occur in patients with:

1) an elevated pulmonary venous pressure due to abnormalities in the left heart such as mitral stenosis, left atrial myxoma, cor triatriatum and left ventricular disease of any etiology;

2) increased pulmonary blood flow from a left to right intra or extra-cardiac shunt such as ventricular septal defect, atrial septal defect or persistent ductus arteriosus;

3) intra or extra-cardiac shunts with pulmonary vascular disease (Eisenmenger syndrome).

These conditions will be dealt with in their relevant sections. This section will deal with other causes:

4) pulmonary embolic disease;

5) chronic hypoxic conditions including diseases of lung parenchyma and high altitude;

6) idiopathic (primary) pulmonary hypertension.

Pathology

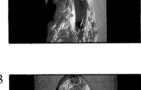

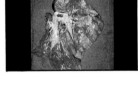

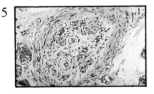

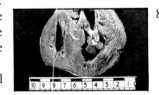

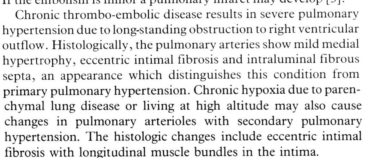

Pulmonary embolism may be massive or minor, acute or chronic. Acute pulmonary embolism usually results from the passage of thrombus originating in a systemic vein [1] through the right side of the heart and lodging in the pulmonary arteries [2]. If the embolism is massive, the right ventricle becomes acutely dilated. If the embolism is minor a pulmonary infarct may develop [3].

Chronic thrombo-embolic disease results in severe pulmonary hypertension due to long-standing obstruction to right ventricular outflow. Histologically, the pulmonary arteries show mild medial hypertrophy, eccentric intimal fibrosis and intraluminal fibrous septa, an appearance which distinguishes this condition from primary pulmonary hypertension. Chronic hypoxia due to parenchymal lung disease or living at high altitude may also cause changes in pulmonary arterioles with secondary pulmonary hypertension. The histologic changes include eccentric intimal fibrosis with longitudinal muscle bundles in the intima.

Some cases of pulmonary hypertension are due to primary disease of the small pulmonary arterioles [4,5] the cause of which is unknown. Histologically, there is medial hypertrophy, concentric and laminary intimal fibrosis, with medial fibrinoid necrosis with or without arteritis and the so-called 'plexiform' lesion. Similar histologic appearances may be seen in patients with the Eisenmenger syndrome. There is an overall decrease in the number of pulmonary arteries with reduction of caliber of the peripheral vessels [6,7].

All cases of long standing severe pulmonary hypertension will result in right ventricular hypertrophy [8].

Presentation

Symptoms

Acute massive pulmonary embolism presents with the features of sudden reduction in cardiac output (collapse and circulatory arrest). Sudden severe breathlessness is another common presentation. Pleuritic chest pain is usually not a feature of acute massive embolism, but there may have been prior episodes of pleurisy due to minor pulmonary embolism. Acute minor embolism usually results in pulmonary infarction with pleurisy and/or hemoptysis being the main features. Usually there is a clear predisposing factor for the development of thrombo-embolism such as surgery, trauma, bed rest, neoplastic disease or severe generalized disease. Chronic pulmonary thrombo-embolic disease presents with the features of severe pulmonary hypertension (exertional dyspnea or syncope sometimes with repetitive episodes of pleurisy and hemoptysis).

If pulmonary hypertension is due to chronic parenchymal lung disease the symptomatology will be dominated by the respiratory abnormality.

Idiopathic (primary) pulmonary hypertension is most frequently seen in young women. The presentation is insidious with increasing breathlessness, occasionally exertional syncope and sometimes hemoptysis. Angina–like chest pain sometimes occurs.

Signs

Massive pulmonary embolism will result in the physical signs of a low cardiac output (peripheral vasoconstriction, hypotension, sinus tachycardia, oliguria, cerebral confusion) and right ventricular failure (elevation of jugular venous pressure, and a gallop rhythm at the left sternal edge). Minor pulmonary embolism causing pulmonary infarction has physical signs confined to the respiratory system such as a pleural rub, lobar collapse or consolidation or a pleural effusion.

Severe pulmonary hypertension as occurs in long-standing hypoxic lung disease, chronic thrombo-embolic disease or of idiopathic etiology gives rise to a loud pulmonary component of the second heart sound usually with normal respiratory variation in the width of splitting. There may be palpable right ventricular hypertrophy. The jugular venous pulse may either show abnormal dominance of the 'a' wave or a frank rise in venous pressure with or without obvious tricuspid regurgitation if there is additional right ventricular failure. Hepatic engorgement and fluid retention characterized by peripheral edema and ascites may be present. Respiratory failure is often present when the cause is long-standing parenchymal lung disease.

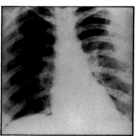

9

Investigations

Radiology

In acute massive pulmonary embolism the chest radiograph shows areas of oligemia due to patchy reduction in blood flow interspersed with areas of compensatory hyperemia [9]. The central pulmonary arteries are not enlarged. In minor pulmonary embolism the chest X-ray may be normal or show features consistent with pulmonary infarction (lobar collapse/consolidation with or without pleural effusion) [10].

In primary pulmonary hypertension the heart and central pulmonary arteries are characteristically enlarged in a non-specific way and the peripheral vessels diffusely reduced in size [11].

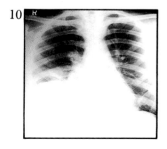

10

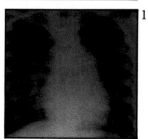

11

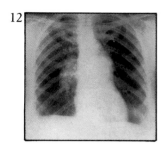

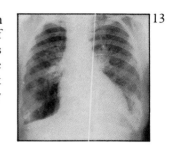

Thrombo-embolic pulmonary hypertension is distinguished from primary pulmonary hypertension by an irregular distribution of the vascular obliteration in the lungs [12]. In parenchymatous lung disease causing chronic pulmonary hypertension the nature of the lung disease may be identified by specific appearances, but the cardiovascular changes are similar to those seen in pulmonary hypertension from other causes [13].

Electrocardiography

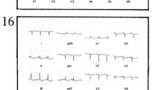

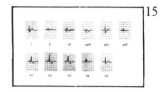

In acute massive pulmonary embolism, the electrocardiogram may show a $S_1Q_3T_3$ pattern [14], right bundle branch block [15], or right ventricular 'strain' with T wave inversion over the anterior precordial leads [14]. In minor pulmonary embolism the ECG is normal. In chronic pulmonary hypertension from any cause, the electrocardiogram usually reflects the right ventricular hypertrophy with right axis deviation, right atrial enlargement and T wave inversion over the right ventricle (anterior precordial leads). The R wave is dominant in lead V_1 and S wave dominant in V_5 [16].

Arterial blood gases

Blood gases in massive pulmonary embolism usually show hypoxia and hypocapnia; in minor pulmonary embolism the gases will be normal. In chronic pulmonary hypertension due to lung disease it is likely there will be hypoxia and hypercapnia; in idiopathic and chronic thrombo-embolic pulmonary hypertension there will be hypoxia.

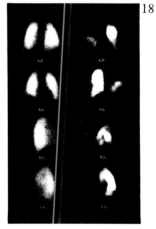

Nuclear Techniques

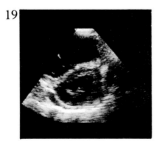

Simultaneous ventilation (using krypton-81m or xenon) and perfusion scans (using technetium-99m labeled macro-aggregated albumin) will permit distinction between primary lung pathology e.g. emphysema (matched ventilation-perfusion defects), and pulmonary vascular disease due to pulmonary embolism (where the ventilation scan is normal but there are variable defects of perfusion [17,18]).

Echocardiography

Long-standing severe pulmonary hypertension gives rise to right ventricular hypertrophy and dilatation and secondary right atrial dilatation. These features may be identified by echocardiography [19]. The M-mode echocardiogram usually shows reversed septal motion [20]. A key role of the echocardiogram is to eliminate left heart abnormalities such as mitral valve disease, left atrial myxoma and left ventricular disease as causes of pulmonary hypertension.

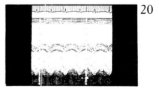

Cardiac Catheterization and Angiography

In acute massive pulmonary embolism there is only moderate elevation of pulmonary artery pressure distinguishing this condi-

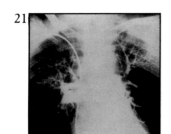

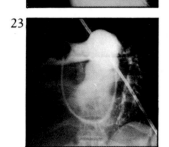

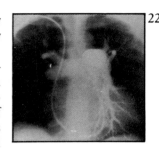

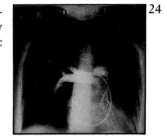

tion from chronic thrombo-embolic disease where the pulmonary artery pressures are usually much higher. In minor pulmonary embolism the pulmonary artery pressure is normal.

In massive pulmonary embolism the angiogram shows obstruction to a major portion of the total pulmonary arterial bed [21]. In chronic thrombo-embolic pulmonary hypertension the pulmonary trunk is enlarged and there is an asymmetric obliteration of pulmonary vessels, those unaffected by thrombus being tortuous and dilated [22]. There is a convex leading-edge to contrast-filled vessels obstructed by thrombus [22] unlike the concave leading-edge in acute embolism [23]. In primary (idiopathic) pulmonary hypertension the pulmonary vasculature shows symmetric peripheral pruning [24].

1   Thrombus in the femoral vein.

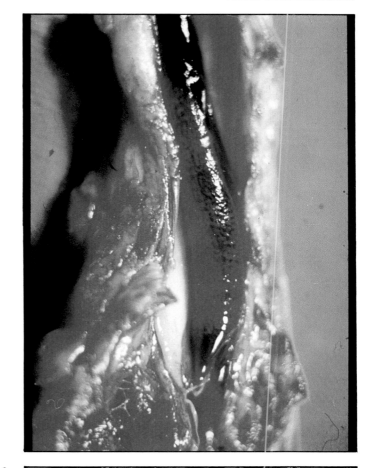

Thrombus

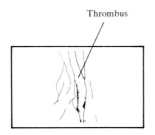

2   Large saddle embolus is seen astride both right and left pulmonary arteries.

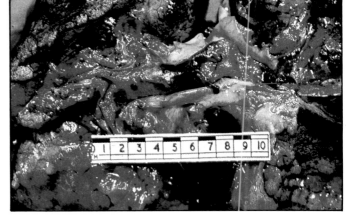

Right Pulmonary Artery   Left Pulmonary Artery

Embolus

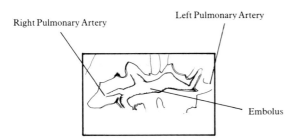

3   Minor pulmonary embolism in the upper lobe arteries resulting in infarction of the lung.

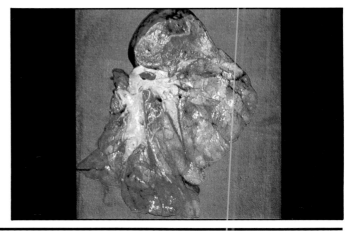

Pulmonary Embolus   Infarction

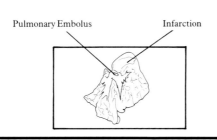

4   Normal pulmonary arteries (left panel) compared with small pulmonary artery affected by intimal fibrosis as a consequence of severe primary pulmonary hypertension (right panel).

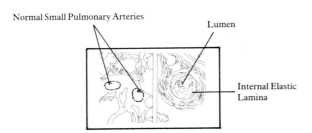

Normal Small Pulmonary Arteries

Lumen

Internal Elastic Lamina

5   Complex angiomatoid lesions in small pulmonary arteries in primary pulmonary hypertension.

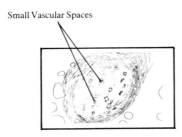

Small Vascular Spaces

6   Normal post-mortem pulmonary arteriogram.

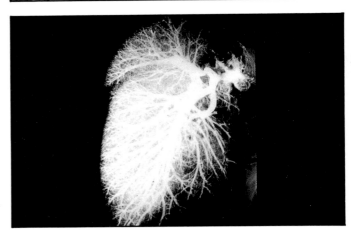

Filling of Peripheral Vessels

7   Post-mortem pulmonary arteriogram in primary pulmonary hypertension.

Peripheral 'Pruning'

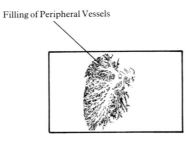

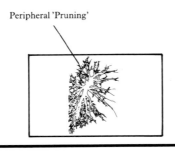

8   Gross right ventricular hypertrophy secondary to primary pulmonary hypertension. The right ventricular wall thickness and size greatly exceed those of the left ventricle.

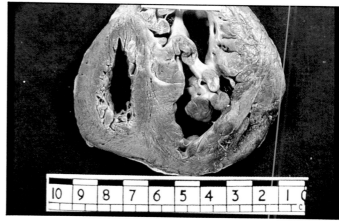

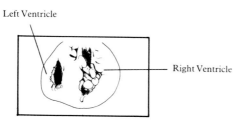

Left Ventricle

Right Ventricle

PULMONARY EMBOLIC/VASCULAR DISEASE

Radiology

9   Chest radiograph of acute massive pulmonary embolism showing oligemia in the right lung with compensatory hyperemia in the left lung.

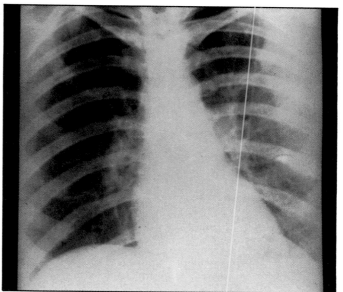

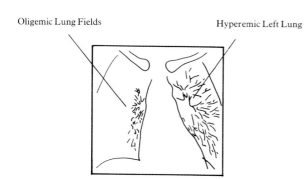

Oligemic Lung Fields

Hyperemic Left Lung

10   Chest radiograph of pulmonary infarction. Note shadow at right lung base and elevated right hemidiaphragm.

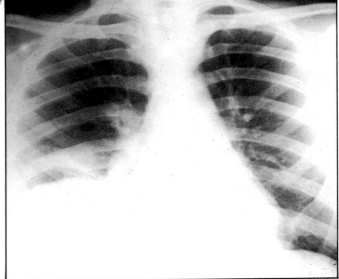

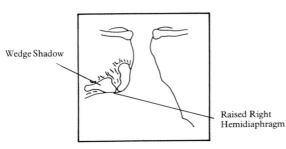

11   Chest radiograph of primary pulmonary hypertension showing large central pulmonary arteries and symmetric reduction in peripheral vessel size.

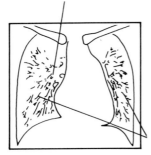

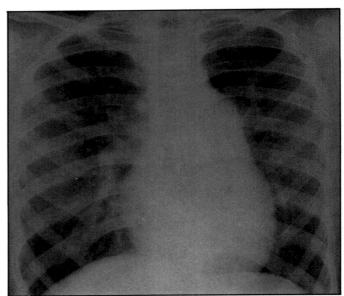

12   Chest radiograph in thrombo-embolic pulmonary hypertension showing large pulmonary trunk and right hilar artery. The left lung is oligemic.

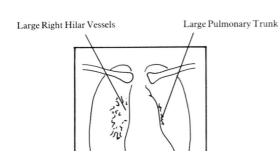

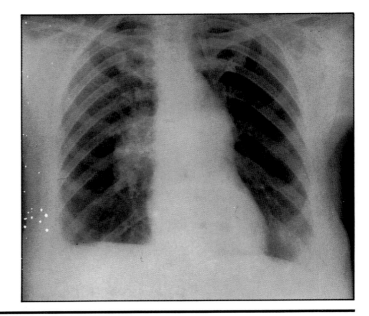

13 Chest radiograph in obstructive airway disease with cor pulmonale showing large heart and hilar arteries with irregular pulmonary vascular obliteration.

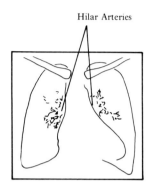

Hilar Arteries

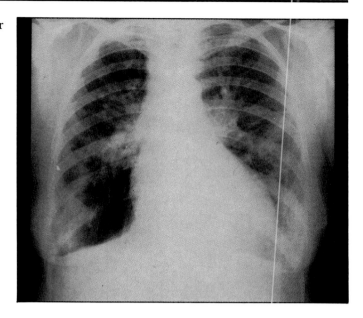

PULMONARY EMBOLIC/VASCULAR DISEASE   Electrocardiography

14

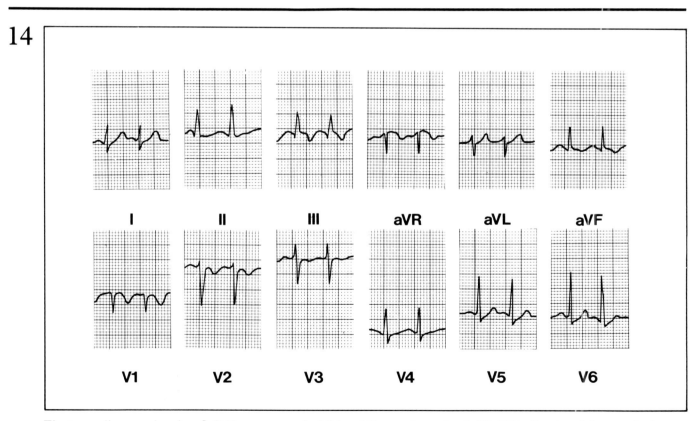

Electrocardiogram showing $S_1Q_3T_3$ pattern and additional T-wave inversion in V1-V3 indicating right ventricular strain.

15

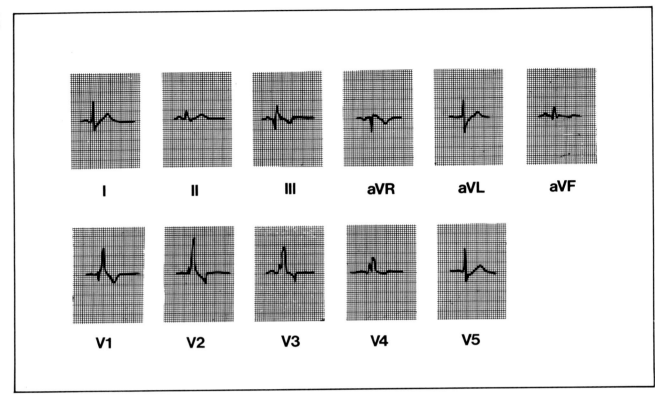

Electrocardiogram showing right bundle branch block.

16

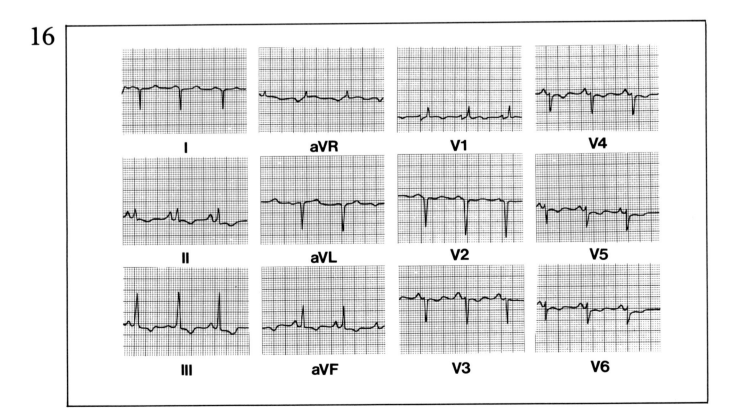

Electrocardiogram showing 'P' pulmonale, right axis deviation and right ventricular hypertrophy.

17 Ventilation [left panel] and perfusion [right panel] lung scans in chronic obstructive airways disease showing matched defects.

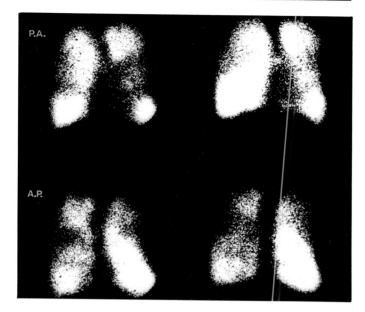

18 Ventilation [left panel] and perfusion [right panel] lung scans in pulmonary embolic disease, showing normal ventilation but multiple perfusion defects.

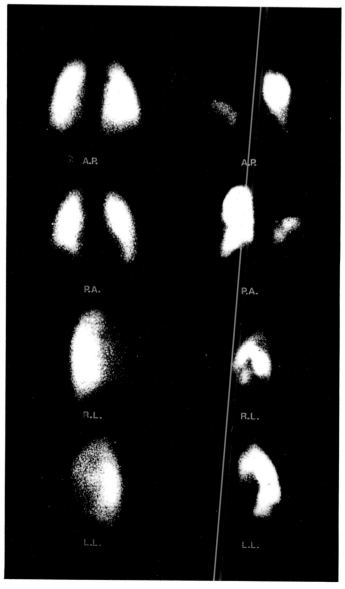

19

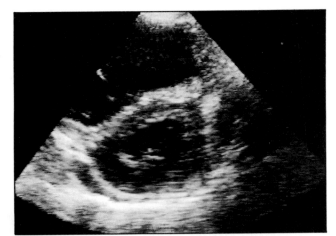
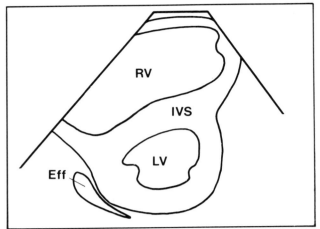

2-D echocardiographic parasternal short axis view of pulmonary hypertension secondary to chronic obstructive airways disease. The right ventricle is enlarged and the left ventricle is small. The interventricular septum is less curved than normal, giving the left ventricle a flattened appearance.

20

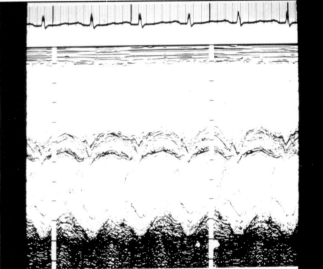

M-mode echocardiogram showing reversed septal motion in a patient with pulmonary hypertension.

21 Pulmonary arteriogram in acute massive pulmonary embolism showing involvement of more than 50% of the major pulmonary arteries.

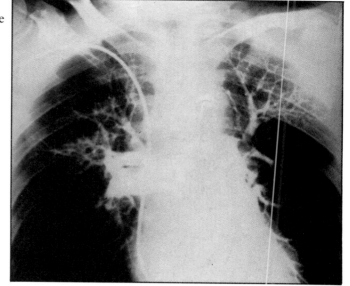

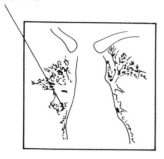

Filling Defects (Acute)

22 Pulmonary arteriogram in chronic thromboembolic pulmonary hypertension. The pulmonary trunk is dilated, and vessels unaffected by thrombus are dilated and tortuous.

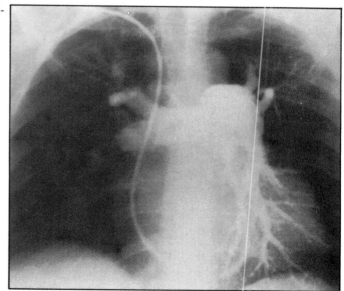

Dilated Tortuous Vessel

Dilated Pulmonary Trunk

Long Standing Filling Defect (Retracted)

23 Pulmonary arteriogram in acute massive pulmonary embolism showing acute thrombus in right pulmonary artery causing a concave leading edge.

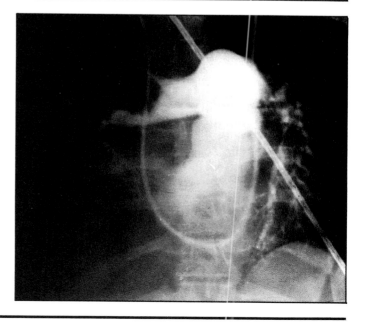

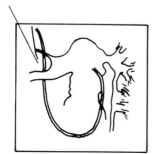

Acute Thrombus

24 Pulmonary arteriogram in primary pulmonary hypertension showing peripheral arterial pruning.

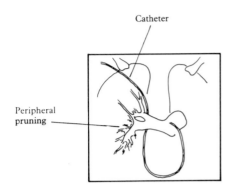

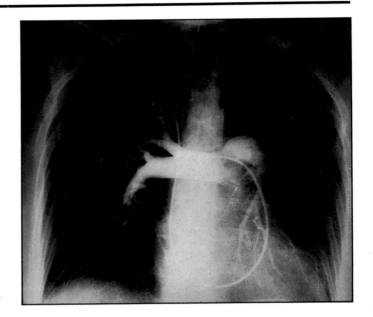

INDEX

INDEX

INDEX

INDEX